Testing Pe

MIKE SMITH WITH PAM SMITH

TESTING PEOPLE
AT WORK

COMPETENCIES IN PSYCHOMETRIC TESTING

BPS Blackwell

BLACKWELL PUBLISHING
350 Main Street, Malden, MA 02148-5020, USA
108 Cowley Road, Oxford OX4 1JF, UK
550 Swanston Street, Carlton, Victoria 3053, Australia

The right of Mike Smith and Pam Smith to be identified as the Authors of this Work
has been asserted in accordance with the UK Copyright, Designs, and Patents Act 1988.

First published 2005 by The British Psychological Society and Blackwell Publishing Ltd

Library of Congress Cataloging-in-Publication Data

Smith, Mike (J. Mike)
    Testing people at work : competencies in psychometric testing
  / Mike Smith with Pam Smith.
        p. cm.
    Includes bibliographical references (p.) and indexes.
    ISBN 1–4051–0817–7 (hbk : alk. paper) — ISBN 1–4051–0818–5
  (pbk : alk. paper)
      1. Employment tests—Textbooks.   2. Employees—Psychological
  testing—Textbooks.   I. Smith, Pam, 1946– .   II. Title.
  HF5549.5.E5S64 2005
  150′.28′7—dc22

                                                              2004022192

A catalogue record for this title is available from the British Library.

Set in 10/12pt Erhardt
by Graphicraft Limited, Hong Kong
Printed and bound in the United Kingdom
by MPG Books, Bodmin, Cornwall

The publisher's policy is to use permanent paper from mills that operate a sustainable forestry
policy, and which has been manufactured from pulp processed using acid-free and elementary
chlorine-free practices. Furthermore, the publisher ensures that the text paper and cover board
used have met acceptable environmental accreditation standards.

For further information on
BPS Blackwell, visit our website:
www.bpsblackwell.com

CONTENTS

PREFACE

In effect, I started writing this book in 1976, when I was preparing my first postgraduate course to qualify people to use psychometric tests in selection and vocational guidance. The theoretical material needed by students was scattered among texts such as Anastasi's *Psychological Testing*, Cronbach's *Essentials of Psychological Testing*, Guion's *Personnel Testing* and a myriad of other books covering topics such as intelligence, personality and motivation. It was even more difficult for students to obtain materials relating to the practical issues of using psychometric tests in industry. Very little information was publically available. It usually existed as notes for courses run by organizations such as the National Institute for Industrial Psychology (NIIP) and the Independent Assessment and Research Centre (IARC).

It was therefore necessary to provide students with a comprehensive set of notes covering the occupational use of psychometric tests. These notes were constantly enhanced in the light of comments from over 800 students on scores of courses within both the private and university sectors. This book could not have been produced without their input. Their comments highlighted the points that were most likely to be misunderstood and those that needed emphasis.

Consultancy experience also played a major part. Individual feedback sessions with over 2,500 clients and experience with devising, setting up or evaluating selection systems for organizations provided a practical perspective. It also provided specific examples that could be used to demonstrate theoretical points.

The third major influence was the guidelines offered by professional bodies. The British Psychological Society's syllabi for their Certificates of Competence in Occupational Testing (Level A and Level B) were a vital influence and it is hoped that the book covers all their required topics. The International Test Commission's *Guidelines for Test Use* were also important in providing a wider international context.

In due course, BPS Publications invited me to turn my materials into an authoritative book on the use of psychometric tests in occupational contexts, and I am delighted that their successor, BPS Blackwell, has continued the project.

The book follows a straightforward, but slightly unusual, structure – a straightforward time line from job analysis to delivering feedback. The only exceptions to this pattern are the initial introductory chapter and the final chapter on ethics. The other chapters are ordered in the sequence in which they are encountered when setting up and delivering a programme of psychometric testing in occupational settings. This pattern might be unfamiliar to some readers who are used to a structure that first deals with theoretical issues such as personality, and then practical issues, with a section on statistics tacked on in an appendix. The present structure is better. In particular, it integrates statistics within the process of using tests rather than treating them as afterthoughts that are not very important for practitioners.

The present volume is the centrepiece of a range of materials. In order to keep down costs and make the book as accessible as possible to as many people as possible, some less essential matter has been placed on a website, which is freely available. It is intended to modify this site as the need arises. However, at the time of going to press, it contains the following:

1 List of additional materials
2 Materials available to people teaching psychometric testing
3 How the contents of this book map on to the requirements of the British Psychological Society's Certificate of Competence in Testing, Level A (ability tests)
4 How the contents of this book map on to the requirements of the British Psychological Society's Certificate of Competence in Testing, Level B, Intermediate (personality and more complex tests)
5 Websites containing ethical codes
6 Further reading on personality
7 Neurolinguistic programming
8 Rarer types of correlations
9 Confidence limits
10 Confidence intervals
11 Non-technical introduction to factor analysis
12 List of test publishers
13 List of psychological societies
14 Cattell's UI factors
15 Method matrix
16 Report to individual client
17 Organizational report

The materials can be accessed by visiting www.blackwellpublishing.com/testing/

Instructors and lecturers can obtain additional materials that they can use on their courses. They include:

- *worksheets* that can be used to assess students' competence in 47 aspects of using psychometric tests
- *answersheets* on which students can record their responses to questions in the worksheets – these have been designed to promote efficient marking
- *marksheets* that contain the correct answers to multiple-choice questions and marking standards for the evaluation of written assignments.

These materials will be available free of charge to at least the first 100 instructors who adopt this text as their course book. The website associated with this book (www.blackwellpublishing.com/testing/) explains how Instructor Materials may be obtained.

My dearest wife, Pam, has made a major contribution to the production of this book, checking hundreds of facts and making detailed comments on its structure, presentation and clarity. It is fitting that this invaluable contribution is recognized by our joint authorship.

Mike Smith

ACKNOWLEDGEMENTS

Many people have commented and improved upon earlier drafts. We are deeply grateful for their comments. However, none of the shortcomings of the book should be attributed to them, since the final responsibility lies with the authors. We are grateful to:

Professor Dave Bartram
Dr Steve Blinkhorn
Dr Roy Childs
Mr John Cooper
Mr David Duncan
Dr George Erdos
Professor Clive Fletcher
Mr John Fordham
Dr Christine Jones
Professor Pat Lindley
Ms Wendy Lord
Ms Amy Luck
Dr Laurence Paltiel
Dr Michael Pearn
Dr Christopher Ridgeway
Mr Andy Roberts
Dr Stuart Robertson
Dr Stevan Rolls
Dr Colin Selby
Dr Viv Shackleton
Dr George Sik
Professor Paul Sparrow
Dr Peter Storr
Dr Paul Sutton
Dr Sue Walters
Dr Charles Woodruffe

This book would not have been possible without the superb support of our colleague Joan Mahon, who provided friendly, patient and efficient secretarial support.

Mike Smith

CHAPTER 1

COMPETENCE IN OCCUPATIONAL TESTING

Psychometric tests are powerful measures of human characteristics. Their results can alter the course of people's lives. Consequently, the sale of tests is restricted to people who can use them competently. This book aims to help practitioners develop a level of competence that qualifies them to purchase tests. No book can achieve this aim on its own. It must be accompanied by good tuition and practical exercises. It must attempt to mirror the requirements of professional bodies. The website associated with this book maps the contents on to the requirements of professional bodies such as the British Psychological Society. This book also aims to provide a source of reference on specific issues. Psychometric tests have four main uses: selection, vocational and careers advice, research, and workforce audits.

1.1 SELECTION

People differ. Some are intelligent, while others are slow-witted. Some are warm-hearted, while others are cold-blooded. Some are motivated by money, while others are motivated by ideas. Jobs differ too. Some require intelligent, warm-hearted people who are motivated by ideas. Others require slow-witted, cold-blooded people who are motivated by money. The task is to measure people's characteristics in some way, so that their characteristics can be matched to the requirements of the job.

Gains from good selection are widespread. *Candidates* gain because the best person is more likely to be hired. They also gain because fewer unsuitable people are appointed and go through the nightmare of failure and dismissal. *Colleagues* gain because they are spared the burden of coping with the mistakes of an incompetent co-worker. *Organizations* gain because they need fewer resources – as a general rule, good selection can increase productivity by 10% of labour costs. *Customers* gain because, other things being equal, they receive a better service at a lower cost. *Society* gains because increased productivity produces a sounder economy and tax base, which can support higher levels of 'social goods' such as hospitals and universities.

However, it is not easy to make good appointments. It has been known for almost a century that traditional interviews are very inaccurate. In 1929, Hollingsworth asked 12 sales managers, who were experienced in interviewing, to interview 57 applicants for a sales job and rank them in order of suitability. If interviews are any good, there should be some concordance in the rankings: a candidate ranked in the top ten by one interviewer should be in the top ten for other

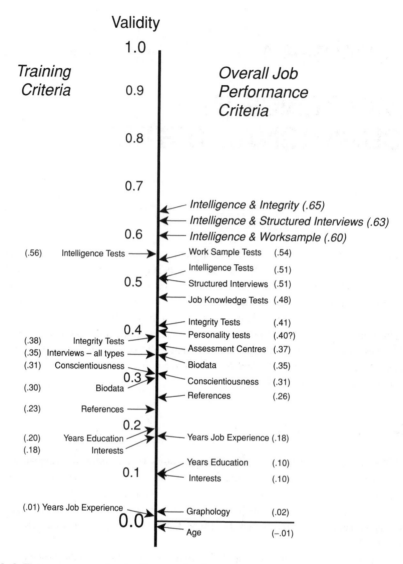

Figure 1.1 The accuracy of selection methods.

interviewers. Unfortunately, Hollingsworth's results showed that one candidate was ranked sixth by one interviewer and 56th by another. Subsequent analyses have suggested that the traditional interview is less than 3% better than chance.

Over the past 90 years, the accuracy of selection methods has been extensively researched. An important paper by Schmidt and Hunter (1998) collated many correlations between (i) different selection methods and success in training and (ii) different selection methods and success in the job. Robertson and Smith (2001) used this collation, together with other information, to produce figure 1.1. The figure shows that psychometric tests are among the best methods of predicting how well a candidate will cope with training and performing the job.

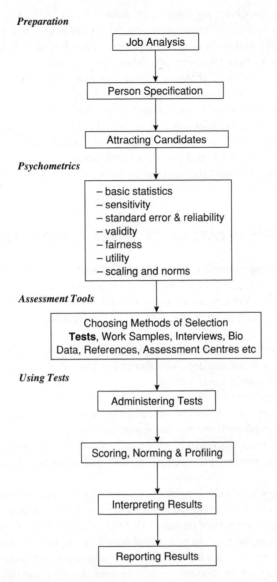

Figure 1.2 The selection paradigm.

Psychometric tests are one of the jewels in the crown of modern psychology. Few other areas of the subject have reached such an advanced, quantitative stage.

Nevertheless, on their own, tests do not result in accurate selection. They should be used, along with other scientific methods, in a systematic approach. This systematic, idealized approach is often called the 'selection paradigm'. It is rarely followed rigidly, but it provides a useful route-map for a selection system. This book is based upon the selection paradigm (see figure 1.2), and it deals with the topics in the chronological order in which they are depicted in the figure.

Good selection involves four major topics: preparation, psychometrics, assessment tools, and the use of tests. *Preparation* consists of analysing the job, drawing up a person specification of the abilities, personality and motives of the ideal person for the job, and then attracting applicants who seem likely to have these characteristics. These topics are covered in the first part of this book. Some methods of choosing among applicants are good, while others are bad. The difference between a good and a bad measure lies in the psychometric properties of the measures. Psychometrics, including basic statistics, is covered in the second part of the book. It is wrong to jump to the conclusion that tests should always be used to select people. Other assessment tools, such as work samples or situational interviews, may be just as good. Various assessment tools, including tests, computer tests and assessment centres, are described in the third part of this book. The final part focuses on the actual use of tests, including test administration, interpretation and feedback of results.

1.2 TESTS IN CAREERS GUIDANCE AND DEVELOPMENT

Tests are used very extensively in careers guidance and development. In selection, tests are used primarily to meet the aims of organizations. In careers guidance, they are primarily used to meet the need of individuals. In development, they are used to benefit both the organization and the individual. There are other, more subtle, differences. In careers guidance and development:

- A wider mix of tests is likely to be employed. Selection uses mainly tests of ability and personality. Vocational guidance will also utilize tests of ability and personality but may also use tests of interests and values.
- Testing sessions tend to be longer.
- Testing is usually done in smaller groups or on an individual basis.
- Feedback to test-takers is much more comprehensive.
- Testing usually takes place within a constellation of other activities, such as counselling, provision of information and coaching in skills such as writing CVs or interviewing.

Guidance is usually given at three points in a career. *First*, vocational guidance is often given at the point of *entry into work or training*. School-leavers, teenagers and people in their early twenties often have no strong idea of the career that they should follow. Tests are used to identify personal characteristics so that they can be matched with those required by various jobs. Test results at this age need to be interpreted with care. Whilst cognitive ability has stabilized, other aspects such as personality may still be in a state of development. Guidance at this stage often involves assessing vocational maturity and providing realistic information about the world of work. Vocational guidance at career entry is often financed by an educational authority, an employment service or by parents, and the resources available for each individual case may be meagre.

Second, career guidance may be provided as a part of a *personal development program* during an early career when people are in their late twenties or thirties. Testing at this stage is often limited to one or two tests of, say, personality and problem-solving style. Feedback is often rudimentary and consists of a profile plus explanatory leaflets. Guidance is often given in a group training context, which involves 'lectures' and sessions where a personal development plan is developed in co-operation with a course tutor.

Third, career guidance is frequently given in mid- or late career, when people are in their forties or fifties. It often forms a part of a *redundancy package* offered by employers. In these circumstances, tests are used to assess the individual's suitability for future jobs. A major benefit of using tests at this stage is frequently to restore a person's self-confidence following redundancy. Guidance at this age may also follow a reappraisal of life goals. Perhaps the most frequent situation arises when people have chosen an initial career in a branch of finance because of the material rewards that it promised. By the time these individuals have reached their mid-forties, sufficient material rewards have been accumulated and they may seek a second career that will provide personal fulfilment. Tests may be used to identify jobs or other activities that are likely to provide this fulfilment. Testing at these stages is usually financed by relatively affluent organizations or individuals. It often forms a part of a Rolls-Royce service offered by an outplacement consultancy. However, tests are frequently used in less auspicious circumstances, for example during rehabilitation following serious illness or accident. In these situations, tests may be used to gauge whether or not someone is capable of performing certain 'new' occupations.

1.3 TESTS IN RESEARCH

Tests are frequently used in research. Research for many masters' dissertations and doctoral theses use tests, because tests are often the most scientific way of measuring the relevant variables. The research use of tests may be divided into three categories:

- *Research into tests* themselves. For example, many researchers have investigated fakeability, fairness, stability and age changes in test scores (see, for example, Warr et al., 2001).
- *Basic research* into other scientific phenomena – especially aspects of work psychology. For example, a test of cognitive ability might be used by an investigation into the relationship between solving industrial problems and intelligence. Similarly, a test of personality might be used to determine whether emotional intelligence is a new concept or merely a repackaging of traditional factors of personality. Further, a test of interests might be used in a study of job satisfaction. However, the use of tests in research is more widespread and it extends outside the arena of occupational psychology. For example, a test of cognitive ability might be used to examine the relationship between intelligence and the electrical activity in the brain (see, for example, Frearson and Eysenck, 1986). Similarly, a personality test might be used to examine whether extroverts are considered by others to be more innovative than introverts.
- *Applied research*, where, for example, a market research organization in the textile industry might examine whether extroverts are more likely to purchase garments that are coloured red or yellow. Similarly, a safety organization might use a personality questionnaire to discover whether tense people are more likely to cut themselves by resorting to knives to open difficult packaging.

Test results obtained in research settings are less likely to result in irreversible decisions that affect people's lives and fewer ethical issues are involved. Further, in research less precise tests can be used because the results of many individuals are aggregated. Mean scores of groups are much more stable than the scores of individuals, even when the actual test is less reliable. Unfortunately, the use of well-standardized tests in research is inhibited by two factors: money and distribution. Good tests cost money that research students and many research grants can ill afford. Furthermore, most research involves postal questionnaires, but the confidentiality of test materials forbids their 'open' distribution by mail. Consequently, there is a great temptation for researchers to substitute naïve questions or homespun scales for proper tests.

 ## 1.4 TESTS IN WORKFORCE AUDITS

A more recent use of tests is workforce audits, where they are used to calibrate other aspects of an organization's human resource system such as an appraisal system. For example, a communications organization noticed that there were large differences in the grades given to employees in different regions. It was therefore suggested that quotas of grades should be imposed on regions and that managers in 'deviant' regions should be retrained to give more 'equal' grades. Before implementing this policy, the organization conducted a survey using standardized ability tests, which suggested that the appraisal grades were, in fact, a reflection of 'reality' and that the pools of ability varied from region to region. It therefore abandoned a programme that would have disadvantaged more able managers in some regions.

A second example of a workforce audit is given by a Manchester organization that was falling behind its rivals despite the fact that most of the senior employees that it was hiring had PhDs. The selection process involved tests of cognitive ability. It was arranged for senior employees to complete a personality test. When the scores were analysed, it was clear that the company was attracting and employing 'intelligent stodge'. When compared to national norms, the senior staff had achieved high scores on intelligence but low scores on imagination and willingness to try new ideas.

The chapters that follow will focus mainly on the common principles that affect all of the four main uses described above, but there will be special emphasis on their use in selection and guidance.

PART I

PREPARATION FOR TESTING

CHAPTER 2

JOB ANALYSIS AND PERSON SPECIFICATIONS

Many organizations rush to advertise a job as soon as an employee resigns or a post is created. This is foolish and it accounts for many of the mistakes made in selection. It is much better to analyse the job coolly and to work out the type of person who would be ideally suited to perform the work. It is true that job analysis requires effort, but it makes selection more precise and saves resources in the long run. Job analysis can also be used for other purposes such as training needs analysis, organizational design, job grading and employee development. Job analysis is so important that it has been called the cornerstone of work psychology.

The rigour of a job analysis will vary according to its use. The most rigorous analyses are needed for research purposes or the design of training. Rigorous job analyses are also usual when many people are employed in a job, when safety is involved or because irretrievable consequences flow from a mistake. Fortunately, selection usually only requires a straightforward approach that identifies about seven important characteristics. The identification of more than seven characteristics may be technically correct, but the greater information often only serves to confuse selectors. The following description offers a straightforward account of job analysis and person specifications.

◣ 2.1 JOB ANALYSIS

Before starting any job analysis, the significance of the job should be subject to strategic review. The main purpose of the job should be identified and it should be confirmed that the job makes a worthwhile contribution to the organization's business plan. Often, there is a committee that reviews the importance of every new job and which only sanctions those that make a positive contribution.

The purpose of job analysis is to achieve an objective understanding of a job, so that critical skills and performance can be identified (Pearn, personal communication, 2001). Job analysis can form a part of the justification, and perhaps legal defence, of a selection process. Job analysis is concerned with *what* is done or achieved. It also describes external factors and data, which are usually obtained from personnel records, including the following:

- job title and grade
- list of Key Result Areas (KRAs)

- workplace location
- hours of work and days of work
- holiday entitlement
- rates and method of pay
- direct supervisor
- assets controlled
- relationships with others
- other benefits, such as a pension.

The tasks involved in a job are more difficult to determine. The simplest method is to ask the superior, and perhaps other people who do the same job, to describe what they do. This information can be supplemented with data from other documents, such as training manuals or operating procedures. A draft job analysis is then circulated for comment. This very simple procedure is quick and involves minimal effort. An example of a straightforward job analysis is given in appendix 2.1. Unfortunately, this simple approach is often adopted by untrained people, and it may be unsystematic, subjective and miss major aspects of the job. If the post is important or occupied by many employees, a more systematic approach is justified. The more systematic approaches can be organized into four groups.

2.1.1 DISCUSSING THE JOB

Three non-technical approaches involve discussing the job with people who know it well:

- *Individual interviews* with job-holders can be more systematic and comprehensive than the simple method. A series of interviews will allow several viewpoints to be captured. The method allows flexibility, so a wide range of data can be collected and a semantically rich analysis produced. However, the method retains a large element of subjectivity because it depends on the synthesis and weighing of information by the analysts. It is also very time-consuming. A further disadvantage of the individual interview is that the job analysis is based on what people say about the job rather than on the actual job itself: the incumbents may inflate the description of their job ('gold-bricking') in an attempt to obtain an advantage.
- *Group interviews* are similar to individual interviews, but they have two extra advantages. First, they are less time-consuming because the views of several people can be obtained simultaneously. Second, synergy between the participants, where one person's contribution stimulates further and richer contributions from others, may result in a fuller description. However, group interviews can be influenced by group dynamics and a dominant person can distort or inhibit the contributions of others. Group interviews also suffer from the subjectivity of individual interviews.
- A group of *Subject Matter Experts (SMEs)* can be assembled, and after several meetings a job description can be produced. A job analysis by SMEs has several advantages. First, the method uses time efficiently. Second, it is appropriate in 'green field' situations where incumbents are not available. Third, a job description produced by a panel of 12 SMEs is resistant to legal attack, because it would be a foolish advocate who attempted to persuade a jury of 12 people that a panel of 12 SMEs was inadequate. Fourth, a job description produced by a panel of SMEs is less likely to be inflated by 'gold-bricking'.

2.1.2 OBSERVING AND PERFORMING

Two non-technical methods of job analysis involve observing or performing the job:

- *Observing the job* has the advantage that the analyst can directly access a wide range of information and thus the results may be comprehensive and less subject to 'gold-bricking'. In some circumstances, observation can be aided by slow-motion video. However, observation is time-consuming and interpretation can be subjective. Furthermore, an observer may alter the way in which the job is performed: employees are more likely to follow official procedures, and increase the quantity rather than the quality of their work. Other disadvantages of this method include the resentment often felt by employees at being watched and the safety issues that might arise due to the observer distracting the worker. Jobs involving confidential meetings or unpredictable hours cannot be analysed by this method. Some of the classic analyses of management jobs have used observation as the mode of analysis (see, for example, Mintzberg, 1973).
- *Job performance* is, in theory, a good method of job analysis. Whilst performing the job an analyst is subject to the full range of information, sensations and perceptions: the possibilities for 'gold-bricking' are very low. However, this method can only be used on relatively simple jobs that require short training. Furthermore, it cannot be used where a 'novice' job analyst could inflict damage on others – very few people would be happy if they were subjected to brain surgery conducted by a job analyst rather than a surgeon!

2.1.3 WRITTEN RECORDS

A range of non-technical methods of job analysis involves asking people to keep written records.

The Diary Method

The diary method asks incumbents to keep a log of their activities. A big advantage of this method is that it requires little preparation and it has a flexible format. However, the diary method has disadvantages. First, the styles that employees adopt may affect responses: some may answer in excruciating detail, while others may prefer a broad brush approach. Second, employees may ignore the diary until shortly before the deadline and then complete it from memory. Other potential problems arise from 'gold-bricking' and from the danger that tasks completed only at specific time or seasons are missed. A final problem is that diaries are very time-consuming to analyse and the process may involve a content analysis that is subjective. Some classic studies of managerial work have involved the diary method (see, for example, Stewart, 1967).

2.1.4 QUANTITATIVE METHODS

Task Lists

If the job is performed by many people, a number of quantitative methods can be used. The simplest method is to send each incumbent a questionnaire that contains biographical questions and ask them to *list ten tasks* that they have done in their job during the past two weeks. It is often useful to add three or four extra lines with the prompt to list tasks that are carried out at other times of the year. The questionnaires can be analysed easily using a spreadsheet.

Checklists

An improvement is to construct a checklist that is then sent to incumbents, who are asked to tick those tasks that are a part of their job. The results can be analysed in terms of the frequencies with which tasks are included in a job. Because the analysis of a checklist is usually restricted to percentages, they are not very useful if the number of job-holders is below 50. Further, the checklist needs to be piloted very carefully to ensure that all possible tasks are included.

Inventories

A checklist can be turned into an inventory by changing the items into a Likert-type scales, such as the following:

0   The job does not involve this task.
1   The task is a relatively unimportant part of the job.
2   The task is a fairly important part of the job.
3   The task is an important part of the job.
4   The task is a very important part of the job.

Sometimes, it is better to use a different scale. It may be more useful to ask about the difficulty of the task or the proportion of the time spent on the task. Inventories are easy to analyse and can obtain useful results with quite small samples.

In an ideal world, all job analysis inventories would be bespoke instruments, developed on site for specific organizations after extensive pilot work and psychometric studies. In most situations, this ideal is impractical: it is too costly, it takes too long and it requires expertise that is not usually available. Therefore, in most circumstances, *'standard' inventories* are used.

Standard Inventories

Standard inventories are used by many organizations. Considerable resources will have been devoted to their development, but they can usually be purchased in a matter of days. The booklets may seem expensive, but they will be professionally produced and an individual user will not have to bear all of the development costs. Many 'standard' job analysis inventories are available. The following descriptions only cover a selection that has been chosen to demonstrate the range of available instruments or a theoretical point.

The doyen of standard inventories is the **Position Analysis Questionnaire (PAQ)**, developed by McCormick et al. (1972). Its origins lay in observations of a very large number of aspects of a very large number of jobs in the United States. The resulting mass of information was reduced to a more manageable volume by the process of factor analysis. Today, it has 162 scales, grouped under the following headings:

- information input
- thinking processes (mediation)
- work output (manipulating objects)
- interpersonal activities (communication and so on)
- the work situation (physical and psychological facets)
- miscellaneous aspects such as work schedules and shifts.

An excellent feature of the PAQ is that each of the 162 scales is benchmarked with explicit examples of what a rating represents. For example, one of the scales concerns 'Finger Manipulation', which is rated on a seven-point scale. The points on the scale are benchmarked as in table 2.1.

Another excellent feature of the PAQ is the database, which contains details for hundreds of jobs. Consequently, a profile can be produced that gives the percentage of jobs where the attribute is less important than the job being analysed. It is then easy to isolate those activities that are particularly important.

The PAQ is a 'broad spectrum' job analysis inventory and is not particularly suited to the analysis of managerial or professional jobs. Therefore another job analysis inventory, the Professional and Managerial Position Questionnaire, which is similar in format to the PAQ was produced. It contains 108 scales and benchmarks that are relevant to six aspects of managerial and professional work:

- planning and scheduling
- processing of information and ideas
- exercising judgement
- communication
- interpersonal activities and relationships
- technical activities.

The **Work Profiling System** (Saville Holdsworth, 1988) is also a well-developed job analysis 'inventory'. The system contains about 800 items, but there are ways of ensuring that any one person is only confronted with the most relevant 200–300 items. The system takes the form of three interlocking inventories, which are suitable for:

- managerial and professional workers
- service and administrative workers
- manual and technical workers.

Table 2.1 Finger Manipulation: the extent to which the job requires making fine movements with the fingers of one or both hands

5	Makes very delicate movements, such as those required by a surgeon conducting a brain operation
4	Makes delicate movements, such as adjusting a camera or adjusting scientific equipment
3	Makes some movements, such as packing small gadgets in boxes
2	Makes some gross movements, such as moving large pieces of furniture
1	Makes no finger movements

The number of items answered can be reduced further because the items are grouped into sections around common themes. There is a system for choosing the eight or so most relevant sections. The inventory takes about 50 minutes to complete and yields so much information that computer analysis is essential. The computer-generated report gives results in terms of 32 generic activities – such as 'planning' – as well as results for more detailed components of these activities – such as 'setting short-term objectives', 'planning a logical sequence' or 'anticipating problems'. A final advantage of the Work Profiling System is a method, described in a later section of this chapter, for using the job analysis to produce an objective person specification.

The **Occupational Analysis Inventory (OAI)** (Cunningham et al., 1983) is a long inventory that contains 622 descriptions of work activities and conditions, which are grouped into five main areas: information received, mental activities, observable behaviour, work outcomes and work context. The inventory was designed for technical jobs but it can be used for more general occupations. OAI is particularly good at capturing the technical content of jobs, but its length means that it is time-consuming.

The **Job Components Inventory (JCI)** (Banks et al., 1982) features almost 400 items, covering tools and equipment, physical and perceptual requirements, mathematical requirements, and decision-making and responsibility. The inventory is particularly strong in the areas of mathematical requirements and the use of tools and equipment. Administration takes the form of an interview with an incumbent, which lasts about 45 minutes. The Job Components Inventory is particular good for analysing entry-level jobs.

Functional Job Analysis (FJA) (Fine and Wiley, 1971) is not an inventory but, rather, a method of analysing jobs using a controlled vocabulary, in which activities are grouped according to whether an incumbent is dealing with people, data or things. Several days of training are needed to master the technique of Functional Job Analysis.

An excellent and more detailed explanation of job analysis is given by Pearn and Kandola (1988). Several authors, such as Campbell (1994), Borman and Motowidlo (1993) and Viswesvaran and Ones (2000), have criticized present methods of job analysis because they are incomplete. Most methods focus upon discrete, specific tasks that produce identifiable results. However, most jobs require a worker to behave in a way that contributes to more diffuse outcomes, such as maintaining morale, courtesy and helping others. These kinds of 'citizenship behaviour' are often missed. A job description should therefore be inspected to check whether these less well-defined activities have been omitted.

▶ 2.2 PERSON SPECIFICATIONS

At the end of the job analysis phase, a recruiter has a very clear idea of the job. This is useful in training, organizational structuring and job grading. However, recruiters have little direct use for job descriptions, because they select candidates on the basis of candidate's knowledge, skills and abilities. The job analysis is only useful because it is an important intermediate step in determining the knowledge skills and abilities that are needed. Statements about competencies form the second important document in selection: the **person specification**. In the past, the distinction between a job analysis and a person specification has been blurred. A job analysis has often been called a 'task-oriented job analysis', while a person specification has often been called 'a worker-oriented job analysis'.

The way in which the person specification is a derived from a job analysis is often more of an art than a science. Usually, an expert is asked to review the job analysis, and on the basis of experience he or she divines the knowledge skills and abilities (competencies) that are needed. An expert's mental database is usually built up over many years. The next three chapters, on ability, personality and motivation, provide some of the facts and theories that experts might use. The remainder of this chapter will be divided into two sections: a straightforward approach to producing a person specification and more complex approaches.

2.2.1 A STRAIGHTFORWARD APPROACH TO PERSON SPECIFICATIONS

An adequate person specification can be produced by taking an interview plan, such as Rodger's Seven Point Plan, and listing the competencies needed under two headings: essential characteristics and desirable characteristics. A simple example is given in figure 2.1. Rodger's Seven Point Plan is a simple framework that systematically covers most of the characteristics that are relevant to work:

1 *Physical make-up* includes health, physique, appearance, grooming, strength, impact on others and speech.
2 *Attainments* include such things as educational qualifications, training completed, licences, membership of professional bodies, offices held, membership of clubs and societies, success in competitions, occupational experience and career progression.
3 *General intelligence* involves the ability to identify key aspects of a problem, the deduction of the relationship between the different parts of the problem and the ability to deduce the next step in the sequence. It is sometimes useful to distinguish between the intelligence that an individual *can* access and how much he or she actually uses in practice. A fuller explanation of intelligence is given in chapter 3.
4 *Special aptitudes* include numerical reasoning, verbal reasoning, memory, mechanical reasoning, spatial reasoning, musical aptitudes, artistic aptitudes and manual dexterity.
5 *Interests* includes a liking for outdoor, mechanical, scientific, persuasive, artistic, literary, social service, clerical, practical, intellectual or medical activities.
6 *Disposition* deals with aspects of personality and includes such things as relationships with people, an optimistic approach, an active approach (extroversion), level emotions, self-assurance, lack of tension and trust (emotional stability). A fuller explanation of personality is given in chapter 4.
7 *Home circumstances* include those aspects of an employee's domestic situation that justifiably impinge on the job. Usually, this involves the ability to work shifts or travel away from home. Great care should be taken with these topics in order to avoid infringing equal opportunities legislation and prying into people's lives – however well intentioned the intrusion might be.

The Seven Point Plan is a well-tried method, but it is not sacrosanct. An example of a simple person specification is given in appendix 2.2, at the end of this chapter. With thought, it can be tailored to meet the precise needs of specific organizations. It is often advisable to omit irrelevant sections. Furthermore, other plans are available. Perhaps the most well known alternative is Munro Frazer's (1966) Five Point Plan, which arranges a person specification under five headings: impact on others, acquired knowledge, innate abilities, motivation, and adjustment.

2.2.2 SOPHISTICATED WAYS OF PRODUCING PERSON SPECIFICATIONS

A person specification based on the Seven Point Plan will be adequate for many situations. However, more sophisticated methods will be appropriate if the job is very important or if it is a job that is done by many employees. In essence, there are four sophisticated approaches: Repertory Grids, Empirical Job Component Analysis, Expert Systems and an Intuitive Method based on theory. The first three of these are described below. The theories on which the Intuitive Method is based are given in the next three chapters.

Repertory Grids

Repertory Grids are probably the most objective and scientific way of deriving person specifications from a job analysis and the method usually proceeds in three stages: task analysis, eliciting competencies and grading the tasks of the competencies.

The process *starts* with a list of the most important tasks performed in a job. This list may be obtained in any of the ways outlined in section 2.1.

In the *second stage*, the competencies are elicited in an ingenious way. Three tasks are chosen at random and presented to incumbents or other SMEs. They are asked to consider the skills, knowledge, abilities or other human characteristics that are required in order to complete each of the tasks successfully. The SMEs are then asked to say which two of the three tasks are most similar in terms of the characteristics needed. The actual nomination is not significant. The important part is the response to the supplementary question, 'What characteristic makes two of the tasks similar but different from the third in terms of skill and competencies need to do this job?' For example, a senior civil servant might be presented with the tasks of appearing before the Public Accounts Committee, giving oral presentations and assessing policies – the first two tasks are seen as similar to each other but different to the third. The response to the supplementary question might be that the first two tasks involve skills in persuading other people. At this point, it has been established that at least one person thinks that persuading people is an important skill for a senior civil servant. This procedure is known as 'triadic elicitation'. It has a very important advantage: subjects may answer in any way that *they* think is appropriate. There is no possibility of the analyst making conscious or unconscious suggestions that are mimicked. Triadic elicitation is repeated with another randomly chosen triads until a SME starts to repeat earlier answers. This is a signal that the SME's mental repertoire has been exhausted and it generally occurs after between seven and 12 triads have been presented.

Third, a grid is constructed, with the tasks along the top and the skills down the side. An incumbent is asked to work methodically along the rows, grading each task on the extent to which it requires the skill or characteristic. Usually, a five-point scale is used, as shown in table 2.2, which is an extract from a larger grid.

The triadic process and grading are repeated with as many SMEs as possible – everyone uses the same tasks, but individuals will nominate different knowledge, skills and so on. A thorough analysis will involve tens of subjects, but quite acceptable results can be obtained from five or six people. The grids are then submitted to a specialized computer package, such as Slater's (1974) Grid Analysis Package, which combines them and performs a factor analysis. The factors that emerge provide an objective and quantitative person specification.

Table 2.2 An example of a Repertory Grid

	Understanding policy	Appearing before PAC	Briefing ministers	Managing area	Financial estimates
Persuading people	1	5	5	3	1
Numerical ability	4	2	1	3	5
Analysing problems	5	4	3	3	3
Foresight	5	3	3	2	4
Motivating staff	1	1	3	5	2
Using Gantt charts	1	1	2	5	1
Assembling facts	2	5	5	2	3

For example, an analysis of the results for senior civil servants might reveal eight significant factors:

1 Analytical ability   23%
2 All oral presentations skills   16%
3 Management skills   9%
4 Detailed specialist knowledge   6%
5 Drafting skills   5%
6 Decision-making skills   4%
7 Breadth of mind   4%
8 Foresight   3%

The method has a number of advantages. First, the information is not contaminated by the ideas of the analyst. Second, the specification is expressed in words that are familiar and 'owned' by incumbents. Third, it gives a quantitative guide that suggests that, for example, a selector should expend approximately four times as much effort assessing analytical ability as examining drafting skills.

Repertory Grid analysis has two other important advantages. The analysis estimates the difficulty of the various tasks. In addition, it allows the skills needed for individual tasks to be specified. For example, it can be estimated that success in appearing before the Public Accounts Committee depends .4 on presentation skills, .3 on specialist knowledge, .2 on analytical ability and .2 on breadth of mind. Few other methods of devising a person specification have so many advantages. Unfortunately, the Repertory Grid method requires specialist statistical skills in order to exploit all the opportunities.

Empirical Job Component Analysis

Considerable empirical data has been collected for job analysis questionnaires such as McCormick's Position Analysis Questionnaire. This data has been linked to worker characteristics by equations. Consequently, the results from a PAQ can be keyed into a computer and the characteristics needed in order to perform a job can be calculated (McCormick et al., 1972; McCormick, 1976). A practical example of this approach is given by Sparrow et al. (1982).

Experts System Analysis

It is tedious and costly to obtain sufficient data for an Empirical Job Component Analysis. An alternative is to ask experts to estimate the skills needed for various tasks. In this approach, the results of a job analysis questionnaire will be shown to a group of experts, who will go through the questionnaire scale by scale and rate the skills needed for each task. Their ratings are incorporated in a computer program. When the results from a subsequent job analysis are entered on the computer, the skills that are needed for that job can be printed out. This approach is less rigorous than one based on empirical data, but it is quicker and cheaper and can be applied more readily in specific situations. A classic example of an expert system analysis is provided by Saville Holdsworth's system, which is based on their Work Profiling System.

2.2.3 COMPETENCIES

The skills, knowledge, abilities and so on that are needed to perform a job are often called competencies. The competency movement was triggered by a book by Boyatzis (1982), which was based on his experience as a management consultant. To many, competencies were merely old wine in a new bottle. To devotees, it was the dawn of a new era in human resource management. Boyatzis defined a competency as an underlying characteristic of a person. Hornby and Thomas (1989) defined them as 'the knowledge, skills and qualities of effective managers and leaders'. One of the best definitions is given by Woodruffe (1992): 'a competency is the set of behaviour patterns that the incumbent needs to bring to a position in order to perform its tasks and functions with competence'. The advantage of this definition is that it features behaviour patterns which vary from individual to individual and that are relevant to the performance of a job.

There are many lists of management competencies. Table 2.3 is based on an analysis, by Bristow (2001), of competencies used by 60 organizations. 700 separate competencies could be categorized into 27 major management competencies. A typical organization uses about 12 competencies. There is a temptation for organizations to produce lists that are too long and impractical. The optimum number of competencies is between two and nine.

2.2.4 FAIRNESS IN JOB DESCRIPTIONS AND PERSON SPECIFICATIONS

Unfair job descriptions are fairly uncommon, because the tasks that are involved in a job and the other details are often objective. Nevertheless, it is worthwhile involving some members of a minority group in any job analysis exercise. Further, job analyses should be scrutinized to see whether the same goals can be achieved in different ways. The assumption that a job must be conducted in a conventional way may discriminate against disabled people who often find ways of overcoming their disability by using innovative work methods.

Unfair person specifications are often produced unwittingly – usually by applying time-honoured practices. A person specification is unfair when it demands a characteristic which is not actually necessary in order to perform a job but that differentiates two groups of people. For example, specifying that a police officer must be 1.8 m (6 ft) tall is likely to be discriminatory

Table 2.3 Competencies used by major organizations

Competency	Components	Percentage of organizations
1. Communication	Written communication, oral communication	97%
2. Self-management	Personal effectiveness, self-control, self-discipline, self-confidence, resilience	75%
3. Organizational ability	Organizational awareness, delegation, control, structure	68%
4. Influence	Impact on others, networking, negotiation	67%
5. Teamwork	Team membership, team leadership	60%
6. Interpersonal skills	Relationships, dealing with individual people	58%
7. Analytical ability	Conceptual thinking, problem-solving	58%
8. Results orientation	Achievement focus, concern for effectiveness	55%
9. Customer focus	Customer service, customer orientation	53%
10. Developing people's potential	Enabling others, coaching	53%
11. Strategic ability	Vision, breadth of view, forward thinking	52%
12. Commercial awareness	Business acumen, market and competitor awareness	48%
13. Decision-making	Decisiveness, evaluating options	48%
14. Planning	Planning and organizing, action planning, task planning	40%
15. Leadership	Providing purpose and direction, motivating others	40%
16. Self-motivation	Enthusiasm for work, achievement drive, commitment, energy, drive, will to win	35%
17. Specialist knowledge	Expertise, professional knowledge, functional expertise, operational understanding	35%
18. Flexibility	Adaptability, mental agility	32%
19. Creativity	Innovation, breakthrough thinking	32%
20. Initiative	Proactivity	31%
21. Change orientation	Change management, openness to change	23%
22. Dealing with information	Information gathering, information processing	20%
23. Concern for quality	Quality focus, concern for excellence	20%
24. Reliability	Accuracy, disciplined approach, procedural compliance, attention to detail, systematic	18%
25. Ethical approach	Integrity, commitment to social and economic equity, valuing people	13%
26. Financial awareness	Financial judgement, cost awareness	12%
27. Negotiating skills		7%
28. Other		15%

because people who are 1.7 m (5 ft 8 in) tall can perform the job adequately. As women are generally shorter than men, this specification would be unfair to women. Similarly, arbitrarily specifying that applicants must be under the age of 30 and have eight year's experience may also discriminate against women. Maternity leave and so on may make it more difficult for women to accumulate eight years' experience before their 30th birthday.

However, it should be noted that requirements that bear more harshly on one group are allowed, provided that they can be shown to be necessary in order to perform the job. For example, in the USA, stipulating that police officers must be taller than 1.6 m (5 ft 4 in) is, apparently, permissible because people who are shorter are unable to perform the vital police activity of shooting a pistol over the top of a car!

Appendix 2.1 An illustrative job description

1	Job title	WOOD MACHINIST (Trencher)

2 Location   MILL SHOP

3 Number in job   8

4 Purpose of job
  - To take pre-cut and pre-planed wood and to cut trenches of specified dimensions at specified positions.

5 Responsibilities
  - Responsible to Mill Shop Foreman.

6 Relationships
  - Works largely on own, but has some contact with the operatives performing previous and subsequent operations. Sometimes required to train new operatives.

7 Physical conditions
  - The Mill Shop is dry, well lit and ventilated, but there is no heating at any time of year; noise levels can be high. Work is performed in standing position. Some lifting and carrying is involved.

8 Outline of job
   1. Transport batch of wood from previous process by pulling along trolley.
   2. Check with specification the position of trenches; change cutters on trencher if necessary.
   3. Take small batches of wood to bench, place in position under trenching machine using preset guides. Pull cutter of trencher forward, keeping hands clear of cutters.
   4. Restack trenched wood neatly and safely.
   5. When batch is completed, pull cart to next operative.
   6. Complete job card and other simple forms.

9 Safety aspects
   The work involves a number of potential hazards:
  - noise from machine
  - falling stacks of wood
  - injury from the cutters of the trenching machine.

10 Salary and conditions of service
   Salary: Flat rate of xxx per week plus monthly group bonus.
   Holidays: Four weeks per year plus bank holidays.
   Hours: Monday–Friday 9.00 a.m. – 5.00 p.m.
                Saturday 8.30 a.m. – 12.30 p.m.
   Breaks: Afternoon and morning breaks of 20 minutes. Lunch break of 1 hour.
   Overtime: Usually available by agreement.

Any job description should always be checked to ensure that it complies with local legislation.

Appendix 2.2 An illustrative personnel specification

Job Title: Upholsterer		Location: Glossopdale

1 Physical characteristics	Essential	•	Able to work in standing position
		•	Able to bend at waist
		•	Free movement of all limbs
	Desirable	•	Normal colour vision
		•	Neat and clean appearance
2 Attainments	Essential	•	Time-served apprenticeship
		•	Member of trade union
3 Intelligence	Desirable	•	Not in bottom third of population
4 Special aptitudes	Essential	•	Spatial ability and ability to work with patterned material – in top 20% of population
		•	Manual dexterity
5 Interests	Desirable	•	Practical and manual interests, especially working with wood or fabric
		•	Interests requiring cleanliness, eye for detail and care over final presentation
6 Disposition	Desirable	•	Self-sufficient approach to life and willingness to work on own, with only infrequent social contact
		•	Willingness to work at a job that offers only a minimum level of variety (that is, not suitable for strong extrovert)
7 Home circumstances	Essential	•	Absence of commitments that could present difficulties to working shifts
8 Contra-indications	Essential	•	Medical history of rheumatic or muscular disease, or back trouble
		•	Working history involving minor accidents

CHAPTER 3

AN INTRODUCTION TO INTELLIGENCE AND COGNITIVE ABILITY

SUCCESS IN DOING THINGS

Intelligence is *the* mega-concept in psychology. No other aspect of human behaviour has been the subject of so many books or articles. No other aspect of human behaviour has been so thoroughly researched. No other human characteristic accounts for so much variation in human behaviour. Intelligence correlates, for example, with the age at which you start to talk, the age at which you learn to read, your educational success, the kind of job you will enter, your occupational success in that job, the person you will marry, the success of your children and your adjustment to life. Intelligence is to psychology what the atom bomb is to physics and the double helix is to biology. Such an important and ubiquitous variable has far-reaching implications for the 'human condition'. No wonder it has been so controversial.

Intelligence has been acknowledged as a key variable in psychology for over 100 years. Furthermore, intelligence has been reliably measured for almost 100 years. Today, only a very few psychologists dispute its existence. However, some people shy away from using the term because they believe that it has negative connotations, resulting from the use of intelligence tests in educational selection and the debate on racial differences. Yet the term is so useful that an alternative is needed. The politically correct term for intelligence is general **cognitive ability**. The topic of cognitive ability can be covered under five main headings:

1 Definition of intelligence
2 The structure of intelligence
3 Measuring intelligence
4 Stability of intelligence, practice and coaching
5 Specific issues and controversies

Many books have been written about intelligence. This chapter gives only a superficial account.

3.1 DEFINITION OF INTELLIGENCE

People with obvious intelligence are said to be *quick*-witted, *quick* on the uptake or smart. People with low intelligence are said to be witless, brainless, addle-headed, *slow* on the uptake or 'plodders'. These common usages would seem to point to the fact that intelligence is concerned with the brain and the speed of thinking. There is also a wealth of evidence that intelligence is related to the functioning of the brain (see Jensen and Sinah, 1993). When intelligent people solve a problem, their brains use up less sugar than the brains of less intelligent people (Haier, 1993). When intelligent people are shown a stimulus, their brains react in a more predictable way (that is, the brain waves are less variable). This probably means that nerve impulses are transmitted in a more dependable way and less time is spent eliminating random signals (see, for example, Eysenck, 1986; Anderson, 1992). When people are given a task that involves passing information from one level of thinking to another, intelligent people transfer the information at a faster rate than unintelligent people. None of these physiological factors has a perfect correlation with intelligence (and therefore cannot be substituted as a measure of intelligence), but they relentlessly point to the conclusion that intelligence has a lot to do with the relative efficiency with which the brain processes information. Intelligence may therefore be defined as:

. . . the relative speed and accuracy with which the brain processes complex information.

Probably one of the best non-physiological definitions of intelligence was given by the pioneer Charles Spearman, who defined intelligence as an amalgam of three mental processes (neogenetic laws):

- The **apprehension of reality**: a person 'looks' at a problem and is able to *identify the most salient elements*.
- The **eduction of relationships**: the salient elements are linked and the *relationships between them identified*.
- The **eduction of correlates**: *existing relationships are extended* into new or future situations, and further steps in the sequence are anticipated.

Spearman's three neogenetic laws can seen in the following problem:

2, 4, 6, 8, . . .   What comes next?

To answer, it is first necessary to realize that the salient elements are numbers (apprehension of reality). Second, it is necessary to realize that the numbers are even numbers in an ascending series (eduction of relations). Third, by extending the relationship, the next number in the series, 10, is deduced (eduction of correlates).

A further example of the neogenetic laws would be:

'hand is to arm as foot is to . . .'

Apprehension of reality gives realization that the salient elements are limbs. Eduction of relations indicates that the hand is at the end of the arm. Eduction of correlates applies the same relationship to the foot, which is at the end of the leg. Neogenetic laws can be applied to spatial problems such as:

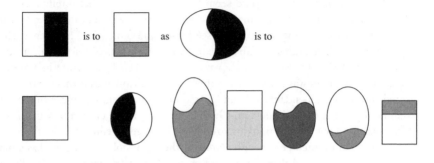

Figure 3.1 A spatial problem.

This is much more difficult because the brain must deal simultaneously with four factors. It must be apprehended that the salient features are shading, proportion and rotation. Then the relationships must be educed: dark goes to grey, half goes to a quarter and rotation is clockwise. Third, the correlates of these relationships mean that only the only figure that satisfies these relationships is the penultimate one.

Spearman emphasized that the neogenetic laws only applied when the problems did not involve specialized knowledge. He called this the **indifference of the indicator**. Most English people would find the following problem easy:

M T W T F . . .   What comes next?

But most English-speaking people would find the following problem much more difficult:

L M M J V . . .   What comes next?

According to Spearman, intelligence is something that helps people to solve problems, where the elements can be apprehended by almost everyone.

◤ 3.2 THE STRUCTURE OF INTELLIGENCE

Probably the first person to examine the structure of intelligence was Spearman, in 1904. In 1923, Spearman noted that when tests of mental ability were correlated, the correlation was always positive. The positive correlation among all measures of mental ability is called the **positive manifold**. The positive manifold indicates that intelligence is a general ability: if you are good at one type of mental problem you will *tend* to be good at all types of problems.

Spearman developed a primitive type of factor analysis (tetrad equations) to test his ideas and he concluded that intelligence consists of one big general factor, which he called 'g'. Spearman's view has received support from recent physiological research. Modern techniques such as magnetic resonance imaging can identify which part of the brain is active when a problem is being solved. The results indicate that the same part of the brain (the frontal cortex) is active even when the problems involve different elements such as patterns, words or numbers. A detailed examination of many aspects of Spearman's 'g' is given by Jensen (1998).

Although hotly debated (for an excellent account, see Blinkhorn, 1998), Spearman's view remained strong until the late 1930s, when it was contested by Thurstone (1938), who maintained that intelligence consisted of several specific factors. A great debate ensued. In the early 1950s, Spearman's analysis was slightly modified by Vernon (1950), who took two group factors into account. The small group factors were v:ed (verbal and educational factors, which are important in educational achievement) and k:m (spatial factors).

A fresh series of factor-analytic studies was conducted by Horn and Cattell (1966), Gustafsson (1984) and Carroll (1993). They suggest a hierarchical structure of intelligence. At the third, and highest, level is the '3g' factor – to all intents and purposes Spearman's 'g'. At the second level are eight factors, two of which are very large:

- **Fluid intelligence (2gf)**, the largest factor, is the basic reasoning ability, which can be applied to a wide range of problems. It is a very broad factor, which is close to Spearman's 'g' and is associated with neuronal efficiency in the cortex of the brain. gf is measured by culture-fair tests, such as Raven's Progressive Matrices, and is close to the ability to educe correlates. Independent researchers such as Undheim and Gustaffson (1987) have also identified one broad factor of fluid ability, which is similar to Spearman's 'g'.
- **Crystallized intelligence (2gc)** is thought to develop from fluid intelligence – up to the age of three years, gf and gc are very highly correlated. But crystallized intelligence develops as the person starts to invest his or her mental abilities in the skills of his or her culture. In the West, these are often the traditional skills of education that are measured by many intelligence tests. Some people suggest that crystallized intelligence resembles Vernon's V:ed.

The smaller factors at level two are:

- 2y (general memory and learning)
- 2v (visual perception)
- 2u (auditory perception)
- 2r (retrieval ability)
- 2s (cognitive speediness)
- 2t (processing speed/decision speed).

Each of the second-level factors, in turn, contains first-level factors (the small boxes in figure 3.1). For example, the small memory factors include memory span, associative memory, free recall memory and so on.

On the basis of Deary (2000), the structure of intelligence may be depicted as shown in figure 3.1.

Thus fluid intelligence is one of the largest factors whose variance is completely shared with 'g'. Crystallized intelligence is of a similar size and about two-thirds of its variance is shared with 'g'. The smaller factors share approximately one half of their variance with the general factor of intelligence. Carroll (1993) suggests that there are few differences in the structure of intelligence according to sex or ethnic group. Bickley et al. (1995) conclude that 'the existence of "g" is difficult to dispute [and there is] compelling evidence that the three-stratum theory

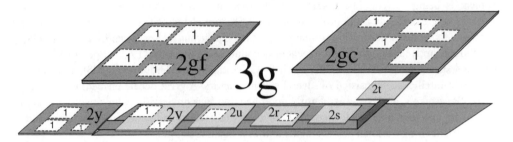

Figure 3.2 The hierarchical structure of intelligence.

may form a parsimonious model of intelligence. The fact that it is grounded in a strong founda-
tion of vast, previous research also lends strong support for the acceptance of the model.'

3.3 MEASURING INTELLIGENCE

The earliest attempts to measure scientifically intelligence were a disaster. In the late 1800s,
Francis Galton attempted to equate intelligence with reaction times, but he failed. Subsequent
attempts have been more successful.

3.3.1 BINET AND SIMON'S TEST

Binet made a breakthrough in 1905. The education authorities in Paris were implementing
a policy of universal education. However a small minority of children were proving difficult to
educate within the resources of the time. Binet's genius was to realize that, in the case of children, intelligence was related to age. If a child of eight could equal the cognitive ability of a
child of ten, that child would be advanced. However, a child of eight who could only equal a
child of six would have problems.

Binet established the mental problems that the average four year old, the average five year
old, the average six year old and so on could answer. He could then administer the questions
to an individual child, compare that child's answers with those of the other children and determine the average age of children of equivalent ability. This was termed the **mental age**. To
obtain an index of a child's mental ability, the mental age could be divided by the actual age
(the **chronological age**). If the result of the calculation was greater than one, the child was
advanced. If the result was less than one, the child was 'backward'. In 1912, Stern invented the
IQ scale by multiplying the ratio by 100 (see Stern, 1965). The formula is:

$$IQ = \frac{mental\ age}{chronological\ age} \times 100$$

A child whose actual age was eight but who could equal a child of ten would have an IQ of
125. The child of eight who could only equal a child of six would have an IQ of 75. When the
IQs of a large number of children had been gathered, it emerged that intelligence was normally
distributed, with a standard deviation of just over 17.

The Binet scale was revised by Terman and Merrill at Stanford University, the revised test is sometimes called the Stanford–Binet test.

Binet and Simon's method worked well with children, but it was hopeless with adults because intelligence is no longer related to age once people are older than, say, 17. Therefore an age-related scale is not appropriate for use with bright people who are older than about 13 years. The modern method of measuring IQ takes this into account and uses norm-referenced IQs based upon the standard deviation (see section 3.3.4).

3.3.2 THE ARMY ALPHA AND ARMY BETA

The mobilization of the American army during the First World War posed a significant problem of classifying soldiers so that the most able could be trained as officers. The army devised two tests, the Army Alpha and the Army Beta. The Army Alpha was used with men who were literate, while the Army Beta was used with soldiers who could not read. The use of the Army Alpha and Army Beta tests was one of the first mass programmes of testing intelligence, and the tests served as a model for many later intelligence tests. Revisions of these tests are still used today.

3.3.3 THE WECHSLER ADULT INTELLIGENCE SCALE (WAIS)

The WAIS was constructed in 1938, on a different principle to the Binet test. It sought to overcome the limitation that the Binet test could not be used with adults. Wechsler devised a test that contained 11 types of problem:

- information – general knowledge likely to be encountered by most people
- comprehension – understanding everyday situations
- arithmetic – solving practical arithmetical problems
- similarities – identifying the link between objects and ideas
- digit span – remembering strings of random numbers
- vocabulary – the ability to verbalize meanings of words
- digit symbol – the input–output speed when coding numbers into simple shapes
- picture completion – identifying the missing parts from sketches
- block design – arranging cubes to reproduce a pattern
- picture arrangement – arranging a series of sketches so that they convey a story
- object assembly – arranging the pieces of a 'jigsaw' to make an object.

Each kind of problem (scale) featured questions that covered the range from very easy to very difficult.

Wechsler administered the test to a large random sample of the population and calculated the standard deviation of their scores. When the test is administered to a single person, it is easy to determine how many standard deviations above or below the mean that person lies. It is also possible to convert the score into an IQ. When Binet administered his test to a large sample of people, he found that the standard deviation was a little over 17. This is an arithmetically inconvenient number, so Wechsler and colleagues adopted a standard deviation of 15. Today, most intelligence quotients adopt a standard deviation of 15, but some scales (notably the Cattell tests and those used by MENSA) have rounded the 17 up to 20 and have a standard deviation of 20. The formula for calculating Wechsler IQs is as follows:

$$IQ = (sds\ from\ mean \times 15) + 100$$

The first six scales all involve words (numbers are a special kind of word) and they can be combined to produce a verbal IQ, which is roughly equivalent to Carroll's gc and Vernon's V:ed. The latter five scales can be combined to produce a performance IQ, which is roughly equivalent to gf.

Like the Binet test, the WAIS is an individual test, where there is one administrator for each candidate. The administrators need training at the highest level, because they need to interpret answers and position equipment. The WAIS is therefore expensive and is used infrequently in industry.

3.3.4 RAVEN'S PROGRESSIVE MATRICES

Raven's Progressive Matrices were developed at about the same time as the WAIS and have been very extensively researched. The results of the research indicate that they are a fairly pure measure of 'gf'. Subjects are asked to look at a 3×3 matrix from which the final object has been omitted. They have to educe the relationships between the other eight objects and then use that relationship to educe the correlate in the ninth box that would complete the pattern. The patterns do not use culturally based questions.

Raven's Progressive Matrices are often accompanied by the Mill Hill Vocabulary Scale, which is a very good measure of verbal ability (gc).

3.3.5 OTHER TESTS OF INTELLIGENCE

Most major test publishers offer a range of intelligence tests. In general, these are tests that measure general intelligence, verbal intelligence and spatial intelligence. A typical test of general intelligence would be the AH4. Most publishers also offer different levels of intelligence tests for use with specific occupations. For example, the AH5 is similar to the AH4, but is more difficult and is probably more suitable for graduates. Many tests of cognitive ability, such as the Watson–Glazer Test of Critical Thinking and Saville Holdsworth's Advanced Managerial Tests, have been designed for use with graduates or managers.

3.4 STABILITY OF INTELLIGENCE, PRACTICE AND COACHING

3.4.1 STABILITY

Despite all their faults, tests of intelligence are some of the best measures available in psychology. Typically, the reliability of intelligence scores is in the region of .9. The WAIS, for example, has a reliability of .97, while the reliability of the AH4 test is .92. These correlations are comparable to those obtained when comparing the lengths of a sample's left and right arms. Whatever they may measure, intelligence tests measure it very consistently!

The stability of intelligence after the age of 20 is also remarkable. Deary (2000) lists 15 studies in which people were retested. The average interval between tests was 23 years and the 'average' correlation was .72. In the case of one data set, people were retested after an interval of 66 years (Deary et al., 2000) and a correlation of .73 was obtained. Converse and Markus (1979) have calculated that the annual stability coefficient for intelligence data is .99. Few other psychological characteristics have anywhere near this level of stability.

3.4.2 PRACTICE AND COACHING

High test–retest correlations do not mean that people's intelligence is immutable. The correlations indicate that people's relative positions remain constant – if everyone's score were to increase by 10, the individual scores would differ but the correlation would be 1. A uniform improvement of this kind is unlikely, but some people might improve their scores as a result of practice or coaching. Repeating the same or a similar test does improve scores by about four IQ points and some of this effect can last for a year or more. The precise level of improvement depends upon the person and the tests.

The biggest gains are shown by *people* who:

- Have no experience whatsoever of testing. Practice effects quickly show diminishing returns: repeated practice has less and less effect.
- Have initial high scores. Bright people gain most from practice.

The biggest gains are shown on *tests* that:

- Have a low loading on 'g'. Tests that are 'g' saturated are more resistant to practice effects.
- Are identical or very similar. The more the tests differ, the lower is the practice effect. Repeating the same test after a short interval can improve scores by eight IQ points. Using parallel forms of a test reduces the practice effect to three or four points. Completing a different test after a long interval is likely to produce a practice effect of less than three IQ points.
- Are timed. These tests increase the practice effects by between 10% and 25%. Untimed tests minimize practice effects.
- Involve materials and equipment that may be unfamiliar.

Coaching consists of someone teaching applicants how to take tests. For example, an applicant may be taught how to analyse problems. The main effects of coaching were outlined as long ago as 1960, by Vernon. In general, coaching is ineffective unless it includes practice on a very similar test. The effects of coaching are highly specific and do not transfer to other types of test. Indeed, coaching may even lower a person's score on another type of test (that is, negative transfer). Furthermore, any gains from coaching fade rapidly.

Practical Implications Concerning Practice and Coaching

Because practice and coaching can have some effect, it is important to equalize applicants' previous experience as far as possible. Much can be achieved by *levelling up* test experience. Candidates should be given practice tests before they complete the 'real' test. This can usually can be achieved by sending practice tests to candidates' homes. Alternatively, practice tests can be given at the start of a testing session. Precautions should also be taken to *prevent practice*, by denying candidates prior access to tests. Tests should be held in a secure place and only issued to qualified personnel. Finally, candidates should be asked point blank *questions about their past experience* with tests in general and with the tests used in particular. Tests that they have completed during the past 12 months should be noted in the test log.

 ## 3.5 SPECIFIC ISSUES AND CONTROVERSIES

Intelligence is such an important topic, with such important consequences, that it has been embroiled in controversy. From time to time, you may read the accounts of some of these controversies, or you may be asked about them by candidates whom you are testing. It is therefore advisable to be aware of the following issues:

- *Boring's epigram.* 'Intelligence is what intelligence tests measure.' Do the tests measure anything that is worthwhile?
- *Multiple intelligences.* Many people do not accept the idea that intelligence is largely a single, general factor 'g'. Thurstone, Guilford, Gardner and Sternberg are amongst those who believe that there is more than one kind of intelligence.
- *The Burt affair.* After his death, Cyril Burt, a pillar of the British psychology establishment, was accused of fabricating data that showed that intelligence is largely determined by heredity. The initial judgement was that Burt did falsify some of his data, and that he invented co-authors to help hide his deception. More recently, doubts about his culpability have increased – especially since the discovery of someone who was probably one of his disputed co-workers.
- *The Flynn effect.* Some research suggests that intelligence increases in each generation. Is this true? How might it be caused?
- *Heritability.* What are the methods and problems in establishing the extent to which intelligence and other psychological characteristics are inherited?

It is not possible to explore these controversies in this volume, but they are covered on the website that accompanies this book.

CHAPTER 4

AN INTRODUCTION TO PERSONALITY

THE *STYLE* OF DOING THINGS

The subject of personality is fascinating and a great deal of time is spent analysing other people's temperaments. Personality is so complex that we do not have enough brain power to analyse each person separately. We save mental effort by developing a few personality theories and then applying these theories to people. Theories that we develop for ourselves are called **implicit theories**. Some theories are worked out in great scientific detail. The accumulated knowledge that is explicitly stated in the literature is called **formal personality theory**. Books on formal personality theory have been likened to a graveyard tour (Singer and Kolligan, 1987) that, chronologically, takes in the work of dead theorists such as Freud, Jung, Maslow, Rogers and so on. These works are little more than updated copycats of an ancient text that divided personality theories into four categories: psychoanalytic theory, trait theory, humanistic theory and cognitive-social theory. This chapter is structured in a different way:

1 Definitions of personality – personality is defined and differentiated from related concepts
2 Does personality exist? – The existence of personality is considered
3 What makes up personality? Traits – The nature of personality is discussed and it is concluded that personality is made up of traits
4 Theories of the determinants of personality – theories of personality are described, this long section being subdivided as follows:
   • *implicit theories* of personality
   • *modern, scientific theories*:
     – biological theory
     – environmental theory
     – the social learning theory of personality
   • *mythological theories*:
     – psychoanalytic theory
     – the humanistic view of personality.

◤ 4.1 DEFINITIONS OF PERSONALITY

The most widely quoted definition is that of Allport (1937): 'the dynamic organization within the individual of those psychophysical systems that determine his unique adjustment to his environment'. Allport also defined personality traits as 'neuropsychic system(s) . . . with the capacity to render many stimuli functionally equivalent, and to initiate and guide consistent forms of adaptive and expressive behaviour'. This definition includes everything about the person – it is so broad that it is almost useless. It makes no distinctions between ability, motives and interests, which are essential in guidance and selection. It is therefore necessary to look at other definitions, such as the following:

- 'That which permits a prediction of what a person will do in a given situation.' (Cattell, 1965)
- '[O]ne's habits and usual style, but also . . . the ability to play roles.' (Cronbach, 1984)
- 'Personality: The characteristics of thought, emotion and behaviour that define an individual's personal style and influence his or her interactions with the environment.' (Atkinson et al., 1990)
- '[M]ore or less stable, internal factors that make one person's behaviour consistent from one time to another, and different from the behaviour other people would manifest in comparable situations.' (Child, 1968)
- '[P]eople's characteristic tendency to behave, think and feel in certain ways'. (Arnold et al., 1992)
- 'Temperament' generally refers to typical or characteristic modes of behaviour – behavioural style, as it were. 'Personality' is usually a more inclusive term encompassing all that is meant by 'temperament' but referring also to more basic theoretical constructs such as needs, defence mechanisms, or emotional states (Guion, 1965).

The recurring elements of these definitions are:

- style or mode
- enduring characteristics that allow prediction
- adjustment (or non-adjustment) to the environment
- personality involves of ways of:
  - thinking
  - behaving
  - feeling (emotion)
- one person's personality is different to that of other people.

Thus personality is not about *what* is done (which usually reflects motivation) or *success* in doing something (which usually reflects ability). It is about the *way* in which things are done. Consequently, personality may be defined as follows:

> the relative consistencies of style that people show in the way they think, act and feel as they respond to their environments

Unlike some earlier definitions, this does not include the terms 'unique' or 'defining' – which would be included in an Allportian, ideographic, definition. Although personality is complex and it will be rare for two people to have personalities that are identical, the possibility cannot be discounted – especially in twins who have identical heredity.

A problem with this definition, and with others, is the differentiation of 'personality' from 'ability' – the introduction of the term 'think' allows potential for overlap. However, ability concerns the efficiency and effectiveness of thinking, whereas personality concerns the style of thinking, such as grounded or imaginative. Of course, the two aspects may be related. Some theorists get around the problem by saying that cognitive ability is a part of personality. This goes against most practical uses, as seen in catalogues, test certification, the organization of testing sessions, academic journals and so on. Because of the potential for confusing personality with other concepts, it is useful to briefly consider these other concepts.

The distinction between personality and ability is fairly easy, and was discussed in detail in a previous chapter. In essence, ability is '*success* in doing things'. The distinction between personality and the motivational concepts of needs, values, attitudes and interests is much more difficult. In essence, motivational factors concern what we *choose* to do and they are discussed in more detail in the next chapter.

▶ 4.2 DOES PERSONALITY EXIST?

A basic question raised by people such as Mischel (1968) is 'Does personality exist?' Various writers have maintained that people behave very differently in different situations and that there are very few regularities in styles of behaviour. This reasoning goes back to the classic work of Hartsorne and May (1928) on cheating. They found that different people cheat in different situations. There was, for example only a low correlation between cheating in examinations and cheating in other situations. Consequently, they argued that there can be no such thing as an honest personality – it all depends on the situation. Mischel's ideas cast a great deal of doubt on orthodox thinking and spawned a great deal of research, which did indeed show that by controlling the situation, people (who should have consistent personalities) could be made to behave in inconsistent ways.

Some researchers, such as McAdams (1990), regard Mischel as a villain who caused personality research to go off course. It has been claimed that the experiments of Mischel and his co-workers were flawed in a way that emphasized the importance of situations. Others have criticized Mischel and his colleagues because:

- they misrepresented trait theory (which *does not* maintain that people always act in the same way)
- their research was shoddy and did not take sufficient measures over a long time period
- inconsistency is *itself* a trait
- situations differ – strong situations that force behaviour patterns are fairly infrequent, while weak situations in which traits are the main influence are relatively common.

Work by Small et al. (1983) flatly contradicts Mischel's views. They observed adolescents over a period of several weeks. They used a series of measures to gauge how dominant and co-operative they were during different situations such as camping, meal times and free time. The correlations were impressive. *Every* correlation was over .3 and three-quarters of the correlations were over .7: the adolescents *were* behaving consistently across situations.

Others, such as McCrae and Costa (1990), have been able to show considerable consistencies in behaviour (that is, personality). There is overwhelming evidence that, after the age of 30, personality is very stable: indeed, it has been likened to something 'set in plaster'. There is longitudinal evidence, particularly from the Baltimore ageing study, that the 30-year correlations are as follows:

- neuroticism   .83
- extroversion   .82
- openness   .83
- agreeableness   .63
- conscientiousness   .79

In general, personality *is* quite constant over long periods. There is weaker evidence that between the ages of 18 and 21 personality changes by about 4% per year, but some of these changes are in opposite directions and cancel each other out. Balanced reviews by Kenrick and Funder (1988) and Funder (1991) have confirmed the view that personality does indeed exist – much in the form outlined by Allport 60 years previously!

The diversion caused by Mischel may seem irrelevant, but users of personality tests need to know the story: opponents of personality tests may use Mischel's early arguments. In fact, Mischel (Wright and Mischel, 1987) himself abandoned the radical situational approach in favour of an interactionalist perspective.

4.3 WHAT MAKES UP PERSONALITY? TRAITS

Once it is accepted that personality exists, a new question arises: 'What makes up personality?' There have been three main suggestions: ideopathic configurations and syndromes, types, and traits.

4.3.1 IDEOGRAPHIC CONFIGURATIONS AND SYNDROMES

Early psychologists took an ideographic approach that has three basic tenets:

- *Personality is unique* – no two individuals are the same.
- *Personality is holistic* – it must be understood as a whole and it cannot be dissected into parts.
- *Personality is dynamic* – it has a past, a present and a future. The present cannot be understood without knowledge of the past. The future cannot be predicted without knowledge of the past and of the present.

In order to understand someone's personality, we must comprehend the unique set of mental processes. Instead of analysing individual variables such as extroversion, we should be using person–oriented analyses (similar to case studies) and Q-sorts (a very flexible method of classification), and looking for patterns. A modern exposition of the ideographic (holistic) approach is given by Magnusson and Torestad (1993).

Once a number of case studies are collected, it is found that certain clusters repeat themselves. In medicine, a cluster of symptoms is called a **syndrome**. One famous personality test, the Minnesota Multiphasic Personality Inventory, tried to measure psychiatric syndromes such as hypochondriasis, psychopathic deviance and hysteria.

Probably the most famous non-clinical syndrome is the **authoritarian personality** (Adorno et al., 1950). An authoritarian personality is likely to show a cluster of 'symptoms', which include:

- willingness to submit to authority
- a rigid moralism
- the repression of disapproved tendencies in the self and others
- placing people in over-simplified, black or white categories
- an ethnocentric view.

The F (Fascism) scale was developed to measure authoritarianism.

Another well-known syndrome is the **anancastic personality** – someone, often a pillar of society, who is always well ordered, tidy, correct, inflexible and mildly obsessive (Psychejam, 2001).

4.3.2 TYPES

Once patterns of behaviour have been grouped into syndromes, it is only a small step to start thinking about personality in terms of types.

The History and Concepts of the Type Approach

Types can be traced back to the work of ancient philosophers, who thought that personality was determined by the four humours (blood, black bile, yellow bile and phlegm). For example, if your predominant humour was blood, you would have a sanguine type of personality, and if phlegm was predominant, you would be phlegmatic and slow. The use of personality types was all the rage during the first half of the 19th century. In the late 19th century, Lombroso (1870) was busy using phrenology to divide people into criminal and non-criminal types on the basis of the shapes of their heads. In the 1920s, Jung was busy dividing people into sensing and intuiting types and so on (see Jung, 1977); and in the 1940s, Sheldon was busy developing types of personality on the basis of their body build (see Sheldon, 1942).

Types can be defined (McCrae and Costa, 1990) as 'distinct groups of people characterised by a unique configuration of features'. Note the use of the words 'distinct' and 'groups', which imply a clear-cut, multimodal distribution as shown in figure 4.1.

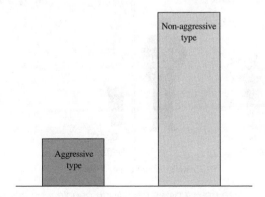

Figure 4.1 The distribution of people into two clear-cut types.

The type approach is clearly justified in the case of some physiological attributes, such as eye colour and blood group. Labelling people in this way is very convenient, both administratively and legally. In industry, many employers hope to select people who are 'leader types' or 'creative types'.

The Advantages of the Type Approach

The main advantage of the type approach is simplicity. Typologies usually offer a simple system that even quite unintelligent people can understand. People who use personality tests based on types acknowledge this weakness, but often justify the test on the basis that they 'find it easy to communicate in an industrial setting'.

The Disadvantages of the Type Approach

The type approach suffers from at least four disadvantages. *First*, it ignores a great deal of empirical evidence that human personality is normally distributed and that people are not divided into just a few groups (see figure 4.2).

Second, dividing people into types can be quite misleading: some dissimilar people can be grouped together, while others who are quite similar can be artificially separated. For example, suppose that three people are divided into small and tall types on the basis of their average height: person A is only 1.1 m tall, person B is 1.8 m tall and person C is 1.9 m tall. Since, in this population, the average height is 1.85 m, persons A and B are called 'short types' and person C is called a 'tall type'. Person B is portrayed as being most similar to A despite the fact that B is actually much more similar to C!

The *third* disadvantage lies in the consequences of labelling people using a simplistic but rigid system. Once you are labelled, it may be very difficult to change the perceptions of others, even if you change quite dramatically! One company used the Myers–Briggs Type Indicator (a personality test based on types – see below) for management development and posted their managers' personality types on the doors of their offices. This practice led to stereotyping and inflexible

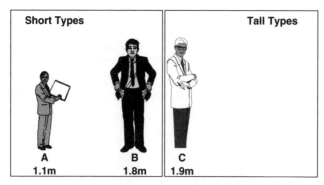

mean height of population

Figure 4.2 Beware. Unwise use of types can divide people who are similar (B and C), while grouping people who are different (A and B).

behaviours – and the stereotyping lasted for many years, despite the fact that some of the younger members had changed.

A *fourth* disadvantage is that we rarely see pure types, so that it is virtually a waste of time to use this way of thinking about personality. Amongst all the people you know, how many are *complete* hypochondriacs, deviant psychopaths, hysterics or hypomanics? There are probably so few that it is not worth your while learning what the words mean.

Measuring Types

Types are often determined by clinicians after an interview or, perhaps a review of life history. They may also be determined by tests. The predominant test that uses the type approach is the Myers–Briggs Type Indicator – although recent modifications allow it to be used in other modes too.

4.3.3 TRAITS

The History and Concepts of the Trait Approach

Trait psychology is usually traced back to the work of Gordon Allport in 1937. Since then, it has been followed by many other people, including Eysenck, Cattell, and Costa and McCrae. Trait psychology is fundamentally based on the idea that personality is made up of a number of characteristics. If we were to measure these characteristics in a perfect way, we would find that people would be distributed on a continuum, probably in a normal distribution, with most people in the centre and fewer and fewer people at the extremes – as shown in figure 4.3.

Traits are neither complex nor profound. A trait is a posh name for a characteristic. McCrae and Costa define a trait as 'a dimension of individual differences in tendencies to show consistent patterns of thoughts, feelings and actions'. Trait theory is based on two self-evident ideas:

- people's thoughts, feelings and actions differ on a number of dimensions
- these dimensions can be measured.

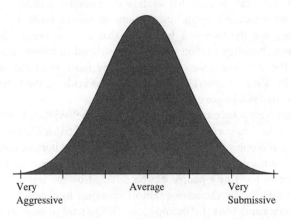

Figure 4.3 The normal distribution of people on the trait of submissiveness.

The trait approach follows the 'natural' order of things. When most human characteristics (for example, height) are measured, they form a normal distribution. When Binet first measured intelligence, it was found to be normally distributed. When extroversion was first measured, it was again found to be normally distributed.

Categories of Traits

Definitions of traits are so broad that they encompass thousands of thoughts, feelings and actions. One count of the English language by Allport and Odbert (1936) identified 16,000 traits. There has been a great deal of effort to reduce or classify traits into a more manageable number. Allport tried to reduce the problem by dividing traits into three types:

- *Cardinal traits* are general and enduring. They are an overriding factor in someone's personality, in the way that hatred of Jews was an overriding factor in the psychological make-up of Adolf Hitler.
- *Central traits* are more common and are the basic units that make up personality. About seven traits describe most of the aspects of personality. They are still general and pervasive but, unlike cardinal traits, they do not swamp all aspects of personality.
- *Secondary traits* are much more specific and localized, such as liking sport, hating curry and handing in assignments late.

Many psychologists, especially Cattell, make the distinction between source traits and surface traits.

Source traits are the basic, fundamental aspects of personality that *direct* the style of behaviour that an individual chooses. They are often given strange names, which may have little direct connection with work behaviour, because the way in which traits are manifested depends on other factors, such as ability and motivation. Furthermore, source traits such as extroversion are multifaceted (Lord, personal communication, 2001). Source traits may often be identified only by **factor analysis**. Some people believe that source traits are more important than surface traits, since they offer greater economy of description because there are fewer of them. Cattell (1950) wrote that 'source traits promise to be the real structural influences underlying personality'. Source traits can be expected to show considerable stability.

Surface traits are produced by the interactions of source traits and other factors such as motivations. They are the forms of behaviour that are observed. They are often given common-sense names, but they explain only a narrow band of behaviours. Surface traits are likely to appeal to the common-sense observer as being more valid and meaningful, because they correspond to the kinds of generalizations that can be made on the basis of simple observations. Surface traits may not be particularly stable.

To confuse matters, one source trait can cause different behaviours. For example, the source trait extroversion can lead to surface traits of liking social activities, such as parties, or it can lead to a surface trait of liking very stimulating activities, such as bungee jumping. To add more confusion, the same surface trait can be directed by different source traits. For example, the surface trait of liking to meet new people can be directed by the source trait of extroversion, but it could also be directed by the source trait of openness to experience – a curiosity about new things. Some personality tests (for example, the OPQ) tend to measure surface traits, while others (for example, the 16PF) tend to measure source traits.

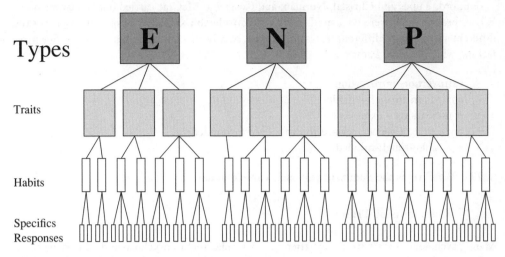

Figure 4.4 Eysenck's structure of personality.

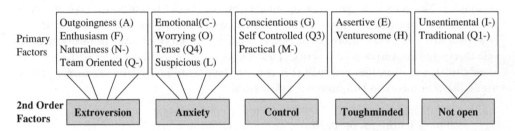

Figure 4.5 Cattell's structure of personality.

A very popular approach to reducing traits to a manageable number is factor analysis. One of the earliest factor analysts of personality was Hans Eysenck, who developed a model that started with specific responses. Responses could be grouped together into habits (which might be similar to secondary traits). A trait is a fairly generalized and consistent set of habits and is possibly equivalent to Allport's concept. The traits in their turn could be organized into types (not in the strict sense of the term), such as 'extroversion'. Eysenck used factor analysis and found that there were three main traits: extroversion, neuroticism and psychoticism. Eysenck's hierarchical structure of personality is shown in figure 4.4.

Raymond Cattell also used factor analysis, but he worked in the other direction. He found that there were 16 primary factors, which could be organized into five second-order factors. A slightly simplified version is shown in figure 4.5.

At first sight, the models of personality seem quite different. However, considerable similarity exists – it is simply that one of the diagrams is upside down. Eysenck preferred to work from the general to the specific and put general factors at the top of his diagram. Cattell thought that the specific (first-order) factors were more useful because the general (second-order) factors were 'a summary too far', since the general factors lost much of the richness needed to understand individual differences (Lord, personal communication, 2001). Consequently, Cattell put the specific factors at the top of his diagram.

Guilford, Tupes and Christal, Norman, and Costa and McCrae carried out similar analyses. When these analyses were compared, there was considerable similarity despite the fact that the different authors used different terms and names. Nearly all of the analyses produced five main factors, which became known as the 'Big Five':

- extrovertion–introvertion
- anxious (neurotic) – stable
- conscientious – expedient
- open to experience – closed to experience (grounded)
- agreeable–tough-minded.

The 'Big Five' is the dominant personality model today.

Criticisms of Traits

Many psychological texts treat **trait theory** in a similar way to psychoanalytic theory or social learning theory. However, trait theory is not a theory of personality at all. It does not claim to say how personality develops. It does not claim to say what is normal or abnormal about personality. Nor does it suggest how personality can or should be changed. Trait theory is atheoretical. It is merely a system for describing and measuring personality – whatever it is or however it may arise. Trait theory can be used in conjunction with psychoanalytic theory, humanistic theory and cognitive-social theories. This annoys some critics. They say that trait theory merely labels and quantifies personality; it does not help us to understand personality. Some would like trait theory to be a little more theoretical.

The Advantages of Traits

An advantage of the trait approach is that, because it is based on the normal curve, it is permissible to use most parametric statistics on trait measures. The multitude of positions along a continuum of a trait means that the richness and variety of humankind can be accommodated.

The Disadvantages of the Trait Approach

A disadvantage of the trait approach is that it sometimes yields a picture of a person that is too complex for some people to remember or understand.

The Measurement of Traits

In principle, trait theorists can use any method of measurement to gauge traits. In practice, the pre-eminent method has been personality inventories, which are based on some kind of factor analysis.

Nearly all of the common personality tests are based on trait theory. Most modern tests, including the 16PF, the EPQ, the OPQ and the NEO, use the trait approach (see chapter 15).

The easiest way to distinguish a test based on the trait approach is to look at the scoring scheme or its norm tables. A trait-based test will probably use scores called **stens, quotients, stannines, T scores** or **Z scores** (see chapter 22). A trait test will have extensive norm tables, rather than one or two numbers that can be used as 'cutting points' to put people into a few groups.

◤ 4.4 THEORIES OF THE DETERMINANTS OF PERSONALITY

Once it has been established that people have traits, it is interesting to determine why one person has more or less of a trait than some other people. There are as many theories as there are people, because as we go about our lives every person constructs his or her own informal and implicit theories, which we use on an *ad hoc* basis. Some theories have been explicitly developed by experts, on the basis of observation, deduction or systematic research. Formal theories can, in turn, be divided into two groups: scientific theories based on modern research and mythological theories based upon the observations and armchair theorizing of the early days of psychology. This section is therefore subdivided into three:

- implicit personality theory
- scientific personality theories – biological theory, environmental theories and social learning theory
- mythological theories – psychoanalytic theory and the humanistic view of personality.

4.4.1 IMPLICIT PERSONALITY THEORY

Implicit personality theory (Bruner and Tagiuri, 1954) refers to the fact that everyone develops a set of ideas (a theory) to explain how people's personality characteristics fit together. Everyone has a common-sense theory of personality. Implicit personality theories tend to describe people in terms a jumble of personality traits, personality types and stereotypes. Examples of implicit personality theories include:

- Good-looking men/women are vain.
- All blondes are bimbos!
- People with close-set eyes can't be trusted.
- Redheads have fiery tempers.

- Americans go on about the slightest thing.
- Germans are authoritarian and have no sense of humour.
- Scotsmen are mean with money.
- The English are snobbish.
- The Irish are stupid.
- Women are born mothers.
- Men are 'strong' and 'masterful'.
- All men are bastards!

- People who are ill in childhood grow up to be dependent adults.
- Brilliant people are emotionally unstable.
- Quiet people have strong emotions.
- People who make friends quickly do not have deep relationships.

It can be seen that most implicit personality theories concern either physical appearances or membership of some group. The psychodynamics of implicit personality theories may be similar to the psychodynamics of stereotyping. A few implicit theories link one psychological characteristic with another.

Implicit theories of personality may or may not be borne out by fact. Consequently, it would be dangerous to base important decisions upon them.

4.4.2 THREE SCIENTIFIC THEORIES OF PERSONALITY

Biological Theory

The biological background to personality is very pervasive, since it persists from culture to culture and from generation to generation. Someone with a deficient thyroid tends to be sluggish whether they live in the Goyt Valley in Derbyshire, Elizabethan England, the Shoganate of Kyoto or a village in the India of the Moguls. However, the biological background is very complex and has at least five aspects:

- genetics
- neurophysiology
- the nervous system
- the endocrine system
- the relevance of biological background.

Genetics

The *basic concepts* of genetics start with the fact that at conception, a person inherits half the genetic material of the father and half the genetic material of the mother. It is important to note that this genetic material is not necessarily the same as that in the father or the mother; some of it may have mutated (usually, the mutations are within the father's sperm cells). The effects of genetics are also sometimes confused with congenital conditions. Congenital conditions are those irreversible conditions that occur during pregnancy or birth; for example, brain damage caused by a forceful forceps delivery. It is important to be able to distinguish between heredity, genetics and congenital conditions. The following may help:

heredity = genetic material passed on from mother and father
genetic = heredity plus mutations
congenital = all characteristics fixed at birth, including genetic and physical factors.

The basic pattern of inheritance is not always obvious. Some genes are recessive and the characteristics that they control may appear to skip generations, thus lowering correlations between parents and children. Some genes are gender-related and mainly appear in males, while some characteristics are controlled by several genes. Furthermore, the influence of genetics involves the influence of differential mating; for example, bright people tend to marry bright people. Many of the critics of the heredity position use a faulty heredity model – that things are passed, directly, on a one-to-one basis from parent to offspring. But this is not what modern genetic theory says – things are much more complex.

Genetic material consists of DNA, which forms chromosomes. The chromosomes control the formation of proteins, which in turn control the formation of body tissues such as muscles and nerves. The proteins also cause the formation of many body chemicals. The mechanisms by which genes influence behaviour have been known since at least the mid-1950s (see Zubek and Solberg 1954) and are as follows:

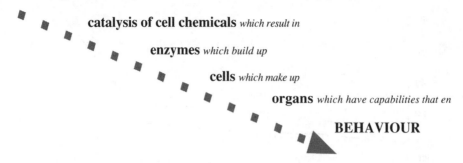

GENES *which control*

catalysis of cell chemicals *which result in*

enzymes *which build up*

cells *which make up*

organs *which have capabilities that en*

BEHAVIOUR

The case for linking genetics to personality is based on two kinds of evidence: animal breeding and epidemiological studies.

Since time immemorial, *animal breeders* have known that temperament in animals can be bred: gundogs such as Labradors have been bred for their placidity, while guard dogs such as Alsatians have been bred for their ferocity. More recent scientific evidence has been provided by Hall (1938), who placed 145 rats in a very large empty container. Some rats responded to the 'open field' test with anxiety and rage, while other rats were placid. Hall interbred the seven most 'emotional' males with the seven most 'emotional' females. He also interbred the seven most placid males with the seven most placid females. The process was repeated for several generations. At the end of the experiment Hall had produced two strains of rats, which differed markedly in their personalities. Care must be taken in generalizing the results of any animal experiment to humans. However, Hall's results shift the burden of proof to those who say that personality has no hereditary basis.

Kallman (1951) conducted a classic *epidemiological* study on the incidence of mental illness among people who were related to each other by different degrees. Whilst Kallman's methods have been refined and developed, his results have withstood critical evaluation. Some of Kallman's results are given in figure 4.6.

As genetic relationship increases, the coincidence of severe personality disorder increases – and it is especially high in identical twins. This is exactly what is predicted by the genetic argument. Many hereditary determinants have been established for vocational interests, job satisfaction (Arvey et al., 1989; Moloney et al., 1991), religious beliefs, attitudes and values (Waller et al., 1990).

Many physical characteristics, such as height, eye colour, curliness of hair, colour blindness and blood group, are directly inherited. There can be no doubt that some mental states, such as the feeble-mindedness associated with **phenylketonuria**, are genetically determined. However, there are many characteristics for which genetics cannot provide the complete answer. It would seem that intelligence has a heritability of .76 in adults (see chapter 3). The heritability of personality appears to be about .45. Bouchard (1996) presents data that allow the following approximate heritabilities of the 'Big Five' personality factors to be calculated as follows:

- extroversion .53
- neuroticism .53
- conscientiousness .46
- openness .52
- agreeableness .45

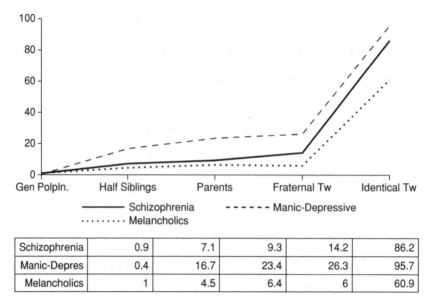

Schizophrenia	0.9	7.1	9.3	14.2	86.2
Manic-Depres	0.4	16.7	23.4	26.3	95.7
Melancholics	1	4.5	6.4	6	60.9

Figure 4.6 Genetic relationship and coincidence of personality disorders.

Scientifically, it is not sufficient simply to establish a relationship. A really convincing argument needs to show a plausible mechanism whereby genes can affect behaviour. The mechanisms that are usually cited include the structure of nerves (neurophysiology), the way in which nerves are organized into the nervous system and the endocrine system.

Neurophysiology

Nerves conduct impulses from the senses to the brain and from the brain to the muscles. All nerves have the same basic parts, as shown in figure 4.7.

Dendrites at the receiving end collect stimulation. This sets off a wave of chemical reactions that produce a minute electrical current, which is prevented from escaping by the insulating sheath of fat. When the charge reaches the dendrites at the other end, the impulse is passed on.

The place where the dendrites of two nerves meet is called a **synapse**. It is important to note that dendrites do not actually make contact with each other, and that the tiny electrical impulse cannot jump the gap, which is called the **synaptic cleft**. When an impulse reaches the end of a nerve's dendrites, it causes the dendrite to release minute amounts of chemical substances called **neurotransmitters**. The neurotransmitters quickly cross the tiny synaptic cleft to the dendrites of the next nerve. When the neurotransmitters reach the dendrites of the next nerve, they cause a chemical reaction, which triggers the impulse again (see figure 4.8).

Neurotransmitters such as dopamine exist in minute quantities but their effect is massive. If anything upsets their delicate balance, the consequences are serious. Further information about key neurotransmitters is given on the website that accompanies this book.

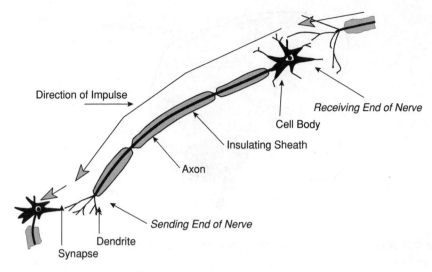

Figure 4.7 A schematic drawing of a nerve.

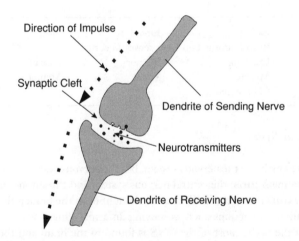

Figure 4.8 A schematic diagram of a synapse.

It is wrong to think that activity at a synapse always helps an impulse. Some synapses have the opposite effect and tend to prevent the transmission of an impulse. Whether or not an impulse is transmitted to the next nerve depends on the balance of activity in the excitatory and inhibitory synapses (Pinel, 1997, 86–9). These effects have a direct relevance to personality. People who have stronger inhibitory processes tend to be extroverts and are less easily conditioned (that is, they are less responsive to the environment and therefore they either create or seek 'loud' environments), while introverts have stronger excitatory processes and are more easily conditioned (Eysenck, 1967). There is a multitude of evidence to support this finding (see Furnham, 1992, 217–20). Thus there may be a biological component for 'extroversion', which is one of the 'Big Five' personality factors.

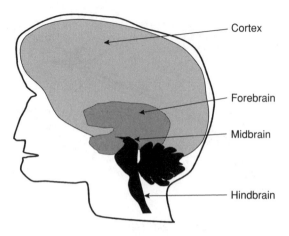

Figure 4.9 A schematic diagram of the main brain structures.

Table 4.1 The functions of some brain structures

Structure	Controls			
Hypothalamus	Eating	Emotions	Sleeping	Homeostasis
Thalamus	Relays information from senses to cortex			Sex
Limbic system	Learning	Memory	Pleasure	Emotions
Basal ganglia	Muscle Contraction	Mood	Memory	

The Nervous System

The individual nerves make up the nervous system, but the nervous system is not one single entity. It is made up of two main parts: the central nervous system and the autonomic nervous system.

The **central nervous system (CNS)** may be thought of as the branch that controls voluntary, conscious thought and actions such as moving an arm. Whilst there are nerves from the CNS in all parts of the body, most of the CNS is found in the brain and the spinal cord. The CNS is so vital to our functioning that most of it is encased in protective bone. The brain is divided into four parts: the hindbrain, the midbrain, the forebrain and the cortex (see figure 4.9).

The activity of the forebrain is also vital to our personality. The forebrain contains a number of structures that control our emotions and motivations, as shown in table 4.1.

When people doze and think of nothing in particular, the cells of the cortex tend to fire in synchrony, at a beat of about 10 cycles per second. These cycles are called **alpha waves**. When people think hard, or where there is a strong stimulus, the alpha waves break up (see figure 4.10). There is some evidence to suggest that there is a direct link between the functioning of the cortex and personality. Cattell et al. (1988) suggest that tough-minded (the opposite of agreeable) people have a cortex that is highly active. The ambient alpha rhythms of their brains are easily interrupted by external stimuli and they tend to have quick reaction times. Thus there may be a biological component to 'agreeableness' – another of the 'Big Five' personality factors.

The **autonomic nervous system (ANS)** controls basic life processes such as digestion and respiration, which *are not usually under conscious control*. It is sometimes called the **peripheral**

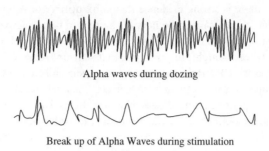

Alpha waves during dozing

Break up of Alpha Waves during stimulation

Figure 4.10 A schematic trace of brain waves.

system, because it operates mostly outside the spinal column and brain. The ANS has two branches: the sympathetic nervous system and the parasympathetic nervous system.

The **sympathetic nervous system** (SNS) goes into overdrive when a person is threatened. It mobilizes the body's energies either to fight the threat or to run away from it. For example, the SNS increases heart rate, dilates pupils and halts digestion if there is an emergency. These reactions usually divert oxygen and energy to the muscles. In some individuals, over-activity of the ANS can produce panic attacks or anxiety disorders. Drugs can be used to overcome the effects of an over-active ANS. Most of these drugs act by blocking the action of neurotransmitters. The **parasympathetic nervous system** (PNS) works in opposition to the sympathetic nervous system and calms the individual down.

The autonomic nervous system is clearly related to personality. In anxious and 'jittery' people, the sympathetic nervous system may be over-active. Unemotional and unreactive people may have an over-active parasympathetic nervous system. Thus there may be a biological component to another 'Big Five' personality factor – anxiety.

The Endocrine System

The endocrine system works by pumping chemicals into the bloodstream. One of the first biological influences on personality to be discovered involved the endocrine system. It was noticed that people whose thyroid was under-active had a sluggish personality. When the thyroid gland is over-active, a person has quick movements and is over-active. More information on the endocrine system is given on the website that accompanies this book. It is important to remember that the relationship between hormone levels is not a simple one and hasty conclusions should be avoided. Whilst it is true that castration always lowers (but not necessarily eliminates) sexual behaviour in men, it is not always true that injections of extra testosterone to men increases their sexual activity.

The Relevance of the Biological Background

The biological background has an inescapable importance in personality theory. There are grounds for believing that several of the 'Big Five' personality factors have *some* biological basis. However, these arguments are poorly understood because many of the details are technical. In comparison, details of environmental determinants are available to anyone who is sufficiently intelligent to read a novel or a newspaper. Consequently, many psychologists focus upon 'easy', environmental explanations because they are more accessible. The effects of this bias can be quite considerable.

For example, today there is strong evidence that **schizophrenia** is, in part, caused by having too much dopamine, which causes the nervous system to be too active and to make associations that do not exist in reality. In the 1960s, this and other biological bases of schizophrenia were not well known. It was thought, for example, that schizophrenia was caused by the inconsistent, intrusive way in which certain mothers treated their children. Many caring, blameless mothers underwent hours of useless therapy to 'correct' their relationships with their children. Many devoted mothers spent years needlessly blaming themselves for the illness of their offspring – all because the biological basis of the personality disorder was not understood. Another example of the importance of the biological background to behaviour is **neurolinguistic programming**, which is described in more detail on the website that accompanies this book.

Environmental Theory

Environmentalists argue that personality is mainly determined by a person's surroundings. Four main features of a person's surroundings are culture, family, people and noxious environmental factors.

Culture and Personality

ANTHROPOLOGICAL STUDIES

Sociologists, in particular, argue that personality is largely formed by culture. Margaret Mead's very influential book *Coming of Age in Samoa* (1928) suggested that adolescent turbulence, which the West attributes to the physiological changes accompanying the start of adulthood, should, in fact, be attributed to cultural factors such as the restrictions and roles placed on adolescents. She reported her 'extensive observations' of Samoan adolescents (who were undergoing the same physiological changes as adolescents in Western cultures) and found that they did not experience an adolescent crisis. She claimed that the difference lay in the culture and, in particular, the social pressures. Samoan culture was reported to be relaxed and did not repress sexual behaviour in young people. Another, very classic, study undertaken by Margaret Mead specifically linked personality and culture. Her book *Sex and Temperament in Three Different Cultures* (1935) described three different tribes:

- *The Arapesh tribe* lives in a mountainous, barren region and is an example of a society in which both men and women adopt what we would consider stereotypical feminine roles:

Men	Gentle, co-operative, nurturent
Women	Gentle, co-operative, nurturent

- *The Mundugumour tribe* lives on rich, fertile, river banks and the people are headhunters. This is an example of a tribe in which both men and women adopt what we would consider to be masculine roles:

Men	Fierce, have violent tempers
Women	Fight husbands, teach sons to taunt husbands, are harsh to children

- *The Tchambuli tribe* are lake dwellers in New Guinea. They are an example of a reversal of our stereotypical sex roles:

Men	Artistic, wistful
Women	Utilitarian, organized work

METHODOLOGICAL WEAKNESSES OF ANTHROPOLOGICAL STUDIES – DON'T BELIEVE MARGARET MEAD!

It should be noted that many of the early cross-cultural studies were of very poor quality. Much of the work has been criticized for subjectivity and for selecting only those aspects of 'primitive cultures' that fitted with the theories – there would be little reason to pay travel and other costs if anthropologists were to find that people in Borneo are much the same as people in Birmingham! The in-built bias towards finding differences meant that the researchers often overlooked similarities. For example, babies of the Hopi Indians spend much of their time bound to cradle-boards and cannot move their legs and feet, but they learn to walk at much the same time as babies who have extensive practice at crawling and standing. Other studies used tiny samples and drew conclusions from a sample of, say, six cultures. Statistically, small samples produce unstable results because of sampling error. Often, sampling error was confused with the reality.

The seminal work of Margaret Mead has been subject to devastating but controversial attacks by Freeman (1996, 1998), who was able to reconstruct her work programme. Mead was sent to Samoa for five months as a postgraduate student. She spent most of her time, without her supervisor's knowledge, working at a museum. When her time was almost up, she interviewed just two Samoan girls about their sexual behaviour. The girls, it appears, decided to tell lies. Margaret Mead did not undertake systematic research on the behaviour of Samoan girls. Franz Boas, Mead's gullible supervisor and a leading light in the sociological circles of the day, vouched for Mead's painstaking research. In the 1934 edition of the *Encyclopaedia of the Social Sciences*, Boas concluded that 'the genetic elements which may determine personality' are 'altogether irrelevant as compared with the powerful influence of the cultural environment'. Boas' conclusion and the faulty works of Mead were rehashed in thousands of undergraduate courses until they became accepted truth.

The Family and Personality

The family is an important influence upon the way in which personality develops. Two findings are that birth order and the absence of fathers have profound effects. Consistent differences have been reported between the personalities of first and latter-born children. It is suggested that earlier-born children tend to be conservative and cautious, whereas latter-born children tend to be rebellious and radical. Latter-born children are said to have personalities that are more sociable and manipulative. Research also suggests that boys in homes where the father is absent tend to be more achievement-motivated and successful – especially if they have an ambitious mother. Theodore Adorno et al.'s classic study of *The Authoritarian Personality* (1950) found that this character type was most prevalent in families with a cruel, dominant father and a mild, submissive mother.

Other People and Personality

Some aspects of personality *are* learnt from others. This learning is sometimes called 'social learning theory' and is discussed below. Of course, some of the most significant people in one's life are one's relations. The influence of other people and the influence of the family show significant overlap. If a father is observed using aggression to resolve problems, it is quite likely that aggression will become a facet of his son's personality.

Frustrating and Noxious Situations and Personality

The economic situation can also influence personality. A classic example was described by Dollard and Miller (1950). They suggested that aggression should increase in communities that were frustrated by economic hardship. They used the size of the cotton crop in the southern United States in a given year as an index of economic well-being. They also used the number of Black lynchings as an index of aggression. They found that in years in which the crop was poor, the number of lynchings increased. This phenomenon is often referred to as the Frustration–Aggression Hypothesis. Other studies suggest that people who consistently face frustrating situations tend to develop anxious and rigid personalities. More recent research has shown that other 'noxious' situations can cause aggression. Physical pain, air pollution, heat and overcrowding tend to produce aggressive individuals. Heat in particular seems to have consistent effects. Even in countries as diverse as France and the USA, indices of aggression such as rape and murder show higher rates in the hotter months of the year and in the hotter regions in the south.

Criticisms of the Environmental Argument

In one way, the heredity–environment debate has been very unfair. It tends to examine the assertions of hereditarians in depth, while excusing the assertions of environmentalists from equal scrutiny. Yet when the environmental case is subjected to close scrutiny, it does not fare well. For example, in the 1930s orphanages were very regimented and children were treated very much the same. If the environmentalists were correct, the range of personalities of children in orphanages should be small because the variation of their environments was small. However, the variance of intelligence and personality of children in orphanages was only slightly less than the variance for the population as a whole.

The Interaction between Biology and the Environment

It is clear that personality is formed by *both* environment and biological factors. Furthermore, the two may interact. The trait of aggression is a good example of this interaction. People may inherit a tendency towards aggression from their parents. They also see their parents solving problems by using aggression and copy them. Consequently, they develop aggressive personalities.

The Social Learning Theory of Personality

Social learning theory, also called cognitive-social theory, was developed by Albert Bandura, George Kelly, and Cantor and Khilstrom. Their work built upon the behaviourist traditions of Skinner. The main work began in the 1960s and the field remains very vigorous today.

Basic Concepts

Social learning theory starts with the basic behaviourist position that behaviour is shaped by the number of times it has been reinforced in the past. Behaviourists would maintain that when we say that someone is aggressive, we are really saying that when someone has been in confrontation situations in the past, that person has been 'rewarded' for acting aggressively, and therefore when he or she encounters a confrontation in the future he or she will react aggressively.

Advanced social learning theory argues that the situation is more complex, because human beings have the ability to reason, remember and think abstractly. We do not simply react to stimuli with a simple response developed through reinforcements. Instead, reinforcements build up cognitive models (sometimes called cognitive maps or schema) of our environment. When we need to react to a situation, we use these models or maps to choose a response. Our behaviours and personalities are usually consistent because our mental maps change very slowly, if at all. In more technical terms, people's actions reflect the schemas that they use in understanding their world.

The question then arises, 'How are these schemas or mental maps developed?' A part of the answer undoubtedly lies in the principles of Skinnerian conditioning. However, a greater part probably depends upon other mechanisms. Bandura (1977) emphasized the part played by observing and copying the behaviour of others – especially others who we believe to be:

- attractive
- powerful
- distinctive
- consistent.

In a series of experiments with Bobo dolls, Bandura was able to show that, in part, people are aggressive because they watch aggressive people.

George Kelly (1955) emphasized the importance of our mental maps or, as he called them, our system of personal constructs. Furthermore, he did a lot of work to link our *personal constructs* with emotions and psychological disorders. According to Kelly, most psychological disorders arise because our mental maps do not accurately reflect the real world. The emotion of dread is generated when we realize that we have no map for the experiences that we anticipate we will encounter. Aggression arises when our map is slightly faulty and we try to force the world to fit into our cognitive system. Therapy consists of giving us techniques that prevent us from building faulty maps.

Researchers such as Julian Rotter maintain that people have been reinforced to build general types of maps. Some people have built up cognitive maps that tell them that they can influence their environment. People with these maps are said to have an **internal locus of control**. Other people have built up cognitive maps that tell them that they are at the mercy of forces in their environment. People with these maps are said to have an **external locus of control**. Similarly, people with high levels of **self-efficacy** have maps that tell them that they have the power to influence events.

Methods Used in Cognitive-Social Theories

The pre-eminent method in cognitive-social theories is the **Repertory Grid** technique developed by Kelly. In addition, there are supplementary techniques such as **'Laddering'**, which can be used to identify core constructs and values. There are many inventories, such a Rotter's I-E scale, which measure the locus of control and the related concept of self-efficacy.

Criticisms of Cognitive-Social Theories

Cognitive-social theories have been enormously powerful in generating effective techniques of changing people's personalities. Brainwashing and B-mod (Behaviour Modification) are based on techniques of conditioning. Many therapies are based on changing people's construct systems.

Many critics maintain that cognitive-social theories oversimplify human behaviour by breaking everything down to expectancies and past reinforcements. Human behaviour is seen as little different to animal behaviour except, perhaps, that it is more complex. This criticism can only be levelled at early versions of cognitive-social theory. Later versions rely heavily upon reasoning and analysis – the very characteristics that are supposed to set us apart from the animals.

4.4.3 TWO MYTHOLOGICAL THEORIES OF PERSONALITY

The determinants of personality were a topic of speculation long before we knew about neurotransmitters, the areas of the brain, learning theory or social modelling. In those pre-scientific times, great thinkers produced colourful and enthralling explanations of personality in the same way that the Greeks produced enthralling explanations of natural phenomena by constructing stories of Zeus, Poseidon and Iris. The Vikings and Celts felt a similar need to explain phenomena when they constructed the myths of Thor, Aegir and the Alcis. In the latter part of the 19th century and the early part of the 20th century, we felt the need to explain personality without the advantage of scientific facts. Two theories, psychoanalytic theory and humanistic theory, were concocted.

Psychoanalytic Theory

The main proponents of Psychoanalytic Theory were Sigmund Freud, Carl Jung, Alfred Adler, Erik Erikson and Karen Horney. The main development took place in the first half of the century – say, between 1900 and 1940.

Basic Concepts

Behaviour is driven by unconscious forces that we may not be able, or may not wish, to recognize. These unconscious forces shape our personalities in a 'normal' way as we develop from childhood to adulthood. However, our progression through the stages of development can go wrong. We can become stuck in a given stage and this produces problems with our personality (complexes). If we have a harsh potty training, we may become stuck in the anal stage and show the traits of anal sadism or anal retentiveness. If we don't get beyond the oral stage, we will show the trait of self-gratification and suck our thumbs!

The basic psychoanalytic position is that, despite the trials and tribulations of life, we must integrate the different elements of our psyche in a lasting way that is in harmony. The main

Table 4.2 The main psychoanalytic explanations of personality

	Freud	Jung	Adler	Horney
Motive force	Sex (the brain is an appendage of the genitals)	Archetypes (for example, male archetype = animus; female archetype = anima)	Innate striving for perfection (superiority)	Anxiety
Division of psyche	Id Ego Super-ego Conscious Unconscious	Personal unconscious Collective unconscious	Conscious more important than the unconscious	Anxiety and hostility combine to give three directions: • towards others • against others • away from others
Stages in development	Oral → anal → phallic → latency → genital	Development continues throughout life	Inferior → superior	Insecure/dependent → secure/ independent
Complexes	Oral and anal fixations Oedipus and Electra complexes Penis envy	Mid-life crisis	Inferiority complex Superiority complex	
Jargon	Defence mechanisms	Personality types	Compensation, overcompensation	

psychoanalytic schools were formed by Freud (1949), Adler (1956), Jung (1977) and Horney (1939). The Freudian theories were the first, and probably most influential, psychoanalytic explanation of personality. Freud's theory is basically biological – functionally, the brain is an appendage of the genitals. **Transactional analysis** is, in essence, a Freudian theory of personality, in which the parent corresponds to the super-ego, the adult corresponds to the ego and the child corresponds to the id.

Different psychoanalytic theorists posit different motivational forces, stages and divisions of our psyche. Table 4.2 contrasts the main psychoanalytic explanations of personality.

Other psychoanalysts include Erich Fromm (2001) and Erik Erikson (1982). Fromm started with the view that the distinguishing feature of the human race is reasoning and self-awareness. These abilities give us freedom of thought. Our personalities are formed by the way in which we react to this freedom. We can shrink from the freedom, mindlessly conform and submit to dictators; or we can embrace freedom, to become creative and constructive. Erikson believed that Freud put too much emphasis on the id. He and other *ego psychologists* claim that the ego is the most important part of our psyche. Erikson developed Freud's stages and maintained that at each stage we need to confront a dilemma. The way in which we resolve each dilemma determines our personality, as shown in table 4.3.

Table 4.3 Erikson's developmental stages

Stage	Dilemma
Maturity	Ego–integrity versus despair
Adulthood	Growth versus stagnation
Young adulthood	Intimacy versus isolation
Adolescence	Identity versus role confusion
Latency	Industry versus inferiority
Locomotor–genital	Initiative versus guilt
Muscular–anal	Autonomy versus shame and doubt
Oral–sensory	Trust versus mistrust

Methods Used by Psychoanalysts

The psychoanalysts were not very rigorous or scientific. Their basic method consisted of some-one sitting in an armchair and theorizing on the basis of case studies. In Freud's case, at least, some of the case studies were fraudulent. Initially, the psychoanalysts used techniques such as free association and interpretation of dreams. Later, projective tests, such as Rorschach inkblots and the TAT (see chapter 5), were used to give some semblance of objectivity. Unfortunately, few projective tests were either objective or valid (see Anastasi, 1988). Another method used by Freudians and neo-Freudians is the life history method, which tries to record formative events in childhood.

Criticisms of Psychoanalytic Theory

Many complain that the psychoanalytic school over-emphasizes childhood. The main criticisms focus on the fact that many psychoanalytic concepts are badly formed, often tautological and untestable. Psychoanalysis is essentially a description of past behaviour and is not much good in predicting the future. The empirical base for Freud's theorizing consisted of about a dozen carefully chosen case studies, in which Freud was hardly an independent observer. It has been suggested (MacDonald, 2003) that he 'reconstructed' his case studies to fit his theory. He may also have knowingly misdiagnosed a case of tuberculosis as a conversion reaction (Eysenck, 1985). Others accuse him of fraud (Crews, 1998) and it has been claimed that 'Opinion is gaining ground that doctrinaire psychoanalytic theory is the most stupendous intellectual confidence trick of the twentieth century' (Medawar, 1975). Nevertheless, psychoanalysis has been enormously influential, not least because writers and literary critics find the theories conducive, and some-times luridly fascinating and compelling.

The Humanistic View of Personality

The main proponents of the humanistic view of personality were Carl Rogers and Abraham Maslow. The main development of the approach took place in the 1950s and 1970s, and the field is still active today.

Basic Concepts

The humanistic view of personality can be thought of as an extension of psychoanalytic theory: Notice how several psychoanalytic theorists, especially Erikson and Horney, posited personality as passing through several stages and ending up with an individual who had maximized his or her potential and was in harmony with his or her environment. Humanistic theorists also emphasize a similar utilization of a person's potential, but they tend to ignore the mumbo-jumbo about penises, inferiority and ancestral archetypes. Humanistic psychologists are less likely to get involved in dividing the psyche up into component parts. Unlike many psychoanalysts, the humanists emphasize the uniqueness of the individual and his or her ability and right to make choices: *free will* is emphasized. Whereas psychoanalysis was largely derived from people who were not functioning properly, the humanistic approach was largely derived by examination of creative 'healthy' people, such as US presidents, who were excelling in their field. Thus both psychoanalytic personality theory and humanist personality theory can be said to be based on extreme, atypical examples.

Humanists argue that we have a **'true self'** (what we naturally are) and a **'false self'** (how we try to make ourselves appear). They argue that we must accept our true selves and the true selves of others for what they are, and that we must value all people, whoever they are and whatever they do. Presumably, humanists would have counselled Vlad the Impaler to see himself as one of humankind's successes and to feel self-actualized when he saw all those bodies on spikes! This warm acknowledgement of the worth of *all* other people is called **'unconditional positive regard'**. Humanists believe that everything is relative.

According to Maslow, each of us strives to be 'the best me I can be'. The humanist approach emphasizes positive attributes of growth, self-expression and self-fulfilment. People who reach this pinnacle of existence are said to be **self-actualized**, and to show the following traits:

- orientatation to the 'real' world
- a high level of spontaneity
- a problem-centred rather than self-centred nature
- autonomy and independence
- capable of experiencing profound 'mystical' experiences
- democratic attitudes
- creativity
- able to distinguish means from ends
- able to transcend the environment rather than just coping with it.

Carl Rogers maintained that a *fully functioning* person would also show the traits of confidence, openness to experience, absence of defensiveness, accurate perceptions, unconditional positive regard and harmonious relations with others.

Unfortunately, we are not born into this blissful, idyllic condition. Carl Rogers was a clinical psychologist and on the basis of his patients he theorized about why some people were not self-actualized. He reasoned that when we are young we are the objects of only *conditional positive regard*. We only receive positive regard from others on the condition that we live up to their standards of dress, attitude and behaviour. Often, we have to suppress our own feelings and actions (our true selves) in order to obtain and retain the high opinion of others. In other words, we establish *conditions of worth* – extraneous standards designed to obtain the approval of others (the false self). Sometimes these standards are in conflict with our true selves, so we start to distort our perceptions and behaviour in order to maintain our supply of positive regard from others. Our personalities are largely determined by the gap between our selves as we are in practice (our true selves) and the people we would like to be (our ideal selves), and by the way in which we try to reconcile the gap. When our real selves and our ideal selves are incongruent, we rely on the defence mechanisms of denial and rationalization that Rogers construed in virtually the same way as Freud. The use of the defence mechanisms increases the level of incongruence and we may become neurotic. If the level of incongruence increases still further our defence mechanisms are overwhelmed, our sense of self becomes shattered and we become psychotic.

Humanistic psychology has been very influential. It is seen in the existentialist writings of Jean-Paul Sartre, where the meaning that we find in life is essentially our own invention and dies with us. Becker developed the philosophy into the belief that the fundamental human dilemma is **existential dread** – the recognition that life has no absolute value or meaning, and that ultimately we all face death. We all spend life denying mortality and the nothingness that lies behind our values and pursuits.

Methods Used in Humanistic Personality Theory

At the risk of not showing much positive regard, one can say that the methods of the humanistic personality theorists were little better than those used by the psychoanalysts. Maslow's work was based largely on armchair theorizing and unsystematic interviews with a small sample of unrepresentative people. His famous hierarchy of needs has not stood up to empirical validation (neither the existence of five needs nor their hierarchical order have been verified). Rogers never clearly defined key concepts such as 'a fully functioning person' and he emphasized subjective experience, which is very difficult to study in a scientific way.

The humanistic approach to personality is ideographic: it insists that everyone is unique and must find his or her individual 'real self'. Consequently, standard methods of measurement would be inappropriate and ideographic (individual) methods must be adopted. The predominant method used by Rogers is the non-directive interview, in which a counsellor merely helps to verbalize, reflects on and summarizes the 'output' of the individual. Other methods that are said to help identify the various selves, especially the 'perceived self', are T-Groups (sensitivity training) and so on. Both of these genres of measures are subjective and unscientific.

However, there are ideographic techniques, such as Stephenson's Q-sorts, which are more objective. Ipsative tests, which only give information about the distribution of characteristics within an individual, could also be said to flow from the humanistic approach to personality.

Criticisms of the Humanistic Theory of Personality

Humanistic personality theory has been criticized because it does not offer a comprehensive theory of personality. Nor does it attempt to develop a body of testable hypotheses and research.

Humanistic personality theory has also been criticized on philosophical grounds. Some say that the humanistic approach lacks balance and is a biased theory, which assumes that human personality is good rather than neutral. This is an unfair criticism. We have no way of knowing whether we were created good, neutral or bad. It is just as much an assumption to say that we were created neutral as it is to say that were created good.

Others criticize the humanistic approach for providing a respectable underpinning for the selfish 'Me culture' of California, which blossomed during the 1960s and 1970s. Very recent research (Begley and Rodgers, 1998) suggests that praising children unconditionally breeds narcissistic adults who are more likely to resort to violence if others cease to render unconditional praise.

This chapter is intended as a primer in personality theory. Further reading is given on the website that accompanies this book.

CHAPTER 5

AN INTRODUCTION TO MOTIVES (NEEDS, VALUES AND INTERESTS)

WHAT WE CHOOSE TO DO

 5.1 MOTIVES

This chapter concerns the motives that can determine people's choice of activities. This contrasts with chapter 4, which was concerned with personality (the *style* in which things are done), and chapter 3, which dealt with ability (the *competence* with which things are done). The following pages aim to provide a working guide to these topics. More detailed information on motives can be obtained from Steers and Porter (1979) and O'Reilly (1991).

5.1.1 THE DEFINITION OF MOTIVES

Motivation is a complex topic that is difficult to define. Some authors often make no attempt, whilst others have put forward a number of definitions:

> . . . contemporary (immediate) influences on the direction, vigour, and persistence of action (Atkinson, 1964)

> . . . how behaviour gets started, is energised, is sustained, is directed, is stopped and what kind of subjective reaction is present in the organism while all this is going on (Jones, 1955)

> . . . process governing choices made by persons or organisms among alternative forms of voluntary activity (Vroom, 1964)

> . . . a set of independent/dependent variable relationships that explain the direction, amplitude and persistence of an individual's behaviour (Campbell and Pritchard, 1976)

These definitions are not adequate. Vroom's definition, for example, could equally apply to cognitive abilities. The other definitions merely consist of a listing of the components of a motive. However, they do give clues that the core of the concept of a motive is:

> a psychological process that energises thinking and behaviour.

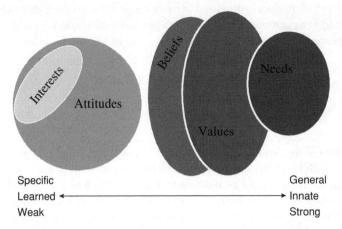

Specific General
Learned ←————————————————————————→ Innate
Weak Strong

Figure 5.1 Suggested relationships between different types of motive.

Motivation is the power source of our actions and it determines three facets of behaviour:

1 The direction of our behaviour – what we try to do.
2 The effort we exert – how hard we try.
3 Our persistence – continuing behaviour in the face of adversity.

5.1.2 DIFFERENT CATEGORIES OF MOTIVE – NEEDS, VALUES AND INTERESTS

Behaviour can be motivated by different sources of energy in the same way that a machine can obtain its power from a battery, a combustion engine or a water wheel. An examination of the literature reveals a wide and bewildering array of motives that include needs, values and interests.

Super (1973) attempted to 'settle the mud surrounding the vocabulary of motivation' by arranging the terms in order of their remoteness from specific activities and objectives in 'actual life'. Super's idea can be used to produce the diagram shown in figure 5.1.

Needs can be satisfied in many ways, making prediction of behaviour from needs hazardous. Values and, to a greater extent, interests, are believed to have a closer relationship with specific activities. They are therefore a more reliable way of predicting the choices that an individual makes (Watts et al., 1981). Values and interests re-state needs in terms taken from the social and work environment. It can be argued that the general–specific continuum suggested by Super coincides with two others: an innate–learned continuum and a strong–weak continuum. Thus needs are general motives with a high 'genetic' component and which energize behaviour very strongly. Beliefs have little intrinsic capability to energize behaviour – which is why they are depicted as lying behind values. Values are fairly general and strong, and at times may be stronger than some needs. The values attached to certain beliefs lead to attitudes towards a wide range of objects and ideas. Some of these objects and ideas concern activities, especially work activities. This subset of attitudes is often called occupational interests. Interests are specific, learned and may be fairly weak motivators.

Each of the types of motives is discussed in more detail in the sections that follow. However, it should be noted here that the relationship between motivation and job performance is complex, and this relationship is considered in greater detail in section 5.7 below.

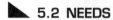 ## 5.2 NEEDS

5.2.1 THE CONCEPT OF NEED

The essential ideas of needs were established over 70 years ago. They start with a person who is at equilibrium with his or her environment. During the course of interacting with the environment, the balance changes and a need develops. For example, well-fed people burn up energy as they go about their lives. This leads to a fall in the blood sugar level, which would be dangerous if it continued. A need to eat develops in order to bridge the gap between the present state and the equilibrium required for survival. People develop a need to eat. Essentially, needs are homoeostatic mechanisms designed to keep people at or near an equilibrium. The process is seen most easily in biological drives such as hunger, thirst, sleep, warmth and so on.

Many needs involve psychological rather than physiological processes but the principle remains the same. There is a desired state, and when a gap emerges the organism is motivated to reduce or eliminate the gap. For example, most individuals have an optimum level for stimulation. If the environment provides too little stimulation, they develop a need to explore or manipulate their environment. If the environment provides too much stimulation, a person develops a need for peace and quiet and uses various mechanisms to damp down the stimulation. The idea of equilibrium can also be applied to the cognitive processes that we use to construct our ideas about the world. Kruglanski et al. (1983), for example, suggest that our thoughts need to have a certain amount of structure, to be in line with what we wish and to be consistent with the evidence that is available to us. If our thoughts do not have structure and correspondence with our wishes or the context in which we find ourselves, we will be motivated to develop another set of ideas that are closer to the optimum. Hence, need theory is closely linked to the ideas of cognitive psychology. The phenomenon of cognitive dissonance, which is an important concept in attitude change, can be seen as an aspect of needs. We have a need for our attitudes to be consistent. If we become aware that one of our attitudes is inconsistent with others, we are motivated to change the attitude so that it is no longer contradictory. Goal-setting theory is important in work psychology and can also be explained in terms of need reduction. Setting participative goals realigns the desired state at a higher level. An individual is then energized to reduce the discrepancy between the existing state and the goal by working harder to achieve greater results.

5.2.2 BIOLOGICAL ASPECTS OF NEEDS

There is some evidence that many needs have a biological basis. Experiments with animals (take great care in generalizing to humans) suggest that certain centres of the brain have a crucial influence on motivation. The centres detect the homeostatic imbalance and initiate behaviour to restore an optimum level. If these centres are damaged or otherwise abnormal, the animals eat too much or, say, drink too much. Neurobiological research (White and Milner, 1992; Eysenck,

1998) suggests that certain parts of the brain, especially the parts of the forebrain called the limbic system, such as the amygdala, play a crucial part in motivation. Nader et al. (1997) suggest that the presence or absence of the neurotransmitter dopamine plays a crucial role. If the action of dopamine is suppressed, then animals (take care when generalizing results) become less motivated. This might suggest that, to an extent, motivation might be a general characteristic.

5.2.3 FUNCTIONAL AUTONOMY OF NEEDS

Biology does not provide a complete explanation of needs. Some needs, especially the 'psychological' needs, develop a life of their own and become independent of the biological equilibrium that they originally served – they become functionally autonomous. For example, a person who grew up in dire poverty might develop the need for money in order to buy food to maintain his or her blood sugar level – exactly as the biological theory of needs would predict. However, after a period of time gaining money might become a need in its own right (that is, functionally autonomous) and the person might work to gain money even though he or she has saved enough to buy food for many years. Furthermore, a need can alter its own equilibrium as the organism habituates to higher and higher levels. This process can be clearly seen in addictions. Initially, there may be little or no need to consume a drug such as cocaine. However, once cocaine is consumed, a person's physiology adapts and requires a regular intake of the drug. As consumption continues, the body's physiology adapts further, and greater and greater doses are required in order to maintain a state of 'peace'. A similar situation may develop with 'psychological' motives such as recognition, where some individuals are driven to obtain higher and higher levels of adulation from more and more people.

Jarvis and Petty (1996) have noted that people have a chronic tendency to evaluate 'psychological objects' and that this indicates that there is a *need to evaluate*. The evaluation of objects appears to be to be ubiquitous, immediate and fast. This evaluative function may have an evolutionary advantage, since it would facilitate approach to objects conferring survival and retreat from objects presenting risk. Jarvis and Petty contend that individuals differ in their chronic tendency to evaluate, and they have developed a scale to measure this tendency. Individuals with high scores are more likely to hold strong attitudes towards issues and to be able to list more evaluative statements about objects and events (see sections 5.4–5.6).

5.2.4 PSYCHOLOGICAL NEEDS

The biological basis of some needs is impossible to ascertain. For example, no one has been able to identify a group of neurons or a physiological process that can account for achievement motivation. However, McClelland (1976) has shown that people tend to have high levels of achievement motivation when their society and upbringing rewards them for taking certain kinds of risk. Rotter (1966) suggests that our environment teaches us to have one of two views of the world. Some people develop motives that are based on the view that they control their own fate and that their own actions and decisions determine events. These people are said to have an 'internal locus of control'. Other people develop motives that are based on the view that our fate is determined by external forces or luck. Such people are often said to have an 'external locus of control'. In fact, most people lie somewhere on a continuum between these extremes.

5.2.5 NEED THEORIES

Many *psychoanalytic theories* of personality can be viewed as need theories. Indeed, according to these theories, personality emerges from an individual's motivational state. For example, according to Freud, personality (the ego) emerges from the battle between biological needs (sex) and higher needs (the super-ego). According to Adler, personality emerges from our need to overcome inferiority. According to Horney, personality is formed by our need to minimize anxiety. According to Maslow, personality is determined by the level of our dominant need in his hierarchy

One of the first theories of psychological needs was developed by Murray (1938). He identified many needs, such as aggression and autonomy. Unfortunately, the list grew longer, until over 30 needs were identified. It became too cumbersome and still did not account for all motives, so it gradually fell into disuse. Nevertheless, three of Murray's needs continue to be used and researched today. The most important of the three, achievement motivation, which is usually referred to as '**n ach**', is probably the most extensively researched psychological need (McClelland, 1976; Koestner and McClelland, 1990). It is the need to accomplish difficult tasks or to accomplish routine tasks in a more effective, better way. People with high achievement motivation aspire to accomplish moderately difficult tasks. They maintain high standards and are prepared to work towards moderately distant goals. They respond positively to competition and are willing to make a lot of effort in order to attain excellence. Studies suggest that a country's economic growth is preceded by a surge of achievement motivation in its population 30 or so years earlier. Companies that employ executives with high achievement motivation tend to grow faster and make more innovations. These effects have been shown to apply in a large number of countries, including the United States, the United Kingdom, Finland, Israel, India and Australia. The effect is very robust. Furthermore, achievement motivation can be trained and has been linked to child rearing practices where children are encouraged to experiment and are praised when they succeed. The need for power, '**n pow**', and the affiliative need, '**n affil**', have also been subjected to considerable research. An interesting set of studies attempted to identify the motivations of people who rise to the top of organizations (The Leadership Motivation Profile – LMP). These people tend to have a high need for power, a low need for affiliation and a moderate need for achievement.

5.2.6 MEASURING NEEDS

Needs are measured mostly in guidance and development situations. They are rarely measured in selection because:

- Needs appear to be unstable characteristics. A person can have a strong need for food shortly before lunch, but an hour later he or she has no need to eat.
- It is thought that needs are easy to fake.
- Few objective measures of needs exist. Needs are routinely assessed at interviews and assessment centres, but tests of motivation are few and far between.

Perhaps the earliest test of needs was the Thematic Apperception Test (TAT), which was developed to measure Murray's needs. The TAT consists of a series of very vague pictures. Clients are shown a picture for 20 seconds and then required to tell a story about it. They may be prompted to say what is happening, who the people are, what has happened in the past and what will happen in the future. The stories are then analysed by trained people, who use a rigorous scoring system. Perhaps the best developed of the systems is the scheme used to score the need for achievement (McClelland et al., 1953). The TAT stories can also be used to obtain scores for *n pow* and *n affil*. Measuring needs with the TAT has two substantial disadvantages. First, the test takes a long time to score. Second, the TAT pictures are not particularly relevant to the world of work and may damage rapport with clients. An occupational test, the Picture Story Exercise, is based on the TAT but uses more relevant pictures.

One of the oldest pencil and paper tests of motivation is Cattell's (1975) Motivation Analysis Test, which measures a number of 'ergs', such as fear, narcissism, sadism assertiveness and pugnacity. Hogan and Hogan (1987) devised the Motives, Values, Preferences Inventory (MVPI), which yields ten scales, including seven that measure the need for recognition, power, hedonism, altruism, affiliation, tradition and security. The MVPI is not specifically designed for occupational settings, but is useful in personal and career counselling. Saville Holdsworth (1992) produced the Motivation Questionnaire, which yields 18 scores grouped into four sets: energy and dynamism, synergy, intrinsic motivations and extrinsic motivations. The test was specifically developed for use in occupational settings and has acceptable validity data. Tarleton's (1998) Motivational Styles Questionnaire is specifically designed to measure motivation at work. It is a partly ipsative test that yields seven scores on the need for achievement, independence, structure, affiliation, systems, people and personal power. The test has moderate reliability, but it is new and evidence of predictive validity in a selection context is awaited.

 ## 5.3 BELIEFS

5.3.1 THE CONCEPT OF BELIEFS

Beliefs are assumptions about the probability that an object or event has certain characteristics – especially the fundamental characteristic of the object's, or event's, existence. The nature of beliefs is seen most clearly in religion: some people believe that God exists, whilst others may believe that God does not exist – and some people may believe that God is 'mild', whilst others may believe that God is powerful. Similarly, some people believe that the Loch Ness Monster does exist while others do not. Some believers in the Loch Ness Monster think that it is green, whilst others believe that it is brown. The dry, cognitive nature of these examples should be noted. Beliefs do not imply any evaluation – there is no emotional reaction to the object or event – they are merely statements of what the holder believes to be true (Rollinson et al., 1998). On their own, beliefs do not strongly energize behaviour and hence they are given only a brief explanation in this chapter. However, there is some motivation to have a system of beliefs that is logically consistent. If our beliefs are illogical, we will experience cognitive dissonance and be motivated to change one or more of them. Nevertheless, beliefs are important to motivation, because there is a link between beliefs and values. For example, if we hold a belief that we then evaluate positively, we will have a positive attitude and tend to favour objects or events linked to that belief.

5.3.2 THE MEASUREMENT OF BELIEFS

In principle, the measurement of beliefs is easy. A person can be asked whether he or she agrees or disagrees with certain factual statements, such as 'Fairies exist' or 'On average, men are taller than women.' In most circumstances, a more sensitive Likert scale (ranging from 'strongly agree', through 'agree', 'uncertain' and 'disagree' to 'strongly disagree') can be used. In other situations, a multiple-choice format can be used to generate questions such as:

> The population of Australia is approximately:
> (a) 29 million; (b) 24 million; (c) 19 million.

5.4 VALUES

5.4.1 THE DEFINITION AND CONCEPT OF VALUES

In section 5.2.3, it was noted that people have a chronic tendency to evaluate 'psychological objects' and that there may be a 'need to evaluate', which may have conferred evolutionary advantage. Nevertheless, values have been the Cinderella of motivational characteristics. They rarely or scantily appear in the literature on selection and assessment. A rather spasmodic interest in values by psychologists makes the definition and elaboration of the concept of values difficult. Perhaps the best definition is given by Rokeach (1973):

> an enduring belief that a specific mode of conduct or end-state of existence is personally or socially preferable to an opposite or converse mode of conduct or end-state of existence.

Rokeach's definition can be divided into two parts. *First*, values are enduring characteristics of individuals that remain stable over long periods of time. *Second*, values concern preferences and notions of desirable states of affairs. They are intimately connected with moral and ethical choices that often determine what people think ought to be done and what they think ought not to be done. Rand (1964) focused upon the evaluative and energizing aspects of values when he defined a value as 'that which one acts to gain and/or keep'. The evaluative element was also emphasized by Locke (1976), who defined a value as 'what a person consciously or subconsciously desires, wants or seeks to attain'. Locke also believed that values are standards in a person's conscious or unconscious mind and are therefore essentially 'subjective' and learned. This contrasts with the 'objectivity' of needs, which are innate and exist regardless of what the person wants. Thus it is possible to define values as:

> enduring, evaluative, but subjective and learned, standards of the preferred state of affairs which a person wishes to achieve or maintain.

5.4.2 THE OCCUPATIONAL RELEVANCE OF VALUES

There is little empirical evidence to link values with job performance. However, there is reason to assume that job performance would be diminished if relevant values were absent. For example, it seems reasonable that a merchant banker who places a low priority on financial values would not contribute as effectively to his or her organization's goals as a colleague who places a high priority on financial values. Similarly, a person who has low religious values is less likely to perform all the responsibilities of a priest as well as a person who has high religious values. The correlation between values and performance is likely to vary from organization to organization. According to Smith's (1994) theory of the validity of predictors, values belong to the relational domain of predictors. This means that effective use of values in selection is likely to require the measurement of the organization's values as well as the measurement of the applicants' values. The extra burden of collecting organizational data is, perhaps, a partial explanation as to why values are seldom used in selection contexts. Furthermore, the relative nature of values means that they are unlikely to emerge as important predictors in clumsy meta-analyses that simply aggregate the correlations across many organizations.

However, there is considerable evidence that values are important in vocational choice (see, for example, Watts et al., 1981) and therefore the measurement of values may be particularly important in careers guidance. Their results provide considerable evidence that values play a crucial role in job satisfaction. Although they differ in the arithmetic processes of combining data, several researchers maintain that job dissatisfaction arises when there is a discrepancy between the values held by a worker and the rewards provided by a job (see Locke, 1976). There is also evidence that dissatisfied workers are more likely to disengage from their work by arriving late, taking unnecessary absences or leaving a job. This suggests that values might be predictive of these, less frequently used, criteria.

At a semi-anecdotal level, Peters and Waterman (1982) suggest that a characteristic of excellent companies is a shared set of values.

Furthermore, values may be particularly important when selecting individuals for work in other cultures or in multinational companies. Hofstede (1984, 1994) suggested that cultures differ significantly in the degree to which they value:

- power distance – the differential between the highest and lowest people in an organization
- individualism
- masculinity
- avoidance of uncertainty
- long-term orientation.

However, the scales produced by Hofstede have been strongly criticized because they have poor psychometric properties (Spector et al., 2001).

5.4.3 THE MEASUREMENT OF VALUES

The doyen of measures of values is the Allport et al. (1960) Study of Values, which is an ipsative test that requires individuals to rank tetrads of statements. It yields scores on six values:

- theoretical
- social
- economic
- political
- aesthetic
- religious.

There is empirical work that links scores on the Study of Values to occupational choice. Furthermore, there is some correspondence between these categories and those used by Kuder and Holland (see 'Interests' below). However, the test appears to be rather dated and it is not particularly appropriate to occupational settings.

A tetrad of statements similar to the Allport–Vernon–Lindzey test

Please rank the following (1–4) in the order in which people should spend most time:

(a)   attending church;
(b)   participating in elections;
(c)   earning money;
(d)   meeting friends.

The Work Values Inventory (Super, 1970) has greater occupational relevance, but is most appropriate for use with people between the ages of 15 and 20. It yields 15 scores on values such as creativity, intellectual stimulation, co-workers, pay, security, prestige and altruism.

Two questionnaires, Schutz's (1989) FIRO-B and Gordon's (1993) Survey of Interpersonal Values (SIV), focus on values that concern other people. The FIRO-B measures how much an individual values (1) inclusion, (2) control and (3) affection. The Survey of Interpersonal Values measures six values: (1) support, (2) conformity, (3) recognition, (4) independence, (5) benevolence and (6) leadership. Gordon (1992) has also published a test to measure personal values. It assesses the values placed upon (1) practical mindedness, (2) variety, (3) decisiveness, (4) orderliness, (5) goal orientation and (6) achievement. Smith (1982) presents a compendium of scales that measures values towards people, risk, ideas, rules and work.

5.5 ATTITUDES

5.5.1 THE CONCEPT OF ATTITUDES

Attitudes are typically defined as the tendency to react positively or negatively to a class of objects or events. Unfortunately, in the context of motivation, this definition is tautological, since anything that produces a tendency to react must, *ipso facto*, motivate behaviour.

5.5.2 THE STRUCTURE OF ATTITUDES

Several researchers (Feather and Newton, 1982; Fishbein and Middlestadt, 1995, 1997; Ajzen and Fishbein, 2000) have suggested that an attitude is the aggregate that emerges when an object or event is evaluated against a person's values (the expectancy-value model). However, this process may be complex, because values may have differing weights and people may have more than one attitude towards an object. Attitudes are thought to have three components: a cognitive component (a person's knowledge of the subject); an affective component (a person's feelings on the subject); and a behavioural component (how a person is likely to act on a subject).

The expectancy-value model of attitudes suggests that we have as many attitudes as there are categories of 'psychological objects'. Some of these 'psychological objects' are more relevant to occupational psychologists than others. The subdomain of 'interests' is of particular relevance to test users.

 ## 5.6 INTERESTS

5.6.1 THE CONCEPT OF INTERESTS

It is often hard to differentiate interests from other kinds of motives. Indeed, several tests, such as the Life Styles Inventory (Lafferty, 1973) and the Motives, Values, Preferences Inventory (Hogan and Hogan, 1987), freely intermingle motives and interests. Interests differ from motives because they have a weaker power to energize action. Indeed, an interest may evoke no action other than thought or contemplation. Interests have a high discretionary element, whereas motives are important in redressing a physical or psychological imbalance that is important to well-being. For example, it is directly vital to our survival to redress an imbalance in our blood sugar level by eating, whereas we would come to no great harm if we were to ignore our interest in, say, gardening. Thus, occupational interests may be defined as:

> A subset of attitudes concerning the evaluations of beliefs about occupational activities. They are discretionary mental processes producing positive (or negative) feelings and arousing a desire to continue (or discontinue) with similar thoughts or behaviour.

5.6.2 THE STRUCTURE AND THEORY OF INTERESTS

Strong and Occupational Keying

The study of interests has largely been driven by pragmatic considerations. One of the earliest investigations was in 1919, by Edward Strong. He assembled a range of about 325 questions, which asked people how much they liked a variety of activities, objects or persons that are commonly encountered in daily living. Strong (see Campbell, 1971) then asked groups in occupations such as architects, editors, engineers, bankers, farmers and so on to complete the questionnaire, and analysed the replies to see which items most clearly differentiated the groups. The first version of the Strong Vocational Interest Blank (SVIB) was published in 1927. A person's answers were checked against each occupational group: if the pattern of their replies matched the pattern of, say, architects, they would be said to have architectural interests. Over the years, occupational profiles have been collected for hundreds of occupations and a person's questionnaire may need to be checked against each profile – a laborious process even with the aid of computers. Nevertheless, Strong's approach gave rise to a whole genre of interest tests, which are usually called '**occupationally keyed** interest tests'.

Kuder and Interest Themes

Kuder (1954) pioneered the other major type of interest test, which is based upon **interest themes**. He identified ten general themes, such as 'outdoor', 'mechanical', 'computational' and

Table 5.1 A comparison of eight interest inventories

Kuder	Rothwell–Miller	Jackson	Thurstone	Closs	Connolly	Thompson	Saville Holdworth
Outdoor Mechanical	Outdoor Mechanical		Biological science	Natural		Biological science	Biology Engineering: • process • mechanical • electrical • construction
Computational	Computational	Communicative Expressive	Computational	Computational	Computational	Mathematics	Non-verbal: • financial • data-processing
Scientific Persuasive Artistic Literary Musical	Scientific Persuasive Artistic Literary Musical		Physical science Persuasive Artistic Linguistic Musical	Scientific Persuasive Artistic Literary	Scientific Persuasive Artistic Literary	Physical science Fine arts	Physics Media Art and design Information
Social service	Social service	Helping	Humanitarian	Social service	Social welfare	Human relations	Caring: • welfare • education
Clerical	Clerical				Clerical		Administration Legal
	Practical Medical	Practical Logical Inquiring Assertive Socialized		Practical	Practical		Medical
			Business Executive				Control
						Commerce	Commercial Managerial
						Government Sports	

so on, that are relevant to many jobs. Scales were constructed for each theme and the scales were combined into the Kuder Preference Record. An updated version of this is called the Kuder Occupational Interest Survey (KOIS). People complete the test and are scored on each theme. The combination of the highest scores is used to identify suitable occupations. For example, someone who scored highly on outdoor, computational and scientific interests might be steered towards a career in agricultural statistics and research, whilst someone with high scores for social service and music might be pointed to a career in teaching dance to infants.

The approach pioneered by Kuder is much more convenient and transparent than the 'occupational black box' approach suggested by Strong. Indeed, later versions of the Strong questionnaire have been adjusted so that they too can be scored in terms of interest themes. The approach suggested by Kuder is now the dominant method of measuring interests and is used in many tests, including the Rothwell–Miller Interest Inventory (Miller et al., 1994), the Jackson Vocational Interest Survey (Jackson, 1977), the Michigan Vocabulary Profile Test (see Guion, 1965), the Occupational Interest Guide (Closs, 1978), the Connolly Occupational Interest Questionnaire (Fox, 1970), and the Managerial Interest Inventory (Saville Holdsworth, 1989), which is a narrow-spectrum test. Most of the other tests are designed primarily for school-leavers or people about to enter a first career. Table 5.1 provides a compilation of the themes measured by broad-spectrum tests.

Table 5.1 would suggest that the 'Big Nine' interest themes are as follows:

- biological and outdoor interests
- computational mathematical interests
- scientific interests, especially physics
- persuasive interests
- artistic interests
- literary interests
- social interests
- clerical interests
- practical interests.

Holland and RIASEC

Holland's (1976, 1996) work has produced probably the most influential theory of the structure of interests. Working on the basis of earlier factor analyses by Guilford (1954), Holland arrived at six occupational categories. He reasoned that the categories were not randomly organized but were arranged in the shape of a hexagon. People could be given a test of interests such as his own system, 'Self-directed Search – SDS' (Holland, 1985), and they could be typified by their three highest scores. Holland's six categories are shown in figure 5.2.

Holland suggests that in many cases the three highest scores of an individual will lie close together on the circumplex. For example, the order of one person's scores might be Realistic, Conventional and Intellectual, and he or she might be classified as an RCI type.

Holland also reasoned that jobs too could be classified into the same six categories according to the nature of the work. For example, the job of a detective might be classified as RCI, because detectives need to deal with gruelling situations as a matter of routine, and follow a conventional set of procedures, while at the same time using their intellectual faculties to interpret clues. A key element of Holland's theory is that when there is a match between a person's interests and the activities of their jobs, they will be satisfied and more likely to remain in that job.

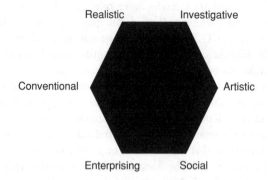

Figure 5.2 Holland's model of the structure of interests.

RAISEC is not accepted by everyone (see Gati, 1991). Some critics have claimed that the factors are a function of an unrepresentative set of questions and that there are high correlations between the themes. Other critics have questioned the number of themes and their arrangement. Prediger (1982), for example, suggests that Holland's model consists of two basic and independent dimensions: people versus things (corresponding to Holland's social–realistic dimension) and data versus ideas (corresponding to a mixture of Holland's conventional and enterprising versus a mixture of intellectual and artistic themes).

5.6.3 THE OCCUPATIONAL RELEVANCE OF INTERESTS

Beyond early adolescence, people's scores on interest tests are highly stable. Researchers such as Tracey and Rounds (1993, 1996) suggest that 20-year test–retest correlations are in the order of .6 and .7. Hanson and Campbell (1985) suggest retest reliabilities of .92, .89 and .87 after intervals of two weeks, 30 days and three years, respectively. Furthermore, the correlation between personality and interests is low (Dawis, 1991).

However, the ability of interest tests to predict job performance or training success seems poor. Schmidt and Hunter (1998) report meta-analyses which indicate that the predictive validity of interest tests for job performance is only .10, while the predictive validity for training success is only .18. The poor validity of interest tests has also been reported by Dawis (1991). In fact, interest tests are used less frequently in selection than either ability tests or personality tests. One possible reason is that interest tests are very transparent and easy to fake.

Nevertheless, interest tests and interest measures can be very useful in guidance situations where there is less likelihood of faking. In guidance situations, the criteria are not the quantity and quality of goods produced but the satisfaction of incumbents and, perhaps, their likelihood of staying in the same job or occupation.

 5.7 MOTIVATION AND JOB PERFORMANCE

Motivation is an essential condition for job performance. A very able employee who has an 'excellent' personality will produce nothing unless he or she is motivated. The relationship between job performance, ability, personality and motivation might be expressed by the following hypothetical formula:

$$job\ performance = (ability + personality) \times motivation$$

It should be noted that motivation is a multiplicative function, and that if it is zero or close to zero, performance will be negligible.

However, the situation is more complicated than the above formula might imply. As long ago as 1908, Yerkes and Dodson noted that motivation had a curvilinear relationship with performance. Low motivation or arousal produces poor performance. But very high levels of arousal can also produce poor performance. Good performance is usually obtained when motivation and arousal are moderately high. Furthermore, there is an interaction between the difficulty of a task and the optimum level of motivation. High arousal or motivation interferes with difficult tasks more than it interferes with easy tasks. Easterbrook (1959) suggested that when people are highly motivated, their breadth of attention is reduced and they use a restricted range of cues. When motivation is low, only a few, largely irrelevant, cues are ignored. However, when motivation is very high, many cues – including some crucial ones – are eliminated and performance declines. Easterbrook's ideas have received empirical support from investigators such as Koksal (1992). Eysenck and Calvo (1992) suggest that high levels of motivation increase the mental resources that a person applies to a task, but that this increase is offset by the mental resources needed to deal with the stress. Eysenck and Calvo's theory of processing deficiency has been supported by the work of MacLeod and Donnellan (1993).

5.7.1 JOB DESIGN AND MOTIVATION

It might be argued that the selection of highly motivated people is not the best way of optimizing productivity. Motivation involves restoring a homeostatic balance between a person and his or her environment. Some people will argue that it is easier to obtain this balance by changing the environment to meet the state of the people. In other words, it is better to alter jobs so that they motivate people. Work by Hackman and Oldham (1976) suggests that motivation can be improved if jobs are altered to involve:

- a variety of skills
- the capacity to complete whole tasks rather than a part of a task
- tasks that are significant
- the freedom how to choose how to do a job
- feedback on how effectively the job is done.

Another major theory of work motivation, expectancy theory (Porter and Lawler, 1965), suggests that motivation will be improved if:

- managers understand that different people value different rewards, and try to establish the rewards that are valued by individual employees
- the specific behaviours that constitute good performance are realistic, clearly defined and understood
- there is a direct, clear and explicit link between good performance and rewards.

As a general conclusion, it is probably better to modify a job so that it is motivating than to attempt to select candidates who are motivated.

CHAPTER 6

ATTRACTING APPLICANTS

Attracting applicants is a vital step. The more effectively the step is conducted, the less import-ant the actual selection becomes. If a firm only attracts six really excellent applicants, it hardly matters whether they select among these high flyers with a bad method, such as using a pin, or whether they choose on the basis of a more scientific method. Similarly, if an advertisement is so awful that it repels all but the most desperate and incompetent people, even the best selec-tion method cannot produce a good recruit. Boudreau and Rynes (1985) demonstrated the point by using utility analysis, which is described in chapter 13, to work out the cash benefits of selec-tion. They imagined a situation in which an organization needed to fill ten vacancies per year. For the sake of simplicity, they also imagined that the vacancies could be filled in two ways. First, the organization could use a good source of recruitment (such as an effective recruitment agency) and then use a poor method of selection, such as traditional interviews. Alternatively, the organization could use a poor source of recruitment (such as newspaper advertising) but then use a moderately good method of selection. Boudreau and Rynes found that in terms of the money returns to the organization, the first strategy was better.

6.1 THE SELECTION RATIO

The number of credible applicants for each post is known as the *selection ratio*. In general, it is best to have a low ratio – in other words, many applicants for each job. However, there comes a point of diminishing returns, where a large number of applicants swamp resources and recruiters are unable to give each application the attention it deserves. Consequently, the quality of selec-tion declines. Some interesting strategies have been adopted to deal with these situations. For example, one government authority received over 3,000 applications for a job that was advert-ised as suitable for a graduate of any discipline and that involved foreign travel. Overwhelmed with the sheer volume of applications, the authority gave each one a number and then selected 20 at random for further consideration. As a rule of thumb, recruiters should aim to achieve about ten credible applicants for each post. An examination of the application form or the CV and changes of mind by some applicants will then produce about six effective applicants, who can be assessed carefully.

▲ 6.2 RECRUITMENT MEDIA

Recruitment media should be chosen carefully on the basis of the type of job involved. The main media are as follows.

6.2.1 INTERNAL ADVERTISING

A memo can be pinned to a notice-board, a notice can be inserted in a company newsletter or notices of vacancies can be e-mailed to employees. Internal advertising has many advantages:

- speed and low cost
- much is already known about the applicants
- there are fewer formalities
- training is reduced, because applicants know the organization
- morale is improved, since the organization is seen to look after its present employees.

Internal advertising may also work, because existing employees pass the information to relatives and acquaintances. This may yield good applicants, since they will make their decisions in the light of realistic information obtained from the existing employees. Such applicants, if appointed, will try hard not to let down the person who recommended them, and the person making a recommendation often acts as a source of informal guidance and discipline.

Unfortunately, internal advertising also has many disadvantages. The long-term consequences to the organization may be particularly dire, because persistent use of this method will deny the company access to new people, ideas and approaches. Internal recruitment can also lead to difficult situations if existing staff are rejected. A high proportion of employees whose internal application is rejected resign shortly afterwards. Internal recruitment often does not solve a selection problem but merely transfers it elsewhere in the organization. Finally, internal advertising may have an indirect effect of being unfair. Internal advertising maintains the status quo and if existing employees are not a fair representation of potential employees, equal opportunity legislation may be infringed.

6.2.2 VACANCY BOARDS

Vacancy boards are traditionally used for unskilled and semi-skilled jobs and they tend to attract local recruits who travel past the premises. Vacancy boards have three major disadvantages. First, they advertise what may be a chronic inability to attract and retain staff. Second, most organizations find it difficult to keep the boards up to date and remove vacancies that have been filled. Third, there may be implications for equal opportunities since the route past the premises may not be used by some minority groups.

6.2.3 FUTURE VACANCY FILES

Future vacancy files are compiled from the applications of candidates for previous jobs, and can be both cheap and effective. However, they need to be managed carefully, with proper classification and indexing – a task that is easily computerized. There must also be effective procedures to remove files that are too old or where applicants have refused several appropriate approaches. If information is kept on a computer, data protection legislation must be observed (see chapter 27).

6.2.4 GOVERNMENT AGENCIES

Government agencies offer free service and they may undertake preliminary sifting of applicants. Unfortunately, government agencies may have a poor image and employers may be reluctant to use them for non-routine jobs.

6.2.5 PRIVATE AGENCIES

Private agencies charge between 15% and 25% of the yearly salary of a successful applicant. The financial incentives mean that the agencies work quickly – agencies can often provide the names of suitable applicants within two hours. Agencies usually specialize in particular kinds of staff, such as accounting staff, drivers, retail staff and lawyers. They maintain a register of potential applicants together with their CVs. If agencies are used with any frequency, their management is a matter of great importance. Often, it is best to trawl a large number of agencies to obtain information concerning their methods, the qualifications of their staff, their compliance with equal opportunities legislation and so on. On the basis of this information, four or five agencies can be chosen as approved suppliers and a strong relationship with them can be established.

6.2.6 HEADHUNTERS

'Headhunters' is the popular name for 'executive search consultants', a particular type of private recruitment agency. They are usually used for top jobs, on the basis that the ideal applicant is not looking for a job and is too busy to read advertisements. Therefore, a prospective employer needs to be proactive and seek out the best person. Headhunters use a variety of techniques to identify potential applicants. Often they use contacts in education, trade associations and professional bodies. Sometimes, headhunters use subterfuge and telephone the switchboard of competitors to obtain the names of potential applicants. Good headhunters build up a database that contains extensive information on key employees in a whole industry. Their database may track high-flyers throughout their careers. Discretion is one of the main advantages of using headhunters, but they are not cheap. Top headhunters have the capability of conducting an international search for the best candidates. Typically, 11% of the year's salary is payable on acceptance of an assignment; a further 11% is payable on presentation of a shortlist and a final 11% is payable on the acceptance of a job offer. Some people regard headhunting as unethical. However, it is also possible to argue that it is unethical for firms to 'hoard' talent when it could be used to better advantage elsewhere. It can be argued that Headhunters are merely helping the labour market to operate efficiently.

6.2.7 PROFESSIONAL BODIES AND TRADES UNIONS

Professional bodies and sometimes trades unions can be a source of good recruits. In many professional bodies, such as the Australian Psychological Society and the Institute of Personnel and Development, the process is highly organized and advertisements can be placed in society magazines, or arrangements are available at meetings and conventions.

6.2.8 THE INTERNET

The Internet is a rapidly growing source of recruits. It can be used to attract candidates in two main ways.

First, a company can include vacancy pages on its own corporate website. Vacancies are often listed under headings such as 'career opportunities' or 'working for us'. Some features of a good corporate website are as follows:

- an attractive, uncluttered design, with images that are relevant and that are changed frequently
- a description of the organization, products, services and locations
- a section that is only one click away from the home page
- details of specific jobs given in such a way that they are easily located by search engines
- extra information such as profiles of current employees, diversity policy (equal opportunities), working here (our values) and career tips also frequently included
- contact details specified – some corporate websites request applications by e-mail or give the telephone number and postal address
- the avoidance of high-tech tricks or images that take a long time to download or distract from the main purpose (applicants prefer a user-friendly site to an eye-catching one).

It is important to keep company sites up to date. The job title should be expressed in several different ways, so that applicants can locate it by using different key words in their search. A good example of a corporate website that includes career opportunities is www.pricewaterhousecooper.com.

Second, an organization can post its vacancy on a specialized website that acts as an agency, advertising the vacancies of many organizations. The most widely known site of this kind is www.monster.com. An exceptionally good, Australian, agency site that offers many other features, including links to e-recruiting organizations, is www.employment.com.au. Some sites, for example www.onetest.com.au, provide online applicant assessment, including tests (see chapter 17).

Some agency sites offer to manage the entire recruitment process from the preparation of 'adverts' to placing them on a server so that they are readily available whenever applicants choose to do their search. They will also allow applicants to submit their CVs online. These agencies automatically acknowledge the receipt of the applications and filter applications using skill matching, key words and location. Most systems track and record each contact with the applicant. The systems also produce statistics and sophisticated reports, so that accurate information is available on the types of jobs filled, the availability of applicants and their sex, age, disability or ethnic origin.

The Internet promises to be the major recruitment medium in the future. The main advantages seem to be:

- cost efficiency (in some situations)
- a lot of information can be made available in a way that the applicants can tailor to their needs or styles
- better reach and exposure, since millions of potential applicants use the Internet
- a faster hiring process.

6.2.9 PRINTED ADVERTISEMENTS

At present, printed advertisements remain the major route by which applicants are attracted. Newspapers tend to specialize in the kind of advertisement that they carry on certain days. For example, they may carry civil service jobs on Mondays, legal jobs on Tuesdays, sales jobs on Wednesdays and so on. The types of advertisements also vary:

- At the basic level are *linage* advertisements, where the cost is related to the number of words or the number of lines used. There is little control over the appearance and there will be little to differentiate one advertisement from the hundreds of others on the page. It is usually best to start a linage advertisement with a word starting in A or Z.
- *Semi-display* advertisements are the next step up. The advertiser pays for a number of column centimetres and has some control over appearance, to make an advertisement a little more distinctive.
- *Classified display* advertisements are the top of the range and are usually spread over several columns. The advertiser has a great deal of control over the final appearance, because photographs, diagrams and logos can be used to project a corporate image. Unfortunately, classified display advertisements can be very expensive.

Printed advertisements can appear in several types of publication. Local newspapers often have a preponderance of linage advertisements. Classified display advertisements usually dominate the quality broadsheets – especially those published at the weekend. Specialist jobs are usually advertised in trade magazines or practitioner magazines published by professional bodies. Unfortunately, these magazines are often published on a monthly basis and when lead times are taken into account there can be a delay of six weeks or more before an advertisement actually appears.

 ## 6.3 THE EFFECTIVENESS OF MEDIA

Different media have different levels of success. The British Institute of Management and the Institute of Personnel Management (1980) surveyed satisfaction with the different media, using a five-point scale. The results were as follows:

internal recruitment	4.1
local press	3.7
national press	3.5
trade journals	3.2

selection consultants   2.8
private agencies   2.7
headhunters   2.5
government agencies   2.2
professional registers   1.9

Media may also vary in the quality of the applicants that they provide. Several people have suggested that informal media yield better applicants. For example, De Witte (1989) found that 51% of applicants located via advertisements left the organization within one year. In comparison, 37% of applicants who made speculative applications, and only 30% of applicants who were recommended by existing employees, left within the same time period.

There has been some speculation about why informal methods attract better applicants. One suggestion is that informal media tend to reach people who are already in work and performing well, while advertising tends to reach people who are dissatisfied with their jobs or who have not been able to sustain satisfactory performance. Another suggestion is that applicants introduced by informal channels have better and more realistic information about the job, so that they only apply if it is likely to be suitable. More recently, the finding that informal media produce better applicants has been questioned. Critics point out that many of the studies are poorly controlled and that extraneous factors may account for the phenomenon. For example, informal methods are more likely to be used in senior appointments that will be filled by older applicants. Since job turnover is strongly related to age, the apparent superiority in turnover rates might thus be a function of age rather than the recruitment medium.

◣ 6.4 SELECTION AS A SOCIAL PROCESS AND APPLICANT IMPRESSIONS

The way in which a job vacancy is communicated can be vitally important in the success of selection, because it affects applicants' perceptions of the job and the organization. Herriot (1989, 2002) has emphasized that selection is a social process, in which both the employer and the applicant must make a series of positive decisions to continue. For example, the first step is taken by the employer when the job is advertised. A potential applicant will see the advertisement and form an impression of the job and the firm. If the impression is positive, the applicant may send in an application form. However, if the impression is negative, the applicant will exit from the process and look for a job elsewhere. When the organization receives the application form, it gains an impression of the applicant. If the impression is positive, the applicant may be invited for an interview. However, if the organization's impression is negative, it will terminate the sequence and consider other applicants. A successful result will only occur at the end of a long chain of such reciprocal decisions, and much of the decision power will lie with an able applicant. Research on the factors that influence applicants' impressions can be organized under six headings:

- *Interviewer behaviour* has a strong effect on the perceptions of applicants (Harn and Thornton, 1986; Thornton, 1993). Interviewers who seem warm and thoughtful engender favourable impressions of the process and the organization. Furthermore, applicants who are interviewed by warm, thoughtful people are more willing to make contact with the organization and feel that they will be made an offer of a job. The behaviour of the interviewer seems particularly important when other information is absent. Applicants who are interviewed by people whom they perceive as cold will only make further contact with the organization if the 'cold' interviewer gives a great deal of information. However, there is some suggestion that the impression given by the interviewer does not affect the 'bottom line' – the applicant's intention to accept or reject an actual job offer. Latham and Finnegan (1993) point out that the expectations of the interviewer and interviewee are different. Applicants want the flexibility to present themselves in the best light and to be able to learn about the job. They also want to feel that the methods of selection are fair. Managers are more concerned about accurately identifying the best applicants, convenience and the ease with which decisions can be defended. Employment lawyers have a third perspective. They value a selection system that is based on job analysis, and where applicants are given a standardized list of questions that are clearly relevant to the job. It is therefore hardly surprising that applicants prefer unstructured interviews while managers and lawyers prefer situational interviews (see chapters 18 and 19).

- *Applicant mood* is thought to be an important determinant of perceptions and it believed that an applicant who arrives in a bad mood will have a less favourable impression of an interview. However, a study by Adams (1987) casts doubt on this notion. He manipulated the mood of applicants by giving them good or bad feedback before an interview and he found that this manipulation had little impact.

- *Labour market conditions may have an important impact.* It may be argued that when jobs are scarce, interviewees are more likely to have a positive impression of the interviewer and are be more likely to accept a job offer. These ideas were investigated by a study where engineering students were given different written descriptions of the labour market their impressions of subsequent interviews were then measured. Contrary to expectations, the labour market conditions did not affect students' perceptions of interviewers or their intentions to accept job offers. This conclusion can only be tentative, since the simulations were not entirely realistic.

- Many organizations emphasize their *equal opportunities policy* in job advertisements. Mondragon and Thornton (1988) suggest that even aggressive positive recruitment (that is, making contact with potential applicants from 'minority' groups) does not affect reactions towards a potential employer. However, if affirmative measures are used in the actual selection or promotion decisions (that is, the choices made), applicants have a more negative view.

- *Realistic Job Previews* take many forms: brochures, a video or a job try-out. Gaugler and Thornton (1990) suggest that Realistic Job Previews do indeed reduce initial expectations – even in those areas that are not covered by the previews themselves. Realistic Job Previews improve the effectiveness of selection primarily because they reduce the initial turnover once a job offer has been accepted. However, there does not seem to be any need to tailor previews to the motives of individual applicants – a general preview is just as effective as one designed for specific groups.

- Several studies have shown that applicants have clear preferences concerning *methods of selection*. In general, applicants like methods such as work samples that have an obvious similarity to the job. They also like unstructured interviews, because they feel that they have some control over the topics discussed and the impression that they make. Applicants tend to dislike tests. In part, this stems from the fact that some tests do not *appear* to have relevance to the job. In addition, applicants may not like tests because they offer little control over the proceedings. Applicants may also fear that tests are more likely to detect their efforts at lying and cheating.

6.5 ADMINISTRATIVE ASPECTS

Applicants may react very quickly indeed. It is important to prepare the response at the same time as an advertisement is placed. It is prudent to inform reception, so that they can help applicants who call in 'on spec'. Similarly, the switchboard should be alerted, so that telephone enquiries can be directed to the correct person. Advanced preparation of an application pack will prove very useful and will give an efficient image. In general, the application pack should contain four items:

- a short letter thanking applicants for their interest, stating the closing date, outlining the selection process that will be used and drawing their attention to any enclosures
- an application form or any instructions concerning the contents and format of a CV
- a job description and possibly a person specification
- a reply envelope.

It is also prudent to make preliminary arrangements for later stages, such as the administration of tests (see chapter 21).

 ## 6.6 FAIRNESS IN ATTRACTING APPLICANTS

The way in which applicants are attracted can lead to unfairness and infringement of the law. Details about a vacancy should be equally available to all subgroups of a population. For example, an advertisement placed exclusively in women's magazines such as *Cosmopolitan* would discriminate against men. In some circumstances, this will mean that organizations will need to make a special effort to advertise a vacancy in publications read by minority groups. Internal advertising or filling a vacancy by word of mouth carries a substantial risk of unfairness. These media tend to perpetuate a status quo that is often biased in favour of a majority group.

Job advertisements can also be biased. An advertisement must not contain a statement such as 'A strong young lad needed', or 'Only Irish people should apply'. This constitutes direct discrimination and is illegal unless, for example, the 'lad' is required for a male role in a play or for a situation in which public decency is involved (for example, a janitor in a male toilet). Job advertisements, particularly display advertisements, can also contain subtle forms of indirect bias. Photographs of existing or potential employees should reflect the racial and ethnic composition of the community. A photograph of, for example, a group of white male employees would be taken to imply that applications from women or from the ethnic minority communities would not be welcomed.

PART II

PSYCHOMETRICS

CHAPTER 7

BASIC STATISTICS 1

THE NORMAL CURVE

Once a reasonable field of candidates has been attracted, the best one must be identified. As chapters 15, 18 and 19 will show, many different methods of measuring their suitability are available and it is necessary to choose the best methods. This is not an easy task, because the proponents of each method will claim that theirs is the best. Some way is needed of evaluating their claims. Later on (see chapters 9–12), it will be shown that measures of people's characteristics can be judged against five statistical properties:

- sensitivity
- validity
- utility
- reliability
- fairness.

Evaluating any method may also involve understanding its construction and the way in which it is scored. These statistical qualities used to evaluate a method of selection are usually called **psychometrics**. Competence in psychometrics is a vital requirement of using tests.

A quick glance at the psychometrics chapters will reveal that they contain a lot of statistics. Consequently, a basic knowledge of statistics is needed in order to choose the most appropriate selection methods for a field of candidates. The aim of this and the next chapter is to give a basic explanation of these ideas. Readers who have studied statistics or psychology are certain to have encountered these ideas before. However, you should not skip the next two chapters unless you are absolutely 100% certain that your statistical knowledge is good!

Basic psychometric statistics fall into two areas: the normal curve and correlations. Normal curves are covered in this chapter and are considered in five sections:

1 The development of the normal curve
2 The characteristics of normal curves
3 The standard normal curve
4 Z scores (Z values)
5 Normal curve tables

7.1 THE DEVELOPMENT OF THE NORMAL CURVE

7.1.1 DERIVING NORMAL CURVES FROM MEASUREMENTS

In order get accurate conclusions, we need to take measurements of people and things. There are usually too many measurements to remember, so we need to summarize them using statistics. The simplest method of summarizing measurements is to arrange them in order and then to count the number of times any measurement occurs. The result can then be displayed as a table or a graph. For example, suppose the height of 47 men is measured to the nearest 2 cm and the following data obtained:

165	167	169	169	171	171	171	171	171	173	173	173
173	173	173	173	173	175	175	175	175	175	175	175
175	175	175	175	175	175	177	177	177	177	177	177
177	177	179	179	179	179	179	181	181	183	185	

The data could be displayed as a table or graph:

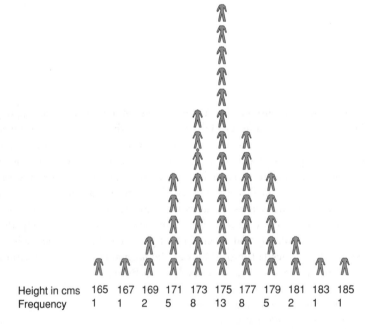

Height in cms	165	167	169	171	173	175	177	179	181	183	185
Frequency	1	1	2	5	8	13	8	5	2	1	1

The lines at the bottom show the number of men in each interval. This is called a **frequency count**. The number of icons in each interval is directly proportional to the numbers in each interval. This kind of chart is called a **pictogram**.

It is possible to replace the pictograms of people with bars of the same height:

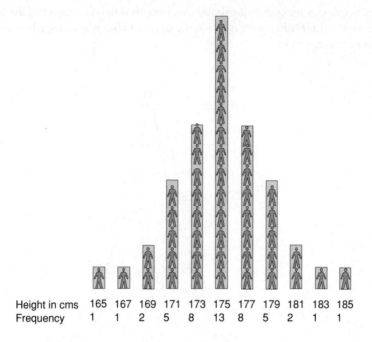

Height in cms	165	167	169	171	173	175	177	179	181	183	185
Frequency	1	1	2	5	8	13	8	5	2	1	1

Diagrams of this kind are called **histograms**. Avoid calling them 'bar charts'.

If the centres of the intervals of the histogram are joined up, a **frequency distribution** is produced:

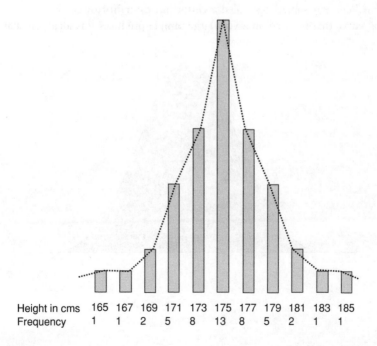

Height in cms	165	167	169	171	173	175	177	179	181	183	185
Frequency	1	1	2	5	8	13	8	5	2	1	1

When the points of a frequency distribution are smoothed to take account of the small sample size and the fact that measures were taken to the nearest two centimetres, a bell-shaped curve, the **normal curve,** is produced:

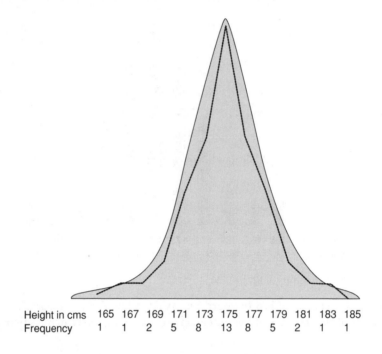

Height in cms	165	167	169	171	173	175	177	179	181	183	185
Frequency	1	1	2	5	8	13	8	5	2	1	1

The normal curve is sometimes called a **Gaussian distribution**.
A normal curve that is based on a very large sample produces this idealized shape:

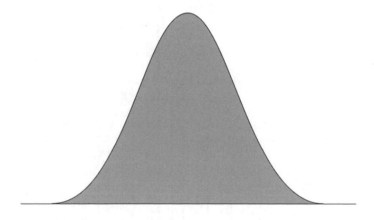

7.1.2 SKEWED DISTRIBUTIONS

In practice, the idealized normal distribution is rarely seen. Often, the curve seems to be slanted to the left or the right. If there is a 'tail' at the lower end, the distribution is negatively skewed. If there is a tail at the upper end, it is positively skewed:

Technically, a negative skew occurs when the mean is lower than the mode or median. A positive skew occurs when the mean is greater than the mode or median. Very often, skews can be statistically corrected.

7.1.3 OTHER DISTRIBUTIONS

Human characteristics are usually normally distributed, but other types of distribution occur. You need to be able to recognize these other distributions, because you can only use certain types of statistics if there is a normal distribution. Two other distributions are as follows:

- A **Poisson distribution** often arises when you count the number of times certain events, such as accidents, occur:

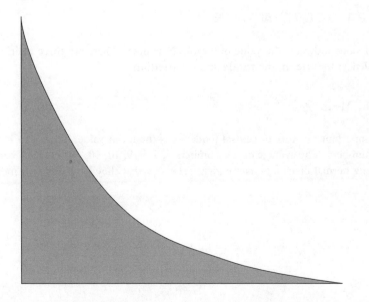

Most people have no accidents in a given year. Some people have one accident. A handful of people have two or three accidents, while just a tiny number have four or more.

- A **bimodal distribution** has two modes. It usually arises when you are measuring the same thing in two distinct groups:

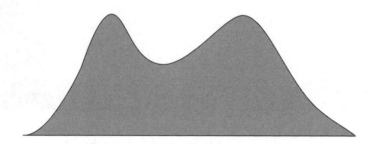

This diagram would probably result if you were to produce a frequency distribution of men *and* women as a combined group.

 ## 7.2 THE CHARACTERISTICS OF NORMAL CURVES

Normal curves are so common that statisticians have established their characteristics in some detail. The two main characteristics are the **central value** and the **dispersion**. If these two characteristics are known, we can accurately recreate the whole distribution.

7.2.1 THE CENTRAL VALUE

The central value indicates the value of a typical member. There are three main measures of central tendency: the **mean**, the **mode** and the **median**.

The Mean

The most important measure of central tendency is the mean value. The mean is the average of a set of numbers. The average of the numbers 5, 7, 9, 9, 10, 10, 10, 11, 11, 13 and 15 is 10. The following normal distributions are identical *except* that they have different means:

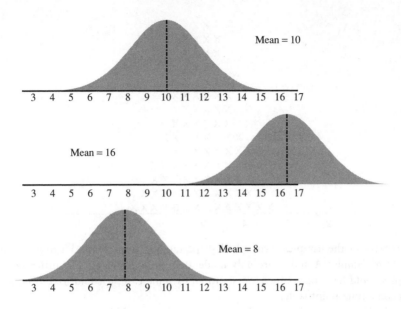

Means (averages) can be calculated from two kinds of list. One kind contains *everyone* in a population (that is, a **census**). For example, an average IQ can be calculated from the scores of *all* 40 accountants in an organization. This mean will be exact and, usually, statistical tests will not be needed.

The other kind of list contains only *some* people – a sample. Often, the mean is calculated for a sample and then used as though it was obtained from the whole population. For example, a hypothetical army might want to check whether an interview is too easy. It could do this by averaging interview scores to see whether the mean is noticeably above 5 (interview performance is rated on a 1–9 scale). However, the army has interviewed 10,000 applicants and it cannot justify the expense of retrieving and analysing data for all applicants. Therefore, the army chooses ten applicants at random (sample A) and calculates their average score. The average is 5.7 and so the army almost concludes that the interview procedure must be made a little harder. In this case, the average for the sample has been used to estimate the average for the whole population. *It is common practice to use a sample to estimate the average for a population, but this can be dangerous – especially when the sample size is small.*

Before a harder interview is instigated, the army decides to cross-check the results by taking the scores of a different sample (B) of ten applicants. This time, it achieves an average of 4.3 – which would lead it to conclude that the interview is a little too hard.

Concerned at the wide discrepancy between the two results, the army decides to repeat the analysis another 98 times – each using a sample of ten. It casts the 100 averages into the following frequency chart, where each cross represents the average for one of the samples of ten, and where the first average is marked A and the second average is marked B:

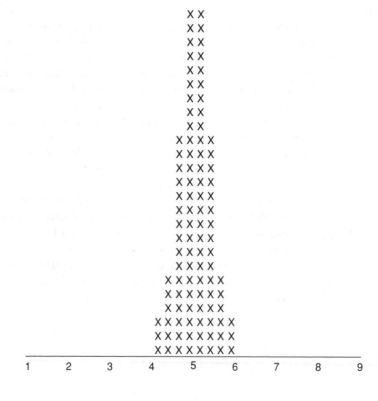

```
                        X X
                      X X X X
                      X X X X
                      X X X X
                    X X X X X X
                    X X X X X X
                    X X X X X X
                    X X X X X X
                  X X X X X X X X
                  X X X X X X X X
                X X X X X X X X X X
                X X X X X X X X X X
              X X X X X X X X X X X X
            X X X X A X X X X B X X X X
  ─────────────────────────────────────────────
    1       2       3       4     5     6     7     8     9
```

The averages of the samples form a bell shape ranging from about 3.3 to 6.6. The values obtained from samples A and B are only moderately different (1.3). The difference between two samples could have been much worse. In an extreme case, it could have been as large as 3.5 points on a nine-point scale.

Intrigued, the army conducts another set of calculations. This time, it draws another 100 samples, but now each sample contains the scores of 20 soldiers. The following diagram results. Notice how the means of the larger samples cluster more tightly about the centre of the distribution. The maximum difference between any two samples is about two points on the nine-point scale:

```
                        X X
                        X X
                        X X
                        X X
                        X X
                        X X
                        X X
                        X X
                        X X
                      X X X X
                      X X X X
                      X X X X
                      X X X X
                      X X X X
                      X X X X
                      X X X X
                      X X X X
                      X X X X
                      X X X X
                    X X X X X X
                    X X X X X X
                    X X X X X X
                  X X X X X X X X
                  X X X X X X X X
                  X X X X X X X X
  ─────────────────────────────────────────────
    1       2       3       4     5     6     7     8     9
```

Intrigued further, the army personnel officer repeats the calculations for a third time: in this case, each of the 100 samples contains the scores of 60 soldiers. It obtains the following diagram. The results for each sample cling tightly to the centre of the distribution. The maximum difference between any two samples is probably $1\frac{1}{2}$ points on a nine-point scale:

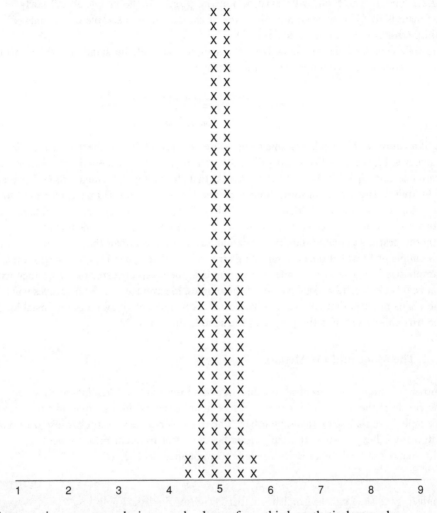

Two very important conclusions can be drawn from this hypothetical example:

1   When an average from a sample is used to estimate the average for a population, it is highly likely that it will contain some error. This error is called the **sampling error** and it causes the different results between samples. The sampling error will often be quite small, but sometimes it will be large and lead to wrong decisions.
2   Sampling error is related to sample size. Small samples contain a great deal of error, while large samples contain less. In many situations, averages based on samples smaller than 30 will contain too much error. If the averages of two small samples (under 30) are compared, any difference is quite likely to be due to sampling error. Decisions based on such differences are likely to be wrong.

These conclusions also apply to most other statistics, such as standard deviations or correlations based on small samples. It is important to remember that results based on small samples are unstable. Another small sample may give quite different results.

The margin of error of a statistic from a sample also depends upon the variability (see section 7.2.2, under 'The Standard Deviation') of the people. If the people are all fairly similar, the estimate is likely to be accurate. However, if the people in a sample differ markedly, the sampling error is likely to be quite large.

The following formula combines both the sample size and the standard deviation of the sample to estimate the sampling error of an average:

$$sampling\ error = \frac{standard\ deviation\ of\ sample}{\sqrt{sample\ size - 1}}$$

Thus, if a sample of 17 people has an average score on a test of 70 and the standard deviation of their scores is 12, the sampling error will be ±3 (that is, $12/\sqrt{16} = 12/4 = 3$). If another sample is taken, one can expect (two out of three times) that the average obtained will be between 67 and 73 – quite a large range in some circumstances. However, if the sample is increased to 145, the sampling error will be ±1 (that is, $12/\sqrt{144} = 12/12 = 1$) and the averages obtained from similar samples can be expected to lie (two out of three times) between 69 and 71.

If another test has a smaller standard deviation, say 6, the average for the population estimated from a sample of 17 will also have a sampling error of 1.5 (that is, $6/\sqrt{16} = 6/4 = 1.5$). Finally, if the sample size is 145 and the standard deviation is 6, the sampling error of the average will be .5 (that is, $6/\sqrt{144} = 6/12 = .5$). Two out of three times, the averages for these samples will be 70.

The major point is that any statistic based on a small sample may be quite unstable. This will be particularly so when the people in the sample differ widely.

The Mode and the Median

The other two measures of central tendency are less important and less informative.

The **mode** is the 'most fashionable' measurement contained in a sample, in the sense that more people have that score than any other. The mode is not very useful because it cannot be used in many other statistics. It simply describes the most frequent measurement. For example, the country of birth of 14 British people was obtained, as follows:

English, English, English, English, English, English, English, English,
Scottish, Scottish, Scottish,
Welsh, Welsh,
Northern Irish.

The modal value of these nominal measures is English, because it occurs most frequently. The mode is of limited value because it cannot usually be used as a part of further calculations. It is useful, however, because it is the only central value that *can* be used with nominal measures such as nationality. The mode certainly *cannot* be used with rank measures and, technically, it should not be used with continuous measures.

The **median** is the middle value of a set of scores. If the scores of nine people for extroversion were arranged in order, the following list might result:

3.5, 3.7, 4.5, 5.0, **5.5**, 8.9, 9.1, 19.5, 90.0.

The median value is 5.5, because it is the middle value. The median is a bad measure of central tendency. Notice how, in the above example, the fact that the numbers above the median are much more extreme than the numbers below the median seems to be ignored. You cannot use the median with nominal measures. Using the median with ordinal measures is a waste of information, and you should rarely use the median when you could use the mean.

The main use for the median is when you are using a scale that is not uniform, as in the case of a logarithmic ('log') scale or correlations. Under these circumstances, it would be misleading to use the mean. You are most likely to come across the median when researchers give a central value for a group of correlations – probably following a phrase such as 'and the median correlation was . . .'.

It should be noted that, like means, modes and medians obtained from small samples are quite variable, whilst those obtained from large samples will be more stable.

7.2.2 DISPERSION (SPREAD)

As well as differing in their central point, normal curves differ in the degree to which the measurements 'cling' to the centre. In some normal curves, the measurements cling quite tightly to the central value. In other normal curves, the measures spread themselves out and are quite dispersed. For example, the normal curves in the following diagram all have the same mean values, but some are more tightly spread than others:

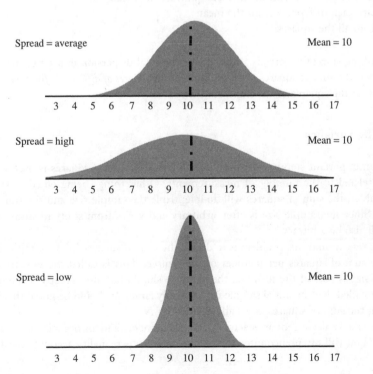

The spread can be described in subjective terms, such as 'average', 'low' or 'high', but a more accurate system is needed.

The Range

There are many indices of the extent to which a set of scores clings to the mean. The easiest index of dispersion is the **range**, which has close relatives such as the **interquartile range**. Measures based on range share the same disadvantage – they depend on the values for just two members in a sample and they may not be representative.

Three better and more important measures of dispersion are the **sum of squares (SS)**, the **variance** and the **standard deviation**. They are related to each other in a systematic way.

The Sum of Squares

The sum of squares is the simplest measure of dispersion, but it is rarely used. However, you need to know about the sum of squares because:

- it is an important step in many statistical calculations and you will encounter it frequently when reading journal articles
- it forms the basis of other measures.

The sum of squares is easy to compute:

1 Take each measurement in turn and subtract the mean.
2 Square each difference from the mean.
3 Add up all the squares.

The resulting sum of squares is a measure of the total dispersion in a set of measurements.

Remember, the sum of squares is the addition of the *squares of differences from the mean*, NOT the addition of the squares of the numbers themselves.

The Variance

Except as an important step in statistical calculations, the sum of squares is useless because it is directly related to the number of measurements. Other things being equal, if the size of a sample doubles, the sum of squares will double; triple the sample size and the sum of squares will triple. Since the sample size is often arbitrary and varies from study to study, the sum of squares will also be arbitrary.

A simple way around this problem is to divide the sum of squares by the sample size, to give the average sum of squares per member of the sample. This is called the **variance**. Because the sample size is part of the formula, the variance should not alter greatly if the sample size changes (provided that the initial sample is reasonably large). It should be noted that if the sample is small, the sum of squares is usually divided by $N - 1$.

Variance is a vital concept in selection and assessment, and in organizational psychology as a whole. You will often encounter statements such as 'personality accounts for 16% of the variance in job performance'. What this means is that if the job performance of a large sample of people is measured (for example, by taking the weekly sales of each salesperson) and the variance turns out to be £100, then if personality could be held constant by recruiting people with exactly the same personality, the variance would shrink to £86. In other words, personality could be suspected of causing 16% of work performance. The objective of most psychological research is to account for as much variance as possible.

The Standard Deviation

The variance is very useful for research problems, but it is useless for practical problems, because the numbers that result bear little obvious relationship with the actual measurements: it is quite possible for the variance to be 10 when the highest possible score is 9. This is because, as a part of the process of calculating the variance, the differences are squared. A simple way of bringing variance back to scale is to take the square root of the variance. The square root of the variance is called the **standard deviation**.

The standard deviation relates directly to the actual scores. In practice, most normal curves are five standard deviations wide (2½ above the mean and 2½ below the mean). In psychometrics, the standard deviation is extremely important, because it gives rise to a measurement system that is almost universal – the system of **Z scores**. A Z score tells you how many standard deviations a person is above or below the mean. Someone with a Z score of 2.5 is two and a half standard deviations above the mean, while someone with a Z score of −.75 is three quarters of a standard deviation below the mean. The following diagram shows the relationships between the mean, the standard deviation and Z scores:

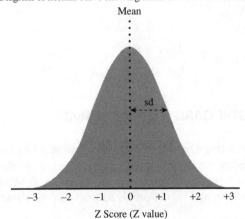

Diagram of normal curve showing mean and standard deviation
Mean

Z Score (Z value)

In order to establish a Z score, you need to know the mean and the standard deviation of the actual data collected. Then you should carry out the following calculations:

1 Subtract the mean score.
2 Divide the result by the standard deviation.

For example, IQs have a mean of 100 and a standard deviation of 15. The steps to obtain a Z score for someone whose IQ is 130 are as follows:

1   Subtract the mean from the score (for example, $130 - 100 = 30$).
2   Divide the result by the standard deviation (for example, $30/15 = 2$).

The Z score of an IQ of 130 is therefore 2.
Z scores are very important for the following reasons:

- They allow different characteristics to be compared. It is possible to say that a person's Z score for age is +1.2, that the person's Z score for income is −.5 and that his or her Z score for IQ is 2.0. The Z scores can be compared and it can be concluded that the most distinctive feature of this person is his or her IQ.
- They have been studied a great deal and so statisticians know the properties of Z scores very well. Tables exist that show Z scores, proportions and ordinates. It is *essential* that you know how to use these tables, and the methods are described in section 7.3 below.

Simplified formulae for the characteristics of normal curves are as follows:

$$\text{the mean} = \bar{x} = \frac{\Sigma x}{N}$$

$$\text{the sum of squares} = SS = \Sigma(x - \bar{x})^2$$

$$\text{the variance} = v = \frac{\Sigma(x - \bar{x})^2}{N}$$

$$\text{the standard deviation} = sd \text{ or } \delta = \sqrt{\frac{\Sigma(x - \bar{x})^2}{N}}$$

 ## 7.3 THE STANDARD NORMAL CURVE

Normal curves can differ in two ways – their mean and their standard deviation. In every other respect, all normal curves are the same. Rather than working out the details for every possible normal curve, statisticians have concentrated on establishing the details for one simple normal curve, so that with basic arithmetic it is possible to work out the details for all other normal curves.

The normal curve chosen as the standard has a *mean of zero* and a *standard deviation of one*, as shown in the following diagram:

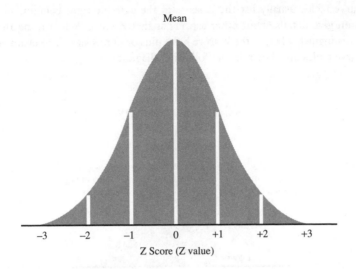

Mean

−3   −2   −1   0   +1   +2   +3

Z Score (Z value)

 ## 7.4 Z SCORES (Z VALUES)

It is easy to convert from any other normal curve to the standard curve – simply subtract the mean and divide by the standard deviation. For example, suppose that someone has an IQ score of 120 and that the IQ scale has a mean of 100 and a standard deviation of 15. Finding the equivalent score on the standard normal curve involves two steps:

1   Subtract the mean from the score (that is, $120 - 100 = 20$).
2   Divide the remainder by the sd (that is, $20 \div 15 = 1.33$).

Thus, someone with an IQ of 120 has a score of +1.33 standard deviations on a standard normal curve. The scores on a standard normal curve are usually called Z scores, but sometimes they are called Z values.

It is as easy to convert the other way – from Z scores to the scale we are using – by reversing the process and first multiplying the Z score by the standard deviation of the scale and then adding the scale's mean. If someone had a Z score of −2, their IQ would be calculated in the following way:

1   Multiply the Z score by the standard deviation (that is, $-2 \times 15 = -30$).
2   Add the mean to the result (that is, $+100 - 30 = 70$).

7.5 NORMAL CURVE TABLES

Statisticians have worked out values for many aspects of the standard normal curve. They have compiled tables that show values for three aspects at each Z score:

• the proportion in the *larger* area of the normal curve 'cut' by the Z score
• the proportion in the *smaller* area of the normal curve 'cut' by the Z score
• the *ordinate* at the Z score.

Normal curve tables usually list the Z score in the extreme right column, and in the suc-
ceeding column give details about other aspects at that Z score. When using the tables, it is
important to distinguish whether the Z score has a plus or minus sign. The characteristics given
by normal curve tables are shown in the following diagrams:

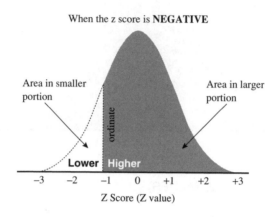

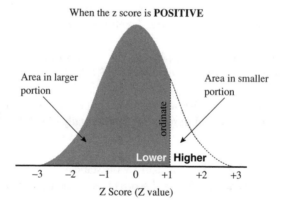

The area in the *larger* portion shows one of two things, depending upon whether the Z score
is positive or negative:

- if the Z score is positive, the larger portion shows the percentage with *lower* scores
- if the Z score is negative, the larger portion shows the percentage with *higher* scores.

The area in the *smaller* portion also shows one of two things, depending upon whether the
Z score is positive or negative:

- if the Z score is positive, the smaller portion shows the percentage with *higher* scores
- if the Z score is negative, the smaller portion shows the percentage with *lower* scores.

Table 7.1 A simplified normal curve table: Z scores (Z values)

Z Standard score Column A	Area in larger portion Column B	Area in smaller portion Column C	Ordinate Column D
.0	.50	.50	.40
.1	.54	.46	.40
.2	.58	.42	.39
.3	.62	.38	.38
.4	.66	.34	.37
.5	.69	.31	.35
.6	.73	.27	.33
.7	.76	.24	.31
.8	.79	.21	.29
.9	.82	.18	.27
1.0	.84	.16	.24
1.1	.86	.14	.22
1.2	.88	.12	.19
1.3	**.90**	**.10**	**.17**
1.4	.92	.08	.15
1.5	.93	.07	.13
1.64	**.95**	**.05**	**.11**
1.7	.96	.04	.09
1.8	.96	.04	.08
1.9	.97	.03	.07
1.96	**.975**	**.025**	**.06**
2.0	.98	.02	.05
2.32	**.99**	**.01**	**.03**
2.6	1.00	.00	.01

Examples:

Z score = +1.64 → 95% lower,   5% higher,   ordinate = .10
Z score = −.5   → 31% lower,   69% higher,   ordinate = .35
Z score = +1.1   → 86% lower,   14% higher,   ordinate = .22
Z score = −2.3   → 99% higher,   1% higher,   ordinate = .03

The ordinate is the *height* of the standard normal curve at a given Z score. The ordinate does not change according to whether the Z score is positive or negative. A simplified example of a Z score table is given in table 7.1. *It is absolutely vital that you know how to use normal curve tables.*

CHAPTER 8

BASIC STATISTICS 2

CORRELATIONS

In selection, we frequently want to know if things are related. For example, we may want to know whether a salesperson's test score is related to the number of sales that he or she will make (validity). We may also want to know whether a score that a person obtains one day is related to their score if they retake the test on another day (reliability). Often, we want to know if someone's score on one personality test will give the same result when a different personality test is used (validity).

Usually, correlation coefficients are used as the index of such relationships. The topic of correlations can be divided into eight sections:

1 Data suitable for correlations
2 Scattergrams
3 Correlations
4 Scattergrams and correlations
5 Factors that reduce correlations
6 The statistical significance of correlations
7 The practical significance of correlations
8 Specialist correlations

 8.1 DATA SUITABLE FOR CORRELATIONS

Some measurements are not suitable for use with correlations, and it is important to distinguish between suitable and unsuitable data. This distinction depends on the types of measurements obtained. For the present purpose, there are three types of measures:

- **Nominal measures** simply put people into categories. The categories are names and they do not imply any size or value. Examples of nominal measures are nationality (English, Irish, Scottish or Welsh) or blood group (A, B, O).
- **Ordinal measures** rank people in some kind of hierarchical order. Ranking measures are bad and can have strange psychometric properties. They should be avoided whenever possible.
- **Continuous measures** are where there are many gradations and there is a clear implication of some kind of size or magnitude. Examples of continuous measures include height,

income, intelligence or emotional stability. With some continuous measures, such as height and income, a zero point is known. With other continuous measures, such as intelligence, the true zero is not known because we have yet to locate a person who has no intelligence whatsoever – although most of us could probably make some nominations.

For the moment, it is convenient to believe that correlations are only permissible when both variables are continuous. The exceptions to this simple notion are mentioned in section 8.7.

 ## 8.2 SCATTERGRAMS

The simplest way to understand correlation is by means of a scattergram, where there are two scores for everyone. For example, five people may complete a maths test and an English test, and we may want to see if the two sets of scores are related. Some fictitious data are given in the following table:

Person	Maths score	English score
Posh	+2	+1
Scary	+1	+2
Sporty	+1	0
Baby	−1	−1
Ginger	−2	−2

A graph with the maths score on one axis and the English score on the other axis can be constructed. We can then place each individual on the graph, at the point at which their scores intersect:

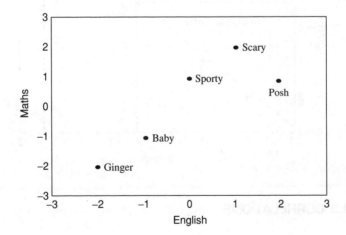

It is possible to draw a trend line through the centre of the points of the scattergram. It would be more accurate to calculate the position of that line, which would then be called the **regression line**:

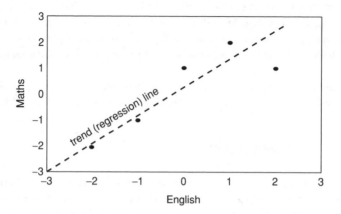

Regression lines are very useful, because they enable us to predict the scores of one test from the scores of another. For example, if someone scores 3 on the maths test, we can draw a horizontal line across the graph from 3 on the maths axis and then down from where it meets the trend line. We can then read off the likely score, 2.6, on the English test.

Predictions can also be made in the opposite direction. If someone scores .5 on the English test, we can draw a line upwards from .5 on the English axis and then across where it meets the trend line, and read off the likely score .7 on the maths test:

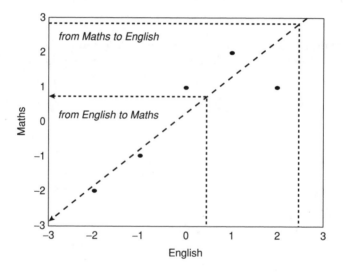

◥ 8.3 CORRELATIONS

It is possible to inspect a scattergram and, on an intuitive basis, decide whether there is a trend between the two sets of scores. In the spicy example above, there is a clear trend. As the maths scores increase, so do the English scores, but the English score increases slightly less than the maths score. In other situations, the trend is less clear-cut and there is room for dispute.

It is better to calculate an objective index called the **correlation coefficient**. There are many types of correlation coefficient. The best and most powerful is the product–moment correlation r, devised by Karl Pearson. The product–moment correlation is amazingly simple. It is merely the average cross-product of the two scores when they are both expressed in as Z scores. As it happens, the scores in our spicy example are Z scores, so the calculation of the product–moment correlation is easy:

Person	Maths	English	Cross-product	Arithmetic
Posh	+2	+1	+2	2×1
Scary	+1	+1	+1	1×1
Sporty	+1	−1	−1	$-1 \times +1$
Baby	0	−1	0	0×1
Ginger	−2	−1	+2	-2×-2
Total cross-products	4			
Number of scores	5			
Correlation	.8	$4 \div 5$		

All other complications contained in the formula for product–moment correlations merely transform the data into standard deviation units.

8.4 SCATTERGRAMS AND CORRELATIONS

Scattergrams and correlations present similar information and it is useful to be able to associate the two. This section describes scattergrams and correlations at different levels, using data on a sample of 31 – a fairly typical sample size for small-scale experiments:

Correlation .9. This is the level of correlation that you can hope to obtain if a good ability test is re-administered to the same sample after a delay of about a month. Notice how the points form a thin diagonal oval with perhaps one or two moderate outliers:

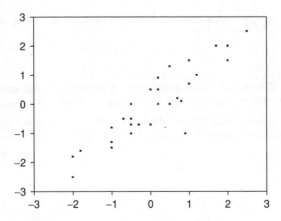

Correlation .4. This is a reasonably good correlation from a validity study. The trend is still just discernable, but the constellation of points is diffuse and there are a notable number of outliers. The points form a diffuse oval:

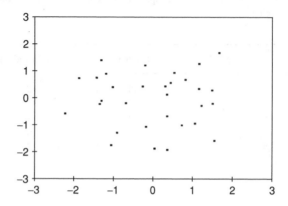

Correlation .0. This is a scattergram of a zero correlation. The points on one variable are at random with regard to the points on the other. There is no obvious pattern, except perhaps that the constellation of points forms a circle:

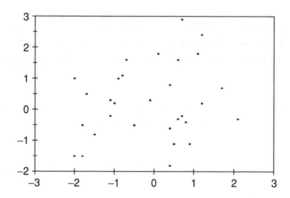

Correlation −.9. Sometimes scores are negatively related – as one score goes up, the other score goes down. An example is a score on a conscientious scale versus the number of mistakes made: the more conscientious you are, the fewer mistakes you make. The following scattergram shows a strong negative correlation (−.9), but negative correlations can range from −1 to 0:

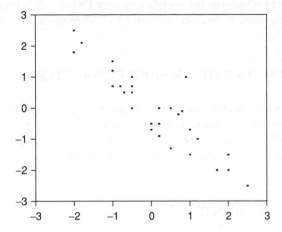

Thus correlations may range from +1 (which shows a perfect relationship in the same direction), through 0 (which shows no agreement of any kind) to −1 (which shows a perfect relationship, but in the opposite direction). It should be noted that negative correlations are as useful as positive correlations in predicting one variable from another.

Sometimes, several estimates of the same correlation are available. For example, a test of empathy may have been administered twice to similar-sized samples of social workers in four different local authorities and test–retest correlations of .4, .6, .8 and .9 obtained. There is a strong temptation to average the correlations to give an average correlation of .68. However, *correlations should not be averaged*, because they are not a uniform scale – the differences between large correlations are greater than the differences between small correlations. It is necessary to stretch large correlations by transforming them into Fisher's Z coefficients (no connection with Z scores), which are averaged, and the average Fisher's Z should then be transformed back into a correlation. The following table can be used to make the transformations to and from Fisher's Z:

r	Z	r	Z
.250	.255	.625	.733
.275	.282	.650	.755
.300	.310	.675	.820
.325	.337	.700	.867
.350	.365	.725	.918
.375	.394	.750	.973
.400	.424	.775	1.033
.425	.454	.800	1.099
.450	.485	.825	1.172
.475	.517	.850	1.256
.500	.549	.875	1.354
.525	.584	.900	1.472
.550	.618	.925	1.623
.575	.655	.950	1.832
.600	.693	.975	2.185

Using the table to transform the correlations into Fisher's Zs, averaging and then back-transforming the Zs yields an 'average' correlation of .78 in the social worker example.

 ## 8.5 FACTORS THAT REDUCE CORRELATIONS

Correlations obtained from ideal studies give an accurate estimate of the relationship between two things. However, ideal studies are rarely possible and the correlations that we obtain in practice usually underestimate the true strength of a relationship. Three factors that reduce correlations are restriction of range, criterion contamination and curvilinearity.

8.5.1 RESTRICTION OF RANGE

In selection, we rarely have the full range of data for our correlations. We rarely hire every-one who applies, and often the very best people leave or are promoted before we can obtain our follow-up data. Consequently, correlations are often based on a restricted range and they underestimate the true relationship. The situation is analogous to the correlation between the engine size and speed of cars. Over the whole range of cars, from a Trabant to, say, an Ferrari, the correlation between engine size and top speed is very high – approximately .8 – and engine size is clearly important. However, if we only collect data for a restricted range of engine sizes – say, between 1,000 cc and 2,000 cc – the relationship does not have 'room' to show itself and a moderate correlation of .3 is obtained. Furthermore, other features – such as aerodynamic styling, the transmission system and so on – are not restricted and show their full correlation of, say, .35. Consequently, restriction of range will not only underestimate the correlation but it may also lead us to conclude that the wrong things are important. The same point can also be made in diagrammatic form. First, here is a scattergram for an ideal situation in which the test results and subsequent performance are known for each of 65 applicants:

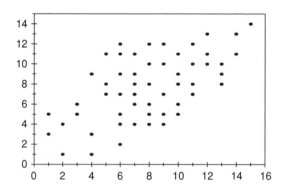

This scattergram shows a correlation of .6 and it suggests that the selection method is very good. The next diagram shows a more realistic situation that is typical of a practical selection situation:

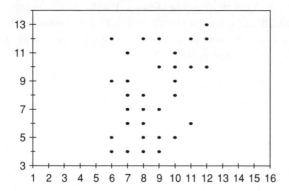

In this case, the nine people with the poorest scores were not hired, and the six best people were promoted before data could be collected on their job performance.

Notice how restriction of range has made the constellation of points look much more round, so that it gives the appearance of a correlation of .45. The restriction of range has made the selection method seem worse. Fortunately, formulae are available that allow the true correlation to be estimated. The use of these statistical corrections is somewhat controversial. As a general rule, you should specify the population that is relevant to your purpose. Then you should examine the population that has been obtained. If the latter has been constrained by artificial factors, then correction is appropriate. In selection, this usually means that correlations *should* be corrected. Whenever corrected correlations are used, a brief explanation of the reason should be given and the raw correlation should also be reported.

8.5.2 CRITERION CONTAMINATION

In selection, we frequently wish to correlate marks at the selection stage with people's performance on the job. However, it is very difficult to obtain an accurate measure of people's performance. Often, we rely on an inaccurate measure such as the supervisor's opinion, which is likely to be contaminated by subjective factors.

The situation may be analogous to calibrating a new thermometer against people's subjective opinions about the weather. The correlation that results might be mediocre – in the range of .3. We might conclude that the thermometer is no good and throw it away. However, the real problem lies in the inaccuracy of our criterion – people's subjective opinions. If we have a perfect criterion, such as data from a satellite, the new thermometer might turn out to be good and produce a correlation of .85.

8.5.3 CURVILINEAR DATA

Correlations are linear statistics. They assume that the direction of a relationship is consistent throughout the range. This may be true for some characteristics such as intelligence where, in most jobs, more intelligence tends to be associated with better performance. However, with some characteristics the direction of the relationship changes. The trait of 'confidence' may be a good example.

In sales jobs, people with very low confidence may be a total failure, people with average confidence may be acceptable, and people with fair self-confidence may be excellent. However, at that point the direction of the relationship changes. People with very high self-confidence may prove to be disastrous, because they are totally insensitive to customers. In this example, there is a clear curvilinear relationship, with an optimum level of self-confidence in the middle. However, the Pearson correlation coefficient is only .08:

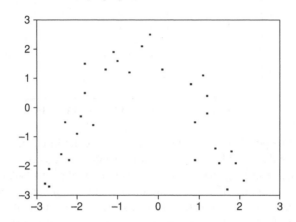

◣ 8.6 THE STATISTICAL SIGNIFICANCE OF CORRELATIONS

Correlations can occur by fluke and this can lead us to conclusions that are false. Fluke correlations are much more likely when they are based on small samples. In this chapter, samples as small as five have been used in order to explain correlations in a clear way. In practice, no one in his or her right mind would use such a small sample. As a rule of thumb, correlations based on samples of less than 30 people are not worth having, correlations based on samples of 65 or more are acceptable, and correlations based on samples greater than 172 are excellent.

A more rigorous approach is to check a correlation's statistical significance. First, you must decide on the level of risk that you are prepared to take – what statisticians refer to as the 'alpha level', .05 being the value traditionally used in research. This means that 5 in every 100 significant correlations will be flukes. The 5% level of significance is quite an exacting level, and the level of risk of accepting a false correlation is fairly small. However, it does mean that there is a substantial risk of rejecting a correlation that is true.

Most computer packages print out the significance level of correlations and most statistics textbooks give a table of correlations that are significant at an alpha level of .05. An abbreviated version of such a table is as follows:

Sample size	Significant correlation	Sample size	Significant correlation
25	.381	90	.205
30	.349	100	.195
35	.325	125	.174
40	.304	150	.159
45	.288	200	.138
50	.273	300	.113
60	.250	400	.098
70	.232	500	.088
80	.217	1,000	.062

In order to be significant at the 5% level, the correlation must be equal to, or higher than, the correlation shown for the sample size.

 ## 8.7 THE PRACTICAL SIGNIFICANCE OF CORRELATIONS

A correlation can be used to make practical estimates, such as the likely level of job performance. A correlation indicates how many standard deviation scores on one variable will increase with each extra standard deviation on another variable. For example, if the correlation between a test score and job performance is .4, every one standard deviation increase in the test score is likely to produce a .4 standard deviation increase in job performance.

Correlations can be used to estimate the benefit of employing one person rather than another. For example, a large currency trading company in Hong Kong has established that a test of mental ability has a correlation of .5 with the subsequent profits made by its traders. There are two candidates for a vacancy. Candidate A scores .3 standard deviations higher than candidate B. The validity of .5 suggests that a .3 difference in test scores will result a performance difference of .15 standard deviations. A standard deviation in the performance of currency traders equals $1 million. Thus, .15 standard deviations are worth $150,000. Choosing candidate A on the basis of the test result is therefore likely to produce an extra profit of $150,000.

 ## 8.8 SPECIALIST CORRELATIONS

So far, this chapter has concentrated on one type of correlation coefficient, the Pearson product–moment correlation, because it is the most widely used and, in most circumstances, it is the best correlation. However, other correlations are used in selection and assessment.

These specialist correlations include **Spearman's rank order correlation** (rho, ρ), which is used when an investigator has been unwise and gathered data in the form of ranks. The rank order correlation would be used, for example, if two supervisors ranked the same group of subordinates and the agreement between the supervisors needed to be estimated.

Other specialist correlations include:

- biserial correlations
- point biserial correlations
- terachoric correlations
- partial correlations.

More details of these correlations are given on the website associated with this book.

CHAPTER 9

THE SENSITIVITY OF SELECTION MEASURES

If a measure is insensitive, most people will have the same or similar scores, and selectors or counsellors will have little information on which to base decisions. If a measure is sensitive, candidates will be spread over a wide range and it will be easy to pick the best. If a measure is sensitive, it will be easier to advise a client exactly where he or she stands relative to other people. Sensitivity is also important in research. Insensitive measures will have little variance and it will be difficult to detect significant relationships. Sensitivity is almost always a 'good thing'.

◢ 9.1 THE INDEX OF SENSITIVITY – THE STANDARD DEVIATION OF RAW SCORES

Sensitivity depends upon the spread of the **raw scores** and is usually expressed as a standard deviation (sd). A sensitive test will have a high standard deviation of raw scores (a large spread), whilst an insensitive test will have a low standard deviation of raw scores (a low spread). It must be emphasized that it is the standard deviation of the *raw scores* that matters. Some test authors scale the raw scores into other systems, so that it *seems* that there is a good spread.

Many psychological characteristics are normally distributed and 99% of people will fit within five standard deviations ($2^{1}/_{2}$ either side of the mean). Each separate category in a scoring system must have at least one mark. So, if the raw score sd of a measure is .4, most people will be covered by two raw scores ($.4 \times 5 = 2$). Therefore, a measure with a raw score sd of .4 can only classify people into 'above average' and 'below average'. Similarly, a measure with a raw score sd of .6 can only classify people as 'above average', 'average' and 'below average'. Table 9.1 shows the minimum raw score standard deviation needed to support up to nine levels of categories. It is highly desirable to exceed the minima given in the table by a considerable margin.

Table 9.1 also indicates the verbal labels that can be attached to categories. It is important to note that these labels are intended in a strict statistical sense. On some scales, such as that for psychoticism, it is better to be below average. Great care must be exercised when using these labels with guidance clients, since the terms 'average' and 'below average' are almost certainly perceived with negative connotations.

Table 9.1 Categories supported by various standard deviations of raw scores

Number of categories	Percentages in categories and possible verbal labels	Minimum raw sd
2	50%:50% Above average/below average	.4
3	20%:60%:20% Above average/average/below average	.6
4	16%:34%:34%:16% Much above average/above average/below average and so on	.8
5	8%:22%:38%:22%:8% Highly above average/above average/average and so on	1.0
6	5%:15%:30%:30%:15%:5% Exceptionally above average/much above average/above average and so on	1.2
7	4%:11%:21%:28%:21%:11%:4% Exceptionally above average/much above average/above average/average and so on	1.4
8	2%:7%:16%:25%:25%:16%:7%:2% Exceptionally above average/highly above average/much above average/ above average and so on	1.6
9	2%:6%:13%:18%:22%:18%:13%:6%:2% Exceptionally above average/highly above average/much above average/ slightly above average/average and so on	1.8

 ## 9.2 BROAD- AND NARROW-SPECTRUM TESTS

Most measures are broad spectrum and attempt to gauge the whole range of the general population. This has the advantage that only one test needs to be developed for all situations.

However, broad-spectrum tests may not be appropriate when candidates are drawn from a narrow range. If broad-spectrum tests are used with narrow groups, they may fail to discriminate between people. For example, a multinational organization operating from Singapore considered using a test of mental ability that, according to the manual, had an adequate sd of raw scores of 6 for the general population. But the organization was prestigious and was able to attract graduate candidates who were in the top 2% of the population. The test was almost useless with this very able group. The standard deviation of their scores was only .5, and the test had great difficulty in discriminating the best graduates from the worst.

Test designers frequently produce tests focused on specific parts of the ability spectrum. Raven's Progressive Matrices, for example, feature the Standard Form, which is used with the population as a whole, the Advanced Matrices, which have difficult questions and are suitable for use with talented populations such as graduates. The Coloured Matrices are used with children or people with learning difficulties. Similarly, the AH series of tests contains the AH4 test, which may be used on the general population. The AH5 test is more difficult and may be used to discriminate between very able candidates. In addition, there are two versions of the AH6 test: one is used to discriminate amongst arts graduates, while the other is used to discriminate amongst science and engineering graduates. Catalogues and test manuals usually state the population for which a test is suitable.

Some test publishers produce narrow-spectrum tests merely as a ploy of their marketing departments. If they can convince a client to purchase several tests rather than a single broad-spectrum test, they increase their profits. However, narrow-spectrum tests are not necessarily best – it all depends upon the sd of the raw scores for the selected group. For example, one publisher promotes a test on the basis that it gives better differentiation between applicants for managerial jobs. An inspection of the manual shows that the sd of the raw scores of the test for this group is 6. However, a standard test – the WAIS – has a standard deviation of 7.4 when used with managerial groups, and therefore this broad-spectrum test provides marginally better discrimination for this population than the narrower-spectrum test.

 ## 9.3 THE SENSITIVITY OF SOME COMMON MEASURES

Table 9.2 shows the sd of the raw scores for some tests and other measures. The analysis is complicated by the fact that many tests yield both global score and sub-scores. The sensitivity of the global scores is nearly always greater than that of the sub-scores. The table gives the sd of the raw scores for the global score and the range of sds for the sub-scores.

Table 9.2 indicates that non-test measures, especially interviews, are generally insensitive and, at best, can only support a four-fold classification. The sensitivity of ability tests is usually excellent. Indeed, ability tests may be so sensitive that they invite over-interpretation. Even the least sensitive personality tests have adequate sensitivity and some – in general, those scales that measure the 'Big Five' personality factors – have good or excellent sensitivity.

Table 9.2 The sensitivity of raw scores of some tests

Scale	Mean raw score sd	Raw score range for sub-scales
Non-test measures[a]		
Group discussions	.84	–
In-basket	.75	–
References	.64	–
Interviews	.54	–
Ability tests		
WAIS	25	2.5–14.0
AH4	14.6	8.3–9.1
Personality tests		
16PF	5.0	3.4–6.2
California Personality Inventory	4.9	3.7–6.3
Hogan Personality Inventory	4.6	3.1–6.9
Myers–Briggs Type Indicator	14.5	11.6–16.3
NEO Five factor Inventory	4.3 (18.6)[b]	3.0–5.3 (15.8–21.2)
OPQ	4.7	3.6–5.7
Quintax	7.9	6.1–10.1
Interest tests		
Rothwell–Miller Interest Test	17.29	13.6–22.0
Management Interest Inventory[c]	5.17	4.7–5.75

[a] Obtained from assessment centre ratings on a 1–5 scale.
[b] The NEO can be scored for facets or the 'Big Five' factors. Data for the 'Big Five' are in parentheses.
[c] Scores for functions.

CHAPTER 10

STANDARD ERROR AND RELIABILITY

Reliability is the second most important concept in psychometrics. It yields precedence only to the concept of validity (see chapter 11). To the lay person, the essence of reliability is the concept of **repeatability** (Guion, 1965).

Repeatability shows whether the same or very similar results are obtained when something is measured two or more times. If different results are obtained each time something is measured, this usually means that the measures are inaccurate and that they are contaminated by error. When reliability (repeatability) is low, it is doubtful whether anything at all is being measured. When reliability is high, it is certain that *something* is being measured quite accurately. However, in itself, reliability does not tell us *what* is being measured. Reliability is a very big topic, which is best considered under seven headings:

1　Definitions of reliability
2　The standard error of measurement (se_m): the preferred index of reliability
3　The reliability correlation: the traditional index
4　Sources of error and systematic variance
5　Confidence limits and confidence intervals
6　Standard errors of *two* scores
7　Three further aspects of reliability

 10.1 DEFINITIONS OF RELIABILITY

Reliability can be defined at three levels: the lay person's view, the conceptual level and the statisticians' level.

10.1.1 THE LAY DEFINITION

The lay person's definition of reliability follows from the introduction of this chapter. To the lay person, *reliability is the extent to which a measure repeatedly produces the same or very similar results*.

10.1.2 THE CONCEPTUAL DEFINITION

The lay definition is acceptable for many purposes, but it is imprecise about the circumstances in which the results are obtained. If two administrations of a test or other measure are separated by, say, six months, reliability takes on the meaning of **stability**. Reliabilities obtained in this way are often called **stability coefficients**, since they show how much a result is likely to change over time. On the other hand, it might be possible obtain two scores almost simultaneously using, say, an interval of a couple of days, which is too short a period for a person to have changed. These indices of reliability are usually called **coefficients of consistency**. Indices of consistency are often obtained by splitting a test into parts and correlating the scores from the different parts. Stability coefficients and consistency coefficients both contain error introduced by random factors. Stability coefficients, however, may also include actual changes in the person being measured.

10.1.3 THE STATISTICAL DEFINITION

A statistical definition of reliability is *the proportion of variance that is not due to random error*. The rationale that lies behind this definition is straightforward and is often called 'Classical Test Theory'. According to Classical Test Theory, whenever we measure anything there is always error. The error may be tiny when, for example, we measure a rod of platinum in a laboratory; or the error may be large when, for example, we try to measure an applicant's intelligence at an interview. Tiny or large, error is always there. It follows that any measurement consists of two parts: the thing itself and error. This leads to the formula:

$$observed\ score = true\ score \pm error$$

This is an important formula and you should remember it. The formula leads directly to the statistical definition of reliability, as the proportion of a measure's variance that is not random error. This can be illustrated by means of variance diagrams.

For the example, suppose that a supervisor estimates the intelligence of a sample of people and that the variance for the whole sample is 100 units. An omniscient deity knows that 36% of these units are caused by random error, such as the supervisor's mood at the time of making the estimates and mistakes in filling in the form. The remaining 64% of the variance

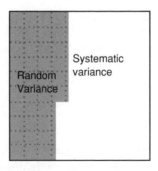

Figure 10.1 A reliability of .64 (64% systematic variance, 36% error).

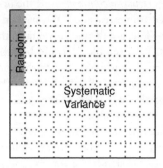

Figure 10.2 A reliability of .95 (95% systematic variance, 5% error).

reflects systematic variance in the intelligence of subordinates. The reliability of the supervisor's estimates is therefore .64, as shown in figure 10.1.

In a second situation, intelligence is gauged with a very good intelligence test, the Weschler Adult Intelligence Scale (WAIS). Again, there are 100 units of variance and the deity knows that five of these units of are due to random events. Systematic variance is reflected by 95 units. Hence, as shown in figure 10.2, the reliability of the WAIS is .95.

◤ 10.2 THE STANDARD ERROR OF MEASUREMENT (se$_m$): THE PREFERRED INDEX OF RELIABILITY

10.2.1 THE BASIC CONCEPT OF THE STANDARD ERROR OF MEASUREMENT

The explanation so far has relied upon information from an all-knowing deity to provide data on the amount of random error in a measure. In practice, this information is not available, so we need to find a way to obtain it. In the past, correlations were used as an index of random error. However, modern opinion is in favour of a different index – the standard error of measurement (se$_m$).

The idea of the standard error of measurement (se$_m$) is easier to explain using an example of measuring a physical object, such as the length of a rod of platinum. It is simple to obtain the standard error of measurement (se$_m$) of the length of a platinum rod: it is measured and re-measured a large number of times under tightly controlled conditions. We are almost certain to find that the measurements form a normal curve. The characteristics of this normal curve can be calculated in the way described in chapter 7.

The first statistic we would calculate would be the average of all the measurements. Provided that we have taken a lot of measurements, the average of all the measurements will be fairly close to the true length of the platinum rod. Because we have measured the rod many times, the transient, random factors that have caused error will have had plenty of opportunity to cancel out. In other words, the average will be very close to the true score known unto the deity.

Then the standard deviation of the many measurements would be calculated (see section 7.2.2). This standard deviation of all the errors will be a good index of how much error was involved each time we took a measurement. The standard deviation of these errors is called the **standard error of measurement (se$_m$)**, and it has two major advantages as an index of reliability:

- *It is in the same units as the original measurements.* If the original measurements are in centimetres, the se_m will be in centimetres, and if the original measurements are in quotients, the se_m will be in quotients. This is a distinct advantage: the standard error can be directly related to a person's score. For example, it would be possible to stay that an applicant's IQ is 124 ± 3 or that a client's sten score on extroversion is $6.5 \pm .9$. In direct contrast, expressing reliability as a correlation of, say, .8 is of little help in interpreting a specific score. This advantage is particularly relevant in guidance, where a client needs to know the margin of error in his or her scores.
- Statisticians have studied standard deviations for many years and consequently their properties are well known. Normal curve tables are available in statistics books. Later in this chapter, it will be shown that the standard error, in conjunction with normal curve tables, can be used to estimate probabilities, cutting points and confidence limits – which are very useful in making objective decisions about candidates and clients.

It must be noted that the standard deviation only equals the standard error of measurement in this very special case. There were repeated measures of the same platinum rod, whose length never changed. Therefore, the only two components in the score that we observed were the true score plus the error. It is much more usual to calculate the standard deviation on things that differ – rods of different lengths, and people of different heights and IQs. *When different things are being measured (for example, different platinum rods or different people), the standard deviation DOES NOT equal the standard error of measurement.*

10.2.2 THE STANDARD ERROR OF MEASUREMENT FROM CORRELATIONS

Whilst making repeated measures of the same thing may be a good method when measuring inanimate objects such as a platinum rod, it is hopelessly impractical when measuring most aspects of human beings. A platinum rod has no objections whatsoever to be measured 100, or even 1,000, times. Furthermore, a platinum rod undergoes practically no change as a result of being measured. In contrast, few human beings would endure completing an intelligence test or a personality test 1,000 times. Even if they could be persuaded to the limits of their endurance, the activity of completing the tests would change the subjects' perceptions and experience of the questions. For example, they would start to remember the answers to questions. The results of the last tests would not be measuring quite the same thing as the results of the first tests.

Consequently, psychometricians have usually employed a second, inferior way of obtaining the standard error – by means of correlation coefficients. In order to obtain a correlation coefficient, it is not necessary to re-measure the same thing 100 or more times: it is sufficient to obtain a pair of scores from 100 or more people – a far easier task.

Fortunately, it is simple to calculate the standard error if the reliability correlation and the standard deviation of a scale are known. The reliability correlation is usually reported in the test manual or, in the worst case, it can be determined by a straightforward study. The standard deviation of a scale is usually known, because it will have been chosen by the user from a limited range of stens, stannines, T-scores or quotients. The formula for calculating the standard error of a score from a correlation coefficient is as follows:

$$se_m = sd_{scale} \times \sqrt{1 - r}$$

where se_m is the standard error of measurement, sd is the standard deviation of the scale, and r is the reliability correlation from the manual or from a study.

The calculation of standard error using even a simple formula can be tedious, and consequently a table showing the standard errors for the most frequently used scoring systems is given in appendix 10.1 at the end of this chapter.

10.2.3 THE STANDARD ERROR AND INTERPRETATION OF SCORES

It is vital that scores are interpreted in the light of the measure's reliability (see chapter 23). The se_m determines the margin of error surrounding a score. If the reliability is high, then small differences between scores are important. If the reliability is low, then even large differences can be due to chance and should not be interpreted.

In approximately two out of three cases, the true score will be within one standard error of the obtained score. In other words, if a score is plotted on a profile and a shaded bar is extended one se_m above and below, we can be 67% certain that the true score is within the shaded area. For example, if an IQ test has a reliability of .91, the se_m will be less than 4.5. So, if someone scores 120 on a test, we can be 67% certain that the true score lies between 115.5 and 124.5. It will therefore be possible to say that it is twice as likely as not that the true score is in the shaded area between the arrows in figure 10.3.

The margin of error depends upon the level of risk that is acceptable. As explained in chapter 8, the level of risk is usually called the alpha level (and it has nothing to do with Cronbach's alpha, which is defined later in this chapter). Research usually adopts an alpha level of .01 (a 1% chance of accepting a false hypothesis) or .05 (a 5% chance of accepting a false hypothesis) – a type I error. But these levels increase the chance of another kind of error – rejecting a true hypothesis (a type II error). In research, it is deemed less important to reject a true

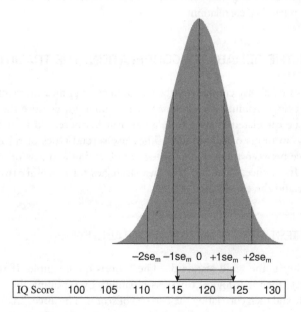

Figure 10.3 Standard error about an observed score.

Table 10.1 Z scores of selected alpha levels

Level of risk – alpha (the probability of accepting a fluke)		Z score
0.5	As likely as not	0.76
0.33	Twice as likely as not	0.96
0.25	Thrice as likely as not	1.15
0.1	Nine times as likely as not	1.64
0.05	Nineteen times as likely as not	1.95

result than to accept a false one: a rejected true hypothesis cannot complain, whereas a publication containing a hypothesis that turns out to be false may be received with derision by colleagues. Consequently, a very stringent alpha level of .05 or .01 can be set. In selection and guidance, the situation is different. The consequences of rejecting a good candidate may be almost as important as the consequences of accepting a bad one. The consequences of missing a good career path may be almost as important to a client as finding a good one. Under these circumstances, an alpha level of .33 or .5 is more appropriate. The choice of the correct alpha level depends on judgement. If a decision is very important and has irreversible effects, a high alpha level should be chosen. In practice, most selectors and counsellors use an alpha level of .33.

To find the appropriate margin of error for the alpha that is chosen, we multiply the se_m by the Z score for the level of acceptable risk. The Z scores for the main alphas are given in table 10.1.

The standard error of measurement is a very important topic, and it will be encountered again in section 10.5 of this chapter that considers cutting scores and confidence limits. However, now that a basic understanding had been achieved, it is necessary to consider the other index of reliability – the reliability correlation.

 ## 10.3 THE RELIABILITY CORRELATION: THE TRADITIONAL INDEX

The modern view of reliability emphasizes the standard error of measurement as the best index of reliability. However, reliability correlations remain important because the standard error of measurement can be calculated from a correlation. Furthermore, old texts frame their treatment of 'reliability' in terms of correlations. They use several types of reliability coefficients. The only difference between them is the strategy of obtaining two lists of measurements that can be correlated. In essence, there are only two strategies for obtaining two lists of data: the test–retest strategy and the consistency strategy.

10.3.1 TEST–RETEST RELIABILITY (STABILITY)

Test–retest reliability is the 'gold standard'. The logic is quite simple. If repeatability is the essence of reliability, then it is logical to assess reliability by repeating the test or measure on a substantive sample and then correlating the two sets of scores. The direct link between test–retest reliability and what a practitioner needs to know – 'Would I get the same result if I were to test this person again?' – is one of its main advantages. However, there are several problems:

1   In practice, test–retest reliability is the most inconvenient method, because it requires contacting subjects twice. Often, this is not easy: subjects may have changed their place of work or residence. Sometimes, lethargy or forgetfulness mean that subjects do not attend the second administration. 25% or more of the initial pool may not participate in the second administration. This may introduce bias.

2   Objectively, exactly the same test may be administered on the second occasion. However, subjectively there may be substantial psychological differences in the second administration. In the same way, when a joke is heard for the second time it may evoke a groan rather than laughter. In addition, an applicant may have learned from the experience of completing the test on the first occasion. He or she may have remembered some answers, or may have looked up some answers. These changes add to error variance but they are not facets of the test itself – they result from the process of establishing a test's reliability.

3   Real changes in the 'subject' are included with the random error. When establishing the test–retest reliability of an inanimate objective such as a platinum rod, this presents negligible problems. However, humans may change. If the test–retest method is used with children and the interval is large, the reliability estimates may be influenced by maturation. Furthermore, initial testing may induce change. Subjects may be sensitized to certain kinds of information. The Hawthorn effect may influence their motivations and satisfaction. Some aspects of people change in a matter of hours. For example, a test might measure hunger perfectly. However, a test–retest study of its reliability where the test for some subjects was taken before lunch and the retest was taken after lunch could produce very accurate but different readings, which would lead to an apparently low test–retest reliability.

The time interval in a test–retest reliability study is crucial. If it is too short, memory and perceptual effects will be heightened. If it is too long, too many true changes such as maturation will be included. In general, an interval of one month is regarded as the optimum interval between the test and the retest.

10.3.2 CONSISTENCY MEASURES OF RELIABILITY

The other class of reliability correlations is concerned with consistency. There are four main types: parallel forms; split-half reliability; item-whole correlations and inter-rater reliability.

Parallel-form Measures of Reliability (Consistency)

Parallel-form reliability is used when there are two versions of a measure. Subjects are given the two versions consecutively and the two scores are correlated. Inter-rater reliability is a special type of parallel-form reliability. From a scientific point of view, parallel-form reliability is probably the best consistency strategy. The parallel versions are independent and the reliability calculation uses the full number of questions. It also reduces memory effects, since each version asks different questions. However, parallel-form reliability has four disadvantages:

- The testing session may be long and scores may be influenced by fatigue, thus underestimating reliability.
- Factors such as poor environment or bad administration tend to be the same for both versions. These influences, which should be regarded as error, may be counted as true variance; thus reliability may be overestimated.
- It requires the extra effort and cost of producing two versions. These extra costs are usually unacceptable and so parallel-form reliability is rarely used.
- It is hard to be absolutely sure that the two tests are, in fact, parallel.

Split-Half, Kuder–Richardson, Cronbach and Inter-rater Reliability

In order to avoid the expense of producing a parallel version of a test, it is possible to produce two scores by splitting a measure in half and calculating scores for each half. The two 'half scores' can then be correlated. For example, an arithmetic test can be divided into two halves and two subtotals obtained: one for the odd-numbered questions 1, 3, 5, . . . and the other for the even-numbered questions 2, 4, 6, . . . The two 'half scores' may then be correlated to produce an odd–even split-half reliability.

Split-half reliability avoids fatigue and memory effects, and also the chore of arranging a second testing session. However, there is a major problem. Reliability is related to test length – other things being equal, longer tests are more reliable than shorter tests. Split-half reliability halves the length of the test and hence will underestimate true reliability. Fortunately, the relationship is well known and a simple formula can be used to estimate the true reliability. The Spearman–Brown formula is as follows:

$$r_{tt} = \frac{2r_{hh}}{1 + r_{hh}}$$

where r_{tt} is the reliability of the full test and r_{hh} is the correlation between the two halves.

Enthusiasts might wish to note that, in fact, it is not essential to split a test into halves. The test can be split into any number of equal fractions and a more general version of the Spearman–Brown formula can be used:

$$r_{tt} = \frac{n r_{nn}}{1 + (n - 1)r_{nn}}$$

where r_{tt} is the reliability of the full test, r_{nn} is the reliability of part of the test, and n is the fraction of the test correlated.

Odd–even split-half reliability is the most frequent type of split-half reliability, but the division of a test in this way is entirely arbitrary. It might be possible to divide a test into the first 50% of questions and the second 50% of questions, or into questions that start with letters in the first half of the alphabet and questions that start with letters from the second half of the alphabet. Each of these divisions is equally valid. To be conclusive, it would be necessary to divide the test in every conceivable way and then take some kind of average of the correlations. While this tactic would be scientifically pure, it would be very impractical indeed.

Table 10.2 A demonstration of item-whole correlation

Person	Total	q_1	q_2	q_3	q_4	...
A	20	1	1	1	1	
B	16	1	1	0	1	
C	10	0	1	0	1	
D	5	0	0	1	0	
E	2	0	0	0	0	
...						
Correlation with total		.6	.5	.5	.1	
Median correlation = .5						

In effect, the **Kuder–Richardson Formula 20** works out the average reliability of a test that is split in half in every conceivable way (Cronbach, 1951; Norvick and Lewis, 1967). The computation of the Kuder–Richardson Formula 20 (Richardson and Kuder, 1939) is very tedious and error prone, and is only feasible with the use of a computer package such as SPSS. The Kuder–Richardson Formula 20 can only be used when the questions in a test are marked on a pass/fail basis. This is straightforward in the case of ability tests, but it can produce problems with personality tests, which are often marked on a five- or seven-point Likert scale.

The solution to this problem was suggested by Cronbach (1951), when he introduced his coefficient alpha, which can be used with continuous data. **Cronbach's alpha** is now probably the most widely used index of internal consistency.

Item-whole correlations are another type of internal consistency. Item-whole correlation starts with the calculation of each person's total score. Then, answers to each question are correlated, one by one with that total. If, for example, there are 20 questions in a test, there will be 20 item-whole correlations. These correlations can be inspected and the median correlation can be used as an index of reliability. The item-whole correlation has a number of disadvantages. *First*, the correlations are inflated, because there is an element of autocorrelation: items are included in the totals against which they are correlated. It is therefore necessary to subtract each item from the total before the correlation is calculated. As shown in table 10.2, this procedure is cumbersome even when computers are used. *Second*, the median item-whole correlation is based on just one correlation and might be unstable from sample to sample. These problems mean that the item-whole correlation is falling into disuse. However, it is important to know its basis, because it is still encountered in some older texts, manuals and research papers.

Inter-rater reliability is the final type of internal consistency, but it is often treated as a separate type of reliability. Inter-rater reliability is used most often with measures, such as behavioural observations or interviews, which may involve subjective judgements. Typically, applicants are interviewed by two people and each person rates each applicant independently. The two sets of ratings are then correlated. Sometimes, inter-rater reliability is called **Conspect Reliability**.

10.3.3 THE EVALUATION OF RELIABILITY CORRELATIONS

When all factors have been taken into account, a reliability coefficient must be evaluated. Table 10.3, which is based on Bartram (1995a), provides rules of thumb.

Table 10.3 Evaluation of reliability coefficients

	Verbal label				
	Excellent	Good	Reasonable	Adequate	Inadequate
Correlation	.85+	.8	.7	.6	Under .6
Percentage of systematic variance	85	80	70	60	Under 60
Percentage of random variance	15	20	30	40	Over 40
Signal-to-noise ratio	5.7	4.0	2.3	1.5	Under 1.5

Enthusiasts may wish to note that reliability may be expressed in several further ways. It may be expressed as the percentage of systematic variance or its complement – the percentage of random variance. The percentage of systematic variance is produced simply by multiplying the correlation coefficient by 100. At first sight this may seem strange, since in most other situations it is necessary to square the correlation before multiplying by 100. The situation concerning reliability is the exception to the general rule. Anastasi (1988, 126) notes that, 'any reliability coefficient may be interpreted directly in terms of the percentage of score variance attributable to different sources. Thus, a reliability coefficient of .85 signifies that 85% of the variance in test scores depends on the true variance in the trait measured, and 15% depends on error variance . . . The statistically sophisticated reader may recall that it is the *square* of a correlation coefficients that represents proportion of common variance. Actually, the proportion of true variance in test scores is the square of the correlation between scores on a single form of the test and true scores which are free from chance errors . . . When the index of reliability is itself squared, the results is the reliability coefficient (r_{tt}) which can therefore be interpreted directly as the percentage of true variance.'

Finally, enthusiasts may also wish to note that reliability can be expressed in terms familiar to those used by sound engineers and information-processing engineers. Dividing the percentage of systematic variance (the signal) by the percentage of random error (the noise) produces a signal-to-noise ratio, which is an index of the accuracy of the measure.

10.3.4 PROBLEMS WITH CORRELATION INDICES: SHAPE, NOT REPEATABILITY

Correlations used to be the accepted indices of reliability and were taught in most basic courses or textbooks. But they have a number of disadvantages, which have led to a fall from favour.

The *first*, obvious, disadvantage is that correlations tell you nothing about an individual score and how it should be interpreted. For example, if a scale of personality test measuring control has a reliability correlation of .75, what does this tell you about vocational guidance client who has a sten score of 7? If, on the other hand, you know that the same scale has an se_m of 1, you know that the odds are approximately 2:1 that the person's real score lies between a sten of 6 and 8.

A *second*, more subtle, disadvantage is that correlations do not give any information on the **repeatability of scores**. The problem arises because correlations are sensitive to shape rather than to the actual scores themselves. Take a simplified hypothetical example with two tests, A and B, and a sample of six people who complete the tests twice with an interval of a month. Any differences between time 1 and time 2 are due solely to error. The scores might be as shown in the following table:

Subject	A	B	C	D	E	F
Test A, time 1	5	6	9	3	2	10
Test A, time 2	7	6	8	5	0	9
Difference	2	0	1	2	2	1
	Average difference 1.3		Correlation .65			
Test B, time 1	5	6	9	3	2	10
Test B, time 2	15	17	19	14	11	2
Difference	10	11	10	11	9	8
	Average difference 9.9		Correlation .97			

The scores for the two administrations differ less for test A, and test A is more reliable than test B: differences between scores for test A are never more than 2, and sometimes the scores are identical. In test B, the two scores are never the same and usually differ by about ten marks. Yet the reliability *correlation* for test A is .65, while the reliability *correlation* for test B is .97.

An alternative index based on actual differences might therefore be useful. Absolute differences cannot be used because they depend, in part, on the width of the scale. A difference of one point on a five-point scale is probably important. However, if the scale has 100 points, a one-point difference is likely to be trivial. Hence it is better to use a standard that takes scale width into account. In general, a reliable scale will have more than 80% of the differences between two administrations within 16% (about one standard deviation) of the scale width. In practice, this would mean that if interviewees' performance is rated on a six-point scale by two interviewers, their ratings should agree to within one point for at least 80% of the interviewees.

10.4 SOURCES OF ERROR AND SYSTEMATIC VARIANCE

Irrespective of whether reliability is measured using the standard error of measurement or a correlation, it is important to be able to recognize the kinds of things that produce the random errors that reduce reliability. Error can be divided into two types: the random, non-systematic error, which reduces reliability; and systematic error, which persists across administrations and which may increase reliability but reduce validity.

10.4.1 RANDOM, NON-SYSTEMATIC, ERROR

Error variance is made up of factors that may differ each time a measure is taken. These influences produce different results when the same thing is re-measured. Sources of error variance have been identified by Jensen (1980) and others. They include the following:

- *Inadequate administration* often decreases reliability, because random differences in administration may make a test easier for some groups of candidates, whilst making it harder for other groups. Typical faults in test administration include:

> – *ad hoc* changes of instructions, so that some candidates get instructions that are more helpful
> – poor time-keeping, so that some candidates get more or less time
> – inaudible instructions to candidates at the back of the room
> – supplying some applicants with marked books that contain helpful (or unhelpful) comments by previous candidates
> – administrators who unwittingly irritate some candidates.

Standardization of test administration is an attempt to improve reliability by eliminating random error.

- *Variation in environment*, such as:
  – poor regulation of temperature
  – noise from an adjoining room or corridor
  – poor lighting
  – avoidable interruptions, such as mobile phone calls
  – unavoidable interruptions, such as fire alarms
  – defective equipment, such as pens or pencils.
- *Scoring mistakes*, such as:
  – crediting marks wrongly
  – wrong addition of scores on sub-tests
  – poor transposition of marks from the answer sheet to the mark or profile sheet.
- *The state of mind of candidates* – some unhelpful states of mind are:
  – preoccupation with other matters, because the candidate has received bad news immediately before the test
  – hostile mood, engendered by over-sensitivity to a remark by the administrator
  – weariness, caused by completing the test at the end of a working day or after a long journey
  – momentary lapses of concentration by the candidate
  – confusion by candidates who fail to synchronize answer spaces with questions or who write answers in a wrong column.
- *Other factors concerning the candidate* include:
  – A candidate forgetting to bring aids such as spectacles to the testing session.
  – Prior experience of the test. Some candidates may have gained illicit access to the test or they may have recently completed the test. Some candidates may even have practised on an identical or similar test.
  – Guessing. In multiple-choice tests it is common for people to guess answers when they do not know the correct response. Guessing has the greatest impact on a test's reliability when it has a true/false format.
  – Background. If candidates are from a wide range of backgrounds, some may attribute different meanings to the words in a question. These meanings may accumulate in a haphazard fashion and therefore influence the answers in a random way. Tests of knowledge and skill that are given later in the academic year tend to have higher reliabilities, because at the end of the academic year students have a longer shared environment that helps to standardize their past experience.

Four important points emerge from this list. *First*, all these sources of error are random events that have nothing to do with a person's characteristics – they are uncorrelated with the score on the test. By the laws of chance alone, some people will be unlucky and suffer from many of these factors, while other people will suffer from only a few. *Second*, the influence of some of these factors may be quite small. A momentary lapse of concentration, a scratchy pen, a shortened test time or an arithmetical slip in adding marks may affect only the answers to one or two questions. However, the effect is cumulative. The combined influence of many sources of error can have a considerable influence on the scores of some individuals. *Third*, many of these factors are controlled by the administrator. A large part of administrator training (see chapter 21) aims to equip administrators with skills to eliminate such sources of error. *Fourth*, random error cannot, by definition, be correlated with a person's test score, but the error in two tests *can* be related. For example, an obnoxious administrator may make all tests in a session harder and this could heighten the apparent correlation between measures taken in close proximity. Similarly, scores on similar selection measures will tend to correlate more highly than measures that are dissimilar.

10.4.2 SOURCES OF SYSTEMATIC ERROR VARIANCE (NON-RANDOM ERROR VARIANCE)

There are many sources of error variance that are not random and that will reappear if the same measure is used again. The main sources of systematic variance are:

- *specialized, technical knowledge or experience*, which is more familiar and easier for some, especially internal, candidates
- *response styles*, such as acquiescence, choosing middle alternatives or choosing socially desirable answers
- *factors in test design*, such as the use of small print that cannot be read easily by all candidates or an answering system that disadvantages certain people, such as those who are left-handed.

Technically, systematic sources of error contaminate a measure and reduce validity. The topic of validity is discussed in the next chapter.

◤ 10.5 CONFIDENCE LIMITS AND CONFIDENCE INTERVALS

The use of standard error as an index of reliability allows confidence limits and confidence intervals to be calculated. Both confidence limits and confidence intervals are important in interpreting scores and using scores to make decisions.

10.5.1 CONFIDENCE LIMITS

A limit is a line – usually dividing people into those who are accepted and those who are rejected. For example, employers may set a limit of 50 on a test. Applicants who score more than 50 proceed to the next stage of selection, while those with a score of less than 50 are rejected. Limits are sometimes called **cutting scores**. Often, the limit is chosen in a very subjective manner. A better way is to calculate the limit. It should be noted that cutting scores have some similarity to one-tailed tests, where all the error is at one end of the distribution.

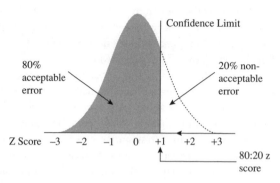

Figure 10.4 A normal curve of measurement error.

The Appropriate Alpha Level

The crux of the calculations to establish a limit is the risk of error that an organization is prepared to accept – the alpha level. This is a commercial and psychometric decision. As noted earlier, in research the alpha level is typically set at .05 – a 5% chance of accepting a fluke result. In commerce, different considerations apply. Few organizations can wait to be 95% sure of success: they will often be driven out of business by an organization that is prepared to act more quickly. Furthermore, the rights of candidates who are wrongly rejected may be as important as the rights of an organization to avoid bad candidates. Hence, in selection and assessment different levels of alpha (.5, .33, .25 or .2) are often used. Figure 10.4 depicts a normal curve of measurement error, where it has been decided that it would be appropriate to accept an error for 20% of the time.

Calculating a Limit

Calculation of a limit usually proceeds in four stages:

1 The appropriate level of alpha is decided.
2 The Z score that divides the normal curve for the chosen alpha is obtained from statistical tables.
3 The standard error of measurement is obtained. Ideally, the standard error of measurement should be determined – usually by reference to the test manual. If the test manual only reports the reliability in terms of a correlation coefficient, the correlation coefficient is transformed into the standard error using the formula given at the end of section 10.2.2.
4 The Z score and the standard error are multiplied.
5 The result is added to (or subtracted from) the score in question.

A specific example might make the procedures for establishing a limit clear. For example, an international firm of consultants calculates that the average IQ of the top managers with whom its consultants deal is 130, and it wishes to ensure that its recruits have at least equal cognitive ability. It *first* takes the decision that it can only accept a one in three chance that a recruit might have an IQ less than 130 and it therefore sets alpha at .33. *Second*, it consults statistical tables and obtains the Z score that divides the normal curve 67:33, which is +.43. *Third*, the firm of consultants knows that the test it uses (the WAIS) is not perfect: random factors will increase or decrease an applicant's observed score. These random factors are likely to be normally distributed and have a standard deviation that is equal to the standard error of measurement. The organization refers to the test manual for the WAIS, where it discovers that the standard error of measurement is 2.6. *Fourth*, it multiplies the Z score by the standard error to obtain a value of 1.1. *Fifth*, it adds the value to its target IQ of 130 and rounds up to the next whole number, to obtain a cutting score of 132. The firm therefore accepts recruits whose score is 132 or more, secure in the knowledge that the chances of it accepting someone whose true IQ is under 130 are less than 33%. In other words, the consultants add 2 to their target score to counteract the chances of applicants being lucky.

A second hypothetical example illustrates a different situation, in which only a reliability correlation is available and it is decided to give the benefit of the doubt to candidates. A local authority has established that an IQ of 124 is needed by people who hold a senior office. The local authority is not in a competitive position, in which it can be driven out of business. Furthermore, it accepts a moral obligation not to exclude people unreasonably. *First*, it decides that it can accept a one in four risk that an officer could have an IQ that is less than 124 and it therefore sets an alpha level of −.25. *Second*, the Z score that divides the normal curve 25:75 is obtained from tables and equals −.68. *Third*, it refers to the test manual. The manual does not give a standard error, but it does give a reliability correlation of .9. The standard deviation of a quotient scale is, by definition, 15. The formula at the end of section 10.2.2 is used to calculate the standard error as follows:

$$se_m = 15 \times \sqrt{1 - .9} = 15 \times .316 = 4.74$$

Fourth, the standard error is multiplied by the Z score to produce a value of −3.22. *Fifth*, the value of −3.22 is subtracted from the target IQ of 124 to produce a minimum IQ of on 120.78, which is then rounded to 121. The local authority is then in a position to accept candidates whose IQ exceeds or equals 121, secure in the knowledge that its chances of rejecting a candidate who is truly able to do the job are less than 25%. Calculating confidence limits can be a chore. Tables on the website associated with this book remove the arithmetical drudgery by giving confidence limits for various scoring systems on the basis of a measure's reliability.

10.5.2 CONFIDENCE INTERVALS

An interval is a gap between two lines. Confidence intervals differ from limits in a very important way. Limits, which are important in *selection*, produce a single line that demarks a single acceptable range and a single unacceptable range of scores.

Confidence limits, on the other hand, are important in vocational guidance and represent **two-tailed tests**. The normal curve is divided into three areas: error within an acceptable range, high unacceptable error and low unacceptable error. The two areas outside the acceptable range represent scores that are too different to be attributed to chance factors. Figure 10.5 illustrates the division of the normal curve into three areas.

A key point to remember is that when calculating *confidence intervals*, **the unacceptable error (the alpha level) needs to be divided by two before the appropriate Z score is obtained from tables**. For example, Chris obtains a sten score of 7 on a test of tough-mindedness that

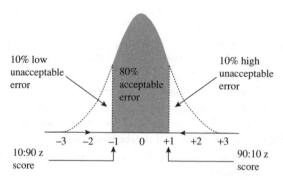

Figure 10.5 Division of normal curves in calculating confidence intervals.

has a standard error of .8. Chris knows that her true score on tough-mindedness is unlikely to be exactly 7 because of random factors on the day of the test. Therefore, Chris wants to know the range of scores that is likely (that is, 50% probability) to contain her true scores. An important fact is that, in Chris' decision, *error has to go in two directions* – the error above the acceptable level and the error below the acceptable level. Hence the alpha has to be divided by two before the normal curve tables are consulted. She is prepared to accept 50% error. In two-tailed confidence limits, half (25%) goes to the top end and half (25%) goes to the bottom. So, Chris looks up the Z score that divides the normal curve 75:25 and this yields Z = .68. The standard error of the tough-mindedness scale is .8, so it is as likely as not that Chris's true score is 7 (her observed score) plus or minus .54 (.8 × .65). In other words, it is as likely as not that Chris' true score on tough-mindedness is between 6.46 and 7.54.

Suddenly, Chris decides to be 'picky' and wants to be fairly certain of the range of her true score. She agrees that 'fairly certain' means that she is likely to be 68% correct and that the chance of being wrong is 32% (that is, alpha equals .32). Because this is a two-tailed test, the error is divided into two and so she looks up the Z score that divides the normal curve 84:16. The Z score at this point is 1. So, the margin of error when Chris wants to be 68% certain is 7 (her observed score) plus or minus .8 (.8 [standard error] × 1 [Z score]). Chris can be fairly certain that the true score lies between 6.2 and 7.8.

The use of the 68% confidence interval is very common. It means that the likelihood of being right is roughly twice the likelihood of being wrong. Furthermore, it is a very convenient figure: the Z score equals 1 and hence the margin of error is exactly the same as the standard error. Often, in vocational guidance or in discussing results with lay people, it is necessary to give a general indication of the accuracy of scores. In many circumstances, it is best to say that 'the margin of error for this test is . . .' and then give the 68% confidence limit – that is, the standard error. Good personality scales usually have reliabilities in the range of .7 to .8, which produces a standard error of just under 1 on a sten or stannine scale. As a rule of thumb, it is possible to tell a client that 'the scores on this test have a margin of error about 1 sten'. Good tests of mental ability have reliabilities of .95, which produces a standard error of about 3 on a quotient scale. Thus it is possible to say to a client, 'your IQ is 112 plus or minus 3 points'. Calculating confidence intervals can be a chore. As mentioned above, tables on the website associated with this book remove the arithmetical drudgery by giving confidence intervals for various scoring systems on the basis of a measure's reliability.

10.6 STANDARD ERRORS OF *TWO* SCORES

Sometimes there are two scores and the standard error involving two measures is needed. There are two situations: two scores can be added together or one score can be subtracted from the other.

10.6.1 THE STANDARD ERROR OF A COMPOSITE (ADDED SCORES)

A person specification may call for, say, spatial ability and numerical ability, and two tests are administered. In order to make a decision the two scores, which must use the same scoring system, are added to obtain a composite. The question arises, 'What is the standard error of this composite score?'

Three pieces of information are needed to answer this question:

- the standard error of the first test (se_1)
- the standard error of the second test (se_2)
- the correlation between the two sets of errors (r_{12}).

The first two pieces of information should be available from the test manuals. The third will not usually be available and two options are possible. First, you can assume that the errors are correlated to the same degree as the tests and use the correlation between the tests. The second, less convincing, option is to assume that the two errors are not correlated at all. This information can be substituted in the following formula for the standard error of a *composite* of two scores:

$$se_{comp} = \sqrt{se_1^2 + se_2^2 + 2r_{12}se_1se_2}$$

Note that a term that involves the correlation between the two errors is added. If you are willing to make the rather improbable assumption that the errors on the two tests are unrelated, the formula becomes:

$$se_{comp} = \sqrt{se_1^2 + se_2^2}$$

For example, a German company hires engineering trainees on the basis of their performance on a spatial test and a numerical test. Both tests use T scores. The se_m of the spatial test is 2 and the se_m of the numerical test is 3. The correlation between the two scores is .4. The standard error of the combination of the two tests is:

$$se_{comp} = \sqrt{2^2 + 3^2 + (2 \times .4 \times 2 \times 3)}$$

$$\therefore se_{comp} = \sqrt{4 + 9 + 4.8} = \sqrt{17.8} = 4.2$$

The German engineering firm has found that successful trainees have a minimum composite score of 60 and it is willing to employ people who have a 3:1 probability of being successful (that is, an alpha of .25). The Z score that divides the normal curve 75:25 is .68. Trainees therefore need to be .68 se_ms above the desired score, which equals 2.9 (.68 × 4.2). The firm therefore sets its cutting point at 63 (60 + 2.9) and offers engineering traineeships to candidates who have a composite score of 63 or more.

10.6.2 THE STANDARD ERROR OF DIFFERENCE BETWEEN TWO SCORES (SUBTRACTED SCORES)

Sometimes, especially in placement and vocational guidance, there are two scores and we want to know if there is any real difference between them.

For example, a firm in Auckland recruits a young graduate, Karen, for one of three posts: accounts, which requires high numerical ability; general administration, which requires numerical and verbal ability; and information officer, which requires high verbal ability. Karen herself has no preference. In order to resolve the issue, Karen takes two tests, a numerical ability test with an se_m of .8 and a verbal ability test with an se_m of .9. The correlation between the two tests is .4. Both tests use the sten scale. The firm reasons that if she scores highest on the numerical test, she should go into accounting; if her test scores are equal, she should go into administration; and if her verbal score is highest, she should go into information work. Karen's numerical sten score is 7.6 and her verbal sten score is 8.6.

The question arises of whether the difference of 1 sten is a true difference or a result of random error. Karen and the company agree that it would be sensible to act on any result that has only a 4:1 probability of occurring by chance (that is, the alpha is .20). The Z score that divides the normal curve 10:80:10 is 1.3.

The formula for the standard error of a *difference* between two scores is:

$$se_{diff} = \sqrt{se_1^2 + se_2^2 - (2r_{12} \times se_1 \times se_2)}$$

Notice that the only difference from the previous formula is that the term concerning the correlation between the two errors is subtracted. Substituting the actual figures for the tests, the equation becomes:

$$se_{diff} = \sqrt{.8^2 + .9^2 - (2 \times .4 \times .8 \times .9)}$$

$$\therefore se_{diff} = \sqrt{.64 + .81 - .576} = \sqrt{.874} = .93$$

The actual difference in Karen's scores is 1 sten, which equals 1.09 se_ms (1/.92). This is less than the Z of 1.3 that divides the normal curve 10:80:10. Both the organization and Karen decide that there is not enough difference in the scores to follow a career that is either verbally or numerically intensive, and she accepts a post in administration.

 ## 10.7 THREE FURTHER ASPECTS OF RELIABILITY

Reliability has three other aspects: test length, relationship with validity and restriction of range.

10.7.1 TEST LENGTH AND RELIABILITY

All other things being equal, longer measures – or at least measures consisting of many constituent parts – will be more reliable than short measures. In general, very short tests, or measures based on only one or two observations, should be avoided. The relationship between test length and reliability is an important consideration in test design (see chapter 16).

10.7.2 RELIABILITY AND VALIDITY

Reliability sets a ceiling on validity. Under most circumstances, a test that is not reliable cannot be valid. The relationship between reliability and the maximum achievable validity is given by the formula:

$$r_{xc(max)} = \sqrt{r_{xx}}$$

In other words, the correlation between a score and a criterion measure cannot exceed the *square root* of the measure's reliability

10.7.3 RESTRICTION OF RANGE AND RELIABILITY

Like all correlations, reliability correlations tend to be underestimated when the sample does not cover the full range. In fact, it is rare for reliability coefficients to be obtained from full samples. It is more usual for reliabilities to be calculated from a restricted group of people, such as students or incumbents in certain occupations. Consequently, many reliability coefficients in test manuals are underestimates. A fuller consideration of restriction of range is given in section 8.5.1.

Appendix 10.1 Reliability correlations and equivalent standard errors on four scoring systems

r	Scale				
	Z score Scale sd = 1	Sten Scale sd = 2	Stannine Scale sd = 2	T score Scale sd = 10	Quotient Scale sd = 15
.02	.99	1.98	1.98	9.90	14.85
.04	.98	1.96	1.96	9.80	14.70
.06	.97	1.94	1.94	9.70	14.54
.08	.96	1.92	1.92	9.59	14.39
.10	.95	1.90	1.90	9.49	14.23
.12	.94	1.88	1.88	9.38	14.07
.14	.93	1.85	1.85	9.27	13.91
.16	.92	1.83	1.83	9.17	13.75
.18	.91	1.81	1.81	9.06	13.58
.20	.89	1.79	1.79	8.94	13.42
.22	.88	1.77	1.77	8.83	13.25
.24	.87	1.74	1.74	8.72	13.08
.26	.86	1.72	1.72	8.60	12.90
.28	.85	1.70	1.70	8.49	12.73
.30	.84	1.67	1.67	8.37	12.55
.32	.82	1.65	1.65	8.25	12.37
.34	.81	1.62	1.62	8.12	12.19
.36	.80	1.60	1.60	8.00	12.00

r	Scale				
	Z score Scale sd = 1	Sten Scale sd = 2	Stannine Scale sd = 2	T score Scale sd = 10	Quotient Scale sd = 15
.38	.79	1.57	1.57	7.87	11.81
.40	.77	1.55	1.55	7.75	11.62
.42	.76	1.52	1.52	7.62	11.42
.44	.75	1.50	1.50	7.48	11.22
.46	.73	1.47	1.47	7.35	11.02
.48	.72	1.44	1.44	7.21	10.82
.50	.71	1.41	1.41	7.07	10.61
.52	.69	1.39	1.39	6.93	10.39
.54	.68	1.36	1.36	6.78	10.17
.56	.66	1.33	1.33	6.63	9.95
.58	.65	1.30	1.30	6.48	9.72
.60	.63	1.26	1.26	6.32	9.49
.62	.62	1.23	1.23	6.16	9.25
.64	.60	1.20	1.20	6.00	9.00
.66	.58	1.17	1.17	5.83	8.75
.68	.57	1.13	1.13	5.66	8.49
.70	.55	1.10	1.10	5.48	8.22
.72	.53	1.06	1.06	5.29	7.94
.74	.51	1.02	1.02	5.10	7.65
.76	.49	.98	.98	4.90	7.35
.78	.47	.94	.94	4.69	7.04
.80	.45	.89	.89	4.47	6.71
.82	.42	.85	.85	4.24	6.36
.84	.40	.80	.80	4.00	6.00
.86	.37	.75	.75	3.74	5.61
.88	.35	.69	.69	3.46	5.20
.90	.32	.63	.63	3.16	4.74
.92	.28	.57	.57	2.83	4.24
.94	.24	.49	.49	2.45	3.67
.96	.20	.40	.40	2.00	3.00
.98	.14	.28	.28	1.41	2.12

CHAPTER 11

VALIDITY

Validity is *the* important concept in psychometrics. It is paramount. Aspects such as reliability and sensitivity are important, *but* the *raison d'être* of testing is to lead us to better decisions. Validity tells us how good the decisions based on any method of selection are – it tells us whether a test measures what it is supposed to measure. Validity is centrally related to many other psychometric concepts: if a measure is valid, it will probably be reliable, and a measure that is insensitive will have difficulty achieving a high validity. A measure that is valid is also likely to be fair.

Even if a measure has every other psychometric property except validity, it will be useless. For example, a ratings-hungry TV game show might try to gauge a person's intelligence by measuring the circumference of a contestant's head. The circumference is, in many ways, excellent. It is sensitive because heads can differ by as much as 75 mm. It is reliable since, with a little care, the same measurement will be obtained year after year. Head circumference is also a practical and cheap measure that even the most inept compère could tackle during a live broadcast. Furthermore, in most respects, the circumference of the head would be a reasonably fair measure in adults: there are negligible differences according to age, disability or sexual orientation, and there are only slight ethnic or gender differences. However, head circumference will be useless because it is not valid: it has hardly any relationship to what the compère is trying to measure – intelligence.

The dangers of using invalid measures are considerable. There are negative consequences for individuals, employers, test users and the community:

- *For individuals*, invalid selection gives a greater risk of being hired for jobs in which they cannot cope. In the worst case, this could mean that they could be a danger and inflict harm on other people. In any event, people hired for jobs in which they cannot cope are likely to experience anguish. Meanwhile, they miss opportunities in other jobs where they would succeed and be happy. The consequence of using invalid selection measures on other candidates is often ignored: invalid measures mean that the best candidate is more likely to be denied his or her due rewards. When invalid measures are used in vocational guidance, candidates may internalize wrong results, start to act them out and otherwise distort their personalities.
- *For organizations*, invalid selection measures mean they are less likely to hire effective workers. In the long run, the organization will cease to be competitive and jobs may be lost.

- *For psychologists and test users*, invalid measures mean that their work will fall into disrepute and a shadow may be cast over other methods that are scientific and valid.
- *For the community and society* as a whole, the use of invalid measures means that the skills and the abilities of the workforce are deployed less effectively and society is less efficient. This will mean that society will be denied social goods – such as hospitals, universities and recreational facilities – that it could otherwise afford.

It is not surprising that such a paramount concept is a very large subject. This chapter attempts to make the huge topic of validity more manageable by dividing it into seven sections:

1 Definitions of validity
2 The trinitarian view of validity – predictive, concurrent and construct
3 Artefacts that mask true validity – including deception
4 Meta-analysis and validity generalization
5 Practical ways of maximizing validity – including lie scales
6 Evaluating validity coefficients
7 Validity imposters – acceptability (face validity) and content validity

 ## 11.1 DEFINITIONS OF VALIDITY

Validity can be defined at on at least three levels: the lay person's level, the conceptual level and the statistician's level.

11.1.1 THE LAY DEFINITION

The easiest definition of validity, which was used before the 1980s, is *the extent to which a score measures 'what it purports to measure'* (Anastasi, 1988). This definition, which is intelligible to a lay person, is enshrined in most undergraduate texts and serves its purpose well. However, this lay person's definition tends to fall down because it is imprecise. Just how do we define 'what a test purports to measure'? What index should be used as a measure of 'extent'? A more precise definition is needed.

11.1.2 THE CONCEPTUAL DEFINITION

A modern definition has been developed by Landy (1980) and others, who assert that validity is *the correctness of the inferences that are made on the basis of test scores*. Up to that date, the topic of validity had been dominated by the trinitarian view that there were three types of validity: predictive, concurrent and construct. According to the trinitarian approach, a test developer needed to carry out a study to obtain good predictive validity, a study to obtain good concurrent validity and a study to obtain good concurrent validity. Landy likens the process to stamp collecting, where it is important to collect stamps for appropriate empty boxes in an album. Landy suggests that all types of validity studies have a common scientific purpose – to gather evidence about the correctness of the inferences that were made on the basis of the test scores.

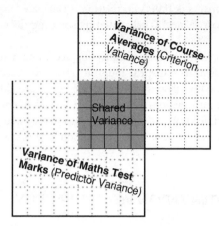

Figure 11.1 Validity is the variance shared between a predictor and a criterion.

It is not necessary to have studies of each type of validity. Instead, it is enough to obtain sufficient evidence, and the category of validation is not important.

Landy's definition of validity as the 'correctness of the inferences' has a huge advantage. It shifts attention from the test to the *uses* that are made of the test score. The same test might have many uses. It might be used to predict examination performance (that is, infer examination grades), or it might be used to select a spouse (that is, infer matrimonial harmony). The same test might be accurate in some inferences, such as future examination grades, but might be useless with other inferences, such as matrimonial harmony. This example highlights a very important point. *TESTS do not have validities. It is the INFERENCES made on the basis of the test scores that have validities.* A test may therefore have as many validities as the inferences that someone may wish to make on the basis of the test score.

11.1.3 THE STATISTICAL DEFINITION

An inference is made whenever a score on a predictor is used to estimate a score on a criterion. For example, a call centre may use a test (predictor) to estimate the number of calls that an applicant will be able to handle per shift (criterion). We can check the accuracy of our inferences by comparing predictions with the number of calls actually handled per shift. The more accurate the predictions (inferences), the higher will be the correlation between the score and the criterion – in other words, the variance in the predictor scores will mirror the variance in the criterion scores. This leads directly to the statistical definition, as *the proportion of the variance of a measure that overlaps with the variance of a criterion.*

Figure 11.1 demonstrates a hypothetical situation in which a large firm of accountants sends middle-level recruits on an intensive course in accountancy techniques. The course is very expensive and consequently the firm does not want to hire applicants who might fail. To screen out recruits who cannot cope, potential delegates are given a test of mathematics. The score on the maths test is used to predict (that is, infer) the mark that they will achieve on the course. To check the validity of the maths test, the firm collects the test scores and the course marks for 172 recruits. In this hypothetical example, the variance of the test scores is 100 and the variance of the course marks is 100. A correlation is calculated and a value of .5 is obtained. The shared variance (the covariance) is calculated by squaring the correlation and multiplying by 100.

All types of validity therefore consist of collecting scores on a predictor, collecting scores on a criterion and then using a statistical index to measure the overlap of their variances. The different types of validity arise simply because there are different ways of collecting the predictor and criterion information. Three main strategies of data collection are commonly used. They are the predictive strategy, the concurrent strategy and the construct. Exhaustive analyses of the theory of validity are given by Guion and Cranny (1982) and by Barrett et al. (1981).

11.2 THE TRINITARIAN VIEW OF VALIDITY

The trinitarian view held sway from the APA's pronouncement in 1954 until Landy's attack in 1980. Even today, the trinitarian view is reproduced in many textbooks. As its name implies, the trinitarian view divides the ways of obtaining data into three: predictive validity, concurrent validity and construct validity. In some other systems, predictive validity and concurrent validity are subgroups of a larger category called **criterion-related validity**.

11.2.1 PREDICTIVE VALIDITY

Predictive validity is the gold standard of validation in selection. Scientifically, it is by far the best method in selection, because it parallels the selection process itself. In an ideal predictive study, a sample of 172 applicants would be given a test that produces a numerical score. All 172 applicants would then be hired without reference to their score: indeed, the scores would be locked away so that they could not influence any decisions. After the applicants have completed training and have settled down into the job, their performance would be assessed against a perfect criterion that produces another numerical score. The two scores are then correlated. The essence of predictive validity is that the scores on the predictor are obtained first – there is then an interval before the criterion scores are obtained.

Unfortunately, predictive validity is rarely used. It suffers from two major practical disadvantages. *First*, it requires employers to *engage all applicants*, irrespective of their scores on the predictor. This would mean that the employers would need to bear the employment costs of some applicants who look patently unsuitable. Only a few very large organizations, such as the armed forces or other governmental organizations, are able to do this. Usually, candidates who appear unsuitable are eliminated from the study and the range of scores of those who remain is reduced. *Restriction of range always makes a correlation coefficient seem smaller.* Consequently, most predictive validity studies underestimate true validity. Fortunately, it is possible to correct for restriction of range using a statistical formula (see section 11.3.2).

The *second* disadvantage of predictive designs is the *time lag* between the collection of data for the predictor and data for the criterion. In some cases, the time lag is unacceptable. For example, a police force might consider a new interviewing method. It would take the force a year to amass data on 172 applicants. Two years would need to elapse while the last of these applicants undergoes training. It would also need to wait for a further period of about six months until the last applicant has settled into his or her job and could be appraised fairly. The total time lag from the collection of the first applicant's interview score to the collection of the last applicant's performance score would be $3\frac{1}{2}$ years. In most situations, such a time lag would be intolerable.

11.2.2 CONCURRENT VALIDITY

Because predictive validity is usually so difficult, a second type of validity, concurrent validity, is used much more frequently. Concurrent validity is similar to predictive validity because it too involves comparison with independent criteria. Hence both predictive validity and concurrent validity are types of **criterion-related validity**. The essence of concurrent validity is that both the predictor scores and the criterion scores are collected at about the same time.

In a typical concurrent study, existing employees are asked to complete a selection exercise. At almost the same time, criterion data are collected. Usually, the criterion is the supervisor's evaluations on an appraisal system, but sometimes a special questionnaire is sent out. In some situations, especially in sales occupations, current sales figures are used as a criterion. The score on the predictor is correlated with the score on the criterion. Although the predictor data and the criterion data are collected at the same time, they are kept separate so that they do not contaminate each other.

Many people feel that concurrent validity is the poor relation of predictive validity, because the predictor is not actually used to select people. The contrived set-up may introduce at least three artefacts. *First*, the *motivation of test-takers*, existing employees, in a concurrent study is unlikely to be the same as the motivation of actual applicants. Employees in a concurrent study might not take the test seriously because they know that it will not affect their jobs. On the other hand, existing employees will probably be less motivated to lie or give socially desirable responses. *Second*, concurrent validity studies always involve **restriction of range**. Current employees exclude the least suitable candidates: some will have been screened out at the selection; others will have quit because the job was too difficult. Concurrent validity also suffers restriction of range at the upper end: the more able employees will have been promoted or will have left for better jobs. Restriction of range is likely to lower the apparent validity. *Third*, the subjects in a concurrent study have *experience on the job* and this may alter the meaning of the questions.

In some circumstances, concurrent validity may be superior to predictive validity. When the inferences involve identifying and classifying individuals into groups rather than future performance in a specific job, a concurrent design may be preferable to a predictive design (Anastasi, 1988). These situations usually arise in clinical settings when a score is used, for example, to decide whether or not an individual is a schizophrenic. In occupational settings, concurrent validation may be more appropriate in vocational guidance or placement decisions.

11.2.3 CONSTRUCT VALIDITY

Practitioners are mainly concerned with predictive or concurrent validity. Researchers are more concerned with a third type of validity – construct validity (Cronbach and Meehl, 1955). Construct validity is, academics loftily claim, concerned with more than 'blind' prediction (that is, actuarial prediction) and focuses upon understanding the psychological 'meaning' of measurements.

A construct is an idea of an attribute or characteristic inferred from research (Guion, 1965). Most tests are designed to measure something intangible – a hypothetical construct. Statistically, construct validity is the degree to which the variance of a measure overlaps with the variance of an underlying construct. Construct validation is a long-term activity that does not depend on a single correlation. It is established by inspecting many correlations and determining whether the pattern is that which would be expected from the underlying construct. Construct validity is not defined by an isolated event, but by a 'nomological network' of associations and situations (Cronbach and Meehl, 1955). Data for construct validity can be obtained in many ways, such as experimental studies together with predictive and concurrent validation.

The simplest way of establishing construct validity is to correlate test scores with data from other established measures of the construct. For example, a new test of intelligence might be contruct validated by correlating the scores that it produces with established measures, such as scores from the Weschler Adult Intelligence Scale, Raven's Progressive Matrices and other well-established tests. Previous research has shown that these measures are highly saturated with the general factor, 'g', of intelligence. If the new measure were to correlate highly, say .6 or more, with each of these measures, it could justifiably be claimed that the new test also measured 'g'.

Construct validity may be determined in four other ways: convergent-discriminant, factorial, nominated group and synthetic validity. Incremental validity is a method that is closely related to construct validity.

Convergent-discriminant Validity

Convergent-discriminant validity (Campbell and Fiske, 1959) is founded on the axioms that a measure *should* correlate with measures that gauge the same construct, and *should not* correlate with measures that gauge different constructs – if the measure correlates with everything, it is likely that it is gauging some artefact such as response style, which is present in all measures. Construct validation should therefore include several measures of the construct *and* several measures of constructs from neighbouring domains. For example, a construct validation of a new test of verbal fluency would include, say, three other measures of verbal fluency *and* measures of other abilities, such as numerical and spatial ability. If the new test is a valid measure of the construct 'verbal fluency', it should have correlations higher than, say, .4 with the first three additional tests and correlations of about .2 or lower with the other tests.

Factorial Validity

Factorial validity is a type of convergent-discriminant validity. Instead of correlating a new test with established tests, a battery of tests, including the new test, is administered to a large sample. The scores are factor analysed. The nature of the factors is inferred from the factor loadings of the established tests. The loadings of the new test are then examined to see if they match the pattern that would be expected.

For example, in a validation study of a new test of numerical reasoning, a battery of three numerical reasoning tests, three verbal reasoning tests, three spatial reasoning tests and two projective tests might be assembled. The battery and the new test are administered to a large sample. Factor analysis might produce the following loadings:

Test	Factor I	Factor II	Factor III	Factor IV
NR1	.3	.5	.1	.1
NR2	.2	.6	.1	.1
NR3	.4	.4	.1	.1
VR1	.3	.1	.3	.1
VR2	.3	.1	.5	.1
VR3	.4	.1	.3	.1
SR1	.3	.1	.1	.5
SR2	.2	.1	.1	.4
SR3	.3	.1	.1	.5
P1	.0	.1	.0	.1
P2	.1	.0	.1	.0
New test	.3	.5	.1	.1

All reasoning tests, but no projective test, load on the first factor, which is clearly a general reasoning factor. Only numerical tests load on the second factor, which is clearly a numerical reasoning factor. Similarly, the third factor is verbal reasoning and the fourth is spatial reasoning. It is expected that the new test should have a moderate loading on Factor I, a high loading on Factor II, and low loadings on the remaining factors. When the loadings for the new test are inspected, they are exactly as hypothesized and factorial validity is good.

Nominated Group Validity

Nominated group validity is used when a construct predicts that groups should have different scores. For example, the concept of extroversion would predict that people who are frequent party-goers are more extroverted than people who avoid parties. It might then be possible to obtain a sample of inveterate party-goers and a separate sample of people who are averse to parties. The two groups could then be given a new test of extroversion and their scores contrasted. A significant difference between the groups would suggest that the new test has construct validity. It should be noted that complete separation of groups will be rare, because it is rarely possible to obtain 'pure' groups.

Synthetic Validity

A fourth approach to construct validation is synthetic validity (Lawshe, 1952), which is an elaboration of the nominated groups approach. Synthetic validity is sometimes called **job component validity**. Synthetic validity is particularly useful in small organizations, where there are small numbers in any particular occupation. The first stage of synthetic validity is to analyse the jobs within the organization and rank them in terms of the degree to which they require the trait gauged by the measure. For example, if a test is believed to measure verbal intelligence, the jobs within the company might be ranked as follows: (1) company secretary, (2) managing director, (3) office administrators, (4) production director, (5) production supervisors, (6) production operatives, (7) security staff and (8) cleaning staff. The test is then administered to everyone in the organization and the occupations ranked on the basis of their average scores.

Finally, the rank of the scores for each occupation is correlated with the expected rank. If the correlation is high, the measure has construct validity.

Incremental Validity

A final type of construct validity is incremental validity. Incremental validity helps us to understand what an extra selection measure adds to an existing battery of measures. Incremental validity is important because it helps us to avoid measuring the same trait many times. For example, a company may have an existing system in which applicants complete tests of general cognitive ability, verbal ability and personality. The human resource manager attends a seminar at which structured interviews are discussed. There is good evidence that the structured interviews have a high validity of, say, .5, and the organization wishes to know whether the structured interviews would improve its existing system. The validity of the existing system is .57. The validity of the existing system plus the structured interviews is found to be .59. The difference between the validity of the new system and the validity of the old system is the incremental validity. In this particular example, it is only .02. A possible explanation is that structured interviews are simply recapturing the variance that is already covered by the test of verbal ability. Clearly, in this particular case, it would not be worth the organization extending its present practices to include structured interviewing. Analyses of this kind should be conducted as a matter of routine whenever additions to an existing system are considered. Otherwise, a selection system might expand to the point at which length jeopardizes rapport and the validity of the system decreases rather than increases.

Some people criticize construct validity as an imprecise idea that leads to woolly theorizing, using a network of naïve rationalizations. They claim that construct validation opens the way for subjective, unverified assertions about test validity (Bechtoldt 1959; Anastasi, 1988). Others criticize construct validity because inferences might become too far removed from actual behaviour. To be useful, the chain of inference must end in some kind of observed behaviour. In the case of construct validity, the chain is simply longer than in, say, predictive validity. But it must ultimately end in some kind of observable event. In this view, construct validity is not a new category of validation – it is merely indirect predictive or concurrent validity.

Construct Validity and Literal Interpretation of Scale Names

Sometimes, users uncritically accept the names given to a scale test and interpret theses names literally. Instead, users should establish exactly which constructs a test measures. Tests may not actually measure what their names say that they measure. Sometimes, a name is inaccurate because the score is contaminated by an unsuspected factor. For example, a short test of arithmetic requiring 20 answers may measure input–output speed rather than numerical ability. Sometimes, a test is measuring a combination of more fundamental traits, rather than the trait implied by its name. For example, a test of 'emotional intelligence' may be measuring an amalgam of extroversion, stability and shrewdness.

Unhelpful scale names may arise due to commercial and marketing pressures. Most personality tests measure the same five traits. However, the publishers of early tests own the copyright on some of the trait names, and more recent tests have been forced to adopt slightly different names that carry rather different connotations. Furthermore, test publishers are, quite rightly, concerned with commercial success and want users to believe that their tests are different to and better than other tests. The strategies adopted are similar to those used in pharmaceuticals to differentiate expensive branded drugs from cheaper, but equally effective, generic drugs: different names, more advertising and glossy packaging. To an extent, differential branding of tests works in the consumer's favour, because alternative measures become available. Competition produces more choice and drives prices down. But beyond a certain point, the process becomes counterproductive. The myriad of names causes confusion and the consumer ultimately bears the costs of too many rival products. To counter these pressures, new tests should not be used until publishers have administered them along with tests of verbal and non-verbal intelligence, and with tests measuring the five main factors of personality. As a generalization, new tests should not be employed if they merely recapture variance that can already be measured by established tests.

The literal interpretation of scale names is a particular danger with personality tests. Scales may not necessarily measure what their name implies. Scale R4 on the OPQ correlates so highly (.74) with another scale (R6) that, in the light of their reliabilities (.82 and .80), they are virtually measuring the same thing, although they are given different names of 'outgoing' and 'socially confident', respectively. Some tests of innovation, for example, may simply be measuring aspects of extroversion. Similarly, many tests of 'creativity' may be measuring the same thing as general intelligence (they generally correlate as highly with intelligence tests as they correlate with other measures of creativity). Decanting the same psychometric wine into different bottles may make commercial sense, but it can also create confusion and duplication.

11.3 ARTEFACTS THAT MASK TRUE VALIDITY

The previous section of this chapter describes the ways of establishing the proportion of the variance that a predictor shares with a criterion. However, the true level of the shared variance can be masked by artefacts that can lead to false conclusions about validity. The artefacts can be grouped according to the way in which they affect the apparent validity:

	Artefact	Effect
1	Small sample sizes	Increase or decrease
2	Restriction of range	Decrease
3	Attenuation of criteria	Decrease
4	Lying and distortion	Decrease
5	Cross-contamination	Increase
6	Use of large matrices	Increase
7	Multiple regression	Increase

11.3.1 SMALL SAMPLES (MAY INCREASE OR DECREASE APPARENT VALIDITY)

Validity studies are usually conducted on small samples. The average validity study in the 1950s used samples of about 76. In the 1970s, the average sample size had risen to 119 (Monahan and Muchinsky, 1983). The reasons are not hard to identify. In many organizations, there are rarely more than 120 people in any given job. Nevertheless, the use of small samples has important consequences. It is a basic law of statistics that estimates based on small samples are inherently unstable – another sample of the same small size is quite likely to produce a noticeably different result (see chapter 7).

An unwary person might therefore look at a validity coefficient for one test administered in one factory, note that it differs from the validity coefficient of a test used in another factory and conclude that the two tests have different validities. In fact, any difference between them may be due solely to the random fluctuations associated with small samples. The impact of small sample sizes is even more important when comparing validities for ethnic groups. A validity estimate for a minority group is often based on a tiny sample of about 20, because there may only be 20 employees of the minority group in the organization. However, a validity correlation based upon a sample of 20 people is highly unstable. Sometimes, by the laws of chance alone, it will produce a correlation that is much lower than the true correlation. An unwary person might conclude that the correlations for the groups differ when, in fact, the low correlation has occurred by chance.

Schmidt et al. (1976) suggest that the sample sizes of most studies are too small to be sure of assessing validity accurately. They show that when the true validity is .5, the criterion validity is .6 and the range of scores has been restricted by 40%, a sample of 172 is needed. They go on to give tables of the sample sizes needed under various conditions.

11.3.2 RESTRICTION OF RANGE (REDUCES APPARENT VALIDITY)

Most validity studies suffer restriction of range, which always reduces the apparent validity. The following hypothetical example illustrates the effect. An organization uses a work sample to test 20 people (A–T) for the job of data entry clerk. Since this is a hypothetical illustration, there is an all-knowing deity who knows the true score of the 20 applicants (that is, a perfect criterion is available). In table 11.1, the applicant rank based on the work sample is given in row 2 and the perfect ranking, known to the deity, is given in row 3. The validity of this test is truly impressive. The rank-order correlation is .80.

However, the company only employs the ten applicants with the highest scores and can calculate validity with this smaller sample, whose range is restricted by 50%. As shown in table 11.2, the rank-order correlation for the restricted sample is only .32.

Table 11.1 A hypothetical example for complete range

	Applicant																			
	A	B	C	D	E	F	G	H	I	J	K	L	M	N	O	P	Q	R	S	T
Rank on work sample	1	2	3	4	5	6	7	8	9	10	11	12	13	14	15	16	17	18	19	20
Rank known to the deity	4	5	1	7	2	10	14	12	6	3	13	9	15	11	8	16	18	20	17	19
Difference in ranks	3	3	4	3	3	4	7	4	3	7	2	3	2	3	7	0	1	2	3	1
Difference squared	9	9	16	9	9	16	49	16	9	49	4	9	4	9	49	0	1	4	9	1

Sum of squared differences = 264; hence 6 × sum of squared differences = 1584

$$r_p = 1 - \frac{6\Sigma D^2}{N(N^2 - 1)} = 1 - \frac{1584}{7980} = 1 - .2 = .8$$

Table 11.2 A hypothetical example of restriction of range

	Applicant									
	A	B	C	D	E	F	G	H	I	J
Rank on work sample	1	2	3	4	5	6	7	8	9	10	
Rank known to the deity	4	5	1	7	2	10	14	12	6	3	Not employed
Difference in ranks	3	3	4	3	3	4	7	4	3	7	
Difference squared	9	9	16	9	9	16	49	16	9	49	

Sum of squared differences = 112; hence 6 × sum of squared differences = 672

$$r_p = 1 - \frac{6\Sigma D^2}{N(N^2 - 1)} = 1 - \frac{672}{990} = 1 - .68 = .32$$

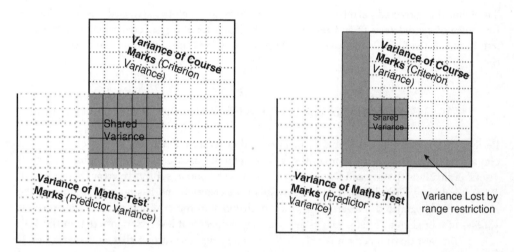

Figure 11.2 The effects of restriction of range.

The firm's conclusion from the restricted sample would be that the work-sample test had only moderate validity, whereas, in fact, the true validity is most impressive.

The reason why restriction of range reduces validity is shown by variance diagrams for another hypothetical situation. The first panel of figure 11.2 is repeated from earlier in this chapter and represents the situation with the full range. The criterion has 100 squares of variance, of which 25 are shared with the predictor. Since the variables share 25% of the variance, the correlation between them is .5 (the square root of .25).

In the second panel in figure 11.2, the restriction of range has been simulated by eliminating the bottom two rows and the corresponding two columns from the criteria. There are now only 64 units of variance in the criterion and only nine overlap with the test. The overlap is now only 14.6% (9/64), even though nothing has changed as far as the test is concerned. The variance of 14.6% indicates a correlation of only .38 (the square root of .146). Thus, the restriction of range in the criterion has reduced the apparent correlation from .5 to .38.

Fortunately, it is possible to correct for restriction of range. There are two possibilities. If the restriction of range occurs in the test (for example, people who do badly on the test are not hired) the appropriate formula is:

$$r_c = \frac{r(\Sigma/\sigma)}{\sqrt{1 - r^2 + r^2(\Sigma^2/\sigma^2)}}$$

If the restriction of range lies in the criteria (for example, the best workers are promoted and the poorest workers leave) the formula is:

$$r_c = \sqrt{1 - \left(\frac{\sigma^2}{\Sigma^2}\right)(1 - r^2)}$$

To obtain the corrected correlation (r_c) it is necessary to know the standard deviation for the full range of candidates (Σ) and the standard deviation for the restricted range of candidates (σ). In effect, the formula increases the correlation obtained in proportion to the restriction in the variance.

11.3.3 ATTENUATION OF CRITERIA (REDUCES APPARENT VALIDITY)

Perfect criteria are never available in practice. All criteria in actual use have their faults and contain random error. For example, the most commonly used criteria in selection are supervisors' evaluations (Landy and Rastegrary, 1989), which contain subjective error (Schwab et al. 1975; Landy and Farr, 1980). The error exists in the criterion and has nothing to do with the measure being validated. Nevertheless, the unreliability in the criterion reduces the apparent validity of a predictor. This is easy to illustrate at an anecdotal level. Suppose that in the 11th century the best thermometer was only 70% accurate. Suppose further that an inventor developed a thermometer that was 90% accurate. The 11th-century inventor would have been forced to calibrate the new thermometer against the best available at the time. Even though the new thermometer was better, when comparisons were made, the new thermometer would only be in 63% agreement with the old one (90% of 70%). The criterion's error would have been wrongly attributed to the new invention.

Attenuation of criteria can be demonstrated by returning to the example of a computer company that is hiring data entry personnel. It will be remembered that there were 20 applicants, whose true ability was 'known unto the deity', and that an impressive validity true of .8 was obtained. However, restriction of range resulted in an apparent validity of .32. Unfortunately, someone in the data preparation room lost the tablets upon which the deity had carved the true criterion scores. Instead, a diligent, careful supervisor was asked to rank the ten people who had been hired and 45% error (which is fairly typical of supervisory ratings) crept in. Table 11.3 calculates the validity against the fallible criteria for the restricted range of applicants.

The situation can be explained with the aid of another variance diagram. It will be remembered that the diagram originally contained 100 units of criterion variation. When the range was restricted, there were only 64 units. Attenuation (thinning) of criteria occurs because there is extra, random variance that thins the criterion. In figure 11.3, the additional random error is

Table 11.3 A table showing the hypothetical effects of restriction of range and attenuation of criteria

	Applicant										
	A	B	C	D	E	F	G	H	I	J	
Rank on work sample	1	2	3	4	5	6	7	8	9	10	
Rank known to the deity	4	5	1	7	2	10	14	12	6	3	
Rank given by supervisor	5	4	1	7	8	2	10	9	6	3	Not employed
Difference: true rank versus supervisor rank	4	2	2	3	3	4	3	1	3	7	
Difference squared	16	4	4	9	9	16	9	1	9	49	

Sum of squared differences = 126; hence 6 × sum of squared differences = 756

$$r_p = 1 - \frac{6\Sigma D^2}{N(N^2 - 1)} = 1 - \frac{756}{990} = 1 - .76 = .24$$

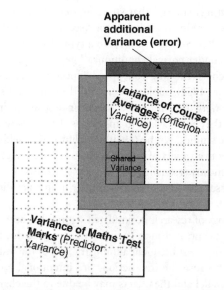

Apparent additional Variance (error)

Figure 11.3 A diagram to represent restriction of range *and* attenuation.

represented by an extra bar attached to the criterion variance. Criterion variance now appears to have increased to 72 units, while the shared variance remains the same, at nine units. Hence only 12.5% of the apparent criterion variance is shared with the test and a correlation of .35 results (the square root of .125). In this example, combined effects of attenuation of criterion and restriction of range have reduced a true validity of .8 to an observed validity of .35.

Fortunately, if the level of attenuation of the criteria can be estimated, a statistical correction can be made to estimate the true validity from an observed validity. The formula is:

$$r_\infty = \frac{r_{xx}}{\sqrt{r_{yy}}}$$

To calculate the unattenuated validity (r_∞), it is necessary to know the reliability of the criterion (r_{yy}) and the correlation between the criterion and the predictor (r_{xx}).

11.3.4 LYING AND DECEPTION (REDUCES APPARENT VALIDITY)

Lying and deception lowers the accuracy of inferences and hence it reduces validity. Dunnette et al. (1962) suggest that about one applicant in seven attempts significant deception. In the past, selectors were highly concerned about the possibilities of applicants faking their responses and hiding their 'real selves', and thereby frustrating effective selection. There appeared to be few problems with ability tests, but distortion of the results of personality tests was thought to be a big problem.

Research Findings

Research in simulated settings showed that students *could* fake personality tests according to the direction to which they were instructed to distort (see, for example, Borislow, 1958; Radcliffe, 1966; Jacobs and Barron, 1968; Strickler, 1967). In a typical study such as Salas (1968), a group of soldiers completed tests under normal conditions. They were then instructed to answer questions in a certain way, such as 'the way you would expect a badly adjusted soldier to answer'. In a similar study (Wesman, 1952), subjects were asked to answer a second administration of a personality test as if they were applying for a 'salesman's position' in a large organization and in a third administration they were asked to answer as if they were applying for a 'librarian's position'. In reviewing the studies, Krahe (1989) concluded that self-report personality inventories 'are highly susceptible to a variety of response biases such as lying, social desirability, extremity and acquiescence . . . most personality inventories . . . consist of scales that are susceptible to faking and response biases which cast doubt on their utility as valid and reliable instruments in personality diagnostics'.

   However, the methodology of research in simulated settings has been heavily criticized (Schwab, 1971). *First,* few studies use control groups, so differences may be due to time effects or increased familiarity with tests. *Second,* the subsequent administrations of the tests are not conducted under the standard conditions, because the instructions are intentionally changed. The two testing sessions are not exactly parallel and the effects may be due to the changed conditions of administration. *Third,* there is always doubt about whether experimental results generalize to conditions in the 'real world'. *Finally,* as the next section will show, there is doubt about whether distortion is necessarily a bad thing. Nevertheless, considerable effort has been expended in order to detect and counteract lying and deception.

A Modern View of Lying and Deception

The modern attitude to lying and deception is much more relaxed, partly because of the reassuring research evidence that has emerged. Rimland (1962) suggested that in natural settings the level of faking was, in fact, much lower than 'experimental' studies would suggest. Faking seemed more likely to consist of shading the truth rather than committing downright lies. Seisdedos (1993) proposed that candidates who distort personality questionnaires are merely showing another of their personality traits – 'an attitude of intelligent adaptation . . . we should not necessarily consider this as a form of insincerity, lying or deliberate faking. It is not necessarily negative from the subject's perspective to show the best "ego", because, in some settings, this could be the way to adapt to the circumstances . . . there are some praiseworthy aspects in this behaviour'. It may be like putting on one's best clothes to go to church on Sunday. It is not lying – it is just another facet of personality. Indeed, it may be an aspect of conscientiousness. Some people are willing to put themselves out more in order to conform to others' expectations. Studies show that it is conscientious, well–controlled, pillars of society who achieve high scores on lie scales. Similarly, Rosenfeld et al. (1995) suggest that impression management can be viewed as a skill that makes interpersonal and social relations in organizations more effective.

Recently, a substantial number of psychologists have suggested that the concern about faking – especially of personality tests – has been overdone. In 1983, Nevid suggested that the issue of social desirability was 'a methodological dead horse'. Hough et al. (1990) came to a similar conclusion when they found that the validity of personality scales was not destroyed even when candidates responded in an overly desirable manner. Furthermore, one meta-analysis (Ones et al., 1996) concluded that social desirability in personality testing for selection was a complete red herring. In itself, distortion does not frustrate good selection. If everyone had a 10% positive distortion, a selection decision would not be altered. Problems would only arise if some people distorted more than others.

There are two other reasons why a more relaxed view of lying and deception has been adopted:

- For some jobs, the ability to distort impressions is an advantage.
- Does it matter when scores are *successfully* distorted? If people can distort successfully on a test, they will be able to distort successfully on the job.

Sources of Deception

In order to understand fully the phenomenon of deception, it is necessary to consider why it occurs. There are three main causes of distortion:

- *Personal gain*. This type of deception may be particularly rampant in selection, but less pronounced in guidance. Some authors, such as Whyte (1957), Huff (1961) and Cohen (1993), give advice to applicants on how to intentionally cheat at personality tests. The desire to mislead in order to achieve personal gain is often called conscious **impression management** (Paulhus, 1984). Impression management is well documented in most social psychology textbooks. Distortions are most likely to occur when:
  - people are aware that they are being assessed
  - assessment is unrealistic and artificial, and where the consequences of atypical actions are slight
  - the assessment has a short duration
  - the assessors are not trained.
- *Desire to please*. **Interpersonal distortion** arises because we generally want other people to like us, even if there is no material gain. Therefore, we generally put our best foot forward and hide our little failures. Sometimes we may distort answers in order to help researchers prove their point (demand characteristics of experiments). Distortion based on the desire to please is usually called **social desirability** and it has been exhaustively examined by Edwards (1957), and more recently by Paulhus (1984), Ganster et al. (1983)

and Rees (1999). Social desirability, it should be noted, often involves a large element of self-deception (Paulhus, 1984).

* *Response sets.* Some people acquiesce and say 'Yes' to whatever questions they are asked. Other people have a distinct tendency to choose the middle response, irrespective of the question's content. Some people even have a tendency to mark the negative answers. All of these response sets add error variance which may reduce the accuracy of inferences made from tests and other measures.

The Vulnerability of Selection Methods of Selection to Lying and Deception

Deception is not limited to psychological tests and is probably a feature of all methods of personality assessment. Table 11.4 summarizes the opportunities for lying and deception in the main methods of selection.

Techniques aimed at reducing lying and deception are discussed in section 11.5.5.

Table 11.4 The vulnerability of measures to distortion

Approach	Opportunities for distortion
Objective and physical measures	Less opportunity than most. Often, it is not clear to the subject what trait the test is measuring and consequently the scope for distortion is limited. *But* Practice and relaxation, or concentration, can distort some measures; for example, lie detectors.
Situational measures	Less opportunity than most. *But* If the situation involves many other people, there will be intense pressure to be socially acceptable. If candidate knows the dimensions assessed, behaviour can be distorted to emit behaviour on these dimensions. The candidate will also tend to emit behaviour that is deemed to be required, rather than 'typical' behaviour.
Self-report tests	In theory, considerable opportunity. *But* The extent depends on the length of the test and the transparency of the questions. Long tests with lie scales reduce the opportunity to fake. Interpersonal distortion is likely to be low. The possibility of distortion from response sets is dependent on that test's construction.
Self-description	The opportunity to distort is very high. Difficult areas may be omitted. Individuals may lack an objective frame of reference.
Clinical interviews	The opportunity to distort is very high and interpersonal distortion could be high. There are few checks, except for the wit and experience of the interviewers.
Projective tests	The opportunity to distort is low, since there is little to indicate what the assessor is looking for and how the responses will be evaluated. Individuals might screen out more bizarre or unusual responses.

11.3.5 CROSS-CONTAMINATION WITH CRITERION (INCREASES APPARENT VALIDITY)

Contamination between the criterion and the predictor occurs when there is some link between the collection of the predictor data and the collection of the criterion data. This usually happens when one or both of the predictor and the criterion are subjective. For example, to validate a test of numerical reasoning, a large company may give a numerical reasoning test to all 60 of its accounts staff. Their boss may collect and collate the test scores. The boss may then rate each staff member according to his or her ability. The ratings are used as the criteria and are correlated with the results from the test. This validation design is poor, because the boss knew the scores before giving the ratings. This knowledge may have a conscious or subconscious influence on the ratings.

Cross-contamination between predictor and criterion may also occur in the other direction; knowledge of the criterion can influence the predictor score. For example, a firm might use the nominated group technique to assess the validity of a certain type of interview in predicting promotion potential. It might select 50 senior managers and 50 junior managers and ask the human resources manager to interview and give each person a score for his or her management potential. If the average for senior managers is significantly higher than that for the junior managers, it might be concluded that the interview is valid. This conclusion might be dangerously false. The human resources manager is virtually certain to know the seniority of the interviewees and this knowledge may have subconsciously influenced the interview scores awarded. To avoid problems of this kind, validations involving any subjective element must ensure that the assessor does not know the other score. It is never permissible to have a validation study where the same person makes subjective evaluations on both the predictor and the criterion. Studies that avoid these problems are called 'blind' validity studies.

Unfortunately, the situation is more complex – especially when promotion record is the criterion. The person making the subjective evaluation may not know the predictor score, but the subjects may know their own scores. Those who have done well may use their high scores to wheedle their way on to prestigious projects and important committees, so that their subsequent promotion is rapid. Similarly, those who know that they had low scores may be reticent, hold back and then be overlooked for promotion. A possible example concerns selection for civil service posts. The competition is open and public candidates have a right to know their own scores, so candidates with high scores are more able to obtain initial postings to prestigious departments such as the Treasury. Early careers in these departments mean that they have a strategic advantage over candidates who receive a low mark and whose initial posting was to worthy, but less powerful, departments. These influences mean that when, in the fullness of time, the scores and the promotion record are correlated, the measure gives a false appearance of validity.

To avoid this type of error, a proper validation ensures that neither the candidate nor anyone making judgements knows the scores. This is called a **double-blind** study.

11.3.6 LARGE CORRELATION MATRICES (INCREASE APPARENT VALIDITY)

Significant correlations are occasionally obtained as flukes. If we keep taking lists of random numbers, one of them will eventually correlate quite well with the criterion and we might think that the random numbers are valid. Section 11.3.1 explains that much depends upon the sample size of the validation study. If our sample size is only ten, we will soon come across a list of random numbers that give a good correlation. However, if our sample size is 172, then we will be generating random numbers for several days before we produce a set that correlates well with our predictor. This example demonstrates that we sometimes obtain spurious correlations even when there is no link at all between the predictor and the criterion, but these 'fluke' correlations become rarer and rarer as the size of the sample increases. Fortunately, statistical tests of significance take sample size into account.

However, a problem arises when validation involves large matrices. If only one statistical test is calculated using random numbers, the probability of a significant correlation occurring by 'fluke' is less than 5% (1:20). However, if 20 correlations are calculated using random numbers as criteria, one of them is very likely to be significant. A personality test may have 20 different scales. A validity study may correlate each scale against, say, five criteria, such as the supervisor's assessment, promotion, productivity, tenure and absences. The validation would therefore involve 100 correlations. By the laws of chance alone, it would be expected that at least 5% of these correlations would be significant at the .05 alpha level. An unwary user could be lulled into believing that the test is valid by a research report that simply reported the five significant correlations.

In fact, the situation is even more complicated. If a validity study involves 100 correlations against random numbers, the most likely result is five significant correlations. However, it is quite likely that six, seven or even eight significant correlations could arise by 'fluke'. At some point, however, there would be just too many correlations for all of them to be dismissed as 'flukes'. The question is, 'Where should the line be drawn?' Fortunately, it is possible to use the binomial distribution to help with this decision. The binomial calculation is simple but tiresome. To avoid the chore of such calculations, the website that accompanies this book gives a table of the number of significant results that are necessary in order to conclude that at least some correlations in a large matrix are genuinely significant.

Sometimes, test producers are not aware of the effects of using large validation matrices and the number of correlations may not be stated clearly. For example, one chapter of a test manual may reveal that the test contains 20 different scales. In a separate chapter on validity, the manual may describe a validation study in which supervisory ratings on, say, 12 different aspects of performance were obtained. The manual will then proudly give a list of the 16 significant correlations as evidence of the test's validity. A canny test user, however, will calculate that the validity study involved 240 correlations. Referring to the table on the website associated with this book, a canny test user will be aware that, with a large matrix of 240 correlations, at least 18 correlations will need to be significant at the .05 level before we can be 95% sure that any of the correlations are not 'flukes'. Consequently, despite the proud claims of the test producer, the 16 significant correlations are not enough to support claims that the test is valid.

Test producers should always provide full correlation matrices that are calculated in a validity study. In a hypothetical example, the 16PF was validated against six criteria for sales staff and the correlation matrix shown in table 11.5 was produced.

The matrix contains 96 correlation coefficients, of which 13 are statistically significant. The number of significant results would need to exceed eight before we could be 95% sure that some of the correlations were genuine. In this case, the number indicated by the binomial distribution would be exceeded and we could be sure that the test had some validity. It is therefore acceptable to inspect the matrix in an attempt to differentiate the genuine from the 'fluke' results. By definition, fluke results will be at random and hence fluke correlations are unlikely to

Table 11.5 An example of a large correlation matrix

Note: 6 × 16 = 96 □ 100	16PF scales														
Six criteria	A	B	C	E	F	G	H	L	M	N	O	Q_1	Q_2	Q_3	Q_4
Supervisor's evaluation	ns	ns	ns	ns	ns	.4	ns	ns	ns	ns	ns	ns	ns	ns	ns
Training success	.4	ns	ns	ns	−.5	.6	.5	ns	ns	ns	ns	ns	ns	ns	ns
Lateness	ns	ns	ns	ns	−.5	.5	ns	ns	ns	ns	ns	ns	.3	.4	ns
Tenure	ns	ns	ns	ns	ns	ns	ns	.3	ns	ns	ns	ns	ns	ns	ns
Volume of sales	ns	ns	ns	ns	ns	ns	ns	ns	ns	ns	.3	ns	ns	ns	ns
Profitability of sales	ns	ns	ns	ns	−.4	.3	ns	ns	ns	ns	ns	ns	ns	ns	ns

This table is for illustrative purposes only. Most research indicates more significant validity coefficients.

show a pattern. A clear pattern *can* be seen in the example: the correlations, especially the higher correlations, seem into be associated with the G (conscientiousness) scale and the F (prudence) scale. The test seems most valid in the prediction of training success and lateness.

11.3.7 CAPITALIZATION ON CHANCE (INCREASES APPARENT VALIDITY)

Capitalization on chance happens when certain statistics, such as multiple regression, are used in a validation study. These statistics 'hunt' through data in order to find the best fit. In their hunt, they take into account random errors that are present in that particular sample. When the same formula is used on a different sample, the random errors are different and a slightly lower correlation is obtained. This effect is known as **'shrinkage'**. Shrinkage is greatest with small samples and when a large number of predictors are used to predict a criterion: it is as if each predictor captures more and more of the random error.

In the past, the strategy of **cross-validation** using 'hold-out' samples was used as a safeguard against shrinkage. For example, if data on five predictors (say, verbal fluency [VF], extroversion [E], stability [S], tough-mindedness [T] and persuasive interests [P]) were used to predict the performance of 172 salespeople, the sample would be divided into two parts. The data from a sample of about 100 salespeople would be used to produce a multiple regression equation such as:

$$Sales\text{-}performance = .3 \times VF + .3 \times E + .3 \times C + .2 \times T + .2$$

The equation might produce a validity of .4. The formula would then be applied to the hold-out sample of the remaining 72 people and a validity of .32 might be obtained – indicating a shrinkage of .08. This approach has fallen into disrepute. Dividing the sample into two smaller ones only creates two less stable estimates of validity. The comparison is only as strong as the validity produced from the, often very small, hold-out sample. It makes better sense to combine all the data into one large sample and then statistically compensate for any capitalization on chance. The formula for estimating the shrunken validity after capitalization on chance has been removed is:

$$cR = \sqrt{1 - (1 - R^2)\left(\frac{N-1}{N-m}\right)}$$

where cR is the corrected multiple correlation, R is the uncorrected multiple correlation, N is the sample size and m is the number of independent variables.

◤ 11.4 META-ANALYSIS AND VALIDITY GENERALIZATION

It is impossible to carry out a perfect validity study. Perfect criteria are not available and often the range of the sample is severely restricted. Usually, the sample sizes of validity studies are small. These imperfections mean that the validity coefficients obtained in practice are often, at best, rough approximations of true validity. A different sample with a different criterion often yields a different validity. Indeed, when validities were collected and catalogued by Ghiselli (1966) and others in the 1960s, the researchers were struck by the range of validity coefficients obtained for similar tests. This led them to believe that the validity of any test is highly idiosyncratic and must be checked in each situation. This became known as the doctrine of **situational specificity**. It was a highly inconvenient doctrine, because the constant need for validation and revalidation involved a great deal of work.

The doctrine of situational specificity also caused theoretical problems. Theorists would try to come to general conclusions about the validity of selection methods. Typically, theorists would review all research papers concerning, say, interviews. Their narrative reviews would collate the different findings, each based on a small sample, and they would usually reveal varying results: as you would expect from small samples, the large random error swamped the true results. Some investigations would show that the measure was valid, other investigations would be inconclusive and yet other investigations would show that the measure was invalid. Faced with apparently conflicting evidence, the reviewers would arrive at the immortal conclusion, 'further research is needed'. Braver reviewers would try to quantify the results by counting the number of positive studies and the number of negative studies. These '**vote counters**' would then adopt the conclusion supported by the greater number of results.

In the mid-1970s, a solution started to emerge. The basic idea was to collect as many studies as possible until there was a respectable combined sample size. Often, sample sizes of more than 10,000 could be accumulated. The average validity coefficient based on such a large sample size would not be as volatile as the validity based on a single, small sample. This combination of many small studies to produce a more accurate estimate is the essential idea of meta-analysis. Meta-analysis confers additional advantages. It also enables the size of an effect to be calculated (Rosenthal, 1991).

The essential idea of meta-analysis was taken by several researchers and refined into a much more sophisticated tool. The main pioneers in this development were Glass (1976), Glass et al. (1981) and Hunter et al. (1982). In selection, the methods developed by Hunter et al. have become the most frequently used approach.

The simplest improvement was to weight the correlation coefficients according to their sample size – after all, a correlation based on a large sample is more accurate than one based on a small sample. The next improvement was to correct correlation coefficients for artefacts such as restriction of range and attenuation of criteria.

Once correlations have been weighted and corrected for artefacts, they can be averaged and a good estimate of the true validity obtained. It is then possible to calculate the distribution of validities that would be expected by chance. The actual distribution can be compared with the chance variance. If they are very similar, any differences between studies are the result of random fluctuations and validity generalizes from one situation to another.

On the other hand, if the actual variation is much higher than the chance variation, there must be some other factor that is systematically influencing validity and a search for the source is undertaken. For example, Barrick and Mount (1991) conducted a meta-analysis on the validity of personality tests. They noted that in some studies the personality tests were chosen on little more than the researcher's hunch. In other studies, however, personality tests had been chosen after a job analysis. They therefore 'coded' studies into two groups: those with a job analysis and those without a job analysis. The meta-analysis was then able to compare the validity coefficients for the two groups of studies. In essence, they found that when the choice of personality test was preceded by a job analysis, the validity was a respectable .38, whereas when the personality test was chosen without a job analysis the correlation was only .12. Other meta-analysts have examined (coded) variables such as the type of criterion used, the industrial sector and the type of job.

Meta-analysis is now a major statistical method in selection and assessment, and throughout Industrial and Organizational Psychology. A basic explanation of meta-analysis is given by Fernandez and Boyle (1996), but for many people the authoritative source is Hunter et al. (1982). An excellent review of meta-analytic procedures is given by Bangert-Drowns (1986).

However, meta-analysis has its critics. Possible criticisms include the following:

- Meta-analyses needs data on artefacts, such as restriction of range and attenuation of criteria. Because many studies fail to report basic data, this information is often not available. Rather than eliminating such studies from their calculations, meta-analysts often estimate the missing values. The estimates may be too generous and therefore the corrected validity coefficients may be too high.
- Meta-analyses can only be conducted on available studies. Validities in published papers may be higher than validities in general, because editors may favour those papers that have striking positive findings. On the other hand, it may be that published validities are lower because editors show a preference for papers that use new or exploratory measures, rather than the tried and tested measures actually used in selection and guidance. Consequently, most meta-analysts devote considerable effort to discovering and including all studies, whether or not they have been published.

As a result of these criticisms, it would seem prudent to prefer results from one or two large-scale studies that have been well designed and conducted. Unfortunately, such studies are rare in selection and assessment, and they are even rarer in other areas of Organizational Psychology, such as guidance. In this majority of situations where good studies are not available, meta-analyses do provide a creditable alternative.

▶ 11.5 PRACTICAL WAYS OF MAXIMIZING VALIDITY

In the past, validity has been considered to be a fixed characteristic and the only role for selectors and counsellors has then been to accept or reject a measure on the basis of a validity correlation. A more proactive approach is now taken to design valid measures. The main strategies are as follows.

11.5.1 CAPTURE THE VARIANCE FROM ALL DOMAINS AND DO NOT RECAPTURE THE SAME VARIANCE

In practice, most selection and guidance systems involve a series of different predictors. For example, a South African mining company might select managers on the basis of school grades, situational interviews, a test of general intelligence, a test of verbal intelligence, a test of spatial reasoning and a test of personality. This procedure will have accumulated over a period of time, during which each successive director of human resources will have added his or her own favourite measure. It is likely that similar accuracy could be achieved with a shorter system. One problem with the mining company's system is that at least four of the measures (school grades, situational interviews and the two intelligence tests) are re-measuring the same characteristic – verbal intelligence. Another problem with the mining company's system is that it omits to measure other important characteristics such as values and motives.

The theory of validity developed by Smith (1994) suggests that there are three main domains that selectors should measure. Characteristics in the *universal domain* lead to good performance in most jobs. They probably include cognitive ability, vitality and work centrality (the proportion of their life space that individuals are prepared to devote to work). Characteristics in the *occupational domain* consist of abilities needed in certain occupations, such as numerical ability (for accountants), musical ability (for entertainers) or empathy (for care workers). The occupational domain also includes specific job knowledge, training and experience. The *relational domain* concerns a person's adjustment to the cultural and interpersonal environment of a particular work setting. Often, the factors within the relational domain are referred to as the 'chemistry' between an employee and his or her organization. It is suggested that the main factors in the relational domain consist of values and an effective sharing of meaning. The validity of a battery will be maximized when the predictors cover as many of the domains as possible. In selection for general entry positions, such as army recruiting or management training, the selection process will largely cover the universal domain. In selection for general occupational posts, such as psychologist, lawyer or teacher, the main concern will be to measure of the universal domain and the occupational domain. For selection to a specific post in a specific team, all three domains – including the relational domain – will need to be covered.

11.5.2 USE A FULL RANGE OF SUBJECTS

In section 11.3.2 it was noted that restriction of range always reduces apparent validity and that most validation studies involve a restricted sample. Consequently, every effort should be made to include the full range of subjects, and where this is not possible a statistical correction should be made.

11.5.3 IMPROVE CRITERIA

In section 11.3.3 it was shown that a poor criterion can reduce apparent validity. The vital importance of choosing criteria carefully is not always recognized. Jenkins (1946) wrote that inadequate criteria are at the heart of much poor prediction and that psychologists in general 'tended to accept the tacit assumption that criteria were either given of God or just to be found lying about'. Most textbooks and journal literature would lead to the conclusion that 'expediency dictated the choice of criteria and that convenient availability of a criterion was more important than its adequacy' (Jenkins, 1946). A good criterion is not too difficult to define in theory. However, in practice it is very difficult to obtain a good criterion. Indeed, probably the most difficult part of any validity study is to get an organization to define exactly what it means by 'a good employee'.

Typically, organizations attempt to define a good employee in terms of three types of data: judgemental data, production data and personnel data (Landy, 1985).

Judgemental Criteria

Judgemental criteria consist of ratings by others. They are usually made by immediate supervisors, but they can be made by subordinates, colleagues, senior managers and customers. One of the best reviews of judgemental criteria is given by Landy and Rastegrary (1989), who suggest that judgemental data are the most frequently used criteria and are found in about 45% of all validity studies. They note that 'supervisory ratings have been variously lionised and maligned over the last several decades . . . they were used extensively in the 1950s and 1960s . . . and vigorously bashed in the 1970s for proneness to errors of judgement'. The main targets for criticism have been their subjectivity and unreliability. Hunter and Schmidt (1989), for example, claim that, 'meta-analysis has shown the reliability of a single rating to be only 0.47'.

Efforts to improve judgemental criteria include Behaviourally Anchored Rating Scales (BARS: Smith and Kendall, 1963) and Behavioural Observation Scales (BOS: Schwab et al., 1975; Latham and Wexley, 1977). A thoughtful analysis of rating scales is given by Handyside (1989). A substantial review of the literature was conducted by Landy and Farr (1980). They concluded that the exact format of the rating scale made little difference *provided that* the scale possessed the following characteristics:

- the dimensions being rated were well-defined
- the scale used for the rating had behavioural anchors
- the number of points on the scale offered a reasonable range; say, between three and nine points.

Judgemental data are sometimes called ratings and they are sometimes used as predictors (see section 18.4).

Production Criteria

Production criteria are often considered to be the Holy Grail sought by all organizations. Consequently, an effort is often made to measure employees' production output in terms of such things as widgets assembled per hour (operatives), sales per month (sales representatives), increase in share price per year (chief executives) or trading profit per year (stockbrokers). Landy and Rastegrary (1989) suggest that 22% of validity studies use production data. Despite their intuitive allure, production statistics have many weaknesses. Production statistics are often unreliable: for example, the correlation between stockbrokers' trading profit in one year and their trading profit in another year is only .2. Also, production statistics are often contaminated by factors beyond an individual's control: for example, a brilliant teacher may obtain a poor pass rate simply because a school is in a poor catchment area and attracts more than its fair share of disadvantaged pupils. A final problem with productivity data as criteria is that for some jobs, such as care workers or middle managers, an objective index of productivity is difficult to devise.

Personnel Data

Personnel data is often obtained from the records that a personnel department maintains on employees. Landy and Rastegrary (1989) suggest that criteria based on personnel data are used in about 20% of validity studies. Typical personnel criteria include:

- attendance, such as days absent, days late and length of service
- career progression, such as job level, promotion record and salary increase
- accidents
- training, such as the length of training to reach a given standard or the marks at the end of training.

Personnel data usually provides a global index of an employee's general suitability. This is an advantage, because fewer criteria are needed and employers are usually more interested in overall performance, rather than performance in one or two aspects of a job. However, the global nature of criteria derived from personnel data has the disadvantage that their exact relevance is hard to trace, and they may be contaminated by influences such as the availability of altern- ative jobs (Stark, 1959), organizational politics and ingratiation (Wallace, 1974).

Training criteria may be one of the best kinds of criteria, because a number of sources of con- tamination seen in other criteria are minimized. Trainees usually have very similar experiences. Trainee performance is usually assessed on reasonably objective standards, by trainers who have little vested interest in individuals. The raters are likely to have some experience in making judge- ments of people. Ghiselli (1966) showed that training criteria are usually reliable. Unfortu- nately, training criteria may be obtained in artificial environments and may be based on only a few weeks' performance. Often, training criteria are reduced to a two-point scale, pass or fail.

11.5.4 USE MULTIPLE CRITERIA – PROBABLY WITH FACTOR ANALYSIS

Because all criteria have deficiencies, validation should usually involve several criteria, so that the random error in one criterion will be balanced by the random error in another criterion. Indeed, the dangers of using one criterion to gauge *the* validity of a test or other measure means that we should adopt the dictum of Dunnette (1963) and junk *the* criterion.

However, the use of multiple criteria can be confusing, because they may give rise to several validity coefficients that conflict. In some senses, the conflict may be a blessing in disguise. An examination of the varying correlations may give some insight into the way in which the measure operates and may enable us to understand the mechanisms by which a predictor works. But, in many situations, the use of factor analysis is needed. First, data on as many criteria as possible are collected. Second, the criterion data are factor analysed to identify a smaller set of factors that are more robust than any individual criterion. Third, the computer calculates each person's score on each of the factors. Finally, the predictor scores are correlated with the factor scores and an assessment of validity is made.

11.5.5 CONTROL AND LIMIT DECEPTION

Distortion is not a major problem in ability tests, because it is difficult to fake the correct answers to objective problems. **Faking bad** is a theoretical possibility, but in the vast majority of selection and guidance situations candidates feel pressure to maximize rather than minimize their scores.

The situation may be quite different with measures of personality and measures of interest. Section 11.3.4 suggests that deception may add error variance, which reduces validity. Consequently, authors and users of personality tests put a great deal of effort into detecting and eliminating deception. There are four main approaches:

- *Establish an atmosphere* in which an applicant believes that distortion is neither necessary nor desirable. Usually, this means establishing a contract of mutual trust, appealing to fairness and pointing out the personal consequences of producing misleading results.
- *Advise of cross-checks*, so that candidates think that lies might be detected.
- *Use lie scales*. There are three main types – those based on unusual responses, consistency and distortable questions:
  - Unusual responses: an example is the lie scale of the Eysenck Personality Questionnaire. Subjects are asked a series of questions to which almost everyone should, say, give a negative reply. For example:

  > 'Have you always paid before getting off a bus?'
  > 'Did you always obey your parents?'

  The number of times the candidate gives an unusual reply is scored, and if the score is above a certain level it is concluded that the person is too good to be true and therefore must be lying. Unfortunately, conscientious people who are very self-controlled tend to produce high scores and be branded liars, even though their responses are genuine.
  - Consistency: in effect, the same questions are asked twice or more during the test and answers are compared. Inconsistent replies are taken as evidence of lying, on the basis that liars cannot remember their previous answers.
  - Distortable questions: it was noticed that when people were instructed to lie on personality tests, the answers to certain questions remained the same while others were distorted. Thus, if these distortable questions are scored separately, they should yield an index of **motivational distortion**. The MD scale on the 16PF was constructed on this basis.
- *Asking forced-choice questions*. It is possible to construct questions where the alternatives are of equal social desirability, and a dishonest person would not know which alternative to choose in order to create the right impression. For example:

  > In each triad, A and B <u>underline</u> the one word that describes you best:
  > A   B
  > warm-hearted   stingy
  > handsome   aggressive
  > experimenting   unsocial

- All of the alternatives in a given triad are carefully equated for social desirability, so it is impossible to fake either good or bad. People tend to dislike forced-choice questions.

11.5.6 USE CORROBORATING INFORMATION

A final method of increasing the validity is to cross-check the scores against other information. This reflects a good psychometric principle – increase the 'test length' to improve reliability and hence the validity. Unfortunately, however, the use of corroborating information has many dangers. Increasing 'test length' only improves reliability *if* the extra items are of equal quality. Stuffing an assessment with irrelevant questions may actually lower reliability and validity.

Often, testing is undertaken in order to escape presumptions embedded in other sources and to obtain a 'fresh and independent assessment' of an individual, which is uncontaminated by prejudice resulting from previous knowledge. In these situations, it is best to eschew corroborating information and make it clear that you are using only the information from the tests, and that all other information except for sex, age and possibly ethnic group has been withheld . The client then knows that your inferences are based only on the test results and that you are not toadying to the views of other people, or to colourful but hearsay evidence of a person's previous history. Some organizations prefer this clear separation rather than having a report that is a *mélange* of sources.

In other situations, it may be desirable to corroborate test results. Care should be taken to avoid contaminating the results of tests or other scientific measures with unscientific information derived from the following:

- *Chance observations*, of *short duration* and in *limited settings*. Many selection decisions have been ruined by trying to corroborate the results of, say, a situational interview with the comments of an untrained receptionist, who observed a candidate while he or she was waiting for the interview. Many selection decisions have also been degraded by the impressions of a senior manager who was able to 'have coffee' with a candidate during a five-minute break in an assessment centre!
- *Old information*. This should not be used – especially with applicants under the age of 30. School reports and recycled school references are a particular danger. Other problems arise when selection decisions are contaminated by reminiscences of previous bosses or colleagues, which are based on events that occurred many years ago in different settings.
- *Subjective information* from people who have a vested interest in perceiving the candidate in a certain way. This may include the opinions of competitors or people who the candidate rightly needed to censure or check. Perhaps the most prevalent source of subjective information is the candidates themselves. Self-assessment has many imperfections. In many situations, it is foolish to adjust an evaluation based on a carefully constructed and administered test because a candidate or a client disagrees with the result. The epitome of such folly must be a counsellor who changes his or her view on a high assertiveness score simply because a client forcibly and vehemently maintains that he or she 'is definitely not as dominant as the test suggests'! However, in deciding *how* to give feedback and on the subsequent actions that should be taken, candidate and client comments do need to be taken into account.
- *Unvalidated or pseudo-measures* that have not been thoroughly researched should not be used to corroborate better measures. Clearly, the results of journalistic quizzes in newspapers should not be used to modify results from more scientific measures. However, in some situations the dangers are less obvious. Sometimes, the results from

an under-researched test being developed as a part of a PhD thesis are wrongly allowed to creep into a decision-making process. Sometimes, the results from a demonstration questionnaire, used by an eminent authority during a training session, are wrongly dredged up and used to modify the conclusions based on well-validated measures.

It is, however, entirely proper to corroborate and modify conclusions if the additional information is:

- recent (say, less than two years old)
- produced by trained 'observers' who have seen all the relevant cohort of individuals in a variety of settings, over a considerable period and who use a consistent rating system
- based on a well-researched instrument whose psychometric properties, especially validity, are known
- provided by people who have no vested interest in the outcome.

 ## 11.6 EVALUATING VALIDITY COEFFICIENTS

When everything is taken into account, validity coefficients need to be evaluated. Two schemes are needed, because coefficients for construct validity are generally much higher than coefficients for predictive and concurrent validity. Table 11.6 adopts the system set out in the British Psychological Society's *Review of Personality Assessment Instruments* (Lindley, 2001), and also used in the Society's *Review of Ability and Aptitude Tests* (Bartram, 1997).

 ## 11.7 VALIDITY IMPOSTERS

Validity is a highly respected concept. Some people have tried to capitalize upon this respect by linking other concepts to validity. Consequently, the literature is peppered with many kinds

Table 11.6 Evaluating validity

Verbal label	Percentage of variance	Correlation
Evaluation of construct validities		
Inadequate	Under 20%	Under .45
Adequate	20–29%	.45–.54
Reasonable	30–41%	.55–.64
Good	42–55%	.65–.74
Excellent	Over 55%	.75 and over
Evaluation of predictive and concurrent validities		
Inadequate	Under 4%	Under .2
Adequate	4–12%	.2–.34
Reasonable	13–15%	.35–.44
Good	16–29%	.45–.54
Excellent	Over 29%	.55 and over

of so-called validity, such as 'social validity', 'impact validity', 'practical validity', 'economic valid-ity' and so on. The concepts behind these new names may be laudable and useful, but none of them has much to do with validity in terms of 'the correctness of the inferences made from a score'. Two concepts in particular have been erroneously considered as types of validity. They are 'acceptability' (face validity) and 'content relevance' (content validity). Since they may be encountered in some older texts, they need to be discussed in more detail.

11.7.1 ACCEPTABILITY (FACE VALIDITY)

The appearance of a test should seem reasonable and acceptable. A test or measure used in selec-tion or guidance should 'look valid' to candidates, clients, untrained observers, administrative personnel and senior managers. If a test does not 'look valid', the people completing the it may not take it seriously and may not give true answers. If a test does not 'look valid', senior man-agers will be unlikely to approve its use. If a test does not 'look valid', it may attract criticism from untrained observers and pressure groups. Therefore, it is highly desirable to use tests that look relevant to the job. This important facet is called **acceptability**. In the past, it was known as 'face validity'. The term 'face validity' is now discouraged. The appearance of a test may or *may not* bear any relationship to the correctness of the inferences made.

High acceptability arises when a test or some other measure is professionally produced and the presentation is modern and appealing. High acceptability also arises when the terms and vocabulary used are appropriate to the people who complete the test. The level of vocabulary should be carefully matched to the verbal abilities of the intended audience. Tests intended for young adults and people whose education and experience has not involved a high verbal content must use short words in short sentences. Tests used in an occupational setting should use terms that are commonly used at work. Where tests will be used with a narrow range of people, such as mechanical engineers, the examples and the questions can be couched in words that are a part of mechanical engineers' argot. However, care must be exercised. Too much em-phasis on acceptability or 'face validity' can lead to tests that are so specific to a particular situation that they quickly become outdated.

Poor acceptability arises if a test designed for one setting is employed in another. For ex-ample, a personality test developed in a clinical setting is unlikely to be accepted when used in an occupational setting. Often, the changes needed to make a test acceptable are cosmetic changes of words. When a test is adapted in this way, it cannot be assumed to have the same validity as the original. It is always necessary to conduct further investigations of validity and reliability.

Acceptability (face validity) is usually discounted as a type of validity, because it is known to be contaminated by a number of artefacts, such as Barnum effects, anecdotal validity, the Pollyanna effect and the effects of authority.

Barnum Effects (Gullibility Effects)

Paul Meehl (1956) was interested in whether the predictions made by clinicians on the basis of their experience were more accurate than those made by statisticians on the basis of an actuar-ial formula. He accused many clinicians of achieving high success rates by adopting the tactics of Barnum. Barnum was a circus entertainer who was able to astound gullible audiences by 'divin-ing' personal information about spectators who he had never met previously (Snyder et al., 1977). Barnum used a simple strategy. He made statements that would be true of most people, such as 'You have just heard from a member of your family – Is that true?' or 'You have just had a disappointment – Is that true?' Meehl pointed out that such prophecies might be very entertaining, but they were useless in making distinctions between people. The Barnum effect is defined as the phenomenon whereby 'people willingly accept personality interpretations comprised of vague statements with a high base-rate occurrence in the general population'.

Forer (1949) demonstrated the Barnum effect in a famous experiment. College students completed a personality test and shortly afterwards were given a personality sketch that consisted of vague statements such as 'while you have some personality weaknesses you are generally able to compensate for them' and 'at times you have serious doubts as to whether you have made the right decision or done the right thing'. All students received the same description, but were led to believe that it only applied to them. When asked to judge the description's accuracy, most students believed that the personality description was indeed accurate. Forer's results have been replicated many times, by Carrier (1963), Manning (1968) and Stagner (1958), amongst others. Barnum statements are most likely to be accepted when:

- they are general in nature and apply to a large number of people
- people are told that they are specifically derived from information about them
- they are favourably worded
- they are based on methods that take little time
- they are given by high-status people, such as clinicians, to people who have much less power, such as patients or students.

Many of these studies took place decades ago, when psychologists and testers were held in awe and candidates were less sophisticated. Most of the subjects were either patients or students. The findings may not generalize to occupational settings today.

The reasoning of Meehl and of Snyder et al. led to a bias against any statement that might apply to large numbers of people. However, some general statements, applicable to large numbers in the population, *are* accurate and correct. A statement such as 'you are neither a total extrovert nor a total introvert but are in the middle of the range' is clearly a Barnum statement. However, it is scientifically the correct statement, because the majority of the population *are* within one standard deviation of the mean. Second, the imprecise nature of psychological measurement means that we cannot make unconditional pronouncements. It is frequently necessary to qualify and use probabilistic statements, as in the example of 'in some circumstances other people may annoy you'. At a superficial level, this statement would also qualify as a Barnum statement. In reports, such general statements are not only technically correct but they are desirable. Other statements in a report provide context that refines and narrows down the meaning of an individual Barnum statement. In this case, the fact that the author of the report has chosen to use a general statement about irritability, rather than a general statement about any one of 10,000 other traits, adds significant meaning. The third justification that is often used for including Barnum statements in vocational guidance reports is that they soften negative information. The use of a statement couched in general terms often means that the recipient is not offended, and hence is willing to accept and take action based upon the results of the tests.

Anecdotal Validity

The use of a selection method will often be justified by examples or instances of the method's spectacular success. These instances are usually dramatic and memorable, but hardly amount to scientific evidence. Dramatic incidents may be 'one-off' random events. It is more likely that they are the result of selective memory. People who are in favour of a particular test will remember and embroider upon its successes, while people who are against the use of the same test will remember and embroider upon its failures. Anecdotes and selective memory are no substitute for a systematic collection of evidence about whether the inferences drawn from a score are correct. Perhaps the most dramatic example of the misuse of anecdotal evidence comes from the history of assessment centres, which began in the German army prior to the Second World War. They were subsequently developed and they have a moderately good validity of about .4. However, the German army abandoned the use of assessment centres after only a few years, on the basis of one anecdotal incident: the son of Field Marshal Keitel attended an assessment centre and failed (Holdsworth, personal communication, 1999). This was taken as clear evidence that assessment centres were invalid and not worth using.

Another glorious anecdote concerning anecdotal validity tells of a merchant bank, whose use of graphology is said to go back to the days of exchange control, when UK citizens were severely restricted in the foreign exchange that they could take out of the country as tourists, but there were no limits for business expenses. One enterprising banker decided to send samples of applicants' handwriting to his aunt in Switzerland. As a business expense, he was then able to circumvent exchange controls and remit a fee to his aunt, who was then most generous whenever he visited. In the fullness of time, individuals who were ostensibly selected by graphology rose to high positions in the bank. Naturally, they came to the conclusion that the selection methods that had chosen them must be accurate. It was only logical that, thereafter, they should choose their subordinates using graphology!

The Pollyanna Effect

Thorne (1961) identified the Pollyanna effect as a component of acceptability. Pollyanna is a character from children's fiction, who always sees everything in a positive, optimistic and enthusiastic light. Researchers such as Sundberg (1955), Mosher (1965) found that people were more likely to agree that positive statements were more accurate descriptions of their personality.

The Acceptance of Authoritatively Given Scores

The basic social psychology of attitude change suggests that people will be more likely to accept random personality descriptions if they believe that the source of these descriptions has high status. Initial attempts to explore this idea involved giving the same general personality statements to people, who would then judge the statements' accuracy as descriptions of themselves. Contrary to expectations, the status of a description's source did not seem to influence the description's perceived accuracy. However, it was found that the initial studies were hindered by ceiling effects: all favourable statements were so readily accepted that a favourable source had little room to improve acceptability still further. Halperin et al. (1976) investigated the possibility of an interaction between the favourableness of a statement and the perceived authority of the source. He found that the likelihood of acceptance of a negative statement was higher if it was thought to arise from a high-status source. Again, this finding arose from a study using clinicians and patients: it must be generalized to the occupational world with care.

Nevo (1985) and Nevo and Sfez (1985) drew attention to the dearth of empirical research on 'face validity' for specific tests. Most test manuals treat 'acceptability' in a very cavalier way.

At best, there is a vague statement that the items were constructed with a certain setting in mind and that the items appeared (to the constructor of the test!) acceptable for this or that audience. It is, however, easy to envisage a benchmark against which acceptability could be assessed. Evaluative panels of 30 incumbents and 30 test users could be asked to complete a test and answer a Likert-style question:

> To what extent do you think this test would be suitable for selecting people for the job of . . . ?
> (4)   Very suitable
> (3)   Suitable
> (2)   Neither suitable nor unsuitable
> (1)   Unsuitable
> (0)   Not at all suitable

For diagnostic purposes, it might be desirable to add a supplementary question, 'What aspects of the test do you think might make it unsuitable?' Responses from incumbents would not be difficult to obtain, because they could be added to the end of any standardization or validity study. Unfortunately, it would be harder to obtain responses from managers and administrators. However, the results could be reported as percentages by dividing the average by 4 and multiplying by 100. As an interim standard, tests and other methods of selection should exceed an acceptance level of 80%.

11.7.2 CONTENT RELEVANCE (CONTENT VALIDITY)

Content relevance is the degree to which the items of a test or other methods of selection accurately sample the subject-matter about which conclusions are to be drawn (Messick, 1975, 1980). For many years, content relevance masqueraded under the title of content validity, because it was believed that if a test replicated a situation, validity would follow as a matter of course. However, a test that does not faithfully reflect a problem domain is not necessarily invalid. *First*, a job may need some underlying ability, which can also be measured by an apparently different task. For example, a test involving the division of numbers may well be valid for a job that involves multiplication, since both division and multiplication depend on general arithmetical ability. *Second*, there is also the problem of determining the adequacy of the sample. An expert may form a judgement, but how can the correctness of that judgement be verified? It would be necessary to establish predictive, concurrent or construct validity – in which case it would have been a waste of time checking the content relevance in the first place!

Checking content relevance does, however, have one big advantage. Courts and jurors seem to be very impressed by content relevance (content validity). A test or other selection measure seems to be much more defensible at law if it can be shown that the questions map on to specific activities involved in a job. Furthermore, content relevance is a crucial step in test construction (see chapter 16).

'Content validity' is another topic that is treated in a cavalier way in many test manuals. Claims of content relevance should be supported by a proper content analysis involving three stages:

1 The test author should describe each of the scales – the descriptions of the scales in the manual could be used.
2 An independent and qualified source that has no prior knowledge of the test should be asked to classify each item according to the scale to which it should belong.
3 The number of correct classifications should be counted and reported as a percentage in the test manual.

CHAPTER 12

BIAS OF MEASURES

Fairness is a broad topic, because discrimination can arise in many ways. It can be caused by faulty job analysis, bad person specifications, poor methods of attracting candidates, or the use of biased tests and methods. This chapter is solely concerned with the last source – measures that have biased psychometric properties. This does not imply that the other sources, mentioned elsewhere in this book, are unimportant. This chapter must be read in conjunction with the appropriate sections of several others. Guidance on avoiding discrimination is available from many sources, such as Saville Holdsworth (1991, 1992), the Commission for Racial Equality (1993) and the Equal Opportunities Commission (1988). It should be remembered that bias can involve discrimination by ethnic origin, gender, age, religion and disability. The topic of psychometric bias can be considered under three headings:

1 Types of evidence
2 Bias in criteria
3 International generalizations

12.1 TYPES OF EVIDENCE

Claims of bias are supported by many different types of evidence. The kinds of evidence can be divided into two groups: evidence that is questionable and evidence that has a scientific basis.

12.1.1 FOUR TYPES OF QUESTIONABLE EVIDENCE

First, *claims by rejected candidates* offer very poor evidence of unfairness. Such claims may be based on a combination of sour grapes or overestimation by candidates of their own capabilities. A rejected job application can engender powerful psychological processes that protect candidates' self-esteem. Often, this involves identifying some imperfection in the selection system and blaming the imperfection for the rejection. In fact, selection is never perfect. The interviews, tests or references for successful candidates are often full of imperfections too. Usually, claims by rejected candidates only give good evidence of unfairness if there is corroborated evidence of a specific, relevant and significant shortcoming.

Second, a claim of unfairness is sometimes made on the basis that the *proportion of employees* who belong to a certain group is less than the proportion of that minority group in the general population. Whilst proportions engaged can be an indicator of a biased selection system, it is far from conclusive: a minority group may choose not to work for a specific employer for religious or philosophical reasons. Furthermore, the local population may contain few members of a minority group. The 4/5ths rule, which was used in the United States, takes the number of applications into account. According to the 4/5ths rule, selection is biased if the selection rate for one group is less than 80% of the rate for another group. For example, if an education authority has 200 female applicants and engages 100 as teachers, while it engages only 35 out of 100 male applicants, it would be deemed to be discriminating against men (100/200 = 50%; 35/100 = 35%; 35%/50% = 70%). However, courts are now less likely to accept the 4/5ths rule as evidence of bias unless it is supported by other information.

Third, especially in the media, it is sometimes implied that *experts can examine a test* or other selection device and judge from the content of the questions whether it is unfair. This has proved to be very unsatisfactory evidence. Even test authors are not good at saying whether a question is or is not biased. There is clear research that psychologists with postgraduate qualifications, who themselves are drawn from a minority group, are not able to identify fair or unfair questions.

Fourth, it is sometimes argued that a test or measure is biased if the *average score* for one group is lower than the average score for another group. This may or may not be good evidence of bias, because we do not know whether two groups are, in fact, equal. There are scores of anthropological studies that show that groups *do* differ from each other. For example, men are, on average, taller than women. Finnish people are, on average, fairer haired than Italian people. There is evidence that, on average, women tend to outperform men on some types of verbal problems. If there are differences between the average scores of groups, we have no way of knowing whether these differences are a reflection of reality or whether they are the result of faulty methods of measurement.

12.1.2 MORE SCIENTIFIC EVIDENCE OF UNFAIRNESS

Because the four types of evidence outlined in the previous section may be flawed, the courts – especially in the USA – place more weight upon other methods: evidence from regression analyses (Ledvinka et al., 1982) and from item difficulty analyses. Both approaches are complex and need further explanation.

The Regression Approach

The regression approach is based upon the widely accepted view that equally suitable candidates should have an equal chance of a job offer irrespective of their backgrounds (Guion, 1965). The regression approach makes no assumptions whatsoever about the levels of ability of various groups and it does not make the unrealistic assumption that the selection system is perfectly accurate. The regression approach is more powerful than quadrant analysis. Furthermore, it has largely superseded the constant ratio approach advocated by Thorndike (1971).

In essence, the regression approach compares selection scores with subsequent work performance. A test score and the work performance for each candidate can be plotted on a scattergram,

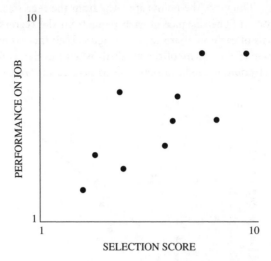

Figure 12.1 A hypotherical scattergram of job performance and selection scores.

as shown in figure 12.1. Each dot represents one applicant. In this example, selection scores range from 1 to 10 and job performance is also on a 1–10 scale. For clarity, only a small sample of ten applicants is shown. In practice, much larger samples are essential.

A line of best fit (a regression line) is then calculated and drawn on the graph, as shown in figure 12.2. The regression line gives the average prediction that can be made from the selection score to the subsequent job performance. In this example, a person who scores 9.5 on the test would be expected to be given a rating of 7.5 for his or her subsequent work performance.

If the prediction were perfect, all of the points on the graph would lie on the regression line. Of course, no selection method is perfect. While most points lie close to the regression line,

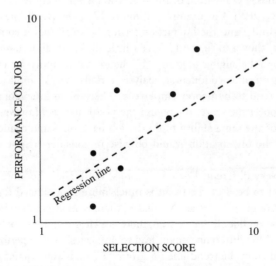

Figure 12.2 A hypothetical scattergram with a trend line.

some are further away. The more the points are away from the regression line, the less accurate is the selection system. The distance of each point from the regression line is called the
residual. The residuals of each point are shown in figure 12.3: the 'average' of these residuals
(statistically, the average of the square of the residuals when the sign is preserved) is an index
of the accuracy of a selection method. Fairness can be defined in terms of the regression lines

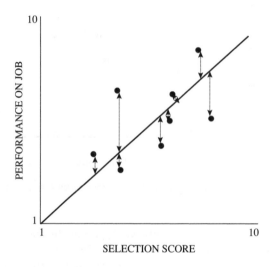

Figure 12.3 Residuals.

and residuals. In a fair system, if the 'average' residual for each group is calculated they should
be equal (and probably zero). However, the arithmetic is clumsy and takes time. Inspecting regression lines is quicker and more elegant. A regression line is fitted using the data from the majority group and a regression line is fitted for the minority group. If the method of selection is
fair, there should be no significant difference between the two regression lines. Thus, without
making any assumptions, examination of the regression gives unequivocal evidence of fairness
(Bartlett and O'Leary, 1969). For example, in figure 12.4, the trend lines for the two groups
'X' and 'Y' are very similar and the interaction term is so small that it could be due to chance.

The next situation, shown in figure 12.5, is a little different. For some reason known only
to the deity, able people belonging to group 'Y' choose not to apply for jobs in this organization. So, when the organization conducts an analysis, it finds that 'Y' applicants tend to do worse
on the test and they tend to be poorer employees. There is no interaction because there is a
uniform effect: the poorer the score, the poorer the performance. However, there is no unfairness because people of the same ability to do the job have the same chance of receiving a job
offer. (Nevertheless, the organization would be wise to consider why it is eschewed by able
people in group 'Y'.)

The third case is very different. For both groups, the higher the score, the higher the job
performance will tend to be. But the trend is much more pronounced for group 'X'. It is as
though the trend is stronger if one is an 'X'; that is, there is an interaction between group membership and the regression line. In figure 12.6, there is a clear difference between the trend lines
for the two groups and the difference might lead to unfairness. If the performance of people in
group 'X' is predicted from the trend line for group 'Y', their subsequent performance will be
seriously underestimated and group 'X' will be disadvantaged. If the performance of group 'Y'

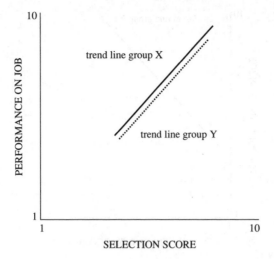

Figure 12.4 Regression lines for two groups, showing that selection is fair.

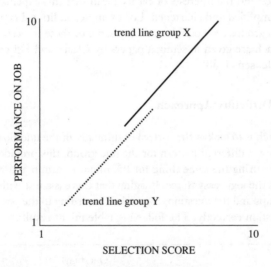

Figure 12.5 Trend lines for groups of unequal ability.

is predicted from the trend line of group 'X', their performance will be seriously overestimated and group 'Y' will receive favourable job offers.

Enthusiasts might wish to note that rather than relying on trend lines drawn by eye, Cohen and Cohen (1983, 313) recommend that an analysis of variance is computed with the selection score and group membership as independent variables. If the interaction term between the two independent variables is significant, the regression lines for the two groups are different, as in figure 12.6. If the interaction term is insignificant, any differences between the two regression lines are likely to be due to random fluctuations.

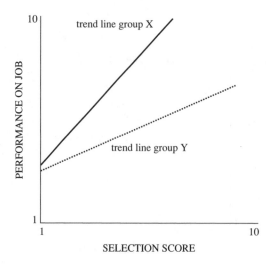

Figure 12.6 An example of trend lines indicating unfairness.

Limitations of space and the interests of clarity mean that this explanation of the regression approach has been simplified and shortened. For example, additional configurations of regression lines for the two groups are possible and only some of these indicate bias. More details of the regression approach are given in seminal papers by Cleary and Hilton (1968), Bartlett and O'Leary (1969) and Jensen (1980).

The Item Difficulty Approach

An alternative approach is to look at the pattern of difficulty of the questions for the two groups. If some questions show a different pattern for the one group, this provides evidence that these questions are not measuring the same thing for the minority group and may be unfair.

An example makes the logic easy to see. Imagine that there is a test with ten questions (A–J). It is given to two groups and the questions are ranked according to the percentage of each group that answers the question correctly. The following table might result:

	Question									
	A	B	C	D	E	F	G	H	I	J
Majority rank	1	2	3	4	5	6	7	8	9	10
Minority rank	1	8	2	4	3	5	7	6	10	9
Difference	0	−6	1	0	2	1	0	2	−1	−1

An examination of the two sets of ranks reveals that nine of the questions show a similar pattern for both groups and only vary by small random fluctuations. However, question B has a very large difference. This suggests that question B is, for some reason, relatively much harder for the minority group – perhaps because it carries a different meaning or it requires specific knowledge.

12.2 BIAS IN CRITERIA

Bias is usually established by comparing selection scores with criteria that represent job performance. However, even near-perfect criteria are rare. There are fewest problems with objective criteria such as attendance or length of service. However, many criteria consist of, say, subjective ratings by a supervisor. It is possible that the supervisor's judgement is biased to the same degree as the method of selection and no bias becomes apparent. For example, a test that is biased against a group by 20% would, in theory, be easy to detect. However, if criterion scores, such as supervisors' assessments, also had a negative bias of 20%, the two sets of biases would match and there would be no apparent discrepancy. The possibility that subjective criteria contain more bias than objective criteria was investigated by Schmidt et al. (1973). Their results indicated that the concerns about subjective criteria were exaggerated and that there was little evidence that they show greater bias. However, it would be wise for investigations of the fairness of measures to include both objective and subjective criteria.

 ## 12.3 INTERNATIONAL GENERALIZATIONS

The overwhelming proportion of the research literature on ethnic bias is based on work from the USA. However, great care needs to be taken in generalizing the research results to other countries, because the national contexts may differ dramatically. With apologies for drastic oversimplifications, the situations in several countries may be summarized as follows:

- *The USA*: the colonists defeated and then dominated the indigenous population, whilst introducing, on the basis of slavery, an ethnic minority of Blacks.
- *Australia and New Zealand*: the colonists outnumbered the indigenous Aborigines (2%) and Maoris (10%).
- *India* historically includes a huge variety of ethnic groups, religions and languages, from the Indics in the north to the Tamils in the south.
- *Malaysia*: Malays (60%) have political hegemony, whilst the Chinese (30%) dominate commercial activities and there is a substantial proportion of people of Indian descent (10%).
- *The Republic of South Africa* has six ethnic groups, four of African origin (Nguni, Bantu, Venda and Thonga) and two of European descent – the Boers (Dutch) and the British.
- *Israel's* situation is perhaps the most complex of all, because shared religious beliefs have attracted immigrants from scores of countries, while the indigenous people are of Arabic descent (Encyclopaedia Britannica, 2000; Whitacker, 2000).

It is very unlikely that all parts of such a varied tapestry woven by the currents of history should conform to the paradigm that is applicable in the USA. Perhaps the best way to understand the differences in national contexts is to contrast the situations in two, very similar, cultures: the United Kingdom and the USA:

- *Size of ethnic minorities.* In the UK, about 7% of the population are from ethnic minority groups. In the USA, about 17% are from ethnic minority groups. This makes research on the topic much more difficult in the UK. A reasonable statistical analysis of fairness will need a sample of about 100 people from minority groups in the same job. A British organization therefore needs to have a job in which 1,500 people are employed before an analysis can be attempted, whereas a similar analysis can probably be conducted in an American organization with about 600 employees in a single job.

- *Origin of ethnic minorities.* The ethnic minority in the USA has a very predominantly African origin – with a rapidly growing number of people with Hispanic origins. In the UK, the origins of ethnic minorities are much wider. The largest group originate from the Indian subcontinent, but there are large numbers of people with Afro-Caribbean backgrounds. There are also notable numbers of Chinese and Irish. The greater diversity of origin adds to the difficulties in conducting research: each subgroup needs a separate analysis and few organizations have sufficient samples.
- *Historical factors.* The main wave of Black immigration to the USA took place predominantly between 1700 and 1860. Black Africans were taken to the USA involuntarily, as slaves, and would have been fairly representative of their 'ancestral' populations. They found themselves in an economic system built on slavery, subservience and rigid segregation (US slavery was abolished in 1863, but there were segregation laws until 1954). The main wave of arrival of UK ethnic groups took place in the 1950s, long after the British had abolished the slave trade in 1807 (France repealed slavery in 1848). There have never been segregation laws in the UK. Almost all of the ethnic minorities in the UK arrived voluntarily. Voluntary immigration probably involved a positive filter and the UK ethnic minorities are unlikely to be representative of their 'ancestral' populations: people with learning difficulties find emigrating 12,000 kilometres too daunting, but bright, able people can rise to the challenge.

The statistical aspects of bias are complex. This chapter has aimed to provide a straightforward explanation of the main approaches. However, when bias of tests or other measures used in selection are a practical issue, a more sophisticated approach and much larger samples, even for the minority group, are needed. It would be appropriate to refer to more specialist texts – especially Cohen and Cohen (1983).

CHAPTER 13

CALCULATING THE STERLING VALUE OF SELECTION (UTILITY ANALYSIS)

One of the biggest psychometric advances during the past two decades is in the methods of working out the cash benefits of better selection. A human resources manager or psychologist can now argue his or her case in the same terms as managers from other functions. This also means that quantitative techniques can guide the use of resources to obtain maximum effect (see Boudreau, 1989).

Before utility analysis, it was necessary to argue for better selection in terms that it was a 'good thing', or quote statistics such as correlation coefficients. Statistics mean little to decision-makers. They make directors' eyes glaze over when they are used to advocate better selection. Utility analysis transforms the situation and enables selectors to talk in a language that all organizational decision-makers understand – money! Many people say that 'money talks'. They are wrong. In most organizations, *money shouts*. Utility calculations may take three forms: individual selections, the Brogden–Hunter method and the Taylor–Russell method.

13.1 CALCULATIONS FOR INDIVIDUAL SELECTIONS

It will be recalled from section 8.7 that a correlation of, say, .5 between predictor and criterion means that every one standard deviation increase in test score will result in an improvement of .5 standard deviations in job performance. In high-value jobs, the standard deviation of performance can be as much as $1,000,000, so the difference between two candidates who are separated by three IQ points can turn out to be $100,000 per year ($3/15 \times 1,000,000 \times .5$) – an excellent return on the costs of testing, which are unlikely to exceed $500.

Worthwhile gains can also be achieved for mundane occupations. A hotel chain had a vacancy for a painter and decorator. By examining its records for all its current decorators, it established that the standard deviation of performance was worth £7000 per year. There were six applicants. After inspection of application forms, references and interviews, there were three who seemed equal. The hotel asked the three applicants to compete a work-sample test that has a validity of .53. The following table was produced:

	Test score Z scores	Likely performance Z scores	Likely money value (£)
Male A	−.5	−.27	−1,855
Male B	.2	1.10	742
Female C	1.0	.53	3,710

Slightly against prevailing tradition, the hotel chain appointed the female, thereby gaining work to the extra value of £5,565 or £2,968 per year, depending upon whether they would otherwise have chosen male A or male B. The gains, which would last as long as the success-ful applicant remained in their service, represent an excellent return on the average cost of £300 for administering the work-sample test.

13.2 THE BROGDEN–HUNTER METHOD

Hunter built on the work of Brogden and devised a formula for estimating the money value of selection if employees can be evaluated on a continuous scale. The formula is:

$$utility = \frac{\theta}{p} \times r \times sd \times t \times n - c$$

where θ is the ordinate at the selection ratio, p is the selection ratio as a proportion, r is the validity of the selection method, sd is the money value of a standard deviation, t is the average tenure, n is the number of posts and c represents the costs.

This formula is initially daunting to anyone without a PhD in mathematics. However, it becomes straightforward if it is broken down into six stages.

Stage 1: Selection at Random

The first stage is to envisage what would happen if the choice between a large group of can-didates was made at random, using a pin. The job performance is likely to form a normal dis-tribution, centred on the mean performance. For convenience, the distribution of performance can be depicted as a standard normal distribution with a mean of zero and a standard deviation of 1, as shown in figure 13.1.

Stage 2: Estimate the Value of Perfect Selection

This starts with establishing the selection ratio (see section 6.1). If the selection ratio is 3:1, a perfect selection process would choose the top 33% (the top .33) of the normal distribu-tion. The question arises, 'What would be the average production of the group who are cho-sen by perfect selection?' Fortunately, an elegant solution exists. The ordinate at the selection ratio is established from normal curve tables and the result is substituted into the following formula:

$$sd\ improvement = \frac{\theta}{p}$$

where θ is the ordinate and p is the proportion (see figure 13.2).

For example, a sanitation services company has three applicants for each sales representative vacancy. Normal curve tables show that the ordinate at the point dividing the normal curve 67:33 is .36. Applying the formula:

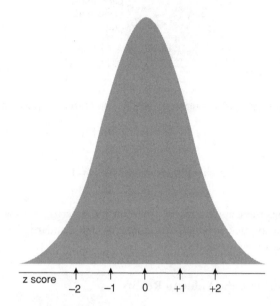

Figure 13.1 Selection at random.

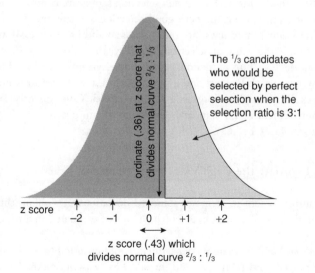

Figure 13.2 Perfect selection.

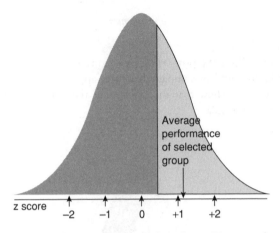

Figure 13.3 The average performance of people selected by a perfect method.

$$sd\ improvement = \frac{\theta}{p} = \frac{.36}{.33} = 1.1$$

So, a company that has three applicants for every job and a perfect method of selection would engage people whose average productivity would be 1.1 standard deviations above those selected at random, as shown in figure 13.3.

Stage 3: Estimate the Value in Reality

At the end of stage 2, the average productivity of those selected by a perfect method is known. However, no selection method is perfect. When selection scores are compared with subsequent performance, the correlation, even for very good selection systems, rarely exceeds .7. Some methods, such as traditional interviews, are quite abysmal and have a measly validity of about .15. In order to estimate the value of selection in reality, the value for perfect selection must be reduced by some factor. The reduction factor is the system's validity. For example, the sanitation company uses an ability test and a personality test that measures integrity to select sales representatives. This combination has a validity of .65. Consequently, perfect selection would yield an improvement of 1.1 standard deviations, but in practice the improvement falls to .72 standard deviations (1.1 × .65).

Stage 4: Estimate the Cash Value per Person per Year

Stage 3 yields an improvement in terms of standard deviations. To obtain the *cash value*, we need to know what a standard deviation is worth. It can be estimated in a number of ways:

- *The empirical method*: the accounts department could be asked to work out the output of, say, 100 employees and then calculate the sd. This was the method used by the hotel chain mentioned in section 13.1.

- *Supervisor estimates*: a sample of, say, 12 supervisors could be asked to estimate the output of an average employee and an employee who is better than 85% of employees. As the 85th percentile is one standard deviation from the mean, it is easy to estimate the value of a standard deviation by subtracting the average value from the value produced by an employee at the 85th percentile. Devotees also ask supervisors to estimate the value produced by a poor employee at the 15th percentile (one standard deviation below average) and they adjust their calculations accordingly.
- *The 40% rule*: on average, a standard deviation of performance is about equal to 40% of the employee's salary. (Enthusiasts might like to note that for a less demanding job the standard deviation of performance is likely to be .2 times the remuneration package, while for highly skilled job the standard deviation of performance is likely to exceed .6 times the remuneration package.) Consequently, the improvement per person per year is:

$$improvement\ pp\ per\ yr = sd\ improvement \times money\ value\ of\ sd$$

The remuneration package for a sanitation sales representative is £30,000 per year. It is not appropriate to ask the accounts department to calculate the standard deviation of sales per representative and there are only four supervisors, so a survey of their estimates would be unstable. Consequently, the company decides to estimate the standard deviation of performance, using the 40% rule as £12,000 (£30,000 × .40).

If the standard deviation of performance of the sales representatives is £12,000 and the average person selected by an ability test and an integrity test is likely to be .72 standard deviations above the mean, the cash value of using the tests is likely to be £8,580 (£12,000 × .72) per person per year.

Enthusiasts might wish to look up other methods of estimating the value of a standard deviation of performance – especially the Casio and Ramos (1986) CREPID method.

Stage 5: Estimate the Value for the Work Group

Selection systems are rarely applied to one person and an average employee rarely stays for exactly one year. Therefore, the result of the previous stage must be multiplied by the number selected and the average tenure:

$$group\ value = value\ per\ person\ per\ year \times N\ posts \times tenure$$

The organization inspects its records and finds that the average sales representative stays with the company for 2.5 years. It anticipates that the selection system will be used to choose ten representatives. Therefore, the group value is likely to be £214,500 (8,580 × 2.5 × 10).

Stage 6: Subtract Costs

A gain of £214,500 seems impressive, but selection systems do not appear out of thin air. The sanitation services company paid a consultant a fee of £12,000 to analyse the job and devise a selection system. The company also paid £9,000 for two members of its staff to be trained to use the system. Furthermore, it costs about £300 to test each of the 30 applicants (£9,000 in total) needed to yield ten suitable representatives. The total cost of selecting 30 representatives is therefore £30,000. This cost must be subtracted from the gains:

$$Organizational\ Value = Group\ Value - Costs$$

The sanitation services company therefore stands to gain £184,500 by selecting sales representatives using the tests rather than selecting them at random.

13.2.1 REFINING THE ESTIMATES

In an ideal world, these results would be refined by taking three more factors into account:

- The *discount rate*, to take into account the effects of inflation. The costs of selection are borne up front, while the benefits accrue over many years, by which time the value of the currency might have declined.
- *Taxes*: because they pay no taxes, selection has a bigger benefit for non-profit-making organizations.
- *Service costs*: good employees usually cost more in terms of support or equipment. For example, good sales representatives may use more literature and claim higher mileage expenses.

13.2.2 PRESENTING THE RESULTS

The results of a utility analysis can be presented in a number of ways. Some organizations prefer results to be presented in terms of the return on investment. For example, other functions in the sanitation services company cost their projects in terms of returns on capital investment. Some organizations prefer to judge investments on the 'payback period'. The sanitation services company calculates that it will take about 16 months for the selection system to pay for itself.

13.2.3 SENSITIVITY ANALYSES

Unfortunately, situations change. The number of recruits may increase or decrease, and salary or selection costs can change. Some kind of sensitivity analysis to establish the likely range of outcomes is therefore desirable. The simplest kind of sensitivity analysis repeats the calculations, using:

- the most *likely* estimates (the central estimate which was obtained in the above calculations)
- the most *pessimistic* estimates
- the most *optimistic* estimates.

13.2.4 COMPARING SYSTEMS RATHER THAN RANDOM SELECTION

Calculations using the Brogden–Hunter method give the improvement over random selection. However, few firms select at random. The sanitation services company currently selects its sales representatives by traditional interviews, which have a validity of about .15. The organization calculates that traditional interviews save about £46,500 per ten vacancies. Thus the gain from scrapping the interview system and installing an ability test plus an integrity test will be £138,000 (£184,500 – £46,500).

Utility calculations can also be used to make strategic decisions about deployment of resources. They can give more objective answers to questions such as whether it would be better to devote £80,000 to develop and install an assessment centre for management, or whether the £80,000 should be used to develop a work-sample test for operatives. Many people believe that the main contribution of utility calculations is to aid such strategic decisions on the deployment of resources.

An excellent description of the historical development of this method, which is often called the Brogden–Cronbach–Gleser method, is given by Schmitt and Chan (1998).

 ## 13.3 THE TAYLOR–RUSSELL METHOD

The Brogden–Hunter method may not be appropriate because performance is not always on a continuous scale. For example, a police officer either 'upholds the law in an appropriate way' or 'does not uphold the law in an appropriate way' – an officer who issues 200 speeding tickets per week is not necessarily better than one who issues only 20 speeding tickets. Similarly, there are many jobs that are automated, and the distinction lies between employees who can keep up with the system and those who cannot. The Taylor–Russell method is an older and simpler way of calculating utility that may be used in these situations. It needs three pieces of information:

- the validity of the selection system
- the percentage of workers who would be satisfactory if they were selected from applicants at random – in essence, this is a measure of the difficulty of the job
- the number of people applying for each job (the selection ratio).

Tables are consulted to determine the improvement produced by the selection device. Full tables, published by Lawshe et al. (1958), are usually reproduced in texts such as Smith and Robertson (1993) and Guion (1965). The extract shown in table 13.1 gives an impression of the fuller tables.

Table 13.1 Expectancies when 30% of those selected by chance would be acceptable workers

Validity	Selection ratio				
	Top 20%	Top 40%	Top 60%	Top 80%	100%
.2	40	37	34	32	30
.4	51	44	39	34	30
.6	64	52	42	36	30

To use the tables:

1   Estimate the level of difficulty of the job by establishing how many people selected by chance could do the job. For an easy job, 70% of people chosen at random could be expected to be satisfactory. For an average job, 50% of people would be satisfactory. The extract shown in table 13.1 gives information for a rather difficult job where only 30% of random applicants would be satisfactory.
2   Estimate the selection ratio.
3   Estimate the validity of the selection system.

It is then possible to locate the percentage of applicants selected by the system who could be expected to be successful. The success rate of the system can then be compared to the success rate of random selection.

For example, a police force may envisage recruiting 100 constables. It is a difficult job that only 30% of applicants can perform. There are many applicants and the force can choose one out of five – a selection ratio of 20%. A combination of situational interviews and written tests with a validity of .6 is used. Tables show that 64% of the applicants chosen would be successful. A commissioner in charge of the finances calculates that each recruit who subsequently fails training costs £10,000. Selecting 100 applicants at random would produce 70 failures, wasting a total of £700,000. The force's selection system of situational interviews and tests produces 64 successes and 36 failures, wasting a total of £360,000. The selection system therefore saves the force £340,000 for every 100 people it recruits.

PART III

ASSESSMENT TOOLS

CHAPTER 14

CHOICE OF SELECTION METHODS

Once the person specification has been produced, it is necessary to decide how each character-istic can be measured. It is best to measure each 'essential' or 'desirable' characteristic men-tioned in the person specification by at least two methods, so that the shortcomings of an individual method have some chance to cancel out.

 14.1 THE AVAILABLE RANGE OF SELECTION METHODS

Many methods of measurement are available and most of them will be described in more detail in later chapters. However, it will be useful if the main measures are listed at this stage, in order to give an overview. They are as follows:

- Written psychometric tests and their construction are described in more detail in chap-ters 15 and 16, respectively. The main types of tests are:
    - psychomotor
    - cognitive ability (intelligence, reasoning)
    - personality
    - motivation and interests.
- Computer-aided testing and e-selection is described in chapter 17.
- Other scientific methods (chapter 18) include:
    - work samples (work try-out or practical demonstrations), such as presentations, in-trays (in-baskets), role plays, leaderless group discussions (LGDs), trade tests (for the job of typist, bricklayer, joiner, mechanic and so on) and trainability tests
    - situational and structured interviews
    - biodata
    - descriptions by others (L data)
    - future autobiographies
    - Repertory Grids
    - objective measures.
- Less scientific methods (chapter 19) include:
    - traditional interviews
    - references

- application forms and CVs
- graphology, astrology and so on.
• Assessment centres, which are described in chapter 20, combine several methods of selection.

• In addition, selection may involve:
  - medical examination
  - special enquiry (for example, security clearance or conviction record)
  - inspection of documents and certificates.

Table 14.1 may help to determine which measures are most appropriate.

14.2 OTHER ASPECTS

Other factors that need to be taken into account when choosing measures are described in greater detail in chapters 9–13. They include the following:

• acceptability to candidate, organization, selector and pressure groups
• practicality (that is, costs, time, equipment, training and flexibility)
• sensitivity
• reliability
• validity
• fairness.

Table 14.1 Appropriate selection measures for points of Rodger's Seven Point Plan

Person specification	Adequate measures (possible measures in parentheses)	Inadequate measures
Physical make-up	Appearance, deportment and diction at interview Medical history Medical examination Colour vision test Strength tests; for example, dynamometer Work samples; for example, firefighter test (References; for example, illness record) (Declaration on application form)	Written tests Some work samples; for example, in-tray exercises
Attainments	Application form Inspection of certificates, licences and membership cards Academic references Situational interviews Attainment tests	All other methods, including 'intelligence' tests Impromptu claims by applicant
General intelligence	Intelligence tests Work samples involving reasoning and analysis Situational questions involving reasoning and analysis (Academic referees)	All other methods

◤ 14.3 THE METHODS MATRIX

One way of making sure that measures are chosen on a systematic basis is to construct a selection matrix with the potential measures down the side and the requirements in the person specification along the top. Suppose, as a simplified example, that the person specification for an assistant personnel officer calls for clear diction, IPD accreditation and Certificates of Competence in Testing (qualifications), high general intelligence, good verbal ability, moderate assertiveness, good team skills and good presentation skills. The matrix shown in table 14.2 could be constructed.

The matrix can be inspected to make sure that each requirement is either measured twice or is measured by one very good index. The matrix also highlights duplication. For example, in the example matrix qualifications are measured three times. It might be possible to rationalize the process by relying on the application form and inspection of certificates, thus making fewer demands on referees. Similarly, the traditional interview duplicates much of the information obtained from the situational interview and the traditional interview could thus be eliminated. Furthermore, the in-tray may be eliminated, because it only measures one characteristic and that characteristic is measured quite adequately elsewhere. A blank copy of the matrix is given on the website associated with this text, and it can be photocopied and used in specific selection exercises.

Thus an appropriate selection process for the position of assistant personnel officer might be a one-day process involving a situational interview, a presentation, a leaderless group discussion, a cognitive test and a personality test. It might also include examination of appropriate certificates.

Table 14.1 *Continued*

Person specification	Adequate measures (possible measures in parentheses)	Inadequate measures
Special aptitudes	Aptitude tests Relevant work samples Relevant situational questions (References) (Application forms)	All other methods – especially naïve questions at traditional interviews
Interests	Interest tests (Application forms) (Probed questions at interview) (References)	All other methods
Disposition	Skilled observation on prolonged work samples or assessment centre Personality tests Tests of motives and values Group discussions (References) (Application form)	Observations in short traditional interviews, informal encounters
Circumstances	Skilful but direct questioning at interview Questions on application form	All other methods

Table 14.2 A methods matrix for the post of assistant personnel officer

	Diction	Qualifications	Intelligence	Verbal ability	Team skills	Assertiveness	Presentation	Times used
Psychomotor test								
Cognitive ability test			✓	✓				2
Personality test					✓	✓		2
Motivation and interests test								
Presentation work sample	✓						✓	2
In-tray work sample			✓					1
Role-play work sample								
Group discussion work sample					✓	✓		2
Trade test work sample								
Trainability work sample								
Situational/structured interview	✓		✓	✓	✓		✓	5
Biodata								
Description by others								
Repertory Grid								
Objective measures								
Traditional interview	✓						✓	2
References		✓						1
Application form and CV		✓						1
Assessment centre								
Medical examination								
Special enquiry								
Inspection of documents		✓						1
Times measured	3	3	3	2	3	2	3	

CHAPTER 15

PSYCHOMETRIC TESTS 1

BASIC CONCEPTS

Tests are one of the most scientifically rigorous methods of measuring peoples' characteristics. They form a very large topic, which occupies several chapters. This chapter deals with the basic concepts of psychometric tests. They are considered under five headings:

1   Definitions of tests
2   Work-sample (analogous) tests versus psychometric (analytical) tests
3   When not to use psychometric tests
4   Types of psychometric tests
5   Choosing between tests

Subsequent chapters explain test construction (chapter 16) and computerized testing (chapter 17).

15.1 DEFINITIONS OF TESTS

The many definitions of texts include the following:

> a standard, portable stimulus situation, containing a standard instruction and mode of response, in which a consenting subject is measured on their response in a predefined way, the measure being designed and used to predict other behaviour elsewhere (Cattell, 1986)

> a systematic procedure for observing behaviour and describing it with the aid of numerical scales or fixed categories (Cronbach, 1970)

> essentially an objective and standardised measure of a sample of behaviour (Anastasi, 1988)

Drawing together common elements, tests may be defined as *carefully chosen, systematic, standardized procedures for evoking a sample of responses from a candidate, which are evaluated in a quantifiable, fair and consistent way*. This definition contains five components that need to be discussed in greater detail:

• Tests are *carefully chosen* and *systematic*. Tests are not haphazard procedures. They are constructed according to rigorous procedures, which should ensure that they are relevant to a clearly defined domain and that the measures they produce have certain desirable properties, such as reliability, validity and fairness.

- Tests follow *standardized procedures*. Tests try to make as many things as possible the same, so that little error can creep in from subtle differences in the way in which people are treated. This standardization usually means that all candidates are:
  - Faced with identical (or at least equivalent) tasks. There is no question of some candidates being subjected to an easier procedure than other candidates. This is dissimilar to traditional interviews, where some candidates may be asked questions concerning easy topics while others may be asked questions concerning difficult and intricate topics.
  - Given identical instructions. There is no possibility that some candidates are given more help than others.
  - Required to perform in very similar settings. All candidates should be tested in a quiet office environment, where there are no interruptions and help is not available.
  - Have their responses evaluated in an identical (or at least equivalent) way. There is no question that some candidates should get an easy marker while others have a strict marker.
- *The questions or other stimuli that evoke responses are only a sample* of all possible questions or stimuli. A typical test of arithmetic will contain, say, 100 questions out of an infinite number of possible additions, subtractions, multiplications and divisions. Other things being equal, a large sample of questions is good. As a rule of thumb, about 19 questions are needed in order to sample a domain reliably (see chapter 16). The comparison between the number of questions asked in a test and the number used in some other selection measures is stark. A typical interview, for example, will devote only two or three questions to a single domain. Personality tests may devote between seven and 19 questions to a domain, while ability tests usually devote more than 50 questions.
- Tests *evoke responses from candidates*, who must do something that can be evaluated. This contrasts with selection methods such as references, biodata and astrology, where the candidate is passive.
- Test scores are compared and *evaluated in the light of scores from a substantial sample that is representative of similar people*. Tests are usually calibrated on a sample of several hundred people (see chapter 22). These comparisons add precision and enable statements such as 'Kiran is in the top 10% of applicants in terms of numerical reasoning'.

When these requirements are not met, the term 'test' should not be used. Instead, 'scale', 'inventory' or 'questionnaire' should be used. Many test publishers reserve the term 'test' for tests of ability, and do not use it in connection with their personality measures.

▲ 15.2 WORK-SAMPLE (ANALOGOUS) TESTS VERSUS PSYCHOMETRIC (ANALYTICAL) TESTS

Two types of measure, work-sample tests and psychometric tests, qualify for the title 'test'.

Work-sample tests simply try to *mimic the behaviour* required in a given job. They do not try to understand the characteristics needed. Often, work-sample tests are more accurate in specific situations because they capture the specific details and context of the job. However, their use is often restricted to a narrow range of occupations, and they may be useless in measuring a candidate's suitability for jobs that appear different but that, in fact, require similar attributes. These tests are often called **analogous** tests, because they simply aim to copy the requirements of a job without understanding them.

Psychometric tests attempt to analyse a person in terms of *fundamental psychological characteristics*, such as ability or personality. This has the advantage that the results can be used over a range of jobs that have different contexts and situations, but which require the same basic competencies. These tests are often called **analytical** tests, because they aim to analyse the fundamental characteristics that underlie behaviour. This and the next two chapters consider psychometric tests in substantial depth. Work-sample tests are considered in chapter 18.

 ## 15.3 WHEN NOT TO USE PSYCHOMETRIC TESTS

Psychometric tests have many advantages. However, they are not a universal solution to a selection or guidance problem. In many situations, other measures will be better. Alternatives should be considered when the person specification calls for the following:

- *Impact on others*, such as creating a good impression, inspiring others, empathy and gaining the confidence of others (although some personality tests may be relevant, because they measure aspects such as energy and emotional responsiveness). In these cases, a role-play or group exercise may be a better measure.
- *Oral communication*, such as giving and receiving directions, or giving presentations. In these cases, a role-play or presentation exercise may be a better measure.
- *Physical ability*, such as physical fitness, and freedom from communicable diseases. In these cases, a physical test such as a dynamometer, a simulation of an arduous physical task (for example, carrying a sack that weighs the same as an adult up a ladder) or a medical examination may be a better measure.
- *Operating specific pieces of equipment*, such as a fork-lift truck or computer. In these cases, a practical demonstration of the use of the equipment may be better.
- *Past experience and employment* record. In these cases, an application form, questions at an interview and referees' reports may give better information.
- *Educational and other qualifications*. In these cases, an inspection of certificates and other documents (originals should be requested) may give better information.
- *Strategic thinking and complex problem-solving*. Elements of problem-solving may be captured by some tests. However, when a strategic view of a complex problem requires the evaluation, integration and synthesis of many elements, other measures such as case studies or report writing may be more appropriate.

15.4 TYPES OF PSYCHOMETRIC TESTS

If it is clear that psychometric tests are appropriate, the question arises, 'Which psychometric test should be used?' Psychometric tests are categorized in three main ways, according to:

- the psychological characteristic measured
- the method of measurement
- the qualifications of the user.

15.4.1 TESTS CATEGORIZED ACCORDING TO PSYCHOLOGICAL CHARACTERISTIC

Most test publishers organize their catalogues according to the psychological characteristic that the test attempts to measure. The categories are usually arranged in the following order: sensory-motor and sensory acuity tests; mental ability tests; personality tests; and tests of interest and motivation. Some of the suppliers of the various tests are indicated by initials in brackets when the tests are mentioned. The full names of suppliers are given in appendix 15.1. More complete contact details are given on the website associated with this book. Tests will, of course, only be supplied to qualified users.

Sensory-motor Ability and Sensory Acuity Tests

Sensory-motor ability is usually required for jobs such as packing where, for example, fairly small cylinders need to be placed quickly and accurately into containers. It is also required for many textile occupations, where yarn or fabric needs to be positioned on to needles, and it is relevant to many assembly jobs – especially assembly jobs in the electronics industry. Sensory-motor ability is also required in technical jobs that involve the setting and calibration of equipment. Some tests of sensory-motor ability are as follows:

- The **Crawford Small Parts Dexterity Test** [PC] measures the ability to use tweezers and small screwdrivers. It is useful in organizations that assemble electrical components.
- **FINDEX** [SHL] is a test of finger dexterity
- **MANDEX** [SHL] is a test of manual dexterity
- The **Hand Tool Dexterity Test** [PC] consists of a wooden 'U' frame with holes through which a range of different nuts, screws and washers are fixed. Candidates are timed as they use spanners and screwdrivers to undo the nuts, screws and washers from the holes on one side of the 'U' frame and assemble them on the other side.
- The **Purdue Pegboard** [RLH] tests the speed and accuracy of finger movements. It is useful in many textile occupations. The Purdue Pegboard is, perhaps, the most frequently used sensory-motor test.

Some organizations have their own tests of hand–eye coordination, which require a candidate to steer an object along a twisting track. These tests are sometimes used to select people for occupations involving the driving of vehicles. Many military organizations have developed their own tests to measure such things as hand–eye–foot coordination in aircraft pilots.

Tests of **sensory acuity** include colour blindness tests. It is vital to use colour blindness tests in most jobs in the transport industry, because it is essential to distinguish between red, amber and green signals. These tests are also vital in many occupations that involve electricity, because it is essential to distinguish between wires that are often colour-coded. Testing for colour blindness is also important in jobs where the product involves some aspect of design, such as floor coverings, furnishing fabrics, clothing and decorations. There are two main types of tests of colour blindness – Isochromatic Plates and Disc Arrangement Tests:

- **Isochromatic Plates** consists of a series of pages, each of which contains a circle that is completely filled by hundreds of smaller circles. These smaller circles are coloured in such a way that to those with normal colour vision a number, such as 29, stands out from the pattern. However, to people who are colour blind, all of the circles appear to be a uniform grey and the number either cannot be seen or a different number, such as 52, is apparent. An Isochromatic Plate test can be used to detect both red–green colour blindness and purple–grey colour blindness. The most famous test of this type is the **Ishihara Isochromatic Plates**. The **Dvorine Isochromatic Plates** are also widely used.

- **Disc Arrangement Tests** are a series of small discs that shade from one colour to the next. They are presented in a scrambled order and the candidate is asked to put them into the right sequence of shades. The candidate's order can be compared to an objective sequence and a numerical score obtained. These tests are useful when it is necessary to place a person's colour acuity on a scale, rather than into simple categories such as 'colour blind', 'colour weak' or 'normal'. Disc arrangement tests have the advantage that it is impossible for a candidate to learn a series of correct answers. **The Farnsworth 100 Hue Test** is probably the best known of this type of test but the Roth 28 Hue Test is also in wide use.

Tests of visual acuity are used to detect, say, short-sightedness, long-sightedness and astigmatism. These tests are specialized, but they are readily available from an optician. Visual acuity is important in many jobs in the transport industry and in jobs that require extensive reading of text and plans. Tests of auditory acuity are also specialized. Some unusual occupations, such as astronaut, deep-sea diver and tightrope walker, may requires tests of the ability to judge spatial orientation and balance.

Tests of Mental Ability

Tests of mental ability are relevant to most jobs, because intelligence (see chapter 3) determines the rate at which people process information. In turn, processing of information controls the rate at which people learn the job (that is, training) and their ability to cope with new novel aspects of a job. Intelligence is more important in jobs that involve abstract thinking and in jobs where change is rapid. It is claimed that intelligence has become more important as computerization and information technology have increased. Many tests of intelligence are available from publishers. It is usually best to start with the most general type of mental ability test. If this is unsuitable, more specific abilities should be considered and, finally, tests for specific occupations and trades can be examined. The classification of ability tests is complicated, because some tests that measure specific abilities also combine the subscores to produce a global score. Furthermore, there are tests for different levels of ability, and some tests measure fluid intelligence while others measure crystallized intelligence. Many people divide ability tests into two types: tests of aptitude and tests of attainment.

Ability tests and **aptitude tests** attempt to measure a candidate's potential. In essence, they are used to predict *potential* and *future* performance. There are often connotations that aptitude tests measure some kind of innate ability. The exact difference between ability and aptitude is hard to discern. **Ability** generally refers to a broad talent that applies to a wide range of tasks: it is measured by 'general' tests that gauge verbal, numerical and spatial reasoning. **Aptitude** is generally a narrower concept that applies to the way in which a skill is actually used – probably in a work setting. Aptitudes are measured by tests that specifically focus upon narrow skills that have a clear connection to the world of work. Examples of aptitude tests would be technical checking and numerical estimation.

Table 15.1 A comparison of aptitude and attainment tests

	Aptitude tests	Attainment tests
Time	Future	Present
Questions	General content	Specific content
Attempts	Usually only one	As many as are needed
Uses	Future performance – the details of the job may change	Immediate performance – the details of the job are static
Typical tests	Many psychometric tests – especially aptitude tests	Many trade tests, work samples, licences

The aim of ability and aptitude tests is to make sure that everyone's experience is equal, through the use of general questions that everyone can comprehend. It is also necessary to ensure that people do not benefit from previous attempts at the test. Ability and aptitude tests are most useful when selection is made on the basis of potential – how someone might perform in the future after, say, a long training programme or after a number of unforeseen changes in the detail of the job.

Attainment (achievement) tests measure *present* performance, irrespective of how the present capability was acquired or how it might progress. They simply state what exists now. Attainment tests are most useful when the selection is made on the basis of who will be the best candidate as soon as they start work. Attainment tests are most useful for jobs that are unlikely to change in a significant way in the future. Attainment tests are suitable in situations in which there are clear, static criteria and in which, once attained, performance is unlikely to deteriorate. The questions in an attainment test will often be quite specific and will involve specialist terms or knowledge. Often, a person can take an attainment tests several times before he or she passes. The driving test is a clear example of an attainment test. It does not matter how long you take to learn to drive; the number of lessons you have or the number of attempts you make. If you pass, you pass. The main distinctions between aptitude and attainment tests are shown in table 15.1.

Unfortunately, the distinction between aptitude and attainment tests is rarely as clear-cut as table 15.1 implies. For example, the same arithmetic test can be used to measure attainment (how well the arithmetic syllabus has been learned) and to measure aptitude (how well a future syllabus can be learned). Some people say that the crucial distinction between aptitude and attainment lies in the *use* of the test, not in the test itself.

Another complication is that aptitude scores are often contaminated by attainment. It is impossible to measure aptitude on, say, verbal logic problems, until there has been adequate attainment in reading. Furthermore, most attainment tests *can* be used to make predictions about future performance. In practice, the distinction between tests of aptitude and tests of attainment is so useless that few test publishers bother. They lump tests into a single category, 'ability tests', and leave the user to sort out which is which. The distinction between tests of attainment and tests of aptitude is being abandoned in favour of the idea of a continuum (see figure 15.1). On one end are culture fair tests of reasoning ability. At the other end are highly specific course tests. The continuum also maps on to the division of intelligence into fluid and crystallized intelligence.

A comprehensive review of ability tests has been edited by Bartram (1997). The following compendium aims to provide a brief guide to some ability tests.

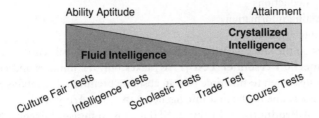

Figure 15.1 The aptitude–attainment continuum.

Some Tests of General Ability

- The **Weschler Adult Intelligence Scale** [PC] is the doyen of ability tests. It contains 11 subscales that capture both fluid and crystallized intelligence, and these are summed to provide a global IQ score. The test is administered on a one-to-one basis and advanced training is needed.
- **Raven's Progressive Matrices (RPM)** [ACER, OPP, NZCER, TA] is an excellent, well-researched test that is saturated with 'g' and fluid intelligence. It is a group test and it involves very little linguistic skill or cultural background. It is therefore very useful when testing people from different countries or backgrounds. It is often used in conjunction with the **Raven's Vocabulary Scale**, which gives a good measure of crystallized intelligence. There are four versions of the RPM test:
  - the **Coloured RPM**, for use with children or lower-ability adults
  - the **Standard RPM**, for use with the general population
  - the **RPM Plus**, a newer standard version, which has more questions at the top end of the ability range
  - the **Advanced RPM**, for use with very able groups.
- The **AH** series of tests [ASE] is used quite widely in industry. There are three versions:
  - The **AH4** is the basic version, for use with the general population. It yields two scores: part 1 gives a verbal/numerical score, while part 2 yields an abstract reasoning score. The two parts are combined to yield a global score.
  - The **AH5** is similar to the AH4, but is suitable for, say, the top 25% of the population.
  - The **AH6** is also similar to the AH4, but is suitable for, say, the top 10% of the population (graduate level). The AH6 is available in two versions. The AH6(AG) is for arts graduates. The AH6(SEM) is suitable for graduates in science, engineering and mathematics because it has a third part, which measures diagrammatic reasoning.
- The **Thurstone Test of Mental Alertness** [RLH] is a good alternative to the AH4. It takes the same length of time, and yields language and quantitative scores that can be combined to provide a global score
- The **Watson Glaser Critical Thinking Appraisal** [PAR, PC] tries to assess the abilities needed for making good decisions. It is a very high level test, which is appropriate to, say, the top 5% of the population. It has five subtests:
  - making inferences
  - recognizing assumptions

- making deductions
- interpreting information
- evaluating arguments.

The scores on the subtests are combined to produce a global score.

- The **Wonderlic Personnel Test** [PAR] takes only 12 minutes and can be used with general groups when testing time is at an absolute premium. It contains 50 questions and its ancestor was one of the first intelligence tests – the Army Alpha.
- The **Test of Productive Thinking** [SHL] aims to measure fluency, breadth and originality in problem-solving. Typically, it is used with managerial populations. Responses are scored on three dimensions: fluency, number of lines of thought and originality. There are several versions of this test.

Some Tests of Numerical Ability

- The **Numerical Test** [ASE] from the General Ability Tests Battery is suitable for middle-range populations below graduate level.
- The **Numerical Ability Test** from the Differential Test Battery [PC] is also suitable for middle-range populations.
- The **NMG 1, 2, 3 and 4** tests from the Management and Graduate Item Bank [SHL] are designed to differentiate candidates in the upper 12.5% of the ability range.
- The **Numerical Reasoning Test** from the Graduates and Managerial Assessment battery [ASE] is designed for use with the top 12% of the population.

Some Tests of Verbal Ability

- The **Verbal Ability Test** from the General Ability Tests Battery [ASE] is suitable for middle-range populations.
- The **Verbal Reasoning Test** from the Graduates and Managerial Assessment Battery [ASE] is designed for used with the top 12% of the population.
- The **Mill Hill Vocabulary Scale** [OPP] is often used to accompany Raven's Progressive Matrices.

Some Tests of Spatial Ability

- The **Spatial Test** is from the General Ability Tests Battery [ASE] and is suitable for middle-range populations.
- The **Space Relations Test** from the Differential Aptitude Test Battery [PC] is suitable for middle-range populations.
- The **Spatial Reasoning Test** (SIT7) [SHL] measures a candidate's ability to visualize spatial relationships and is relevant to people working in technical occupations, such as designers and CAD/CAM operators.

Some Tests of Mechanical Reasoning

- The **Vincent Mechanical Diagrams Test** [NFER] is one of the best tests of mechanical reasoning. It gives diagrams of a contraption with levers and pulleys, and asks the candidate to predict what will happen if something is altered or changed in a specified way.

- The **Bennett Mechanical Comprehension Tests** [PC] are mid-range tests and have parallel forms (S and T) .
- The **Mechanical Reasoning Scale** from the Differential Aptitude Test [PC]. This seems more like an attainment test from a school physics course than a test of mechanical aptitude.
- The **Mechanical Reasoning Test** [ACER, NZCER] is primarily suited to school-leavers.
- The **Mechanical Comprehension** tests MTS3, MT4.1 and MT4.2 [SHL] measure the understanding of mechanical principles. The first of these tests is suitable for process control operators and technicians, while the latter two are parallel tests suitable for people with good school-leaving certificates.

Test Batteries for Specific Occupations and Trades

There are several major batteries of tests that can be used for specific occupational skills in sectors such as clerical occupations, information technology and computing skills:

- the **Revised General Clerical Test Battery** – GCT-R [PC]
- the **Modern Occupational Skills Tests** – MOST [ASE]
- the **Personnel Test Battery** – PTB [SHL]
- the **Computer Programmer Aptitude Battery** – CPAB [RLH]
- the **Information Technology Test Series** – ITTS [SHL].

Tables 15.2 and 15.3 indicate which batteries have tests that measure various occupational mental abilities.

Table 15.2 Tests measuring clerical abilities

	GCT-R	MOST	PTB
Checking	✔	✔✔✔	✔✔
			✔
Filing	✔	✔	✔✔
Calculation	✔	✔	✔✔
			✔✔
Error location	✔		✔✔
Estimation	✔	✔	
Problem-solving	✔		
Spelling	✔	✔	
Vocabulary	✔	✔	
Language use	✔		
Comprehension	✔		
Decision-making (applying rules)		✔	

Table 15.3 Tests measuring computing and IT abilities

	CPAB	ITTS
Verbal reasoning (using DP terms)	✔	✔
Reasoning (DP context)	✔	
Number ability	✔	✔
Diagramming	✔	✔✔
Computer checking		✔✔
Spatial reasoning		✔

In addition, SHL offer a number of tests for specific occupations:

- The **Automated Office Battery** has three parallel sets of tests suited for occupations such as account clerks and clerical supervisors. The three tests are numerical estimation, computer checking and coded instructions.
- **The Work Skills Series** consists of two suites of tests. The first is designed for use in *production situations* and has three tests: understanding instructions, working with numbers and visual checking. The second suite is designed for use in the *transport industry* and contains four tests: using information, number skills, working with words and checking information.
- The **Customer Contact Aptitude Series** (CCAS) contains two verbal tests (VCC1 and VCC3) and two numerical tests (NCC2 and NCC4) that can be used with sales and customer-facing staff.

Tests and Inventories of Personality

Tests of personality may be useful because some jobs require different styles of behaviour. A fuller discussion of personality theory is given in chapter 4. A style of behaviour might arise in two main ways:

- It is a stable function of personality and is an aspect of the person. It is likely to endure over a significant time and over a wide range of circumstances. This kind of behaviour pattern is usually called a **trait**.
- It is a transient state that reflects the environment and will only endure as long as the perception of the environment remains the same. This kind of behaviour pattern is usually called a **state**.

To illustrate the distinction between trait and state, the classic example is anxiety. **Trait anxiety** arises because a person has an anxious personality and exhibits anxiety in many situations, over many years. It is sometimes called endogenous anxiety. In selection, trait anxiety might be important when choosing people for a job such as airline pilot. **State anxiety** arises from an uncertain or threatening environment (for example, a painful, medical operation or perhaps unwanted redundancy). Anxiety is not present in other situations and it passes once the environment returns to 'normal'. It is sometimes called exogenous or reactive anxiety. In selection, state anxiety (for example, test nerves) is regarded as a nuisance and a source of error variance,

Table 15.4 A comparison of tests of traits and states

Feature	Trait questions	State questions
Transparency	Opaque – the meaning is not obvious to the test taker	Transparent – the point of the question is obvious to the test taker
Range of questions	Cover a wide range of situations and may therefore have low internal consistency (for example, alpha) but high test–retest reliability	Cover a narrow range – often there is rewording of the same situation; both alpha and test–retest reliabilities will be very high
Focus of questions	Ask people how they generally behave	Ask people how they feel or behave now or at a stated, specific time

which we try to combat by calming applicants down and establishing rapport. Measurement of state anxiety is generally important in gauging short- and medium-term effects of interventions such as counselling or experimental treatment. There may be an *interaction* between trait and state anxiety. An anxious person facing a threatening environment may 'go through the roof' and exhibit exponential debilitating, anxiety. A stable person facing a benign environment may lapse into complacency. If a candidate is likely to be rejected because he or she has high anxiety, the environment should be checked for anxiety-provoking events and an allowance made. However, almost all candidates will claim an anxious environment if it means a better-paid job, so allowances should be infrequent. No allowance should be made for state anxiety aroused by testing. Testing should be a standardized situation – differences between candidates therefore reflect trait anxiety or wider environmental factors. Tests of traits and states may be contrasted as shown in table 15.4.

A number of questionnaires have been developed by Speilburger to distinguish trait and state personality characteristics. They are usually used in a clinical setting and they include:

- the State–Trait Anxiety Inventory (STAI)
- the State–Trait Anger Scale (STAS)
- the State–Trait Anger Expression Scale Inventory (STAXI).

McReynolds (1968) developed an adjective check-list to measure state characteristics. It gives people a long list of adjectives and asks them to tick those that describe the way they feel *now*. It is claimed that projective tests such as the TAT are particularly sensitive and useful in detecting personality states. Tests of personality states are rarely, if ever, used in selection. They may be used in a small minority of counselling situations, where it is important to chart a client's progress. They may be used more frequently in research – especially when the research is evaluating treatments or experimental manipulations.

The measurement of traits is dominated by the 'Big Five' factors. Many trait tests that originated before the 'Big Five' can use equations to produce 'Big Five' scores. The main difference between the personality tests lies between those that simply measure the 'Big Five' factors and those that measure subcomponents of the 'Big Five'. In general, it is better to start with tests that focus upon the 'Big Five' factors, because they are simpler to use and may give a clearer picture.

Some Tests of Personality Giving Subscales for 'Big Five' Factors

- The **16PF** [ACER, EdITS, NZCER, OPP] has a long history, the current version being the fifth. The test reports 16 factors of personality that can be combined to give scores on the 'Big Five' personality factors and impression management. The items are rather less transparent than those of the OPQ. This test is supported by an unparalleled amount of research evidence. The scales of the **15PF** [PT] have similarities to those scales of the 16PF, but there is no measure of intelligence.
- The **Occupational Personality Questionnaire** [SHL] is a suite of questionnaires that include some ipsative versions. Probably the most widely used is the Concept 5 (now OPQ32n), which is non-ipsative and reports 32 aspects of personality in three domains: relationships with people, thinking style and emotions. It also has a scale that measures social desirability. The OPQ is very attractively produced and has excellent support, but is expensive and requires an annual licence fee. The vocabulary is appropriate for a work setting, but the questions are very transparent. Norms are good.
- The **NEO Five Factor Inventory** [ACER, ASE, NZCER, PAR, TA] was specifically devised on the basis of research findings. It gives scores for the five factors and their components. It is relatively little used in the United Kingdom and the norms are American.

Some Personality Tests that Give 'Big Five' Scores

- The **Eysenck Personality Scales**, mainly the EPQ-R [ACER, EdITS, HS, NZCER], takes only 10–15 minutes to complete and is useful when time is at a premium or where a second personality test is needed as a cross-check. It gives scores for extroversion, neuroticism and psychoticism, and a lie scale.
- The **Quintax Personality Questionnaire** [SR] yields scores for each of the five main personality factors plus a score for social desirability. The test has 72 questions and takes 15–20 minutes to administer. A very useful feature is a series of excellent feedback sheets, which cover all combinations of factors.
- The **Hogan Personality Inventory** [HAS, PSC, RH] is a well-established test that yields eight scores. Five of these scores are closely related to the 'Big Five' personality factors. The remaining scores concern scholarship, ambition and a validity scale that checks whether the test has been completed properly. The primary scores can be used to obtain occupational scores such as Service Orientation, Clerical Potential, Sales Potential and Managerial Potential. It is also possible to obtain scores for Stress Tolerance and Reliability. The test has 168 items and takes about 50 minutes to complete (Hogan and Hogan, 1992a).
- The **Myers–Briggs Type Indicator** [NZCER, OPP] is widely used but measures only four of the 'Big Five' Personality factors (it omits one of the largest factors, emotional stability). Furthermore, despite recent revisions it is based on a psychoanalytic-type theory that is now in some doubt. The test also rather rigidly places people in one of 16 pigeon-holes.

Some personality tests focus on the disposition needed for specific occupations. These are called **narrow-spectrum personality tests**, and they include the HJ5 test, which is designed for the selection of staff involved in sales or service, and SHL's Customer Contact Styles Questionnaire. Narrow-spectrum personality tests usually yield subscores with titles such as:

- people focus – CCSQ [SHL]
- people manager [ASE]
- persuasive confidence [HJ]
- likes people, happy to serve [HJ]
- information handling – CCSQ [SHL]
- dependability – CCSQ [SHL]
- responsible, tidy-minded [HJ]
- stable [HJ]
- energy – CCSQ [SHL]
- alert [HJ]
- cross-cultural adaptability [RLH].

Narrow-spectrum tests have two main advantages. *First*, they are shorter than broad-spectrum tests, because questions on irrelevant facets of personality are eliminated. *Second*, the questions can be made more germane to specific occupations. This may increase acceptability and validity. Narrow-spectrum personality tests also have two disadvantages. A firm may need to purchase and keep stocks of an expensive array of personality tests in order to cover important occupations when, probably, a single broad-spectrum test could produce results of equal accuracy. Furthermore, narrow-spectrum personality tests have more limited use in vocational guidance and placement decisions.

Some narrow-spectrum personality tests are as follows:

- The **HJ5** [HJ] is a straightforward personality test for selecting staff for sales and service jobs. Administration takes 20–30 minutes and five scores relevant to these types of job are produced.
- The **Customer Contact Styles Questionnaire** [SHL] has two versions. It is based on an explicit competency model and yields 16 primary scales, which can be grouped into four broader areas, such as 'people focus' and 'dependability'.
- The **Element B** is a development of the **FIRO-B** [ACER, APP, CPP, OPP]. It focuses upon interpersonal behaviour, but it ignores other aspects of personality. Interaction at work.
- The **Kirton Adaptation Innovation Inventory** [ORC] measures cognitive style on an adaptation–innovation continuum.

Some other personality tests are as follows:

- Gough's **Adjective Checklist** [OPP] of consists of 300 adjectives or phrases, and people are asked to endorse those that apply to them. The test yields 37 scales, which include measures of needs, interpersonal relationships, thinking style, criterion scales and response styles.
- The **California Psychological Inventory** [OPP] is a well-established test. There are two versions, which yield scores on 20 dimensions of personality plus three 'type' scales. The longer version yields a further five indices, such as managerial potential, work orientation, leadership potential, social maturity and creative potential.
- The **Gordon Personal Profile Inventory** [ASE, CP] consists of 38 quasi-ipsative questions and returns scores on eight traits: responsibility, ascendancy, emotional stability, sociability, cautiousness, original thinking, personal relations and vigour.

- The **Morrisby Objective Personality Tests** (MO) are unusual because they are based on objective rather than self-report measures. There are four relatively short tests, which measure conceptual speed, perseveration, word fluency and fluency of ideas. The scores on these tests can be used to obtain scores on three personality dimensions: mental flexibility, type of confidence and balance of confidence.

Detailed examinations of a wide range of personality tests are provided by Bartram (1995a) and Lindley (2000).

Tests of Motivation and Interests

For many years, there was a dearth of good *motivation tests*. During this period, the best measure of motivation was probably the **Picture Story Exercise (PSE)**. The PSE was a development of the TAT projective test and gave scores for *n-ach*, *n-power* and *n-affil*. The results were acceptable, but the test took a long time to analyse. However, there has long been a good selection of tests of values. Tests of motives and values include the following:

- The **Motivation Questionnaire** [SHL] yields 18 scores divided into four domains: energy and dynamism (achievement, commercial outlook, fear of failure, level of activity, competition, power and immersion), synergy (affiliation, recognition, personal principles, personal growth and security), intrinsic motivations (interest, flexibility and autonomy) and extrinsic motivations (material reward, progression and status).
- The **Motivational Styles Questionnaire** [PC] is a new test, which is divided into two halves (Tarleton, 1998). The first half yields scores for needs in seven areas (achievement, independence, structure, affiliation, systems, people and personal). The second half yields three scores on the way in which a person will tackle everyday tasks (focus, caution and rate of starting).
- The **Motives, Values, Preferences Inventory** [HAS] has 200 items, which measure 'needs' for recognition, power, hedonism, altruism, affiliation, tradition, security, business, culture and rationality (Hogan and Hogan, 1996). The UK version is supported by good norms. The manual contains an excellent review of the concepts of interests.
- The **Rothwell–Miller Values Blank** [ACER, MT, TA] is an ipsative test that requires respondents to rank ten pentads according to their importance. The scale is very easy to administer and is quick to complete. It yields ipsative scores on five work values: financial rewards, job interest, security, pride in work and autonomy.
- The [Gordon] **Survey of Interpersonal Values** [ASE, RLH] is an ipsative test that measures the relative importance to an individual of support, conformity, recognition, independence, benevolence and leadership.
- The [Gordon] **Survey of Personal Values** [ASE, RLH] complements the Survey of Interpersonal Values. It is an ipsative test that measures the relative importance of values concerning practicality, achievement, variety, decisiveness, orderliness and goal orientation.
- The **Values at Work Test** [SHL] contains 72 items, which measure 12 values: influence, achievement, self-direction, wealth, enjoyment, adventure, harmony, aesthetics, diversity, affiliation, respect and certainty. The test is very new and a considered opinion is not yet possible. However, so far, it is looking good!

The choice among *interest tests* is wide. Care should be taken when using interest tests for selection. Many interest tests have items that are so transparent that they are easy to fake. Many interest tests are broad spectrum and are most appropriate to those who are looking very widely at jobs – typically young people between the ages of 16 and 25, who are entering or who have just entered the labour market. However, a few tests have a narrower spectrum and focus upon, say, advanced jobs or management jobs. Some interest tests are as follows:

- The **Career Pathfinder** [SHL] is a new test of interests that yields 30 scales, which can be grouped into six major domains: people, enterprising, data, resources, ideas and artistic. Each scale contains only five items, which aim to sample a whole domain, such as medical and health, sports, law and policy-making, entertaining and performing, and so on.
- The **Management Interest Inventory** [SHL] was unrivalled for use with management groups. It yielded both interest scores *and* experience scores for both functional areas (for example, production and finance) and management skills (for example, representing and collecting information).
- The **Kuder Interest Survey** [NCAS] is a well-established interest test that measures ten interests: outdoor, mechanical, computational, scientific, persuasive, artistic, literary, musical, social service and clerical.
- The **Rothwell–Miller Interest Inventory** [MT, TA] must represent the best value in terms of information yielded per minute of testing time. Although the test is ipsative, the large number of scales means that the dangers of ipsative tests are minimized. This is a general-level test that is most suitable for school-leavers, but it can be used on the general population.
- The **Strong Interest Inventory** [ACER, APP, OPP] is a classic, well-researched inventory that can be used in a wide range of settings. It provides a range of types of scores:
  - 25 areas of work; for example, data management
  - six themes; for example, investigative, social and enterprising
  - comparisons with scores for 211 occupations
  - four personal styles; for example, risk-taking and leadership style
  - seven administrative keys to identify invalid profiles.

15.4.2 CATEGORY OF TEST ACCORDING TO METHODS MEASUREMENT

Tests may also be categorized on the basis of the methods that they use to obtain data from candidates. Most categories are self-explanatory.

Group Tests versus Individual Tests

The vast majority of tests, such as Raven's Progressive Matrices, the 16PF, the OPQ or the FFI, used for selection purposes can be administered to several candidates simultaneously in a traditional examination setting. They are called 'group tests' and they are generally much cheaper than 'individual tests' such as the WAIS, which require one administrator to each candidate. Generally, group tests are pencil-and-paper tests, while individual tests usually involve equipment and testers trained to a higher level of competence.

Pencil-and-paper versus Apparatus Tests

Most tests used in occupational settings are pencil-and-paper tests. In general, these tend to be group tests. The use of apparatus tests is largely confined to tests of sensory-motor abilities or tests of sensory acuity.

Transparent versus Opaque (Direct versus Indirect)

Tests vary in the extent to which the questions are clearly related to the characteristics that they measure. At the transparent end of the spectrum are tests such as an arithmetic test, where the characteristic being measured is clear to all. Projective tests lie at the opaque end, where the link between the completed task and the inferences made from the responses are a mystery to all except those trained in projective testing. Opaque tests may be resistant to distortion. Since the candidate has little knowledge of how the test might work, he or she will find it difficult to manufacture the correct answer. However, very opaque tests may buy their resistance to distortion at the expense of acceptability and validity. Personality tests lie in the middle of this spectrum. Usually, it will be clear to a candidate that his or her personality is being measured, but the facet to which a question relates may be less clear. Some personality tests are more opaque than others. In general, tests developed specifically for occupational settings and tests that measure surface traits will be more transparent, and probably more susceptible to faking, than less opaque tests of personality.

Typical versus Maximal Performance

Some tests measure how a person usually reacts (typical performance), while others measure how people perform when they are trying to do their best (maximal performance). Measures of **typical performance** usually attempt to assess characteristics that affect *the way* in which we do things, such as:

- personality
- motivations
- interests
- beliefs.

Questions in typical performance tests ask us how we would *usually* behave, or what we would *normally* do, or how we would respond in *a large number (the majority)* of situations. There are usually no right or wrong answers in a strict sense. Tests of typical performance do not have rigid time limits and they usually encourage the person taking the test to be as honest as possible.

Measures of **maximal performance** usually attempt to measure *the best* we can do when we are making a conscious effort. They are concerned with characteristics such as:

- strength
- endurance
- speed of reasoning

Table 15.5 A comparison of typical and maximal tests

	Typical performance	Maximal performance
Characteristics measured	Personality, motives, interests and values	Physical power, logical power
Type of question	Asks how we usually do things	Ask us to do things
Type of answer	No right or wrong answers	Right and wrong answers
Time limits	Usually no time limits	Usually strict time limits

- power of reasoning
- volume of creativity.

Tests of maximal performance do not ask us how we usually do things; they ask us to show *what* we can do when we try hard. There are usually right and wrong answers, and the tests usually have strict time limits. Some maximal performance tests measure how quickly we solve problems (speed tests), while other maximal performance tests try to establish the difficulty level of the problems that we can solve (power tests). Typical and maximal tests are contrasted in table 15.5.

15.4.3 IPSATIVE TESTS (SELF-REFERENCED TESTS)

Some psychologists have fought battles, if not wars, over the merits of ipsative tests. The name comes from the same Latin root as the phrase '*ipso facto*', which means 'the truth is within itself'. Ipsative tests yield scores that are similarly self-contained within one person. They tell us about how a facet (such as interests) is distributed within one person, but they tell us nothing about how that facet compares with other people. Tests in which people are asked to rank items are nearly always ipsative. For example:

> 'Rank the following leisure activities according to the order of time you spend on them: Daydreaming; Watching Television; Stamp collecting; Gardening.'

A layabout who has 100 hours of leisure time per week, and might spend 10 hours daydreaming, 70 hours watching television and 20 hours stamp collecting, would rank those activities in the order 3, 1, 2. A university lecturer who might have only 10 minutes of leisure time per week and might spend 1 minute daydreaming, 7 minutes watching television and 2 minutes stamp collecting would also give a rank order of 3, 1, 2. Because the pattern of scores is the same, the results of this question could not differentiate between these two, very, very different, individuals. In other words, ipsative tests are sensitive to the variance *within* individuals, but they are totally insensitive to the variance *between individuals*.

Another form of ipsative question can be demonstrated by means of an imaginary test with four scales to measure the above interests, and which asks the following questions:

In each of these pairs of activities, <u>underline</u> the one on which you spend most time:

A daydreaming   A watching television
B gardening   B stamp collecting

A stamp collecting   A watching television
B gardening   B daydreaming

A watching television   A daydreaming
B gardening   B stamp collecting

Sometimes, ipsative questions have a more complex format using tetrads, and ask questions such as:

<u>Underline</u> the two leisure activities on which you spend least time:

A daydreaming   B watching television
C stamp collecting   D gardening

The scores in all three examples share two characteristics. *First*, the sum of all the scores on the test is always the same – 10 in the first example and 6 in the second. *Second*, the scores are not independent. Once 'watching television' has been chosen for the first rank, the scores on the other activities must be reduced. Hence ipsative tests may be defined as:

> tests which are insensitive to differences between individuals, where the sum of the scores on sub-scales is constant and where scale scores are not independent.

Some questions might look as though they are ipsative, but this may be misleading. For example, suppose that a test aims to measure people's liking for work involving quality control, marketing or finance, but no other preferences are measured by the test. Respondents might be asked to underline the members of the following pairs of activities that they would like the most:

A marketing   A giving talks   A finance
B research   B quality control   B training

This test would not be ipsative. Only one item in each group is relevant to a person's score. The other items are distractors and do not receive a score if they are chosen. Consequently, the total scores of individuals will differ and the scores on the scales will be independent.

Ability tests are rarely ipsative. Many personality tests are ipsative. They include Edward's Personal Preference Schedule and the Gordon Personal Profile and Inventory. Other personality tests such as the Myers–Briggs Type Indicator are partly ipsative, while some personality tests such as the OPQ have ipsative forms (Concept 4), which are paralleled by normative forms (Concept 5). Many interest tests, such as the Kuder Inventory and the Rothwell–Miller, are ipsative.

Advocates of ipsative tests (for example, Saville and Wilson, 1991) contend that they are better than normative tests because they are more resistant to deception. Questions can be framed where the alternatives have equal social desirability. Candidates could be asked, for example, to underline the statements in the following pairs that best describe themselves:

A. I am charming	A. I am deceitful
B. I am honest	B. I am rude

Candidates would find it hard to anticipate whether alternative A or alternative B would produce the 'best' score. Whilst advocates of ipsative tests accept that the interdependence of scales is a fatal flaw when there are only a few – say, two or three – scales in a test, this is of little consequence when a test contains many scales. For example, if a test has 32 scales, the influence of any one scale upon another is only 1/31th.

Critics of ipsative tests (for example, Johnson et al., 1988) point out that because ipsative tests are totally insensitive to the differences between people and their scores on the subscales are artificially related, there is a danger that they produce spurious results.

It can be concluded that ipsative tests should be rarely, if ever, used in selection, since differences between candidates are central and fundamental aspects of selection. Ipsative tests, especially interest tests, may be useful in guidance situations where the focus is upon one individual. However, even in guidance situations, ipsative tests will often be less informative than normative tests, because they do not give useful information about the client *vis-à-vis* potential competitors. The use of ipsative tests is, perhaps, most justifiable when they are used in development situations. The emphasis here may be on the detection of a relative 'weakness' that may be limiting the development of other characteristics and abilities.

15.4.4 CATEGORIES OF TESTS ACCORDING TO QUALIFICATIONS NEEDED

In order to maintain confidentiality and eliminate incompetence or misuse, test publishers restrict the sale of tests to those who are suitably qualified. Tests are usually divided into four categories according to their complexity and the level of skill that they require. The four categories are as follows:

- *Level 1* consists of very simple tests that require minimum knowledge and that are unlikely to be used for any major decision where the consequences would be irreversible. Often, these tests are called inventories and are used solely as a basis for discussion, counselling or development. In these situations, any errors may be reversed very easily. Learning-style inventories or questionnaires concerning vocational readiness are typical level 1 measures. These measures are released to educated and responsible users such as teachers and personnel officers.
- *Level 2* consists of relatively straightforward tests of ability and attainment, which yield one or two scores that are easy to interpret. Examples of this category are tests of arithmetic, spelling or typing ability. This category also includes straightforward measures of intelligence. Training courses to qualify people to use this category of tests will last about five days and will cover basic statistics, psychometrics and the preparatory stages

of selection, as well as training in the administration, interpretation and feedback of the test results from these straightforward tests. This level corresponds to level A as defined by the British Psychological Society.

- *Level 3* consists of more complex tests, which may yield a series of subscores that need careful integration and interpretation. The use of these tests will require a deeper know-ledge of the principles underlying testing, together with an understanding of some of the more intricate aspects of psychometrics, such as dealing with distortion. Most personal-ity tests fall into this category. Training to use this level of tests will require the train-ing for level 2 plus an extra five days, and then a further follow-up day after an interval of several weeks so that practical experience can be gained. This level corresponds to level B as defined by the British Psychological Society.
- *Level 4* concerns specialized and intricate tests that require extended and specific train-ing. In general, these are individual tests, where decisions need to be made about the questions to be administered and whether or not answers can be accepted as correct. Many of these tests are used in clinical settings. The Weschler Adult Intelligence Scale is, per-haps, the level 4 test that is most likely to be encountered in occupational settings.

15.5 CHOOSING BETWEEN TESTS

Once it has been established that tests should be included in a selection system, it is necessary to choose a specific test. This process usually proceeds involves six stages:

1 The Initial Trawl

Drawing up a shortlist of likely tests involves wading through the publishers' manuals and websites. The addresses of most UK test publishers are given on the website that accompanies this book. The initial trawl will aim to produce a list of tests that measure the relevant charac-teristic, at the appropriate level, take a reasonable length of time and have reasonable costs. The initial trawl will be aided by constructing a matrix with columns for each of these facets.

2 Elimination on *a priori* Grounds

Once the shortlist has been compiled, it can be refined by eliminating some tests on two *a priori* grounds. *First*, consult promotional material. If it is freely available to anyone without any, or with only cursory, training, it is probably better not to use the test, since it may have been purchased by some candidates. It is also worth checking whether the test is freely available on the Internet. Do not use freely available tests for selection. *Second*, consider the test length. Tests with very few questions are unlikely to be reliable. As a rough guide, you need more than 19 questions for each scale on an ability tests and about seven, quite different, questions for each scale on a personality or interest test.

3 Elimination on Psychometric Grounds

Some of the surviving tests can then be eliminated on psychometric grounds. You can usually eliminate tests where:

- a validity greater than .8 is claimed
- validity is greater than reliability (except for some tests of motivation)
- the standard deviation is very small – less than, say, three raw scores.

4 Eliminate Tests that are Unfair

In theory, the test manual should contain details about unfairness. Technically, the intercept and the slope of regression lines will be the same for majority and minority groups if the test is fair. Differences in average scores for subgroups are not evidence of unfairness (see chapter 12).

Unfortunately, very few manuals actually give the information that is needed to make an educated judgement on the basis of the available information and perhaps an inspection of the test.

5 Make the Final Choice on the Basis of Validity

The final stage is to evaluate detailed information about validity. This stage requires very detailed information. You will probably need to obtain specimen sets of the tests that you are considering and you will probably need to refer to reviews of tests in *Buros* or the British Psychological Society's Reviews (Bartram, 1995, 1997; Lindley, 2000). The information from reliability and validity should be consistent but in the case of conflict, validity is more important than reliability.

Collate as many validity studies as you can find in the manual and other sources. Then eliminate any studies that seem weak or inadequate. You then need to combine the results from the studies that remain. The best way of combining several validity studies into a single index is to take the average weighted by the sample sizes. In general, you should choose the test with the highest aggregate validity. However, do not follow this rule slavishly. If one test seems slightly more valid than another but is twice as long or inconvenient, it will make sense to choose the slightly less valid test and invest the time and effort liberated in some other way that improves selection.

6 Norms

In most selection situations, norm tables are not a very important consideration – as long as the test is valid and fair, it always makes sense to choose the person with the best score. If you are employing a steady stream of people, the best result is obtained if you set the limit at a point that just allows you to fill the vacant posts. However, you do need norms if you are giving vocational advice or if the test is unfair to certain groups (see chapter 22).

Appendix 15.1 Key to test suppliers

ACER	Australian Council for Educational Research
APP	Australian Psychologists Press
ASE	Assessment and Selection in Employment
CPP	Consulting Psychologists Press

EdITS	Educational and Industrial Testing Service
HAS	Hogan Assessment Systems
HJ	Hatfield Jefferies
HS	Hodder and Stoughton
MT	Miller & Tyler
NCAS	National Career Assessment Services
NFER	National Foundation for Educational Research
NZCER	New Zealand Council for Educational Research
OPP	Oxford Psychologists Press
ORC	Ohio Resource Center
PAR	Psychological Assessment Resources
PC	Psychological Corporation
PSC	Psychological Consultancy
PT	PsyTech
RH	Ramsey House
RLH	Pearson Reid London House
SHL	Saville Holdsworth Ltd
SR	Stewart Robertson
TA	The Test Agency

CHAPTER 16

PSYCHOMETRIC TESTS 2

TEST CONSTRUCTION

The development of tests is a scientific procedure that requires great care and skill. A simple test will involve about two months' initial effort, followed by several months work establishing the test's psychometric properties. Test construction involves the dogged application of a series of logical steps. Straightforward descriptions of these steps are given by Smith and Robertson (1993), Bethell-Fox (1989) and Guion (1965). A rather more complex description is given by Kline (1986). Books by Adkins (1974), Gulliksen (1950), Cronbach and Glesser (1965) and Lord and Novick (1968) outline the methods in all their gory complexity. The description of test construction given here has very limited aims. It is intended to provide test users with an overview of test construction, so that the terms used in a test manual can be understood and an informed decision made on whether a test is soundly constructed. The chapter is divided into two main sections:

1   Constructing ability tests
2   Constructing personality tests – rational versus factorial scales

◤ 16.1 CONSTRUCTING ABILITY TESTS

The construction of ability tests usually proceeds in six main stages.

Stage 1: Define the Domain

Probably the most important point is to define the aims of the test. Definition of the domain is a crucial stage upon which all else is built:

* Exactly *what* needs to be measured? A specific statement is required. Rather than specifying, say, 'arithmetic', the exact operations should be given (for example, 'add', 'subtract', 'multiply', 'divide', 'exponentiate').
* Exactly *who* is to be measured? Again, a specific statement is needed (for example, 'the adult population', 'adolescents', 'rocket scientists').
* Exactly what is the *purpose* of the test (for example, 'selection', 'guidance', 'development', 'audits' or 'research')?

Once the aims have been agreed, the test content can be specified. In general, the content can be divided into two parts: the subject-matter and the mental operations. For example, the content of an arithmetic test can involve money, length, weight or time, and each of these content categories can be subject to the mental operations of addition, subtraction, multiplication and division, to produce 16 different types of problem. The domain of arithmetic for shop assistants would focus on addition and subtraction of money. The domain for highly skilled engineers would involve operations involving length, weight, time and, preferably, money.

Clear thinking at this stage should help to ensure that the test neither includes irrelevant aspects nor excludes important ones. A test's manual should give an explicit and clear definition of its domain. Usually, the definition is found under a heading 'Scope of Test' or sometimes 'Rationale of Test'.

At this stage, it is often best to draw up an item budget. The total test length is likely to be determined by practical considerations, such as the available time. Administration and practice items require about 10 minutes. During the test itself, subjects could be expected to answer at a rate of about six questions per minute. An item budget for a half-hour arithmetic test for sales assistants might be 10 minutes for administration and 20 minutes for about 120 questions, as follows:

- 19 additions of two amounts under £1
- 19 additions of one amount under £1 and one amount over £1
- 19 additions of two amounts over £1
- 19 additions of three or more amounts
- 11 subtractions of two amounts under £1
- 11 subtractions of an amount under £1 from an amount over £1
- 11 subtractions of mixed amounts
- 11 other arithmetical operations.

There are no hard and fast rules concerning the number of questions to be allocated to each subdomain, but 19 is a good number (enthusiasts might care to speculate why 19 is a good number). All other things being equal, tests containing many questions are better than tests with few questions. Another rule is that more questions should be devoted to the more important subdomains. In the example, a job analysis had established that sales assistants calculate additions twice as often as subtractions. Therefore, approximately twice as many items were allocated to additions as to subtractions.

Stage 2: Specify the Type of Question

There are two major types of question – open-ended and multiple-choice:

- *Open-ended questions* can vary from asking for several sentences on a topic (for example, what has been happening to the people in the picture), to the answer to an arithmetic problem (for example, $194 + 78 = ?$). Sometimes a subject is merely asked to fill in a missing word, such as in 'Up is the opposite of . . . ?' Open-ended questions have the great advantage that the subjects' responses are not limited by the viewpoint of the test constructor, and the subject is required to produce the answer rather than just recognize it. Open-ended questions have the great disadvantage that, except in arithmetical problems, they are very difficult to analyse and score.

- *Multiple-choice questions* usually have between two and five alternatives. Multiple-choice questions limit the replies that a subject can give, so their preparation needs great care. They are, however, easy to score and analyses. The multiple-choice format usually consists of a question (the stem) plus a numbered list of alternatives, one of which is correct. The others are wrong, but plausible, answers (distractors). It is best if one distractor has a phonic or typographical similarity to the correct answer. Subjects are asked to write the number or letter of the alternative that they think is correct. This type of response has three main advantages: the time taken to answer each question is approximately the same; little time is spent in writing and the answer sheet is quick to mark, either mechanically or by computer. The three most frequent formats of personality tests are as follows:

Format A
☐ Yes
☐ No

Format B
☐ Yes
☐ ?
☐ No

Format C
☐ Very true
☐ True
☐ Uncertain
☐ Untrue
☐ Very untrue

The response mode must be determined. In personality and interest tests, answers usually take the form of placing a cross (a cross is better than a tick because it has an intersection, which avoids the ambiguities of exuberant ticks). Another question is whether subjects should give their answers on the test booklet or whether separate answer sheets should be used in order to reduce costs.

Stage 3: Assemble Items According to the Test Specification

It must be anticipated that many of these items will not survive subsequent stages. Initially, about three times the number of final items is needed. For the sales' assistants arithmetic test, with 120 questions, a pool of about 360 items would be needed. The origin of the questions depends upon the purpose of the test. In most occupational tests, the items should be derived from either a job analysis or from actual problems encountered by those employed in the job. With attitude tests and personality tests, ideas for questions can be obtained from similar existing tests, books, magazines, articles in learned journals or discussion groups.

Usually, at this stage, the questions are cast in an open-ended format. The directions for administering the test are drafted. Question-writing is tedious and detailed. A panel usually considers the first draft, question by question. Some hints for drafting questions are as follows:

- Avoid questions where the purpose is obvious to the candidate (for example, 'Are you usually the life and soul of a party?' – on a test entitled 'Extroversion').
- Avoid questions that rely on a flash of insight for their solution (for example, '1 + 1 = (a) 1, (b) 10 or (c) 11' – unless you twig that the question involves binary arithmetic, the question is drivel).
- Questions should refer to specific rather than general behaviour (for example, 'Do you enjoy sport?' – it depends upon which sport!).
- Each item must make only one statement or ask only one question.
- Avoid terms of frequency (for example, 'Do you come here *often?*' – it all depends upon what you mean by often).
- Avoid double negatives (for example, 'Did you not fail to turn up?').

At this stage, the reading level of the questions is checked. Usually, items needing a reading ability higher than that of the average 11 year old are eliminated.

In personality tests and interest tests, there should be roughly equal numbers of positive and negative answers. Kline (1986) gives more detailed advice on the writing of questions.

Stage 4: Trial the Large Initial Pool of Items on a Relatively Representative Population

Care should be taken to include appropriate numbers of minority groups and a realistic balance of genders. In some locations, the sample should also use people with an appropriate mix of religions. Even if the test is to be timed, a time limit is not imposed at this stage. Instead, subjects are merely asked to mark where they are at various intervals. The test manual should clearly state the size and nature of the sample used in the trial stage.

Stage 5: Item Analysis of the Responses Obtained in the Trial Stage

Item analysis is often very complex, but it usually starts by obtaining a total score. With ability tests this is very easy, because a panel of experts armed with reference books or calculators can determine *the* right answer. Responses to each question are then correlated with the total score (the **item-whole correlation**). In order to avoid correlations that are inflated by auto-correlation, each score is subtracted from the total before it is correlated with the total. The procedure is shown in table 16.1, which, for simplicity, shows the scores of just ten people (A–J) on an item pool of five questions (Q1–Q5).

The scores on each question are shown in the block on the left and person A's scores are 1, 1, 4, 3, 3. The block on the right contains the totals, but each column has a different score omitted. The first column in the right block shows the totals but with the score from question 1 omitted. A's score in this column is 11 (that is, $1 + 4 + 3 + 3$). The scores for question 1 are then correlated with the total where question 1 is missing and the correlation is .50.

Negative correlations indicate that the scoring system for that question is the wrong way round and the scores need to be **reflected** (that is, 1 becomes 5, 2 becomes 4 and so on). The whole process is repeated and a new set of correlations produced. Here, we will pretend that the correlations are unaffected by the process of reflection, except that −.43 becomes +.43.

Questions with low correlations are eliminated because they are probably measuring something different to the other questions. In our example, question 5 would be eliminated.

Table 16.1 A demonstration of item-whole correlations

Person	Scores on questions					Totals *except*					
	Q1	Q2	Q3	Q4	Q5	Except 1	Except 2	Except 3	Except 4	Except 5	Grand total
A	1	1	4	3	3	11	11	8	9	9	12
B	3	3	1	2	2	8	8	10	9	9	11
C	2	1	2	3	3	9	10	9	8	8	11
D	2	3	3	4	4	13	12	12	11	12	15
E	3	3	2	4	2	11	11	12	10	12	14
F	4	5	3	4	2	14	13	15	14	16	18
G	3	2	1	5	3	11	12	13	9	11	14
H	5	4	2	5	3	14	15	17	14	16	19
I	4	4	1	5	4	14	14	17	13	14	18
J	3	4	1	5	5	15	14	17	13	13	18
	.50	.6	−.43	.6	.1	Correlations – extent to which same thing is measured					
	3	3	2	4	3	Averages – difficulty level					

Finally, item analysis looks at question difficulty. Question difficulty can be gauged by cal-culating the average score. A high average score indicates an easy item and a low average score indicates a difficult item. Questions are chosen so that the final questionnaire includes some difficult items, some average items and some easy items. In our example, questions 2, 3 and 4 would be retained. Item one would be eliminated, because it has the same difficulty level as question 2 but has a slightly lower correlation with the total. At the end of item analysis, we are left with a pool of items that are measuring the same thing and that cover all levels of difficulty. For an excellent discussion of item analysis, see Guilford and Fruchter (1978).

Stage 6: Final Formatting of the Test for Publication and Research into its Psychometric Properties

A manual should give clear information about reliability, validity and fairness. To establish these properties, the final version will need to be administered to a large (100+, preferably 200+) representative sample of the population for whom the test was designed. This sample is called the **standardization sample**. The test norms will be based on the results obtained from the standardization sample.

 16.2 CONSTRUCTING PERSONALITY TESTS

The basics of constructing personality tests are very similar to those for constructing ability tests. Both involve six essential stages:

1　Defining the domain.
2　Deciding on the type of question.
3　Assembling items.

4   Trialling a large pool of questions.
5   Item analysis.
6   Standardization and psychometrics.

The main difference lies in the fact that personality seems more complex and it is necessary to construct several scales simultaneously. There are other differences depending upon whether the tests are devised on the basis of classification, rationality, or factor structure.

16.2.1 CLASSIFICATORY TESTS

Scales for classification usually arise out of a practical need to speed up the classification of people or make the process more objective. Many of these scales have their origin in clinical psychology, where there is a need to diagnose people into groups according to their illnesses. The classic example of a classificatory test is the Minnesota Multiphasic Personality Inventory (MMPI).

Defining the general domain is easy – it is usually to measure the type of mental illness. Defining subdomains is a little more complex. After consulting textbooks and case files, experts meet to decide on the types of illness to include. The designers of the MMPI (Hathaway and McKinley, 1940), for example, decided to include scales for:

*   hypochondriacs
*   depressives
*   hysterics
*   psychopaths
*   paranoiacs
*   psychasthenics
*   schizophrenics
*   hypomanics
*   social introverts
*   masculins and feminins.

On the basis of clinical experience, a pool of 550 statements was produced and, for example, given to a group of paranoiacs and a sample of 1,500 'normal' people. The responses to each question were analysed. The analysis might have included the following:

Statement	Percentage saying yes	
	Paranoids	Normals
1 I am being plotted against.	67	12
2 I shop at Woolworths.	40	37
3 I have many vague symptoms.	11	11
4 People often stare at me.	59	3

Items that show big differences between the groups were retained for the paranoia scale: in this hypothetical example, the first and the last questions would be combined to form the paranoia scale. The scores for a group of hypochondriacs were then obtained, and might be as follows:

Statement	Percentage saying yes	
	Hypochondriacs	Normals
1 I am being plotted against.	12	12
2 I shop at Woolworths.	30	37
3 I have many vague symptoms.	60	11
4 People often stare at me.	9	3

The hypochondria scale would consist of statements like 'I have many vague symptoms'. Classification tests are fairly rare in occupational psychology.

16.2.2 PERSONALITY TESTS BASED ON LOGIC AND DEDUCTION

'**Rational tests**' is a euphemistic name for tests based on judgement and logic – usually the judgement and logic of experts. Unfortunately, experts differ and the tests may not be as rational as their authors would like us to believe. Rational tests are sometimes called 'deductive' or 'conceptual' tests.

Rational tests start with the decision to measure some domain that is theorized as being structured in a certain way. Sometimes the decision is capricious and subjective, where some guru feels that a measure is needed in order to bolster his or her pet theory. More rarely, the decisions are the result of careful research and deliberation. A good example of the careful approach is the Occupational Personality Questionnaire (OPQ). In developing the OPQ, the authors amassed information from:

- existing personality inventories
- a review of company documentation
- Repertory Grid studies
- discussions with representatives from 53 companies.

This information was synthesized over an extended period that involved many meetings. A model with three levels emerged. At the top level, personality at work was divided into three very large domains: relationships with people; ideas and cognitive style; and feelings. Each of the three domains was subdivided. For example, feelings are divided into anxiety, energy and self-concept. The subdomains were in turn divided to produce a total of 32 traits. For example, the energy subdomain was divided into the traits of active versus passive, proactive versus reactive and disillusioned versus optimistic.

The second stage of developing 'rational' personality scales is to develop items that measure each of the traits in the model of personality. A wide range of sources may be used, but the authors will tend to focus on those items that seem to best represent their construct. In order to focus upon the construct, they may include some 'marker variables'. These marker variables will be questions, observations or other data that are almost certain to be true indices of the trait in question.

Item analysis for 'rational scales' usually consists of correlating the results obtained from a large and diverse sample. The matrix is inspected and the questions grouped into clusters. The correlations of each item with the other items in a cluster are examined. Those that do not correlate with the other members and with the relevant marker variables are eliminated. Next, the correlations with items from other clusters are examined. If the correlations with other clusters are higher than the correlations within its own cluster, the item is either rejected or reallocated to another trait. In this way, groups of highly interrelated items emerge. Indeed, one of the criticisms of rational scales is that the items are too interrelated and therefore only measure a narrow range of behaviours. It may be that several rational scales are measuring almost the same thing. Again it should be noted that while statistical information is used, the final result depends upon the skill and evaluation of the test author. The pre-eminent 'rational' test is the OPQ.

16.2.3 PERSONALITY TESTS BASED ON FACTOR ANALYSIS

Today, factor analysis is the pre-eminent mode of constructing a personality tests. Factor analysis forms the basis of several tests, such as the Eysenck Personality Inventory, the Guilford Zimmerman Temperament Survey, the Comrey Scales and, above all else, the 16PF.

With the factor analytic approach, the stage of determining the domain is easy. All that is needed is a broad definition, such as 'a broad-spectrum test of adult personality'. It is not necessary to propose either the number of traits or the structure of personality.

In principle, the stage of assembling items is also easy. All that is needed is a fairly large pool of questions that are representative of all the behaviours that might be caused by personality. In practice, it is hard to find an independent sample frame. Cattell, the author of the 16PF, solved this problem by using a previous, independent study by Allport and Odbert (1936). Allport and Odbert collected all of the trait names contained in the English (American) dictionary and the psychiatric and psychological literature. The thousands of trait names were far too many to handle. Furthermore, so many were synonyms and derivatives of the same trait that it was unwise to try to handle them. The first step was to eliminate duplication by combining obvious synonyms and derivatives. The result was 171 semantically different trait names.

Cattell obtained ratings of 100 men by their colleagues on the 171 traits (L data) and factor analysed the ratings. The results of the factor analysis enabled him to shorten the list. He then obtained colleague's ratings on the shortened list for 208 men. The factor analysis of the second set of ratings led to the identification of the primary source traits of personality. The L data studies were supplemented by studies using questionnaires (Q data) and laboratory measures (T data). Twelve traits were clearly identified and there were indications from the Q data that four more may exist (Q_1, Q_2, Q_3 and Q_4). Three further factors (D, J and K) were seen primarily in children. Scales for factors D, J and K are omitted from the adult version of the test. Cattell did most of his work before the wide availability of computers. Much of the factor analysis was done graphically, in a way that minimized the influence of 'rogue points'. Modern computer programs tend to give a lot of emphasis to 'rogue points', because they square any differences from the mean. The 16PF was based on the factors that Cattell had identified.

16.2.4 THE BASICS OF FACTOR ANALYSIS

Factor analysis is such an important technique in the production of tests that it is essential to develop a basic understanding of the process. Enthusiasts might also like to read the more mathematical explanation given on the website that accompanies this book.

The first step in a factor analysis is to correlate every variable with every other variable, to produce a matrix. A computer scans the matrix of correlations, looking for an underlying trend. It then locates an axis similarly to the way in which a trend line can be fitted to points on a graph. Once the trend line is in place, the position of each question can be plotted. The questions near the trend are those that are the best measures of the trend and they are collected together to form a scale. Those questions that are far away from the trend are eliminated, or allocated to another trend. A simplified example of ten questions in a personality test might make the procedure clear. First, the intercorrelations between questions are plotted:

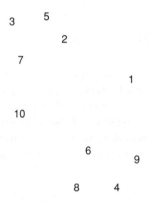

The points fall into two main clusters. Trend line I can be drawn through one cluster and trend line II can be drawn through the other. The trend lines are factors that reflect the fundamental, underlying, natural structure of the data. They have not been decided in advance by an armchair theoretician: they emerge from the data itself. The following figure illustrates how the trend lines might appear:

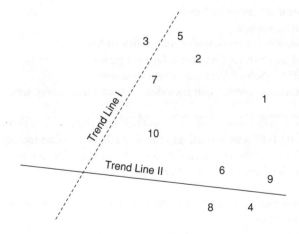

If a personality test was foolishly produced from such a small amount of data, it would have two scales. Scale I would contain questions 2, 3, 5 and 7. Scale II would contain questions 4, 6, 9 and 8. Questions 1 and 10 would be abandoned. In practice, the situation is more complex.

16.2.5 OBLIQUE VERSUS ORTHOGONAL FACTORS

In this example, the trend lines form an acute angle and are not at right angles – they are **oblique**. This means that the trends are related. Some methods of factor analysis insist that the trends are *not* related and the trend lines are therefore at right angles – they are **orthogonal**. This is one of the major differences between various personality tests based on factor analysis. Eysenck, for example, uses orthogonal axes, while Cattell uses *non-orthogonal* (oblique) axes. The issues are complex. There is no reason to believe that in nature trends cannot be related, and oblique axes make the fewest assumptions.

16.2.6 SECOND-ORDER FACTORS

In the 16PF test, several of the factors have quite high correlations. For example, A, F, H, N and Q_2 have notable intercorrelations. Factors C, O, L and Q_4 are also intercorrelated (see Conn and Reike, 1994). With non-orthogonal tests it is therefore possible to create a second correlation matrix that shows the relationships between factors. In its turn, this second correlation matrix can be factor analysed to produce secondary factors, which are called **global scores**. The global scores correlate with the 'Big Five' factors – extroversion, anxiety, tough-mindedness, independence and self-control.

16.2.7 VERSIONS OF THE 16PF

The 16PF was first published in 1949, and it was revised in 1956, 1962 and 1970. The fourth edition (1970) existed in several versions:

- form A – the standard version
- form B – a parallel version to form A
- form C – a short version
- form D – a version for those with reading difficulties
- HSPQ – the High School Personality Questionnaire
- ESPQ – the Early School Personality Questionnaire
- E16P – an expanded version that included abnormal personality traits.

By the 1990s, the fourth edition was looking dated and the test was losing out to commercial rivals. In 1994, the 16PF was revised into the fifth edition – coincidentally at the same time as the rise of the 'Big Five' theory of personality. The fifth edition combined the 'best' items from the versions of the fourth edition. There were attempts to:

- increase the internal consistency of scales (a particular criticism of previous editions)
- remove dated content

- remove content that might have gender, age, race or disability bias
- make the test more 'business friendly'.

There is generally a reasonable correlation of about .5 or more between the fourth and the fifth editions. The narrower, more focused nature of the fifth edition has resulted in lower correlations for factors M (.17), N (.26) and Q_1 (.31). Some practitioners are less happy with some of the changes. There is no longer the convenience of the parallel forms as there was in the fourth edition. Further, the nature of the traits measures seems to have moved away from being source traits towards being surface traits (Tyler, 1996).

Graphical explanations of factor analysis give a reasonable understanding of the principles, but it is usually more accurate to use mathematical calculations. In addition, graphical methods become extremely difficult when there are more than three factors, since more than three factors are hard to represent in three dimensions. Today, most factor analyses are conducted on a mathematical basis and a short explanation is given on the website that accompanies this book.

CHAPTER 17

E-SELECTION

COMPUTER-BASED ASSESSMENT AND INTERPRETATION

Traditional tests obtain data either by pencil and paper or by simple equipment, such as the Purdue Pegboard. Traditional media have proved amazingly convenient, robust and economical, but it is claimed that their long-standing hegemony will be eclipsed by the computer. Computer-based testing and interpretation (CBTI) give a modern aura to the testing process. Furthermore, computerized tests have commercial advantages for publishers. They command higher profit margins and they are more resistant to unauthorized copying. It is therefore no surprise that computerized testing is increasing and most new tests are now released in formats that involve computers.

Computers can play an important part throughout the recruitment process. Word-processors are used to prepare key documents. Jobs can be advertised on the Internet and information can be gathered automatically from potential applicants. Some computerized selection systems suggest appropriate interview questions. Indeed, computer programs are available that manage the whole recruitment process in an efficient and seamless way. Computers can also play a part in the assessment process itself – especially with regard to psychometric tests – and the issues are often complex and technical (see Bartram, 1989, 1994). Computer-based testing and interpretation is often divided into eight facets:

1. The candidate perspective on computer testing
2. Computers as display devices
3. Computers as response devices
4. Controlling testing and adaptive tests
5. Computerized scoring and calculations
6. Computer interpretation and reports
7. e-Recruitment and selection
8. Ethical issues

 17.1 THE CANDIDATE PERSPECTIVE ON COMPUTER TESTING

One of the early fears was that candidates would have a negative view of computer-based testing. It was thought that, without the presence of another person, they would have lower motivation and would dislike the tests. Subsequent research has not supported this pessimistic view (see Klinger et al., 1976; Bartram, 1989). It would seem that in many circumstances people prefer to answer questions posed by a computer. Contrary to expectations, candidates with lower abilities have the more positive view of computer testing. They like not having to write the answers out in longhand and, unlike the more able candidates, they do not mind being paced by the computer or frustrated by other restrictions (Johansson, 1992).

Now there is the worry that positive candidate attitudes plus perceptions of modernity and the infallibility of computer testing can lead to sloppy test administration. In almost all computer-aided testing situations, it will be necessary to have a human being who:

- extends a warm greeting
- confirms the identity of the person presenting themselves
- explains the reasons for testing
- uses a password to gain access to the system (unrestricted access invites serious problems)
- demonstrates the equipment
- assesses the candidate's readiness for testing
- answers any questions that the candidate may have
- monitors and troubleshoots problems that may arise
- closes the system at the end of testing.

A human being helps to ensure that the testing area is kept in good order. He or she may also be needed to explain the next stages in the process, and perhaps give feedback. The human touch can also reassure candidates over minor worries. The omission of such 'personal touches' can lead to a bad test-taking attitude, and candidates might conclude that their potential employer will treat them as a machine rather than as a person.

17.2 COMPUTERS AS DISPLAY DEVICES

The essence of all tests is the presentation of a stimulus to which a person responds. Typically, the stimulus in computer testing is a display on a monitor, but computers can control other stimuli – especially sound.

Displays on a monitor offer much wider capabilities than a printed page. They can be dynamic and involve movement, cueing or fading. A measure of the perceptual rigidity, for instance, could start with an unambiguous drawing of a dog, which slowly fades and becomes an unambiguous drawing of a cat. The subject could be asked to press a button when he or she first perceives a cat. Another example is a vigilance test developed by Schuhfried (1997). The monitor displays a circle of dots, which are illuminated in sequence, so that the bright spot appears to travel clockwise around the circle. The subject is required to press a key when the illuminated spot appears to travel at twice the normal speed. Computer monitors also permit a high level of interactivity. The display can respond to the subject, and it can be made to provide more or less information at the candidate's request.

The added flexibility provided by a monitor can be a disadvantage. It allows more freedom to commit errors whilst the test is being constructed. This may result in an incomprehensible display or may involve mental operations that are different to the psychological characteristic being measured. Furthermore, the monitor display will generally need to include elements such as navigation buttons to go forwards or backwards, in addition to the test stimulus. A number of guidelines and regulations have been drawn up to ensure good practice in the development of test displays, such as the European Directive 90/270/EEC on computer monitor use – especially EN 9241 Part 10 (see Booth, 1998).

17.3 COMPUTERS AS RESPONSE DEVICES

Tests also require responses. In traditional pencil-and-paper tests a person writes the answer longhand or chooses from alternatives by, for example, checking a box. When a test is administered by computer, the response must be input in a way that can be recognized by the system.

Probably the first attempt at capturing candidate responses by computer was to *retype* a candidate's responses into a data file. The process is expensive, time-consuming and error prone but, even today, it is a reasonable solution in situations where the volume of testing is low. *Mark sensing* was developed for situations in which there is a high, recurrent demand. Candidates are required to indicate answers by making heavy pencil marks at predetermined positions on a printed sheet. Mark sensing takes a long time to set up and requires candidates to be very accurate in positioning their responses. Furthermore, it requires special equipment that is often expensive and temperamental. Usually, the marked answer sheets are sent to an agency to be scored – a process that can take several days and it is expensive.

Sometimes, computers require candidates to respond using a *QWERTY keyboard*. A decade ago, there were concerns that scores were contaminated by differences in typing ability. However, there is little evidence that it makes much difference. The introduction of a *mouse* as a pointing device did not change matters. Skills in using a mouse take time to develop and people who have had considerable experience of using a computer may have an advantage. *Light pens* can be used to indicate the chosen answer by touching a 'button' displayed on a monitor or screen. However, they can produce 'arm ache' if used in long testing sessions. Touch-sensitive screens are perhaps the most 'natural' response method – especially when screens are placed horizontally. The development of *voice recognition* software means that subjects are now able to dictate answers. This is a more natural response and is less likely to confer an incidental advantage to those who have prior experience. Voice recognition would not be appropriate in group testing situations.

The use of a computer to capture candidates' responses has one big advantage – the response times for individual questions can be measured accurately. Sometimes, the speed of answering is useful information. In ability tests, quick answering might be related to higher ability. In personality tests, a slow response might mean that a subject is having difficulty choosing the best answer, and it may indicate that a subject is not giving the true answer. Kline (1986), for example, suggests that the disturbing items on a personality test should have longer response times and that neurotics should have higher response times to questions that measure neuroticism. Jensen (1980, 1982) suggests that reaction times to judging the length of lines and choice reaction time are, imperfectly, related to intelligence.

 ## 17.4 CONTROLLING TESTING AND ADAPTIVE TESTS

Computers have been used not only to present information and capture responses, but also to make important decisions about the testing process. Computer decisions are much more consistent than decisions made by humans. The consistency of computer decisions has both advantages and disadvantages. It is an advantage that the decisions are made on the basis of strict, explicit information. This means that the decision is transparent and open to examination. The resulting decisions will be fair in the sense that they will be applied impartially to all. Hence computer decisions probably have a high level of legal defensibility. However, the application of rules means that the decisions will be accurate for the majority of situations envisaged by the rule-makers, but they will take no account of unusual, unanticipated circumstances in which judgement is needed. In a significant minority of situations, proper compensatory adjustments will not be made. The balance is hard to assess. It seems probable that it lies with the advantages, because the adjustments made by human administrators will, to an extent, be arbitrary and merely add error variance to a selection system. Computers have been used to make two types of decisions: which tests should be used and which questions should be presented.

17.4.1 DECISIONS ABOUT TESTS

Some computer packages cover the entire recruitment process, from job descriptions and personnel specifications to recommendations for employment. They provide a seamless process whereby the information in the job description is translated into the competencies set out in the person specification. The system translates and then suggests methods by which the competencies can be assessed. For example, if the person specification indicates that the job requires considerable abstract intelligence, the system may recommend the use of a high-level test of intelligence, such as the AH5 or the advanced version of Raven's Progressive Matrices. Similarly, if the person specification indicates that the job requires sensitivity to distraught clients, the system may suggest a test of insight or a role-playing exercise.

Decision rules can depend on the quirky understanding of the person who writes the program. Fortunately, it is more likely that the rules were obtained from a reasonably large sample (12 or more) of experts and the rules will be less idiosyncratic. The exact nature of the experts might be important. In order to obtain a sufficient number of experts at a cost that will yield an acceptable profit margin, the software company, or test publisher, may include a number of people who have excellent research qualifications, but who are in the process of obtaining sufficient practical expertise. Their inclusion might dilute the accuracy of decision models. The problem of **expertise levelling** is discussed by Rolls (1993). A test manual should specify the size of the sample and the minimum qualifications (probably in terms of the number and types of cases experienced) that the experts have. The sample of experts should be reasonably heterogeneous. It would be dangerous if all of the experts were employees of the same consulting or publishing group. The procedures used to capture the decision rules should be specified and should be reasonably objective.

17.4.2 CHOICE OF QUESTIONS

Computers are better than humans in remembering previous responses and then estimating the level of a person's ability. This makes computers ideally suited to the administration of **tailored tests**.

In traditional ability tests, questions are usually arranged in order of difficulty. People start at the beginning and trudge through easy questions (perhaps making a careless mistake or two) until they reach the items relevant to their level of ability. The score on many ability tests is determined by the last five or so questions attempted. The remainder of the time is wasted, while candidates wade through easy items on the way to the appropriate questions. In a tailored test, such as the Selby–Millsmith adaptive tests, the computer makes an initial estimate of a candidate's ability and administers an appropriate question – say, at the 50% difficulty level. If this question is answered correctly, the computer makes a revised estimate of the candidate's ability and administers another question – say, at the 75% difficulty level. If the second answer is correct, a question at the 87.5% difficulty level is given . . . and so on, until the system has homed in on the individual's level of ability (in fact, it would be dangerous to use only one question at each decision node, since such a system would be highly unstable). The system would then saturate the appropriate difficulty level with six or more questions, which would give a more precise estimate of ability than a test that is ten times longer. Adaptive testing has been taken up with enthusiasm by several armed forces, since it leads to a considerable reduction in the time needed to test large numbers of people. Also, in the forces, large sample sizes are available to derive statistically sound decision rules. Examples of the use of adaptive testing in the armed forces are given by Steege (1986) and by Mardberg and Carlstedt (1998).

Decision rules governing the choice of questions are much more scientific than the rules governing choice tests. In general, the choice of questions is made on the basis of a rigorous statistical model – usually the Rasch model. This model is too complex to present here, but an exposition is given by Rasch (1980). Rasch's model has been severely criticized (see, for example, Chopin, 1976; Nunnally, 1978; Lord, 1980 – but for a defence, see also Wright, 1968; Andrich, 1978) and other models are available.

Another possibility is to allow computers to devise the questions presented to candidates (Rust and Golombok, 1989). Computer generation of questions goes back to 1969, when Atkinson and Wilson designed programs to check whether material had been learned. Such programs break questions down into component parts. Simple programs merely vary the parts. More complex programs are able to vary the difficulty of the components. Kline (1986) suggests that the following elementary cognitive tasks might be a useful alternative to traditional paper-and-pencil tests of cognitive ability:

- A **perceptual closure task** requires subjects to recognize degraded stimuli. The stimuli can be visual or auditory. The computer would add, say, 50% random information in the form of randomized pixels. The random information would be decreased slowly until a candidate recognizes the picture.
- In a **lexical decision task**, a group of letters is briefly presented and the candidate is asked to decide whether the letters form a word. A variation of this task would be to present a series of words and ask the candidate whether they form a meaningful sentence.
- An **identity task** presents the candidate with a picture and a name. The candidate is required to decide whether the name and the picture refer to the same object. The time taken to answer is recorded.

◤ 17.5 COMPUTERIZED SCORING AND CALCULATIONS

Computers excel at calculating scores. Provided that answers are correctly input, computers provide accurate scores almost instantly. Scores can be readily transformed from one scoring system to another – say, stens to quotients – without much effort. Computers can also be used to evaluate complex equations, so that higher-order scores can be constructed from several primary scores. Furthermore, computers can handle, without error, very complex scoring systems that involve, say, different weights for different questions. The advantages of computers scoring tests were recognized from an early date. This was one of the first uses of computers in testing.

Initially, the advantages of computer scoring were restricted to greater accuracy and greater speed. However, a number of other advantages have emerged. Computers can be programmed to detect many kinds of response bias. They can, for example, detect acquiescence (the tendency to say 'yes') or dissent (the tendency to say 'no'). Huba (1987) suggests that computer scoring can detect response styles such as responding at random, agreeing with even-numbered items of a test while disagreeing with odd-numbered items, agreeing with the first half of the test while disagreeing with the second half, and so on. Without a computer, it is virtually impossible to screen for all of these distortions. Computer screening for distortions can become a matter of routine. A good example of the possibilities is given by Rust (1996), who developed a personality test in which respondents' answers are keyed into a computer. The scoring process includes a response audit that checks for lying and distortion, contradictory answers, faking and inattention.

Sometimes, it is useful to compare one profile with another. For example, in careers counselling it may be useful to compare a client's profile with profiles of occupations (such as accountancy) that might offer suitable employment. The formulae for profile matching are complicated and error prone, and only a few such calculations can be attempted 'by hand' (for formulae, see Huba, 1987; Cattell et al., 1988). In the past, a counsellor needed to use intuition to narrow the field to a few occupations. With the aid of a computer, such calculations can be done at will. A client's profile can be compared to every one of a bank of, perhaps, 100 occupational profiles.

However, computerized scoring has a serious disadvantage. It can make the scoring system totally opaque to the test user. The identity of the questions that contribute to a scale may be hidden inside the workings of the computer program. It is more difficult for the user to understand the nature of the scale or trace the answers in order to locate the cause of an anomalous score. Information about the samples used to provide norms is also hidden within the workings of the program and the risk of using inappropriate or inadequate norms is increased. This disadvantage is easily overcome if the relevant information is contained in the test manual. Unfortunately, for commercial reasons, the information is often restricted. Except in the most unusual circumstances, tests with computer scoring should not be used unless the details of the scoring system are explicitly stated in the manual or other publications. At the very least, arrangements should be made so that commercially sensitive material should be scrutinized by an independent professional expert and the review should be in the public domain (see Eyde and Kowal, 1987).

 ## 17.6 COMPUTER INTERPRETATION AND REPORTS

Interpretation of test results and writing reports often takes more time than test administration. Furthermore, it is difficult to delegate these aspects to people with lower levels of training. It is not surprising that considerable effort has been devoted to getting computers to interpret results and write reports.

17.6.1 COMPUTER INTERPRETATION

In some situations, interpretation of test results by computers is very easy. Where a comprehensive testing programme has been validated on large group such as a government agency, multiple regression equations can be established. In this context, a multiple regression equation is called a **prediction equation**, because it forecasts the likely success of candidates in a job. The following example of a prediction equation is based on one given by Cattell et al. (1988, 166):

$$\textit{Sales Effectiveness} = .4 \times A + .3 \times L + .4 \times Q_2 - 3.4$$

where A means warm, L means suspicious and Q_2 means self-sufficient. Note that this formula is an approximation, for demonstration purposes only.

If the selection is to be made on a top-down basis and all other information is equal, the candidate with the highest predicted score is chosen.

17.6.2 COMPUTER-GENERATED REPORTS

The use of computers to generate reports is quite common and a wide variety of reports can be produced. Bartram (1995b) noted that computer-produced reports can vary in many ways, including the following:

- *Media*: the use of words, graphs or tables.
- *Complexity*: the mechanical substitution of phrases for scores or text that relate to patterns or configurations of scores.
- *Modifiability*: whether the report can be changed on a word processor in order to make it more appropriate for the purpose.
- *Level of finish*: whether the text is merely a number of points as notes, or is in the form of a final report.
- *Sensitivity to context*: whether the report uses the language of the recipient.
- *Transparency*: the extent to which the link between a score and the text is obvious.
- *Guidance given*: whether the report merely states the scores or also suggests further actions.

Computer-generated reports aim to simulate narrative reports written by psychologists. An excellent description of computer-generated reports is given by Rolls (1993), on which a large part of this section is based. Rolls characterized computer-based test interpretations (CBTIs) as a structured set of rules that vary in the degree to which they apply objective procedures to select text from a database. Thus CBTI systems have two components: a bank of phrases and a set of rules.

The bank of phrases and sentences is usually derived from three sources:

- the test manual
- research findings and reports
- the experience of practitioners.

The rules are used to choose which phrases or sentences appear in a report. Wiggins (1973) identified three types of rules. In descending order of scientific rigour, the three types of rules are actuarial rules, practitioner rules and descriptive rules.

Actuarial Rules

Actuarial rules are derived from multiple regression equations. The actuarial approach, which is similar in many ways to using a computer to make a decision (see section 6.1), was championed by Meehl (1954). It has been stigmatized as leading to 'cookbook reports'. In selection and assessment, actuarial reports are usually very short and consist of a short piece of text recommending the hiring or rejection of a candidate, plus possibly one or two reasons in support of the decision.

Actuarial rules are rarely used to choose between passages of text, because very large samples are needed in order to obtain valid formulae (Vale et al., 1986). At the very minimum, data is needed on at least 20 subjects for each predictor used (Cohen and Cohen, 1983). This would mean that, for example, a decision rule for use with the 16PF would require about 320 subjects. Actuarial rules have another important disadvantage. They may be situationally specific. A rule developed in one situation may not be applicable in another.

Practitioner Rules

An alternative way of deriving rules to select passages of text is to mimic the thought processes of experts. Wiggins (1973) called these reports automated **clinical reports**. Typically, an expert will be asked to write reports on a series of test profiles. The series of profiles is carefully chosen to represent a wide array of scores and configurations. Preferably a lot of independent, objective and relevant information will be available about the people who provided the test data. The reports will then be decomposed into individual statements, and the expert will be asked to explain the basis on which he or she decided to make each statement. In fact, the process is repeated with a respectable sample of experts (at least 12). Much of this procedure was developed in clinical settings and then extended to occupational settings.

Obtaining rules from practitioners requires much less effort than the actuarial method. Furthermore, the practitioner approach is able to capture many of the contextual considerations and even the argot of specific groups, which would be bleached out by the 'averaging' processes inherent in multiple regressions. Unfortunately, obtaining the rules from practitioners also has substantial disadvantages. It may be costly to make extensive use of expensive experts and there may not be enough of them available. Consequently, there may be the temptation to include people who do not have sufficient knowledge and experience. Their inclusion may mean that accuracy may be diluted. Another problem arises because experts' verbal accounts may not actually reflect the way in which experts make decisions in practice (Hoffman, 1960).

Descriptive Rules

Actuarial reports tend to be very specific. Their specific nature is a handicap. A new formula needs to be developed for every situation and thus they are of limited use in varied counselling situations such as careers guidance. Descriptive rules do not suffer from these disadvantages. They are probably *the* most widely used type of computer-generated report in occupational psychology (Vale et al., 1986). Generally, descriptive rules aim to give a structured and full account of a person's psychometric characteristics, which the reader then reinterprets according to his or her own situation and purpose.

Descriptive rules are compiled, often by experts, on the basis of three kinds of evidence:

- the descriptions of the scales given in the test manual
- a compilation of results of research reported in learned and practitioner journals
- the experience of the experts and their general knowledge of test 'lore' (Matarazzo, 1986).

Rolls (1993) notes that the descriptive systems can use either single scores or configurations (syndromes) to provide a picture of the person. Descriptive rules usually produce long reports, because they systematically consider the test results scale by scale, and they may devote several paragraphs to each score. For example, the OPQ contains 32 scores and gives several composite scores. If just half a page is devoted to each score, a 20-page report is easily achieved.

Descriptive systems have been heavily criticized because they are at the mercy of the 'lore' on which they are based (Jackson, 1985). Others, such as Lanyon (1987), suggest that some CBTIs are unethical, because unvalidated – but plausibly worded – reports might be used by non-professionals who are unaware of the limitations of the system. Critics go further and describe some CBTI reports as 'self-serving statements of validity and glossy promotional literature masquerading as scientific data'. Supporters reply that at least with CBTIs the rules are clearly enunciated and open to examination (Harris, 1987). However, Harris then goes on to criticize the developers of CBTI systems because 'most test user documents are nothing more than operation manuals that share little relevant information with the user, thereby causing the user to implement the programme largely on faith. Without access to the relevant data, it is inconceivable to think that the user can take full advantage of the programme'. Harris notes that 'with the proliferation of inadequately documented automated interpreted programs, fears of litigation will grow . . . especially now that CBTI reports are admissible in some court proceedings'. The British Psychological Society (1999) has published *Guidelines for the Development and Use of Computer-based Assessment*.

17.6.3 WIDER ISSUES OF CBTI

In fact, most computer reports are a *mélange* of the three approaches. The largest part of a report will be a descriptive element, based mainly on a test manual. Certain aspects, such as leadership, creativity or team roles, will be actuarial and based upon empirical multiple regressions. Other aspects such as recommendations for a career path or personal development may be based on rules derived by experts.

Financial Advantages of CBTI

CBTI has a number of substantial advantages. They are usually cheaper to produce, and cost perhaps £40 for each report, in contrast to £400 for each one that is produced manually. If the software is loaded on a local computer, the turnaround for a report can be a couple of hours, in comparison to perhaps a week for an individually written report. Because the computers can scan a profile relentlessly for even obscure patterns, as well as doing the 'donkey work', they leave a counsellor free to undertake other activities, such as communicating and explaining the results or concentrating on making good decisions (Jackson, 1985).

Consistency of CBTI

Another potential advantage of CBTI is consistency. The production of a report is 'mechanical' and, given the same information, an identical report will be produced the second time. The increase in reliability should lead to greater validity. Research, mainly in clinical settings, has suggested that reports produced by CBTI are more valid than reports produced in the traditional way (Hoffman, 1960; Ben-Porath and Butcher, 1986). However, the consistency of CBTIs may not be as advantageous as it seems. Consistency can mean that the system is insensitive and unsubtle. Furthermore, consistency can mean that a system is static and unresponsive. Some of the apparent inconsistencies in traditional reports may arise because the human interpreter learns and develops their interpreting skills. As a result, the second, 'inconsistent', report may be better than the first attempt. In contrast, some computer-produced reports may be consistently bad!

One of the major problems with CBTIs is their relative inflexibility. A system takes a long time to develop and involves very high set-up costs. It is usually only feasible to develop one system for each test or battery of tests. The one Procrustean system must then be applied to many different purposes in many different organizations in many industries. It is likely that the system will be designed to meet the lowest common denominator in all situations – applying in part to every situation, but rarely fitting each situation in full: rather like a one-size boiler suit designed to clothe an entire workforce. Recipients who have spent several hours completing questionnaires are likely to be less than impressed when they receive a report that is a mere pastiche of phrases and sentences that appear with monotonous regularity in the reports of their workmates.

Appropriateness of CBTI Reports

The basic aspects of a CBTI report will be well structured and accurate. But it is unlikely to be focused on the specific purpose for using tests. Even if the main purpose for testing is addressed in the report, it is likely to be embedded in a mass of distracting material that has secondary or tertiary relevance, and an expert might be needed to sift the wheat from the chaff. A good report should reflect the style and argot of the organization. CBTI reports are, of necessity, written in a bland style that avoids causing offence to anyone, but that also often fails to make an impact. Traditional reports are often very good in incorporating such subtle factors and varying them to meet the specific situation. The optimum solution, which is adopted by some systems, might consist of a computer producing a report in the form of a word-processing file. An expert can then edit the file to refine and tailor the presentation to the specific purposes and argot of the client. An expert can also incorporate information that might emerge at a feedback session.

Accuracy of CBTI Reports

A further question concerning CBTI reports is their accuracy. This is not an easy question to answer, because there is no report that is universally accepted as perfect that can be used as a standard. Four approaches have been used to validate computer-produced reports – customer satisfaction; correlation with diagnoses; 'blind matching' and recovery of original scores:

- *Customer satisfaction.* One way of assessing the accuracy of CBTI reports is to use customer satisfaction studies, in which the person commissioning the report assesses whether or not it is accurate. Rolls (1993) and Moreland (1987) give details of ten customer satisfaction studies on CBTI reports used in a clinical setting. The ten studies involved 3,750 reports, of which 81% were thought to be accurate. These results seem impressive, but Harris (1987) points out that many studies have methodological flaws, such as failure to give an operational definition of what is meant by 'accurate', poorly designed rating scales and poorly trained raters. Studies of this kind essentially hinge upon

subjective ratings by the subject of the report. The positive results from customer satisfaction surveys might arise not from the accuracy of the CBTI reports, but from the Barnum
effect (see chapter 11). This could be investigated by giving an individual two reports,
one of which would be true while the other would be generated from Barnum statements.
O'Dell (1972) conducted an investigation of this kind and found that subjects rated
'true' CBTI reports as less accurate than those generated using Barnum effect statements.
He concluded that reports 'would have been most successful from the subjects' point of
view, by using nothing but Barnum interpretations in the statement library' (quoted by
Rolls, 1993).

- *Correlation with diagnoses.* More rigorous designs can be used in clinical settings, where
the CBTI reports can be checked against confirmed diagnoses. Moreland (1987) compared the diagnoses made by nine CBTI systems based on the Minnesota Personality
Questionnaire (MPI) scores (see chapter 4). The data were collected from five studies
and a weighted average correlation of .36 was obtained. In occupational settings, the CBTI
reports could be checked against future performance or appraisals.

- *Blind matching.* Kellett et al. (1991) used a different approach. CBTI reports were generated for members of a work team and the identification was subsequently removed. The
team members were then asked to say which report referred to which person in the team.
Correct identifications were made in 75% of cases. Unfortunately, even studies of this
kind are not conclusive. The reports did not use all of the possible alternatives and statements in the library. The unused statements are likely to have been the descriptions that
are encountered less frequently by experts and hence they may have poorer accuracy.
Bartram (1995b) reports a small-scale study comparing users' evaluations of personality
test reports. Five reports were shown to subjects. One report was based upon the actual
test scores, a second was based upon the person's self-ratings, a third report was based
on a random mixture of average scores (stens of 5 or 6), a fourth report was based upon
a random selection of extreme scores (stens of 1, 2, 9 and 10) and the final report was
based upon a mirror image of the true score. The results showed that the reports based
on the true profiles (test scores or self-ratings) were considered to be more accurate than
the reports based on the false profiles: 57% of subjects (20/35) considered that the reports
based on their test results were best, compared with 26% who favoured the reports based
on self-ratings; and 74% thought that reports consisting of text were easier to understand than graphical reports.

- *Recovery of original scores.* One way of checking the accuracy of computer-generated test
reports is to give experts copies of reports and then ask them to estimate the original
scores. This process is analogous to 'back translation', where a text is translated into another
language and the translation itself is then translated back into the original language. The
two copies in the original language are then compared: any difference between the original and the recovered text has twice the level of error involved in the translation from
one language to another. Vale et al. (1986) followed this approach using 18 CBTI reports
based on the Executive Screening Battery. They also obtained traditional written reports
from experts. A panel of judges was asked to estimate the original scores. In addition,
judges were asked to rate the reports on how well they had covered the important issues.
The results of the study were clearly in favour of the CBTI reports.

Some writers have commented upon the dangers of using computer-based test interpretation because of the damaging effects if CBTI reports fall into the hands of those not qualified

to understand them (Matarazzo, 1983, 1986). Others have argued that access to CBTI software should be restricted. Bartram (1995b) wrote, 'it is acknowledged that CBTI may be far more open to abuse than systems that are dependent on reports written by human experts'.

 ## 17.7 E-RECRUITMENT AND SELECTION

17.7.1 CYBER-HYPE

Astonishing predictions for the use of computers in selection must be viewed critically. Over-estimation is inherent at the start of most developments, when enthusiasts perceive the possib-ilities of 'laboratory versions' but underestimate the commercial and practical difficulties. Often, the data given by enthusiasts are contradictory. For example, an excellent paper by Bartram (2000) gives three separate estimates of the number of people 'online' in the United Kingdom in 1998. They are 7 million, 8.1 million and 10.6 million – a range of 3.6 million, or 51% of the lowest estimate. Estimates with a potential error of over 50% must be treated with con-siderable caution. This is not an isolated incident. Bartram also quotes two estimates of the reduc-tion in recruitment cycle. One study suggests that the Internet has reduced the recruitment cycle from 32 days *to* 16 days, while another indicates that e-recruiting has reduced the recruit-ment cycle *by* 60 days. These results are incompatible.

Statistics of the number of 'hits' obtained on a recruitment site are of dubious value. An employer might boast that a site has been accessed by 300 candidates. However, research (ERI, 2000) suggests that the large majority of hits are not made by candidates. They are made by people who are not looking for new jobs, but who wish to make comparisons with their present jobs. The site will have achieved perhaps 117 true 'hits' out of the 300 claimed. Unfortunately, the attrition does not stop there. One study of recruitment sites of top organ-izations such as Cisco, Proctor & Gamble and Citibank – whose recruitment sites will be difficult to surpass – showed that 74% of job seekers experienced difficulties with online applications and 40% of these were total failures. The recruitment site might therefore have yielded only 38 useful 'hits'. A glimmer of hope, however, is given by evidence that the applications that do survive may be of higher quality than the applications made by traditional methods (Asso-ciation of Graduate Recuiters, 2000). Perhaps Internet recruiting is a substitute measure of intelligence – only the brightest make it to the end!

17.7.2 SUCCESSES OF INTERNET RECRUITMENT AND SELECTION

The Internet has been successful in three main areas of recruitment: advertising, application data and administration.

Recruitment Advertising

Advertising was one of the first uses of the Internet by recruiters. Organizations simply needed to add a 'Join Us' page to an existing website. The advantages are obvious: it is cheap; more information can be given than in, say, a newspaper advertisement; there is total control over the content; and entries or changes can be made quickly without the delay associated with news-paper advertisements. Many companies now find that their vacancies page is the most frequently visited area of their website. However, there is a disadvantage – job seekers must know that the company exists and must believe that the company might have suitable vacancies. There is the additional danger that job seekers might tire of clicking before they reach your company's website.

'Job Boards' were developed to overcome these problems. For a reasonable fee, which is significantly less than the cost of a newspaper advertisement, the details of vacancy can be 'posted' on a site that is devoted to jobs. Because of their specialization, the sites are known and frequently accessed by candidates. The candidates can then search the database to locate relevant vacancies. It is believed that over 5000 job boards, such as www.monster.com and AOL Workplace, exist.

'Join Us' pages and 'Job Boards' have two disadvantages: they leave the initiative in the hands of the job seeker and the volume of applications may overwhelm an organization. It is conceivable that the first problem can be solved by the adoption of marketing techniques. Provided that data protection legislation is observed, it should be possible for recruiters to identify potential candidates from, say, their buying patterns stored on the computers of supermarket chains. For example, it may be possible to identify senior engineers by the level of the total spend and the frequency with which they purchase magazines concerning engineering. It might also be possible to track suitable candidates by their past history of searching the company website. The problem of an overwhelming number of applications could be solved by developments in online application forms.

Online Application Forms

Online application forms have been another big area of success. Once a job seeker has logged on to an e-job advertisement, it is a simple step to ask him or her to complete a form on line. This avoids losing a good candidate who might become too busy to initiate an application at a later time. It also removes the delay in posting documents. Initially, online application forms were mimics of their paper counterparts and merely collected the standard information on qualifications and so on. However, it is an easy step to incorporate an electronic Biodata Questionnaire. Typically, these questionnaires ask for details of qualifications, job history, offices held and hobbies. In addition, a candidate is asked to write a paragraph or two about a topic. As soon as the form is submitted, the Biodata Questionnaire is scored by a computer. Top candidates are immediately informed of their success and invited to the next stages of selection. Sometimes the available days for, say, interviews will appear on the screen and a candidate will be able to reserve an appropriate date. An unsuccessful candidate will also receive prompt notification of the result. The online applications of borderline candidates will be forwarded to a recruiter who will read the paragraph of text and decide upon the appropriate response. Many employers, especially those recruiting large numbers of graduates, have embraced these systems. Indeed, many of these employers now only accept online applications.

Online Administration

Internet recruitment may bring about major improvements in the administrative efficiency. Each stage of the process is logged. The person in charge of recruiting may readily access data that allows him or her to review the way in which the system operates and then decide whether changes are needed. In particular, capturing data in this way makes it much easier to monitor the fairness of the system. The ability to capture and store data obtained from the Internet works in favour of the applicants too. If they raise questions about their applications, they can be answered quickly and authoritatively.

17.7.3 PROBLEM AREAS IN INTERNET RECRUITMENT

Internet recruitment can present problems in four areas: test administration, security, feedback, and legal jurisdiction and repute.

Test Administration

Superficially, it is easy to administer tests to a client or applicant at home with a personal computer. Unfortunately, this idea presents serious difficulties. First, it is difficult to standardize the equipment. For example, some applicants might have state-of-the-art computers that have excellent graphics facilities, while other applicants may have out-of-date computers with poor graphics displays, which make it more difficult to see the elements of a problem. Fortunately, this difficulty is diminishing as the specifications of home computers improve. Furthermore, an organization's server can determine the configuration of a home computer and adjust the marks or procedures accordingly.

The second problem is impersonation. It is vital to ensure that it is the candidate who is actually providing the answers. Administering tests in uncontrolled environments makes such authentication impossible. The person sitting at the PC may not be the real candidate, or there may be someone in the background giving help. Most methods of authentication, even fingerprint methods, can be circumvented. Consequently, test administration by the Internet could only take place at authorized centres where a human invigilator is present. If an invigilator needs to be present, the advantages of Internet-administered tests over traditionally administered tests are likely to be marginal. This is likely to limit Internet test administration to large organizations such as the armed forces or utility companies, which have at least a regional network. It is possible to set up Internet testing centres in a network of institutions and colleges, but the costs would be substantial.

Security of Information

Early fears that it would be easy for people to obtain candidates' scores as they are transmitted over the Internet have proved unfounded. Passwords and encryption mean that information stored and transmitted between computers is more secure than information sent by mail and stored in filing cabinets.

There are major concerns about security of test materials. Candidates might take a test several times under different aliases and eventually obtain details of every question. With traditional testing, the logistics of attendance and the danger of recognition by an administrator make such attempts unlikely. However, this danger will be reduced in the future. Some systems use tests where the computer generates questions according to a set of rules. Consequently, each candidate gets a different, but equivalent, test. It would take a very long time indeed for a rogue candidate to capture the details of all possible questions. Furthermore, it is possible for a computer to detect multiple attempts from the same user address.

Hackers also present a danger for administration of tests over the Internet. A candidate who is disgruntled because he or she does badly on a traditional test is unlikely to break into the organization and alter or sabotage the test booklets. However, it is not impossible to envisage a disgruntled computer science student hacking into an organization's computer to sabotage a test that is administered over the Internet.

Feedback

In most situations, feedback should be given to candidates. However, when e-selection is used, feedback may involve serious issues. It is technically possible to provide candidates with automatic feedback within seconds of completing the procedure. But there will be little control over the circumstances. For all an organization might know, the person who has completed an Internet test might be someone who is encountering severe psychological problems. He or she may have completed an Internet questionnaire in the vain hope that it would provide help, when in fact specialist advice is needed from a clinical psychologist. Automatic feedback might be misinterpreted: it might make the problems worse or delay the person from seeking appropriate help. Alternatively, automatic feedback could be so bland that it is useless.

Jurisdiction and Repute

A potential advantage of e-selection is that candidates from far-flung regions or countries can be assessed. In the case of e-selection for a job with a Dutch company in Amsterdam, candidates would be on the same footing irrespective of whether they lived in Ghent, Glenelg, Glossop, or Grenoble. But suppose that something went wrong. Suppose that the software company producing the system, based in Granada, was unaware of equal opportunities legislation in the UK or New Zealand. Under which country's legal system could a wronged candidate seek redress? Would the Dutch company be liable for the mistakes of the Spanish programmers?

The often anarchic nature of the Internet could also cause problems. The 'entry price' for setting up an Internet test publishing house is low and the mortality of dot-com companies is high. There is little to stop disreputable people from forming an Internet publishing house that offers useless or even dangerous tests in the hope that enough gullible recruiters will use their system. Tests offered by 'Internet cowboys' could bring testing into disrepute – to the disadvantage of individuals, organizations and communities. An enthusiastic amateur could obtain a test and place it on the Internet without fully understanding the implications. In comparison, publishers of traditional tests have higher 'entry costs' and are more stable. They depend upon establishing a long-term, reputable relationship with test users.

17.7.4 FUTURE POSSIBILITIES FOR INTERNET SELECTION

Video interviews might reduce costs. They could be conducted over the Internet – especially if the speed of picture transmission is improved. These would be as difficult to fake as traditional interviews, and they would avoid the need for candidates to travel long distances. However, it is doubtful whether video interviews could replace actual interviews (Kroeck and Magnusen, 1997). Similarly, it is now possible to arrange a group discussion, where participants from widely separated locations communicate with each other via the Internet.

The Internet could also be used to produce 'virtual' work-sample tests, in which a candidate, after putting on a visor and gloves, is asked to deal with a situation that would be a critical aspect of a job. Virtual work samples would probably be most useful in jobs involving danger and where it would be unsafe to expose candidates to real situations. For example, an applicant for the fire service could participate in a virtual work sample that involves a burning building; or an applicant for a police armed response unit could participate in virtual work samples of incidents involving guns. Virtual work samples would be costly to set up, but once they had been produced they could be reused many times, in many locations.

17.8 ETHICAL ISSUES

Ethical issues are not restricted to computer-assisted testing and interpretation (see chapter 27). Some ethical principles, such as self-regard and informed consent, are little affected by the use of computers. Other ethical principles may involve substantial additional facets when CBTI is involved. For example, when the data from tests are stored on a computer, data protection legislation will be involved. Similarly, a candidate's freedom to withdraw could be curtailed by an operating system that refuses to 'exit' unless all questions have been answered. Some ethical principles are profoundly affected when testing and interpretation involves computers. Two areas that fall into this category are (1) competence and responsibility and (2) the qualifications of users.

17.8.1 COMPETENCE, RESPONSIBILITY AND CBTI

Rust and Golombok (1989) ask who is responsible for the proper use of a system that involves computer-assisted testing and interpretation. They question whether the computer, the programmer, the person who authorized the system or the person who administered the system would be responsible for any errors.

Since computers cannot be held accountable in law, responsibility might pass to the test constructor or programmer, who would clearly be responsible if they provided or implied information that could lead a reasonable person to use a system inappropriately. The test constructor or programmer would also be responsible if they made an error of omission or failed to point out the constraints of their system.

The administrator would be responsible if he or she ignored instructions or acted irresponsibly.

However, a program that is perfectly justified for one type of use might be dangerous for other uses. Under most circumstances, the person who authorizes CBTI will be held responsible if things go wrong. That person is responsible for choosing the system, and should satisfy him- or herself that it is reasonably valid and appropriate in the circumstances. He or she should have read the manuals and ensured that they contain sufficient information for the system to be evaluated fully. If the information is not comprehensive, additional details should be requested from the publisher. Those who authorize the use of the system should ensure that there are appropriate administrative procedures, training for administrators and appropriate quality control.

The allocation of the prime responsibility to the professional who authorizes the use of the system is noted by Eyde and Kowal (1987). After reference to the standards of the American

Psychological Association (APA), they conclude that 'a public offering of an automated service is considered a professional-to-professional consultation. In other words, the offering of an automated service cannot be assumed to be suitable for "retail" use – although as a few minutes browsing will establish "retail" tests are available on the web. Professionals must be able to produce appropriate evidence for the validity of the programs and procedures used in arriving at interpretations. They must be able to verify the validity of interpretations for the particular test used. They must educate the employers about the limitations of interpretative test services, terminating those services that do not provide decision rules and other scientific evidence . . . in an employment setting.'

Standard 6.13 of the APA states that 'Test users should not use interpretations of test results, including computer-interpreted test results, unless they have a manual for that test that includes information on the validities of the interpretations for the intended applications and on the samples on which they were based.' Considerable professional judgement is needed to use computer-based interpretations appropriately. Consequently, the APA's standard 5.11 stipulates that 'organisations offering automated test interpretations should make available information on the rationale of the test and a summary of the evidence supporting the interpretations given. This information should include the validity of cut scores or configurable rules used and a description of the samples from which they were derived.' When commercial interests mean that this information cannot be made public, 'the rules should be made available for independent, professional review'.

Eyde and Kowal (1987) believe that 'Psychologists exploring the possibility of using computerized psychological interpretations should evaluate these interpretations, on an experimental basis, for persons with well-documented case histories, before using them for decision-making purposes.' This would mean that interpretative systems should be evaluated with a bare minimum of six known profiles. Three should be fairly typical of profiles likely to be encountered. The other three should be more extreme and represent 'the worst cases' of the profiles likely to be encountered. The evaluation of accuracy and value of the interpretative reports should be made by a disinterested but qualified professional. Unfortunately, it is likely that those people who find computer-assisted testing and interpretation most attractive are those people who have the least knowledge and ability in the area of psychometrics. There is therefore the danger that the use of computer-based testing and interpretation will be evaluated by selectors who are least able to do so (Eyde and Kowal, 1987, 406).

17.8.2 USER QUALIFICATION

The qualification of users of computer-based testing and interpretation has been an area of considerable concern. Because computers may make testing and interpretation seem very easy, there may be a temptation to make programs freely available. Even where the sale of computer tests is restricted to qualified professionals, there is the danger that some will divulge passwords and other security safeguards, thus opening up access to less qualified personnel. The American Psychological Association (1981, ethical principal 8f) gives very clear guidance: 'Psychologists do not encourage or promote the use of psychological assessment techniques by inappropriately trained or otherwise unqualified persons.' In addition, American Psychological Association (1985) standard 5.4 states that 'Test manuals should identify any special qualifications that are required to administer a test and to interpret it properly.' Such statements should identify the specific training, certification and experience needed. The statement on qualifications should clarify the eligibility of borderline groups, such as the clergy, teachers and health-care workers such as psychiatrists and psychotherapists.

The qualifications needed by users of computer-aided testing can be reduced by careful system design. APA standard 3.16 indicates that 'the score report forms and instructional materials for a test, including computerized reports and materials, should facilitate appropriate interpretations'. The designers of computer-assisted testing and interpretation systems must therefore ensure that the reports generated by their systems will be difficult to use for inappropriate purposes. Often, it will be necessary to list prominently inappropriate uses on the printout. An accompanying explanation should list some examples of interpretations that cannot be made from the printout of the results. In particular, where a system has been developed on the basis of a sample of the general population, warnings should be given about using the results for certain minority groups.

Equally serious are recruitment agencies that make tests freely available as a marketing ploy or a loss leader. Uncontrolled, 'retail' access of tests on the Internet has particular dangers. If it trivializes psychometric tests, the public standing of testing will be reduced. If it provides free access to tests that are used for selection by other organizations, the usefulness of tests will be reduced. An organization that selects using tests administered in an uncontrolled environment is inviting abuse, fraud and impersonation. It may well end up being staffed predominantly by liars and cheats.

Free access to computer tests presents a danger to individuals. A proper testing environment includes the presence of a person who can detect non-verbal cues that a candidate may be worried or confused. The administrator can explain again or offer appropriate counselling. There is no way in which a computerized system can exercise such interpersonal sensitivity. Misunderstandings may remain or multiply in the candidate's mind. This may have quite serious consequences. Often, vulnerable and unstable people will seek out tests and complete them, perhaps in the isolation of the lonely bedsitter, in the hope that they will solve the problems that they face. Sometimes, results presented in a thoughtless and mechanical way can make problems worse and could trigger behaviour that places a person danger. Alternatively, inappropriate exposure to freely available tests could delay someone from seeking proper help and advice. Fortunately, such instances will be rare, perhaps only once in every 1,000 test administrations; but if the test is accessed by 10,000 people, there are likely to be ten severe reactions. To increase concern, an Internet tester has no control over the testing context. It could be that an unreasonable employer is forcing vulnerable individuals to complete the test under duress. That unreasonable employer could then use the results, to the detriment of those vulnerable individuals, against their wishes.

CHAPTER 18

OTHER SCIENTIFIC METHODS OF SELECTION

Tests are probably the most scientific methods that can be used to select personnel and guide clients. Knowledge of the details of tests and their construction will certainly aid understanding of the technical aspects of many other methods. Indeed, the technical standards of tests should be the gauge by which other techniques are evaluated. Nevertheless, many other scientific assessment techniques exist. Depending upon the situation, they may be as appropriate, or more appropriate, than tests. In fact, it is probably unwise to use any single method, even tests, when an important decision is being made. No method is perfect. Unless there are exceptional circumstances, it makes sense to use several methods, so that the weaknesses of any single method are mitigated. This chapter gives a *brief outline* of the scientific alternatives. It cannot give them a comprehensive treatment. Detailed reference *must* be made to other sources. The main alternatives to tests are:

1   Work samples
2   Situational and structured interviews
3   Biodata
4   Ratings by others (L data)
5   Future autobiography
6   Repertory Grids
7   Objective methods (T data)

Some guidance on the selection of an appropriate combination of methods is given in chapter 20, on assessment centres. There is also a collection of other pseudo-scientific methods, such as traditional interviews, references and graphology. These are described in chapter 19.

18.1 WORK SAMPLES

18.1.1 THE CONCEPT OF WORK SAMPLES

Work samples are very widely used as a method of selection, and good work samples have validities that rival and may exceed the validities of tests. In practice, however, many homespun work samples are unscientific. Typically, an applicant for a word-processing job is seated before a word-processor and is asked to retype the first printed material that comes to hand.

Although very unsystematic, this example illustrates the essence of work samples: candidates are asked to perform a miniature version of the job itself. There is 'point-to-point correspondence' between what happens in selection and what happens on the job (Asher and Sciarrino, 1974). Work samples do not try to understand the job; they merely seek to mimic it. They are an analogous selection method and they operate in a way that is equivalent to the hands of an analogue clock rotating on a dial, blindly mimicking the movement of the earth without analysing the basis of time. Realism is an important feature. Work samples should involve realistic situations that evoke realistic responses. Research evidence is highly favourable to work samples. Hunter and Hunter (1984) suggest that they are among the most valid methods of selection. Their meta-analysis, based mainly on operative work samples, suggests that they have a validity of .54.

18.1.2 ADVANTAGES AND DISADVANTAGES OF WORK SAMPLES

The realism of work samples confers an additional *advantage*: a good work sample acts as a 'Realistic Job Preview', giving the candidate high-quality information about the job. Many candidates use the information to self-select themselves. Furthermore, Realistic Job Previews reduce the number of recruits who leave the organization within the first few weeks of employment. Candidates tend to like work samples, because they can see their relevance to the job. Another advantage is that the point-to-point correspondence between the selection process and the job makes work samples easy to defend against legal challenges.

However, realistic tasks suffer from disadvantages. There is an inbuilt bias in favour of candidates with previous experience. This favours the status quo, which might be unfair to minority groups. Furthermore, a work sample takes a considerable time to develop and requires resources in terms of equipment, accommodation and administration. Indeed, work samples are probably more resource intensive than psychological tests. A final disadvantage also arises from their realism. Realistic work samples are usually specific to a narrow range of jobs and an organization may need to develop many different work samples. In contrast, one or two tests of, say, intelligence can cover the majority of jobs. Unless a whole range of work samples can be administered, work samples are less suitable for guidance, or for situations in which candidates are hired for their general capability and later placed in one of many possible jobs.

18.1.3 TYPES OF WORK SAMPLES

Work samples may be classified according to their occupational group (for example, operative, clerical, interpersonal, and managerial and professional). The following work samples are given as *examples*. Details of the construction of work samples are given in section 18.1.4 below.

Work Samples for Operatives

In a typical work sample for an operative, an applicant for a *bricklaying job* would be taken to a mock-up of a building site, which would contain a standardized pile of bricks and tools. He or she would be asked to build a wall to certain specifications, which might include, for example, a Flemish bond, a corner, a supporting pier and a window frame. After, say, exactly 90 minutes, the wall produced would be judged against a set list of criteria.

A work sample for a *carpenter* would follow a similar pattern. A standardized work area, wood and a set of woodworking tools would be provided and the applicant would be asked to produce a simple construction involving, say, a lap joint, a mortice joint and a dowel joint in 60 minutes. The results would again be judged against a list of set criteria.

An *auto-mechanic* work sample would probably involve a car into which known faults, such as a fault in the ignition system, a low level of coolant in the radiator and a loose battery connection had been introduced. After a standard explanation, the applicant would be given an hour to identify and rectify as many faults as possible. The number and quality of the repairs would be checked against a standard list.

In the mail-order industry, customer satisfaction is greatly influenced by the accuracy with which *pickers* retrieve the correct goods from the warehouse, and the skill with which the *packers* wrap the goods for despatch. Short and effective work samples can be devised for both jobs. A corner of the warehouse can be set up with typical storage racks. An applicant picker is given a list of orders to retrieve. The list has been carefully devised and contains items where the specifications and size are likely to be confused. The corner of the warehouse also contains a typical packing bench and a standard array of packing materials. Applicant packers are asked to pack a series of parcels. The contents of the parcels have been carefully chosen to include both routine items and irregularly shaped items that are likely to be damaged in transit. The efforts of the applicant pickers and packers are judged against carefully worked out standards.

Work Samples for Clerical Occupations

The archetypal work sample is the typing test. However, a proper work sample for a *typist or word processor* will be much more systematic than reaching for the nearest piece of printed paper and asking applicants to 'do their best' to reproduce it. The work of a typical word-processing operative is first analysed. Those items that a less able typist finds difficult are identified. Finally, a portfolio of routine and difficult items is assembled. The portfolio might include a routine letter, a price list involving many tables, a routine memo, a heavily amended draft and an almost illegible manuscript, scrawled by a chief executive.

Another work sample is relevant to jobs that involve *clerical procedures*. One Australian insurance company examined the procedures that had to be adopted by claims clerks who processed claims made by a parcel delivery company. It developed a set of simple rules, that was similar to those applied by actual clerks. For example, the first check was to verify that the claim was against that particular company, rather than against another, rival, insurance company. Next, it was necessary to check that the claim had been made within the specified time limit, and that the weight of the parcel and the nature of the goods fell within the terms of the policy. On the basis of this information, the applicant would be able to determine which of five possible outcomes would be correct. A dossier of claims was prepared for each applicant to process, as correctly as possible, within a 40-minute period. Other clerical work samples involving filing have also been developed.

Work Samples for Interpersonal Occupations

Interpersonal occupations are characterized by the large proportion of time at work that is spent dealing with other people. Interpersonal occupations cover a wide range, from sales staff to carers. Most work samples for interpersonal occupations involve role plays.

A typical role play for a *salesperson* involves three elements. The first is a description of the product, and of the organization and its aims. The second is a description of the client, together with details of the client's problems and his or her organization. The third is a role-play exercise in which an actor follows a standardized sequence, acting as a buyer. The sequence usually involves passivity, over-enthusiasm and then antagonism. A trained observer assesses performance on a carefully constructed scale.

Interpersonal role plays can involve a multitude of situations. One scenario involves a nurse who is confronted with someone who has a minor problem, but who believes that he or she has a life-threatening disease. A work sample for librarians consists of a series of encounters with borrowers. The first is a researcher with very specific technical requirements. The second is a master's student, whose self-disorganization means that he or she only has two days to conduct a literature review for his or her dissertation. The third borrower is a professor, who wants a briefing for his or her latest four-second slot on a TV programme. The final borrower is a highly motivated, very intelligent first-year student, armed with an extensive reading list.

A work sample for lecturers typically asks applicants to give a lecture before a group consisting of their prospective colleagues (it would be more realistic if the lecture were to students!). A small number of colleges and universities present applicants with a set of student assignments to mark. The role play consists of giving feedback to a marginal student who is worried about his or her progress.

Work Samples for Managerial and Professional Staff

There is a very wide range of work samples for managers and professional staff. The main types are as follows:

- group exercises
- presentations
- written reports
- in-tray exercises
- role plays.

Group Exercises

Most managers spend the majority of their time in meetings and groups (Mintzberg, 1973). The simplest type of group exercise is the Leaderless Group Discussion, where a group of, say, five candidates are seated around a circular table and asked to discuss a topic. The contributions of the candidates are observed and recorded by assessors, who sit unobtrusively behind the candidates. To provide cross-checks, each candidate is usually observed by two assessors and each assessor generally observes two people. The assessors have previously been trained to look for overt behaviours and to use a carefully devised scoring scheme.

The nature of the task before a leaderless group can vary. In general, it should be work related, but this gives an advantage to those with experience of the job. Sometimes, it is better to use a neutral task. For example, the group can be provided with a box of LEGO® bricks and asked to build the tallest tower that they can manage. Another neutral task is to cut up and scramble copies of several newspapers and then ask the group to reassemble the originals. Tasks of this kind often seem childish to managers. In order to maintain rapport, a brief rationale of their use should be given.

Leaderless Group Discussions can be divided into co-operative or competitive scenarios. The type chosen will depend upon the demands of the job.

In the *co-operative scenario*, the aim is to arrive at the best solution. A typical example is the 'Office Relocation' problem. Candidates are given a description of an organization and an inventory of the office furniture. It is explained that the office is to be relocated, usually to Bootle, 200 miles away, in three months time. The group's task is to plan the move so that disruption is kept to a minimum. When there are a series of group discussions, candidates may take it in turn to be nominated as the chairperson.

In a *competitive scenario*, the aim is to prevail over the other members of the group. A typical example is the 'Budget Meeting Scenario'. Each candidate is allotted a role, such as director of production, sales, finance or human resources. They are given a briefing, which explains that each director has a development project that would cost, say, $1 million. The organization only has development funds of $3 million. The meeting needs to allocate the limited resources. Each candidate is expected to obtain as much funding as possible for his or her own project.

In some situations, group exercises have a *physical element*. For example, a group of candidates may be taken to a rural location, given a collection of planks, ropes and tarpaulins, and asked to move a piece of heavy equipment across a fast-flowing river. Each candidate is assessed on the contribution that he or she makes to achieving the objective. However, to qualify as work samples, exercises with a physical element can only be used for jobs, such as those in the armed forces, which involve physical tasks. The health and safety implications of group exercises involving physical tasks need to be thought out with care.

Finally, *social events* such as behaviour at a dinner might be used as a work sample for a job that involves a substantial element of entertaining business clients. Such events are generally disliked by candidates, and they involve considerable ethical and technical issues. The behaviour of candidates at 'informal' social events should not be taken into account unless the candidates have been informed in advance. From a technical standpoint, it is almost impossible to standardize such social events to ensure that candidates are treated in a fair and equal way.

Group exercises have the advantage that they can gauge the interpersonal skills that are important in many jobs. However, they also suffer from a number of disadvantages. In competitive group exercises, it is very difficult to devise roles that are equally difficult. As a consequence, some candidates are allocated easier tasks than others. The interactive nature of group exercises also presents difficulties. Group members affect each other's performance. For example, it is difficult for an innovative person to show his or her abilities if he or she is placed in a group where all the other members are extremely pedestrian. Often, it is difficult to separate the effect of such group dynamics from the abilities of an individual.

Presentations

Most managers and professional people need to give talks. There is therefore point-to-point correspondence in asking applicants to give a presentation. The length of presentations varies from, say, five minutes for very junior posts to an hour for posts such as lecturing. In general, candidates are given time to prepare their presentation, and visual aids are inconspicuously available for those candidates who are aware of their usefulness. Presentations can be divided into two categories: free-choice and fixed-choice presentations.

Free-choice presentations allow a candidate to talk on any topic. They are highly unstandardized, and unless the candidate chooses a relevant topic, the point-to-point correspondence with the job will be weakened. Some candidates will choose topics that are not very amenable for verbal presentation, but, as they have chosen the topic, any unfairness is the responsibility of the candidate.

Fixed-choice presentations are more standardized and point-to-point correspondence can be increased by choice of a relevant topic. When the topic is closely related to the job, there is the danger that people who have done similar jobs will be at an advantage. Thus the status quo will be perpetuated, perhaps to the disadvantage of minority groups.

In-tray Exercises

Managers spend about a tenth of their time doing desk work (Mintzberg, 1973). In some professional groups such as university administrators, the time spent on desk work will be higher. Consequently, a work sample that mirrors desk work is a common component of selection systems for managers and professional workers. These work samples are usually called 'in-trays'. Sometimes, they are called 'in-baskets'.

In a typical scenario, the candidate is asked to imagine that his or her boss has 'departed' the organization unexpectedly, late on a Friday afternoon, and that he or she has to deputize until further notice. It is 11 o'clock on the following Saturday. The candidate must leave for the airport at midday, to travel to an unbreakable commitment. Since it is Saturday, no one else is in the building and so he or she decides to spend the hour completing as much desk work as possible. Thankfully, the secretary has collected all of the outstanding paperwork into a single in-tray. The material consists of about 16 items, such as memos, notes, letters, press cuttings, messages and a diary. Two items will be distractors, which have no relevance. About half of the items will deal with routine matters. Superficially, three will appear to be unconnected problems, such as a complaint to the chief engineer about machine down time, a quality control report highlighting an increase in the rate of defective products, and a protest by worker's representatives that since the change to a new supplier production schedules are too tight. In fact, these problems are interlinked and they are scattered about the in-tray to see if the candidate is able to identify the common thread – the poor quality of raw materials from the new supplier. There will be one or two items dealing with isolated problems and one item dealing with a crucial matter such as health and safety. This crucial item must be dealt with urgently and fully; otherwise, the organization or other people could suffer a major loss. The items will usually contain several meetings that need coordinating in order to avoid a diary clash.

Traditional in-trays have good point-to-point correspondence, except that real managers are interrupted, on average, every nine minutes, whereas classic in-baskets (Fredericksen et al., 1957) allow a whole hour of peace and quiet. Lopez (1966) and others have tried to include a series of interruptions and telephone calls. Whilst interruptions add to realism, they require more resources and they are hard to standardize.

When time is called, candidates are asked to stop work and number the documents in order of priority. The candidates' responses and their orders of priority are evaluated against a detailed marking scheme. Sometimes it is recognized that the in-tray items may be competently handled in ways not envisaged by the marking scheme. Consequently, some practitioners add a face-to-face meeting with each candidate, so that the rationale behind their responses can be explained and evaluated.

Role Plays

A typical management role play is a disciplinary interview with an underperforming subordinate. The candidate is given the subordinate's personnel file, which contains background information plus documentation that provides details of the areas of poor performance. The candidate is allowed, say, 20 minutes to read the file and plan the interview. The candidate is then asked to conduct the interview with a 'stooge', who has been carefully briefed by the selector. Typically, the 'stooge' will have been briefed to be helpful and constructive for the first five minutes, passive for the middle five minutes, and argumentative and threatening for the last five minutes. The proceedings are observed by assessors, who grade the applicant's efforts on a carefully devised marking scheme.

Trainability Tests

Trainability Tests are a special kind of work sample developed by Sylvia Downs (1973). Whilst they do have some point-to-point correspondence with a job, their main point-to-point correspondence lies with the *training* for the job. The development of a trainability test starts with an analysis of effective and ineffective trainees. On the basis of this analysis, a miniature training session is devised. A typical example is the 'Bags Test', developed to select applicants who could assimilate the training to become a sewing machinist.

The candidate is given an oblong of fabric:

and is asked to fold it in half and then sew down one side, across the fold and up the other side, to form a bag:

The effort is then marked against a carefully devised scoring scheme. The initial score is put to one side and the applicant is given a short training session on how to start a seam, how to keep it straight, how to turn a corner and so on. After practising the points that have been demonstrated, the candidate is asked to sew a second bag, which is scored in the same way as the first. The absolute scores for the two bags are not of primary importance: it is the improvement from the first bag to the second bag that matters. The point-to-point correspondence lies between the Bags Test and the training that follows.

18.1.4 THE DESIGN OF WORK SAMPLES – A BRIEF INTRODUCTION

The design of a work-sample test usually involves five stages, which are directed by a steering group:

1 A *job analysis* to identify the key parts of the job that will be encapsulated in the work sample.
2 *Developing the scenario*. It should be realistic, but it should not require specialist, 'in-house', knowledge or technical jargon. The difficulty of the exercise needs to be judged with care. It must be neither too easy nor too difficult for a good applicant, who should find the work sample just a little hard. The work sample should produce a spread of scores, which will enable the organization to differentiate the best candidates without presenting weaker candidates with an ordeal. Sometimes, work samples are used in order to gauge the personal development needs of existing employees. Exercises designed for these purposes can be made quite difficult. The scenario should not depend upon one critical insight for its solution; otherwise, there is the danger that a bimodal distribution of scores (those who did and those who did not have the insight) will result.
3 *Developing materials* for the candidate. There should be a brief, about three-quarters of a page long, that specifies, among other things:
   • the goal to be achieved
   • the time limit.
   The materials for candidates may also include:
   • maps
   • files of information
   • reports
   • balance sheets
   • audiovisual materials
   • research papers
   • computer printouts
   • personnel records
   • LEGO® bricks and Sellotape®
   • oil drums, tarpaulins, ropes and planks!
4 *Critiquing the scenario*. Is it realistic? Is it practical? The initial critique will be by the steering group. A second critique will be more independent. An important part of the critique focuses upon style and formatting, which should be consistent with the style and formatting of other work samples administered to the candidate. Stage four also includes the redrafting of the scenario to take the criticisms into account. Draft instructions and the marking scheme are also developed.

5   *Trying out the work sample* on five or six individuals. The timescale, instructions and
    marking scheme may need to be modified in the light of the information gained.

◤ 18.2 SITUATIONAL AND STRUCTURED INTERVIEWS

It has been known for over 70 years that traditional interviews are not a good way of selecting
people. Typical validity studies for interviews give measly correlations of about .15. Consequently, considerable effort has been expended in improving the interview as a selection device.

Two factors seem to make the interview much better. They improve validity to at least .3,
and in favourable circumstances validities of .5 can be achieved. First, *only ask questions that
relate to the job itself.* Questions about hobbies, family background, early childhood and so on
do not seem to help to select the best candidate. Second, *develop an interview structure and ask
all candidates similar questions.* It is impossible to make accurate comparisons if some candidates
are interviewed for 10 minutes about their leisure activities, while others are interviewed for
30 minutes about their early childhood. These basic points have been used to develop more
specific types of interviews: situational interviews and criterion-referenced interviews.

18.2.1 SITUATIONAL INTERVIEWS

Situational interviews were pioneered by Latham and Sari (1984, see also Latham et al., 1980).
They can be considered as verbal work samples – they attempt to predict how a person will
perform in a job not by *observing* what they *do* in a *sample of the job*, but by *saying* what they
would do in response to *a verbal description* of a *sample of the job*. For example, a candidate sales
representative might be given the following situation, which a job analysis has shown to differentiate good from poor sales representatives:

> You have arranged to meet the chief buyer of an important customer. You turn up at the appro-
> priate time and are told by the buyer's secretary that the last meeting is running over time and you
> are asked if you would like to wait. Time passes and just as you are obliged to leave to go to your
> next appointment the door of the buyer's office opens and the buyer emerges with the representat-
> ive of a rival company. What would you do in that situation?

The candidate's answer is noted and compared with model answers in a carefully devised
marking scheme.

A variation, called **behaviour description interviews**, attempts to overcome the hypothetical
nature of situational interviews. In a behaviour description interview, the same scenario would
be described, but the final question would be 'What is the nearest situation that you have faced
to the one I have described?' The candidate's response would then be followed by a series of
supplementary questions, such as:

- What led up to the situation?
- What did you do?
- How successful was your response?
- What was the reaction of others?
- What did you learn from the situation?

Some people maintain that behaviour description interviews are better, because the questions probe actual rather than hypothetical behaviour. However, they can only be used with candidates who have experience of the same or similar jobs.

Advantages and Disadvantages of Situational Interviews

Situational interviews and behaviour description interviews share many advantages with work samples. They can be good predictors. Candidates like them because questions are clearly relevant. They can also act as a Realistic Job Preview and reduce turnover in the immediate days after engagement. Situational interviews and behaviour description interviews require as much preparation as work samples. Both types have one advantage over work samples: they make fewer demands on special facilities and staff time.

However, situational interviews are more indirect than work samples. They involve a mere *description* of job behaviour and the results may be contaminated by the verbal ability. Subtle cues and information contained in a practical work sample may be missed. Furthermore, the replies of the candidates may not be accurate reflections of what they would actually do in practice. Because of their verbal nature, some people contend that situational interviews are merely measures of verbal intelligence (plus a test of specialist knowledge), and that it would be quicker and cheaper to use an off-the-shelf test.

Situational interviews and behaviour description interviews share a major constraints of work samples – they are specific to a single job or a narrow group of jobs. Each will need its own work sample. Every time the job is substantially modified, the interviews must be modified. They are inappropriate where people are recruited for their potential to perform a wide range of rapidly changing jobs.

The Construction of Situational Interviews

The preparation of both situational interviews and behaviour description interviews usually proceeds in five stages:

1   The *job is analysed*, usually by a panel that consists of Subject Matter Experts (SMEs) (see chapter 2). Each member of the panel is asked to nominate, say, four situations. They are collated and those that arise most frequently are chosen for further development. Some infrequent suggestions may be retained because they represent particularly crucial aspects of the job or because they are aspects that are likely to increase in importance.

2   *Scenarios are drafted* and redrafted to make them unambiguous and realistic. Typically, the situations are typed one to a page. They should also be screened for aspects that might unfairly disadvantage members of minority groups. Usually, this stage involves further consultation with the panel of SMEs. At the end of this stage, about 20 scenarios will remain under consideration.

3   *Typical responses* to the situations are obtained. SMEs are asked to provide a description of what a good employee would do, what an average employee would do and what a poor employee would do in response to each situation. Replies are collated and edited into their final form.

4   *The responses are scaled.* A final questionnaire is circulated to the SMEs, who are asked to rate responses to the scenarios on, say, a seven-point scale. The mean and standard

deviation of each response is calculated. Responses with a large standard deviation are eliminated, since this indicates that the panel cannot agree on the merit of the response. Then, the averages of the remaining responses are scrutinized and those responses that cover the range are converted into a behaviourally anchored rating scale:

7	
6	Explains own prompt arrival for appointment and that it is now necessary to leave in order to avoid inconveniencing another customer. Briefly engages in conversation to find out what has been discussed in previous meeting.
5	
4	Restrains feelings of anger. Pleasantly exchanges courtesies and makes another appointment.
3	
2	Tuts audibly and openly shows feelings. Promises to phone later in the day to make a new appointment. Leaves without adequate explanation.
1	

5 *The situations are used with applicants.* The final 12 situations are assembled into, say, a booklet and about six are chosen to be put to a candidate. The candidate's responses are noted and compared to the benchmarks. Finally, the data should be systematically archived so that when a sufficient sample has been accumulated, the situational interviews can be checked for reliability, validity and fairness.

18.2.2 CRITERION-REFERENCED INTERVIEWS

Criterion-referenced interviews are the other main type of structured interview. The aim is to try to establish whether candidates have enough of an ability to perform a job adequately. The intention is not to locate the best candidate: every candidate could 'pass' provided that he or she possessed enough of the required skills. Candidates are asked specific questions in order to extract information about the level of their skills.

For example, suppose that a job involves giving presentations to aggrieved customers at short notice. This competency may, for example, be typical of holiday representatives who need to explain to travellers why the hotel of their choice is no longer available. The interviewer explains the situation and asks the candidate to describe how they would handle it. The candidate's responses would be checked against the way in which competent holiday representatives would reply.

Advantages and Disadvantages of Criterion-referenced Interviews

Criterion-referenced interviews are very similar to situational interviews and share many of their advantages. Often, decision-making with criterion-referenced interviews is easier, because they involve only the pass/fail borderline rather than graduations on a finer scale. However, criterion-referenced interviews could result in too many or too few candidates being accepted.

Establishing the criterion is not just a thorny problem – it is a major problem. If too many candidates 'pass', the standard is said to be too low and it is raised so that an acceptable proportion succeed. Contrariwise, if too few people pass, the criterion is relaxed. The criteria on which the interviews are based are not as objective as many might wish. Criterion-related interviews can quickly become out of date if the criteria become generally known. Candidates focus upon the criteria, improve their competencies and pass in greater numbers. In normative interviews, this is not a problem, since interviewers simply raise the pass mark to take account of the strategies of interviewees.

The Construction of Criterion-referenced Interviews

The construction of criterion-referenced interviews is very similar to that of situational interviews. The main difference is that instead of identifying good, average and poor responses, an effort is only made to determine the borderline between adequate and inadequate performance. Often, the definition of adequacy relies upon guidelines by the appropriate professional body such as the British Psychological Society or the Institute of Chartered Accountants in Australia. Unfortunately, these bodies do not have God-like wisdom. A set of guidelines depends upon the views of a given group of people on certain days. Other groups of similar people, on a different day, would probably produce rather different criteria.

 18.3 BIODATA

Biodata uses information such as qualifications, job history and stability of residence in a formula to predict job success. This must not be confused with biorhythms or skimming an application form and making some intuitive judgement. Biodata is characterized by formal numerical data collection and the use of a statistical formula. This is a sophisticated technique that is moderately valid (about .35). A detailed discussion is given by Drakerley (1989).

Biodata is widely used by car insurers, who predict the likelihood of a claim and adjust premiums on the basis of about five pieces of information, such as age, previous claim history, type of car, risk address and garage parking. Similarly, credit agencies predict the likelihood of default from postcode, house ownership, previous court judgements, stability of residence and stability of employment. There is an amusing, probably untrue, anecdote that one credit card company refused the Duke of Edinburgh on the basis that he had no official employer, lived in an inner city and had not previously managed credit!

Biodata is based upon one of two suppositions:

- The life we lead makes us the person we are. Therefore, it is possible to deduce the person who we are by examining relevant milestones in our life. Biodata is like footprints left behind as we stumble through our formative experiences.
- The person we are makes us lead the life we do. It is possible to deduce our characteristics by examining the milestones that we have passed.

Whichever supposition is better, the same conclusion follows.

Biodata is normally used as the first screen in selection. The technique is rarely, if ever, used in guidance. Biodata is often used by blue chip organizations that find it impossible to interview, or test, all graduate applicants. They therefore use a points system, such as the following:

- up to five points for each of the three main school-leaving subjects, counting pairs of closely related subjects, such as 'maths and further maths', as one (A = 5, B = 4 and so on) and subtracting one point for each subject taken in modular format
- up to five points for degree or expected degree results (70% + = 5, 60 – 69% = 4 and so on)
- up to three points for work or vacation experience (relevant job held for an equivalent period of 3 months = 3; relevant job for under 3 months = 2; work experience of some kind = 1)
- up to three points for extracurricular activities (for example, a major role such as captain in significant society or team = 3; a significant role such as treasurer = 2; active membership = 1).

All application forms are sent to an assessor, who uses the framework to score the forms. Applicants scoring 22 or more are invited to the next stage of selection. Some organizations, such as one large brewing company, have further automated the process. Graduates are asked to respond to over 50 biographical questions using a 'mark sense' questionnaire. The answer sheets are evaluated by a computer, which generates either a 'regret letter' or an invitation to an interview on the basis of the score.

These examples highlight two features of biodata. First, it tends to be used as an initial filter when the number of applications is so great that it threatens to overwhelm the resources available for selection. Second, this method of selection can be conveniently outsourced to an agency or computer.

The questions contained in a biodata questionnaire should not be chosen at random. There should be some rationale linking them to the characteristics needed in the job. For example, extracurricular activities of graduates might be relevant, because they might indicate vitality or leadership ability.

Biodata questions may be divided into two types: hard and soft. *Hard* items are those such as tenure in previous jobs, qualifications and home ownership, which *could* be externally validated from an independent, preferably documentary, source. *Soft* items involve subjective questions such as 'What subject did you enjoy most at school?' or 'Which do you value most, money or fame?' Some critics question the use of soft items. They claim that these questions are no different from questions in tests of personality or interests.

Advantages and Disadvantages of Biodata

The main advantages of biodata are cost and speed. Once the system has been set up, each candidate can be processed in minutes, at a low cost.

There are three potential disadvantages. Whereas the marginal cost is low, the *set-up costs* are high, and setting up can take six months. Consequently, biodata is only suitable for jobs where there are over 100 applicants per year and where the applications need to be processed very quickly. Another disadvantage is the *specificity* of biodata questionnaires. A scoring system that seems to work in one organization is said to be unlikely to work in a neighbouring one. Consequently, each organization must develop its own system. Furthermore, biodata systems are said to *decay rapidly* over time. A system that works today may not work in a few years' time. Consequently, biodata systems need to be checked every, say, two years and updated if necessary. Recent developments, however, suggest that a generalizable biodata questionnaire may be possible. A final disadvantage is that careless construction of biodata systems may include items that are *unfair* to certain groups. The use of a postcode *may*, for example, be unfair to minorities who congregate in certain areas of a city. However, fair biodata systems can be developed provided that sufficient care is taken.

The Construction of Biodata

The construction of a biodata system usually proceeds in six stages.

First, there is a *job analysis to identify the competencies* that are needed to perform the job.

Second, the list of competencies is used to *devise relevant questions that MIGHT predict success*. For example, if numerical ability is required, items such as liking quantitative subjects at school, gaining high marks in exams in quantitative subjects, previous work experience in a 'quantitative job', and reading quantitative newspapers such as the *Financial Times* or *The Wall Street Journal* might be among the bank of questions. Multiple-choice responses are developed for each question.

Third, the bank of items is tried out on a *pilot sample* of, say, 12 people. A major aim of this pilot study is to check for misunderstandings of vocabulary. Another aim is to check whether people find the questions unduly intrusive. A third aim is to ask if there are any other items which members of the pilot group consider relevant. Often, some of the best items of a biodata questionnaire are those suggested by the pilot group. The draft questionnaire is revised in the light of the information from the pilot study, and at the end of this stage it should contain about three times the number of items required for the final questionnaire. Thus if a final questionnaire of ten items is needed, the draft questionnaire will contain about 30.

The fourth stage is to *try out the questionnaire on a large standardization sample*. The sample size should be at least three times the number of questions. The sample should be made up of people who are as similar to the applicants as possible and it should include members of minority groups. The sample should also be made up of people for whom criterion data is available. It is often difficult to obtain a standardization sample that is the right size and that contains the right people, for whom the right criterion information is available. Compromises are inevitable. Usually, it is necessary to settle for a large sample of existing employees for whom only judgmental data is available.

The fifth stage consists of *analysis* to identify the items that predict which candidates will be good employees. Usually, the multiple regression technique is used. In stepwise multiple regression, the computer, in effect, correlates each question with the criterion to find out which question best predicts – that is, has the highest correlation with – the criterion. It then calculates a regression equation with which a predicted score (PS) can be calculated. An example of a regression equation might be:

$$PS = Q4 \times .30 + Q26 \times .28 - Q7 \times .22 + Q15 \times .19 + 2.2$$

This means that the points gained on question four are multiplied by .3 and added to the points gained on 26 multiplied by .28, and so on until a final constant of 2.2 is included. Usually, such predictions are made on the basis of raw scores and use unstandardized weights.

Finally, in stage six, *the questionnaire is reprinted with only the significant items* and the biodata questionnaire is administered to subsequent applicants.

18.4 RATINGS BY OTHERS (L DATA)

Ratings can rarely be used in selection, since raters are not available to a prospective employer. However, ratings are often used in promotion decisions and they may be available in some guidance situations. Often, data on personal characteristics that are gathered by means of ratings is termed **L data**. Ratings are somewhat unusual, because they may also be used as criteria (see section 11.5.3) as well as predictors. The only real difference is whether they are used to predict other information or whether other information is used to predict the ratings.

Ratings can be provided by a wide range of people. However, all ratings share several common characteristics. First, they are usually based on the *raters' memory of a series of unsystematic observations*. They are therefore dependent on the raters' powers of observation, interpretation and memory. Second, *raters are rarely impartial*. A superior may have a vested interest in suppressing a talented subordinate. A colleague may denigrate a competitor for promotion. A customer may seek to negotiate a lower price. A clinician may have a vested interest in maintaining his or her reputation and pet theory. Third, judgements by others are often flawed by well-established *rating errors*. The main rating errors, which are described in most introductory texts on social psychology, are the halo effect, the leniency effect, the central tendency effect, the contrast effect and the 'like me' effect.

Judgements by others can be divided into two main types, free form and ratings. In the **free form**, the person who is providing the information can use any format that they like. Theoretically, the most suitable format will be chosen to capture the 'true' characteristics of the person being rated. Probably the most frequent format is a narrative one, which requires no specialist training from either the writer or the reader. In practice, the free format has two very important disadvantages. First, the *format chosen is severely constrained by the abilities of the rater*. The portrayal of the person being rated depends upon the descriptive power of the rater. Second, *raters have different standards*. For example, a person with moderate conscientiousness might be described as very conscientious by a rater who is slapdash, but be called slipshod by another who is a perfectionist. Furthermore, these descriptions rarely have any linkage to a theoretical or scientific basis of personality, such as the 'Big Five' personality factors. Third, free-form descriptions are extremely *difficult to analyse* and compare. The user is often reduced to reading a free-form description and then translating it into his or her own evaluation with a greater or lesser degree of accuracy.

In **ratings**, the format is standardized and information can be readily compared. The possibility of different meanings can be mitigated by providing extended definitions. To an extent, the use of different standards can be reduced by providing Behaviourally Anchored Rating Scales (BARS), such as the one illustrated in section 18.2.1. Ratings also equate the writing skills of the raters and demand less time of them. It is also easy to develop a set of rating scales that reflects the latest research findings and theories. However, rating scales may be too crude to capture the nuances of an applicant's personality. They might be designed in a way that results in most people receiving identical ratings. Perhaps ignorance of the job might lead to the omission of some key characteristic.

18.4.1 RATINGS BY SUPERIORS

Ratings by superiors are commonly used in promotion decisions. Indeed, the first port of call by many promotion committees is the applicant's supervisor, whose view will have a crucial impact on the final decision. Where one supervisor is able to report on all applicants, problems are minimized, but when several supervisors are reporting on applicants, the problems are quite substantial.

There are many other problems. *First*, supervisors spend very little time – probably less than 10% of their time – with any individual subordinate. The sample of behaviour that they observe is very limited and probably atypical. It is natural for employees to want to be seen in the best light; consequently, they actively filter information by hiding their mistakes and amplifying their successes. The supervisor's opinion will be based on this filtered information. It may be that a supervisor's rating is more a reflection of a subordinate's ability at impression management than of his or her ability to do the job. *Second*, in some situations, it may have been many years since the supervisors did the job themselves. If the job has undergone subtle changes in the interim, the supervisors' ratings may be based on out-of-date job requirements. *Third*, supervisory ratings are also subject to many effects such as leniency, the central tendency effect and the contrast effect. *Fourth*, different supervisors may have very different standards. It may be a matter of luck whether a candidate is rated by a harsh supervisor or by a lenient one. These problems mean that supervisor assessments have, at best, merely adequate reliability (under .7) and their validity will be much lower.

18.4.2 COLLEAGUE RATINGS

Colleague ratings are also called **peer ratings** and **buddy ratings**. They are perhaps most frequently used in selection for promotion, but they can be used at entry level. In group exercises, for example, candidates may to be asked, on a confidential form, who they think made the major contribution to the group's effort. In principle, peer ratings should be accurate, since peers will have up-to-date knowledge of the job. Peers usually observe their colleagues for a considerable time and therefore it is much harder for unfavourable information to be filtered out. Furthermore, peer assessments are obtained from several people and individual subjectivities should cancel out. Analyses by Reilly and Chao (1982), Hunter and Hunter (1984) and Schmitt et al. (1984) suggest that peer ratings have a validity of about .5 in predicting who will be promoted. The validity for actual job performance seems somewhat lower (about .35).

There are however, problems with peer ratings. First, they have substantial correlations with friendship and this has led peer rating to being dubbed 'mere popularity contests'. Second, there is a marked tendency for people to give others of their own race and socio-economic group higher ratings. Lewin and Zwany (1976) suggest that racial bias is generally to be expected in peer evaluations. Third, peer ratings give considerable scope for tactical voting and 'cutting one's buddy by the throat'. There can be quite strong reactions against the system by peers who do not like rating each other. Finally, peer ratings may damage team co-operation, especially if someone is known to have been rejected for promotion on the basis of peer nominations – the working atmosphere can become very fraught!

18.4.3 RATINGS BY SELF

Conceptually, self-assessment is quite different to ratings by other people, but since both share several technical aspects it makes sense to discuss self-ratings in this section. Self-assessment is very straightforward and has many appealing aspects. The individual should have a large database on his or her own behaviour, on which to base an opinion. Self-ratings are very easy and cheap to obtain. Furthermore, they are very unlikely to be challenged by an unsuccessful candidate.

However, a less superficial analysis shows that for self-ratings to be accurate a chain of three circumstances must be in place. *First*, candidates must know the characteristics and standards needed for the job. *Second*, they must have sufficient self-insight to be able to gauge how their behaviour compares to that of others. *Third*, they must be prepared to be honest and tell the truth. In practice, not all of these requirements may be present. In selection or promotion situations, the requirement of honesty is particularly troublesome and has led to most of the criticisms against this technique. Research has suggested that (surprise, surprise!) self-ratings suffer from leniency effects and inflation of experience and ability. Meyer (1980), for example, found that 40% of applicants put themselves in the top 10% of workers in terms of performance. Only 2% rated themselves as below average. In general, studies such as Reilly and Chao (1982) and Hunter and Hunter (1984) find that validities for self-assessment are near zero. They conclude that 'self assessment appears to have no validity in operational settings'. Indeed, it has been suggested by Mabe and West (1982) that self-assessments discriminate *against* people who are intelligent, honest and achievement-motivated, and who have high self-esteem.

Fletcher (1985) demurs and concludes that 'self-assessments of ability and performance can be very accurate and can even be superior to other, more conventional, assessment techniques'. Mabe and West suggest that self-ratings are improved if the candidate thinks that he or she will be validated against other sources, the instructions explicitly require comparisons with other people and the self-ratings are gathered under promises of anonymity.

18.4.4 RATINGS BY SUBORDINATES

Ratings by subordinates are restricted in their application to promotion and placement decisions within an organization. They are quick and cheap to obtain. It is difficult to hide mistakes from subordinates, since they usually bear the consequences. Unfortunately, subordinates may not have sufficient insight to arrive at balanced decisions or have sufficient experience to apply the correct standard. Subordinates may also lack knowledge about the requirements of the superiors' jobs. In some organizations, subordinate ratings are 'politically' unacceptable and are seen as a threat to the authority structure. However, more and more organizations are adopting systems of 360° feedback, which includes an element of appraisal by subordinates. 360° feedback is usually concerned with team improvement or performance on a present job, and the technique may not generalize to selection or promotion decisions: a subordinate whose frank appraisal denies a superior a promotion is unlikely to be as frank on the second occasion if, as is almost certain, the superior finds out who gave what rating!

18.4.5 CUSTOMER RATINGS

A few organizations, such as banks, obtain ratings of those employed in customer contact jobs, such as tellers, from the customers themselves. In training and higher education it is a very common practice to ask students for their opinions of their teachers. Customer ratings are easy and cheap to obtain. However, customers do not necessarily have the insight to evaluate the information that they obtain and they may see only a small part of the job. They may not be able to adopt a standardized scale of evaluations.

In some situations, customer appraisals are positively dangerous. In sophisticated service products, the consumer may respond to easily observed but peripheral aspects of the service. For example, they may rate a gushing insurance salesperson more highly than a dour one who sells them the correct product. In education, student evaluations can lead to teachers dumbing down the syllabus in order to gain student approval. A slight variation can lead to customer evaluations that avoid these difficulties. Many firms employ 'mystery shoppers'. Mystery shoppers are trained to present situations that demand skilful responses, which are evaluated on a carefully developed scale.

18.4.6 RATINGS BY CLINICIANS

Ratings by clinicians are rarely used in selection. They tend to be used in extreme situations where the consequences of a breakdown would be catastrophic, such as the selection of astronauts, nuclear submarine commanders or scientists on an Antarctic expedition.

Clinician ratings are usually based on interviews that typically last for one or two hours, but may extend to more than two days. A clinical interview will trace a person's memories from infancy until the present day. It will also cover topics that have been known to cause problems either for the individual or those who have previously held the job. These other areas may include relationships with others and reactions to traumatic events. Often, questioning will be indirect or non-directive and, it is claimed, the interviewee is unlikely to know what the clinician is seeking. The clinician will be aware of hesitations, obfuscation and gestures that transcend the actual words that are used, and that give insight into topics that are being repressed and aspects of the subconscious. If a question is misunderstood, it can be rephrased. If answers are inconsistent, they can be probed. It is claimed that clinical interviews have all the advantages of self-reports. The clinician is able to build a 'theory' of an individual that is less susceptible to faking and goes deeper than the superficiality of reports by others. Classic examples of clinical interviews are the '**Life Interviews**' of Levinson et al. (1987).

Despite these apparent advantages, the clinical interview still depends upon human judgement (McCrae and Costa, 1990). The process is subjective when compared to the systematic tabulation of answers to a personality inventory. Clinicians may impute to answers conclusions that are not justified. A restless movement of a leg may mean the onset of pins and needles engendered by sitting for too long, rather than a repressed, unhappy memory: 'Clinicians are trained to see pathology, and see it they will, even in the best adjusted of subjects. Since theorists have a vested interest in finding evidence for the ideas they have advanced, the data they find in support of their own ideas must be taken with a certain amount of scepticism' (McCrae and Costa, 1990). Indeed, a cynic might quip that a clinical interview is merely a projective test that we administer to clinicians. A further problem with clinical interviews is that many clinicians work primarily in . . . clinics! Their knowledge of the job for which they are screening applicants may well be sparse. Often, only a small part of a clinical interview will deal directly with aspects of the work environment – point-to-point correspondence may be very low.

Evaluations by others invariably involve an element of subjectivity and a degree of insight in evaluating the information that is available. However, they differ on other facets, as shown in table 18.1.

Several investigators have examined the correlation between different ratings. Schuler and Schmitt (1987) have summarized the mean intercorrelations between, supervisor, peer and self-ratings in, presumably, occupational settings as follows:

- self–peer   .41
- supervisor–self   .31
- supervisor–peer   .22

McCrae and Costa (1990) provide the correlations shown in table 18.2 for self–peer ratings, obtained in a research context for the 'Big Five' factors. Interestingly, they also provide correlations with spouse ratings.

If they are taken as reliability coefficients, the correlations, especially the correlations from an occupational setting, are not impressive.

Table 18.1 A comparison of six sources of ratings

	Superiors	Peers	Self	Subordinates	Customers	Clinicians
Used for entry positions		✔	✔✔			✔
Used for promotion and placement	✔	✔	✔	✔	✔	✔
Accurate and comprehensive data	?	✔✔	✔✔	✔✔	✔	?
Accurate knowledge of job concerned	✔	✔✔	✔✔	✔	✔	✔
Standardized scale for judgements	✔ (if trained)	?	?	?	✔	?
Acceptability	✔	✔	✔✔	✔	?	✔
Susceptibility to distortion	✔	✔	✔✔	✔✔	✔	?

Table 18.2 Intercorrelations between types of ratings

	Extroversion	Neuroticism	Conscientiousness	Openness	Agreeableness
Peer–Peer	.41	.36	.45	.46	.45
Peer–Self	.44	.37	.49	.63	.57
Peer–Spouse	.26	.45	.41	.37	.49
Spouse–Self	.53	.53	.57	.59	.60

 18.5 FUTURE AUTOBIOGRAPHY

Future autobiographies are unusual, because they are one of the few selection devices that are future – rather than past-oriented. They are based on the humanistic view of personality (see chapter 4). In essence, this maintains that life is a process of moving nearer and nearer to our true selves. Consequently, if we wish to know how applicants will behave in a new job, we should try to access their view of their future selves. This is accomplished by asking them to imagine themselves in, say, five years' time, and then asking them to write a description of what has happened to them and their career in the intervening years. The responses are content analysed according to a strict scheme. Future autobiographies are rarely used. One documented application involves sales positions (Tuller and Barret, 1976). Validity ranged from .17 to .39.

◣ 18.6 REPERTORY GRIDS

Repertory Grids were developed by Kelly (1955) to map personal construct systems. They are used in selection on the basis that the construct systems of successful candidates would differ from those of poor candidates. They may be particularly useful in guidance situations, because they give a client and a counsellor an explicit picture of how a client construes career choices (Smith et al., 1978).

In a nutshell, a Repertory Grid consists of two things, the elements (the objects of thought) and constructs (perceived qualities of the objects). Some domains of objects that are relevant to selection and guidance are the work people, work organizations and work tasks. A very simple way of assessing candidates is to ask them to list elements in a domain and then judge the elements in terms of quantity and quality. For example, if the chosen domain were work tasks, it is easy to ask candidates to list all the tasks they would have to do in the job. Quantification is also easy. The number of tasks that they nominate can be counted. The quality of the elements can also be judged against a carefully devised set of criteria.

A rather more complicated approach would be to assess constructs. To assess constructs in the domain of organizations, candidates could be given a standard list of employers (the elements). The qualities that they use to contrast employers (constructs) could be elicited by one technique, triadic elicitation. For example, candidates for a job in Australia could be given a standard list of employers. Three – say, Broken Hill Properties, Australia Post and the Flying Doctor Service – would be chosen at random from the list. Candidates would be asked to consider these three organizations in terms of, say, their values and nominate which organization was the 'odd one out'. Their actual nomination is not important. What is important is the reason they give when they are asked to explain why the other two are the same and one is different. For example, it could be said that two are the same because they are efficient and the odd one out is inefficient. Thus, without prompting in any way, it has been elicited that the candidate thinks in terms of efficiency and uses the construct to differentiate between well-known Australian employers. The process is repeated with different triads until the person starts to repeat earlier constructs. The candidate's list of the constructs can then be evaluated.

Up to this stage, the method is merely a type of structured interview. However, the process can be continued to a quantification stage. The elements and constructs can be cast into a grid with the elements along the top and the constructs down the side. Each element can then be rated on each construct, using a seven-point scale:

	BHP	Australia Post	Flying Dr	etc
Competitive	7	5	1	
Efficient	6	4	6	
Compassionate	4	4	7	

etc

The grid of numbers can be analysed in very sophisticated ways that provide indices of fineness of construing and the structure of the construct system. A particularly interesting possibility arises when a similar grid is obtained from the organization's perspective. Typically, a group of managers can complete the same grid and the average results are used to represent the organization's view. The organization's grid can then be compared to the individual's grid. In an investigation involving three organizations, Smith and Ryder (2000) found that the correspondence between an applicant's grid of organizational values and the corresponding grid from the organization yielded a validity of .35. Furthermore, this validity was incremental validity, over and above what had been obtained from a battery of ability and personality tests.

 ## 18.7 OBJECTIVE METHODS (T DATA)

Objective methods need to be carefully differentiated from objectively scored tests. *Objectively scored* tests can involve very subjective decisions, but the answers are made so that the scoring is objective. For example, a question such as 'To what extent are you an honest person? (A) Always; (B) sometimes; (C) never?' is subjective and yields objective answers. These kinds of test are technically called **conspective tests**, because two different psychologists would agree on the result. However, they depend upon some kind of subjective answer by a person (Schmidt, 1988).

Objective methods involve some kind of *overt behaviour* that is also objectively recorded or scored. Data from objective measures is usually termed **T data**. Objective methods measure either perceptions or motor responses. It is assumed that either or both are closely related to personality. There is no doubt that perceptions and responses are related to personality, but the relationship may not be strong.

A classic example of an objective measure is the *body sway test*, which might be used to select applicants for jobs where it is important not to be influenced by what others say. The candidate is asked to stand in the middle of dimly lit room and an infra-red source is clipped to his or her body. The candidate is blindfolded and a tape is played, which repeatedly suggests 'you are swaying, you are swaying'. A detector records the movement of the infra-red source and the degree to which the candidate starts to sway. The body sway test is used (very infrequently) to measure suggestibility, and it incorporates two distinguishing features of objective methods – overt behaviour and objective recording.

Another objective method, often cited in the literature but rarely used outside laboratory studies, is the *rod and frame test* of field independence – the ability to resist the disrupting influence of contextual cues. The person is seated in a dark room and asked to look at an illuminated rod that is surrounded by an illuminated square frame. The rod is at an angle and the frame (the field) is perpendicular, but the candidate can adjust the rod so that it is upright:

After several practice sessions, the frame is twisted so that it is not perpendicular:

The question is whether the context of the frame, which sets the perceptual field, will alter the candidate's perception of when the rod is upright – if the frame is twisted to the left, many people perceive that the rod is upright if it is slightly twisted to the left. A final laboratory method is the *Witkin Chair* (Witkin and Goodenough, 1977), which is often used in conjunction with the rod and frame test. The chair is initially in the upright position:

The chair has a rotating mechanism, so that it can be set at an angle. Then, it may further distort a subject's field when judging whether a rod is perpendicular:

Objective measures do not necessarily involve complicated equipment and many use only paper and pencil. For example, the Gottschaldt Embedded Figures test attempts to gauge an individual's ability to pick out a figure hidden among distracting and confusing details. A typical question might be:

The Gottschaldt Embedded Figures Test contains many of these kinds of questions, and the final score has been shown to correlate with a number of personality characteristics, such as a participative approach in learning situations.

Another example of an objective measure is a test of rigidity. A series of pictures starts with a clear drawing of a dog, which slowly changes from picture to picture until it is a clear drawing of a cat. The person is shown the picture of the cat and it is explained that the next pictures will contain some changes. The person is asked to say when the picture changes to a picture of some other animal (see section 17.2). The person who waits to the last picture is thought to have rigid perceptions, whereas the person who identifies the change to a dog on the third or fourth picture is thought to have very adaptable perceptual processes.

A further example of an objective test is designed to measure perfectionism. Candidates are shown simple line drawings. They are asked to copy each one exactly, making as many attempts as they wish. The number of attempts that they make before they are satisfied is used to gauge the level of their perfectionism.

Objective tests have used:

- cartoons – extroverts are said to prefer cruder jokes (Cattell and Luborsky, 1947)!
- pictorial designs – creative people are thought to prefer more complex designs (see Barron, 1965; Worland, 1985)
- agreement with famous sayings – which claims to measure traits such as hostility, fear of failure and conventionality (Bass, 1958).

The Morrisby Tests (Morrisby and Fox, 1995) contain several objective personality tests that aim to measure variables such as ideational fluency, innovativeness, commitment, tenacity and awareness.

Cattell (see, for example, Cattell and Schuerger, 1978) coined the term and advocated the use of T data (objective test scores). He tried for years to set up Universal Index (UI) Factors, based upon factor analysis, which paralleled the 16 personality factors obtained from Q data (self-evaluation questionnaire data). Each UI factor was intended to have several objective marker tests. The UI factors are frequently quoted in the literature supporting the 16PF test. Lists of the UI factors are not readily available, but one is given on the website associated with this book. The relation between these factors and the factors obtained from personality questionnaires is very weak (Schmidt, 1988). The high water mark of objective testing was probably in the 1970s, but there has been a recent reawakening of interest (Schmidt, 1988; Miller, 1996; Parkinson, 1996; Parkinson and Fox, 1997).

Objective personality measures have one big advantage over other methods: they are less easy to fake. Their resistance to distortion stems from two facets. *First*, they are presented in such a way that is difficult for a candidate to guess what aspect of personality is being measured. *Second*, some of the objective measures are, in effect, tests of maximal performance, where it is very difficult to manipulate scores upwards. The embedded figures test, for example, requires candidates to identify the maximum number of patterns contained in complex diagrams. Another big advantage of objective tests is that they can usually be used in different cultures without encountering the usual problems of translation.

Objective personality measures also have some important disadvantages. *First*, many, such as the Witkin Chair, are cumbersome, expensive, time-consuming and difficult to use outside a laboratory. These disadvantages rule them out for use in most occupational settings. *Second*, their opaqueness, which gives some protection against faking, often means that candidates consider them irrelevant and lacking in 'face validity'. *Third*, validity studies in occupational settings are very sparse. Indeed, the low correlations with personality test scores suggest that their construct validity is low (or vice versa!). However, Schmidt (1988) provides results that suggest that in clinical settings T data are superior to Q and L data in diagnosing clinical syndromes.

This list of non-test measures of personality is not exhaustive. There are other measures that have a poorer scientific base. These are briefly outlined in chapter 19, on less scientific measures. There also remains the issue of combining several measures in selection, guidance or research. When several measures are used, they are usually called an assessment centre, and this is described in chapter 20.

CHAPTER 19

LESS SCIENTIFIC METHODS OF SELECTION

Many selection methods with low validities claim to be scientific. These pseudo-scientific methods vary enormously in their popularity. The estimated percentage use of various selection methods in the United Kingdom and in a combination of six countries – France, Germany, Israel, Netherlands, Norway and the UK – is shown in figure 19.1 (Smith and Abrahamsen, 1992).

It can be seen that the less scientific measures are more popular than the scientific ones. In fact, Smith and Abrahamsen calculate that there is an inverse correlation (–.4) between validity and frequency of use. Smith and Abrahamsen speculate that frequency of use is more related to tradition and the lack of technical knowledge, rather than the accuracy of the selection method.

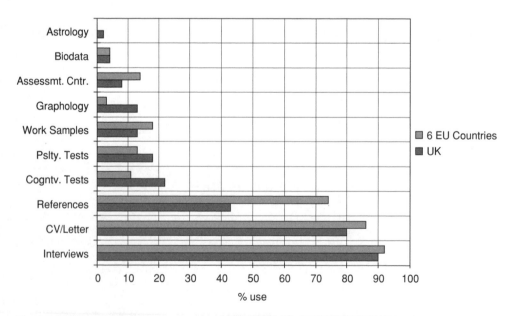

Figure 19.1 The use of selection methods in the UK and some European countries.

19.1 TRADITIONAL INTERVIEWS

Traditional interviews must be distinguished very carefully from the more scientific structured interviews described in the previous chapter. In traditional interviews, candidates are expected to respond to whatever questions pop into the interviewer's head. The traditional interview can take many forms, such as the one-to-one interview, the tandem interview and the panel interview. It is inappropriate and impossible to review all of the extensive studies of traditional interviews here. Readers should refer to reviews and meta-analyses such as Wagner (1949), Mayfield (1964), Ulrich and Trumbo (1965), Arvey and Campion (1982), Reilly and Chao (1982) and Hunter and Hunter (1984). More recent meta-analyses by McDaniel et al. (1994) and Weisner and Cronshaw (1988) give a more favourable view of interviews. However, it is important when reading these reviews to untangle traditional interviews from structured interviews. In general, research into traditional interviews can be divided into two main types: macro-studies and micro-studies.

Macro-research on traditional interviews addresses global issues such as frequency of use, or their reliability, validity and fairness. Macro-research also concerns interviewers: Are some people better interviewers than others, or does training improve the accuracy of interviewers? As simplifications, macro-research has shown that traditional interviews are:

- The most widely used method of selection in almost all countries.
- Not very good at distinguishing between applicants. Leniency effects and halo effects combine to produce a situation in which most applicants are placed in the top two categories of a five-point scale.
- Not very reliable. Typical reliabilities are about .3.
- Not very valid. Typical validities are about .15.

Traditional interviews are liked and accepted by candidates – possibly because they give them the illusion that they are able to control the outcome to some degree.

Micro-research has examined facets such as the time that the participants spend speaking, the influence of non-verbal behaviour, the influence of negative information, order effects and the influence of interviewer behaviour. Some of the main findings are as follows.

Obtaining sufficient and accurate information:

- Interviewers talk for about 57% of the time and candidates talk for 30% of the time (Daniels and Otis, 1950).
- A substantial proportion of interviewees (perhaps a seventh) give misleading replies to questions.
- Interviewers often make up their minds before the interview ends. Springbett (1958) suggests that they make up their minds in the first four minutes and then exhibit confirmation bias (looking for evidence to support their decisions).
- Interviewers can only recall a small fraction of the information given by interviewees (see Snyder and Swan, 1978; Anderson, 1988). It is probable that interviewers try to reduce their cognitive load by resorting to some kind of stereotyping (Webster, 1964; Hewstone and Giles, 1986; Arvey and Faley, 1988).

Weighing and evaluating information:

- Interviewers cannot be relied upon to weigh information accurately. They may give too much emphasis to negative information or actions that are 'out of role' (Bolsher and Springbett, 1961; Webster, 1964; Richey et al., 1967). However, Sackett (1982) found that interviewers search for positive information, and Keenan (1989) even found that when interviewees revealed a weakness there was a tendency for interviewers to change the subject!
- Interviewers are influenced by non-verbal cues such as eye contact, smiling or energetic style (Alafito and Kalt, 1977; Forbes and Jackson, 1980; Gallaher, 1992). Later research suggests that there is an interaction between verbal and non-verbal cues. Good non-verbal cues are only helpful if the candidate's verbal replies are good (Rasmussen, 1984). Baron (1989) contends that interviewers are aware of attempts at impression management. Above a certain level, changing non-verbal cues may be counterproductive.
- Interviewers are influenced by paralinguistic cues. People who are fluent (Lay and Burton, 1968), talk more (Byrd, 1979), have a standard dialect (Edwards, 1982) and who do not hesitate (Breakwell, 1990) tend to be favoured by interviewers.
- Interviewers are subject to 'similar to me' effects. The greater the similarity in speech (Street and Bradley, 1982), education, religion and social class (Griffit and Jackson, 1970), the higher is the interviewer's evaluation.
- Interviewers are subject to contrast effects. An average applicant who follows three good ones gets an unduly poor evaluation, while an average applicant who follows three poor candidates gets an unduly good evaluation (Wexley et al., 1972; Schuh, 1978; Ivancevich, 1983).

However, results of micro-studies should be viewed with caution. Many were obtained from simulations involving students, not from 'real interviews'.

In general, research indicates that, as a selection device, the traditional interview is a 'basket case', which should not be used. However, this is very difficult to reconcile with data that shows that it is *the* most popular method of selection. Partial explanations of the continued use of traditional interviews are custom and inertia. The face-to-face nature of the traditional interview and the power it gives the interviewer to ask any question he or she likes provide very powerful stimuli that engender commitment. Probably the most important reason is given by Herriot (1989a), who suggests that the traditional interview serves many other functions, such as allowing applicants to ask about the job, checking whether applicants will 'fit in with the organization', building an image of the organization and negotiating terms of possible employment.

It would seem that the best strategy is not to abandon the traditional interview, but to reform it. A useful improvement is to place any traditional interview at the end of a selection process, where it can do the least damage. It is a basic principle of selection system design that the most valid methods are used first. By the time an invalid method is used, all of the 'surviving' candidates are likely to be good. Second, the nature of the interview needs to be changed. It should concentrate upon giving the candidate information, answering questions, negotiating terms of employment and building commitment and loyalty to the organization.

 ## 19.2 REFERENCES

References or recommendations are one of the most frequently used methods of selection – especially in the UK. References have a validity of about .26. To be effective, referees must:

- *Be willing to reply*. Mosel and Goheen (1959) obtained a response rate of only 56%. Carroll and Nash (1972) obtained an initial response rate of only 35%, which increased to 85% after a reminder.
- *Know the person they are recommending*. Often, this is barely the case. Referees are often chosen for the prestige of their position. Candidates usually avoid nominating their immediate supervisor, who is probably the person best placed to give an opinion of their behaviour at work. In establishments of higher education, some referees have scant knowledge of students who they are recommending.
- *Know the job requirements*. This is a problem when people are changing careers or moving out of education. Employers often try to overcome this difficulty by enclosing a copy of the person specification with the reference request.
- *Be able to articulate their thoughts*. The quality of a reference may depend more on the verbal skills of the referee than the suitability of the applicant.
- *Be objective and able to overcome their vested interests*. For example, lecturers have a vested interest in providing excellent references for their students, and a superior of an incompetent subordinate has a vested interest in helping the subordinate find another job! Consequently, many references show strong leniency effects. Most gradings fall in the top two categories and show little sensitivity (see chapter 9).

A further problem is that those evaluating the reference must be able to compare and *evaluate the information* that they are given. This task is particularly difficult when the references are collected in free form and referees are able to reply in any way that they wish.

It is very rare indeed for these conditions to be satisfied. It is not surprising that references are not very valid. Although validity is low, references can have significant knock-on effects. Reading a reference before interviewing candidates creates expectancies, which influence the decision as to whether to hire an applicant (Tucker and Rowe, 1979).

Advice concerning references mirrors that given for traditional interviews. They should be placed at the end of a selection process, where they can do the least damage. It is recommended that references are used only to verify objective facts given on the application form. Furthermore, applicants should be informed that references will be used to check the facts of an application. Indeed, probably the most important function of a reference is that the level of lying by candidates is reduced if they know that references will be taken up.

 ## 19.3 APPLICATION FORMS AND CVS

Application forms and CVs are used in about 80% of appointments, and they are a relatively efficient way of collecting background information about candidates. This information is integrated in an essentially subjective fashion and used as the first sift in the selection process. This prime position gives them enormous influence compared to better methods used later in the selection process. Amazingly, there is very little research indeed into the way in which application forms and CVs are prepared or evaluated. In Herriot's (1989c) 800-page book on selection and assessment, neither application forms nor CVs are given a single mention in the index. Most of the available research concerns the fairness of application forms and CVs. In general, application forms and CVs are liable to sex bias (Haefner, 1977; Arvey, 1979; McIntyre et al., 1980; Reilly and Chao, 1982) and age bias (Rosen and Jerdee, 1976; Haefner, 1977). The evidence on ethnic bias in application forms and CVs is mixed. There might be indirect bias caused by information contained in an address or even the name of a school (Pace and Schoenfeldt, 1977). More direct discrimination against black applicants has been found by McIntyre et al. (1980). On the other hand, Newman (1978) found some bias in favour of blacks. Wexley and Nemeroff (1974), Rand and Wexley (1975) and Haefner (1977) found little or no evidence of racial bias with application forms.

Deception is a major problem with both application forms and CVs. For example, Goldstein (1971) compared the information given by candidates with the information subsequently provided by employers:

- 57% claim higher salaries and/or different job responsibilities
- 57% overstate the duration of employment
- 50% understate the number of full-time jobs (Cascio, 1975)
- 37% of the reasons given for leaving are not corroborated by previous employers
- 33% give incorrect information about their marriage date
- 17% claim 'previous' employers who say that the candidate has never worked in their organization.

Opportunities for deception in CVs are high (Walley and Smith, 1998). Their open format allows negative information to be withheld. Leisure interests and memberships may be exaggerated. Keenan (1983) found that only a third of graduates tried to be 'as honest as they could'. Sixty-two per cent adopted the strategy of telling employers what they wanted to hear. Indeed, to adapt Mark Twain's famous saying, it would appear that there are 'Lies, damn lies and CVs!'

 ## 19.4 OTHER PSEUDO-SCIENTIFIC METHODS OF SELECTION

Other pseudo-scientific methods include graphology, astrology, palmistry, somatotyping and numistry. With the exception of graphology, they are rarely used and will only be mentioned briefly here:

- *Graphology*. Graphology (handwriting analysis) is used by about 2% of UK organizations – usually those that have some connection with France. This level of usage has been fairly static for at least 15 years. In France, however, graphology is widely used and may play a part in 20% or more of appointments. Graphology is certainly systematic and it is reliable in the sense that people will agree what constitutes, for example, extrovert handwriting. However, the evidence for its validity is very sparse. The evidence that does exist is not encouraging. It suggests, at best, that graphology has a validity of about .02. Further discussions of graphology are given by McKenzie et al. (1982).
- *Astrology* is rarely used in selection, but its informal use in guidance may be a little more common. Astrology is systematic and reliable. It also shares graphology's weakness in having poor validity. Astrology involves more than simply looking up the star sign under which one is born. Serious astrology takes a person's date, time and place of birth and plots the configuration of stars at either at the horizon or overhead. This part of astrology is rigorously scientific. However, the next stage is to infer personal characteristics from a celestial configuration. This process is essentially holistic and subjective. Many different schools of astrology exist. The main conceptual problem with astrology is to explain, without resorting to mystical influences, *how* the position of a star a thousand

light years distant can influence a person's character. However, the notion of astrology cannot be dismissed entirely. Careful research by Gauquelin (Gauquelin et al., 1979) has shown some very weak, but significant, trends. There *is* a very weak tendency for physicians to be born when Mars or Saturn were either just above the horizon or overhead. Although Gauquelin's work is beyond scientific dispute, the practical importance of astrology is slight. The tendency is so weak that if it were used, many incompetent physicians would be appointed.

- *Somatotypes* were made famous by Sheldon (1942), who developed a method of codifying body shape by using three indices: ectomorphy, mesomorphy and endomorphy. He then tried, with only slight success, to relate body shape to personality.
- *Phrenology* was an attempt to gauge personality by the size, shape and location of bumps on the head. A hundred years ago, Lomboroso unsuccessfully tried to use the method to identify criminals. Phrenology is not used in selection.
- *Palmistry* involves attempts to divine character from the lines on the palm of the hand. There is no evidence of its validity and it is not used in selection.
- *Numistry* takes the letters of a person's name and uses them to infer characteristics. There is no scientific basis for its validity – which is a pity, because all manner of personality defects could be cured by a simple change of name.

19.4.1 CONSEQUENCES OF USING POOR METHODS OF SELECTION

Pseudo-scientific methods may be interesting, but their use can be damaging to candidates, organizations and the community.

Damage to Candidates

The biggest danger of using poor selection methods is the harm caused to candidates. If a pseudo-scientific method selects a candidate whose true ability is one standard deviation below the mean, that candidate's subsequent failings will be very noticeable and dire consequences are likely to follow. The person, who may have been successful in his or her previous job, will be fired or his or her probationary period will be allowed to lapse. The person's self-esteem will suffer and he or she will need to endure the stresses and expenses of job hunting. Any period of unemployment between jobs will involve a loss of income. It should also be noted that the use of bad selection methods may mean that good candidates are denied the jobs that they deserve.

Damage to Organizations

If a poor method of selection is used, the organization loses because it will hire less productive employees. The financial consequences can be estimated using utility calculations (chapter 13).

Nevertheless, a significant number of organizations experiment with pseudo-scientific methods. Such experiments often arise when untrained selectors feel a need to prove that they are open-minded to new or unconventional ideas. Usually, these experiments are discontinued when they produce poor results. However, by the laws of chance, 1 in 20 pseudo-scientific selections will appear to be successful in the same way that about 1 in 20 people who take snake oil *do* notice an improvement. When an excellent person is selected by chance, they are held up as evidence of the method's accuracy, and the anecdotal evidence may be used to perpetuate and extend the use of the pseudo-scientific method. The problem is at its greatest when a very senior figure is selected by a poor method. The person appointed to this senior post is very unlikely to believe that he or she obtained the position by good luck. Cognitive dissonance will lead to the belief that the method is good. The use of the pseudo-scientific method becomes institutionalized and is perpetuated. There is an amusing anecdote concerning a prominent merchant bank that used graphology to select its senior executives. According to the story, the use of graphology started when Harold Wilson's Labour government imposed exchange controls in the 1960s. Business expenses abroad could be paid in full, but a personal traveller faced a limit of £35 per week – which did not go very far if one lived in the style of a chairman of a merchant bank. It is said that one enterprising chairman of the merchant bank hit upon the scheme of sending applicants' handwriting to his aunt in Switzerland for graphological analysis. As a business expense, the money could be sent out of the UK. The aunt was then free to set up a fund (minus commission, of course) to allow her nephew to travel in the style to which he was accustomed. The use of graphology became institutionalized in the bank, and was used in the selection of senior executives for many years after exchange controls were abolished.

Dangers to the Community

Poor selection methods also disadvantage communities. For every 100 vacancies, the gain in productivity from using even a moderately good predictor is about £1.3 million. If the rate of income tax is 30%, government coffers gain almost £400,000 – enough to pay the wages of, say, 20 teachers or 20 nurses. In an economy such as that of the United Kingdom, the United States, Australia or Singapore, there will be hundreds of thousands of jobs filled each year. The gains from using scientific methods of selection will be very large indeed. Any economy that favours pseudo-scientific methods of selection will be at a huge competitive disadvantage.

CHAPTER 20

ASSESSMENT CENTRES

An assessment centre is not a place: it is a process that involves several selection methods. Assessment centres are widely used to select and promote staff. More recently, amended versions have been used as means of staff development. By far the best explanations of assessment centres are given by Woodruffe (2000) and Feltham (1989). Woodruffe's book gives a great deal of practical information, whilst Feltham's chapter has a more general focus. Older, but very useful, guidance can be obtained from Bray and Grant (1966), Moses and Byham (1977) and Thornton and Byham (1982).

◣ 20.1 THE CONCEPT OF ASSESSMENT CENTRES

Assessment centres are based on two main ideas. First, *no single method of selection is perfect*. Consequently, it is desirable to use several different methods. If the combination of methods is carefully chosen, the strengths of one method should compensate for the weaknesses of another. Second, most person specifications show that *more than one ability or competence is needed* to achieve success and that success can be achieved in many ways. For example, one person may achieve success by deploying a quick wit (intelligence). Another person might achieve equal success by working long hours. Consequently, it is important to assess several different traits. Therefore, assessment centres use several methods to measure several traits. In the jargon, the essence of assessment centres is that they are a *multi-trait, multi-method technique*.

Assessment centres take many forms: the archetypal version lasts for two days and takes place away from the workplace, in a residential centre such as a conference centre. In the early days, many were held in country houses: as a result, assessment centres are sometimes nicknamed 'country house selection'. Typically, eight participants who have been sifted by other methods, such as supervisor ratings or written examinations, are invited to attend. An archetypal assessment centre also involves four assessors (drawn from senior management), a psychologist and an administrator. Candidates are required to complete a range of tasks, such as an interview, a group discussion, several tests, a written report and a presentation. On the third day, the assessors meet to integrate the accumulated evidence and make final decisions. The assessors' meeting is colloquially called 'the wash-up session' because, presumably, it is a chore that needs doing after guests have departed. In practice, this archetypal format can be varied in many ways. Assessment centres can last from less than a day to over ten days. Spychalski et al. (1997) report with alarm that some procedures lasting a mere one and a half hours have been called assessment centres.

20.2 THE HISTORY OF ASSESSMENT CENTRES

Assessment centres originated in the German army in the 1930s. They consisted of a three-day board for the selection of officers (Vernon and Parry, 1949). It is rumoured that they were discontinued in 1941 after Field Marshall Keitel's nephew had obtained poor marks (R. Holdsworth, personal communication, 2002)!

In 1941, the British War Office became dissatisfied with its existing method of officer selection, because many of those appointed had to be 'deselected' after proving unsuitable. With the aid of a military attaché who had been stationed in Berlin, an assessment centre based on German methods was developed. The British version, called the **War Office Selection Board**, is referred to as **WOSB** ('Was be') by the *cognoscenti*. WOSB was a great success, since there was a substantial decrease in the number of new officers who were returned to the 'ranks' because of unsuitability.

At the end of the war, the United Kingdom faced the task of reconstituting the top levels of the Civil Service. The Labour government felt that the existing method of selection by a series of essay-type examinations was unfair to candidates who did not have an Oxbridge education. The new method (Method II) consisted of an assessment centre modelled on the lines of WOSB, but without overt measures of physical fitness. The new method was named the **Civil Service Selection Board** and is referred to as **CSSB** ('Sis be') by the *cognoscenti*. For many years, candidates could choose which method of selection they would take, but Method II proved so successful that eventually the method using essay examinations was discontinued. The work of CSSB was followed up for 30 years and a validity of .64 was obtained (Anstey, 1977). The work of both CSSB and WOSB continues today, except that WOSB is now known as the **Regular Commissions Board (RCB)**.

The American armed forces learnt of the British experience and took up assessment centres, especially for specialist units such as the OSS (Office of Strategic Services) during the latter part of the war. Previously, American spies had not been recruited from top universities on the British model but from the criminal fraternity, on the assumption that it takes dirty people to do dirty work. The new OSS procedures reduced the contribution of interviews in favour of work simulations. This difference between British and American assessment centres is still evident today. The book that describes the OSS work, *Assessment of Men* (Office of Strategic Services, 1948), is a classic description of assessment techniques and is still worth reading. American corporations noted the success of military assessment centres and adapted them for the selection of senior executives. Corporations that took up the use of assessment centres included Standard Oil, IBM, General Electric and Sears. Of particular importance was the work at American Telephone and Telegraph Company by Bray (Bray and Grant, 1966; Bray et al., 1974). Bray found impressive levels of validity, equal to those obtained by Anstey (1997).

The impressive results obtained in America attracted the envious attention of European, especially British, companies. Many assessment centres of varying quality have been developed in recent decades. As they started to be used more widely, an additional use became apparent. Even candidates who had not been promoted often gave good reports of the assessment centres. They often said that the centres had shown clearly what competencies were needed and how they compared with other people. In other words, the assessment centre had been a developmental event in its own right. Some organizations henceforth de-emphasized assessment aspects and redesigned the centres to emphasize the developmental aspects. Assessment centres redesigned in this way are known as development centres. An account of the main differences between assessment centres and development centres is given later in this chapter.

◤ 20.3 ADVANTAGES AND DISADVANTAGES OF ASSESSMENT CENTRES

Assessment centres are more costly than most other methods of selection and they should not be used unless their benefits outweigh the extra costs.

20.3.1 ADVANTAGES

Assessment centres are said to have four main advantages, as follows:

1 *Better selection.* Assessment centres were once thought to be amongst the best ways of assessing managerial and professional people. This belief was supported by the impressive validities of about .6 obtained by Anstey and by Bray. However, a meta-analysis by Gaugler et al. (1987) suggested that the validity of assessment centres was moderate, and an 'average' validity of .37 was obtained. However, Gaugler et al.'s results need to be seen in the light of two pieces of information. While the average validity was .37, there was an unusually wide range of validities from individual studies. Furthermore, the samples included in Gaugler et al.'s study contained some short assessment centres that may not meet everyone's criteria of an assessment centre. Schmitt et al. (1990) performed another meta-analysis to investigate the factors associated with higher assessment centre validity. They found that better validity did not result from having a high ratio of assessors to candidates or subjecting the assessors to a long period of training. However, better validities were associated with:
   * more, rather than fewer, exercises
   * a high proportion of women assessors
   * a low proportion of ethnic minorities
   * the involvement of psychologists
   * the inclusion of peer ratings.
   The advantages of assessment centres are not restricted to their direct effects. They often calibrate the rest of the assessment system. For example, in many organizations promotion is a two-step process, in which the general appraisal system is used as a first sieve. Appraisals are often carried out in diverse situations or locations and it is difficult to guarantee their equivalence. However, when candidates reach the assessment centre, one who received a rating of five from a manager in Kuala Lumpur can be directly compared with one who received a rating of five from a manager in Kota Kinablu. Over a period of time, it is possible to determine which managers are operating severe standards and which are using lax standards. Training can help to ensure more even standards across the organization.

2 *Better specification of competency models.* Assessment centres force organizations to analyse and make explicit the qualities that they require from its managers. Often, this is the

first time that an organization considers its competency model carefully and logically. This often results in a more refined model and clearer decisions. Assessment centres are attended by candidates and assessors from all levels in the organization, and consequently the competency model is effectively communicated throughout the organization; and this may produce improvements in other HR activities, such as training, placement and organizational design.

3   *A higher profile for the selection function.* An essential feature of most assessment centres is that assessors are drawn from practicing senior managers. This ensures that selection decisions are integrated with the organization's goals and business plans. The involvement of senior managers gives them a vested interest in the assessment centres and they are likely to act as their champions.

4   *Acceptance by candidates.* Assessment centres have clear point-to-point correspondence with jobs. Candidates can see the direct relevance to the work that they will have to do. They also give candidates the impression that they have been assessed comprehensively and in depth. Since all candidates are asked to do the same tasks under the same conditions and are judged by independent assessors, there are fewer grounds for feelings of resentment or unfairness and, consequently, assessment centres are well accepted by candidates.

20.3.2 DISADVANTAGES

Unfortunately, assessment centres have two very big disadvantages: cost and disruption. Assessment centres are not cheap. In addition to the marginal costs of accommodation, catering and consultants' fees, organizations have to bear the employment costs of the assessors. The costs of an assessment centre can easily equal 50% of the yearly salary for the job concerned. Assessment centres can also cause considerable disruption. In the archetypal assessment centre, the four senior managers who are acting as assessors will be away from their offices for three consecutive days.

 ## 20.4 THE BASICS OF ASSESSMENT CENTRE DESIGN

Assessment centre design has evolved to the point at which explicit standards exist (Task Force on Assessment Centre Guidelines, 2000). Descriptions of specific centres are given by Feltham (1989) and by Russell and Domm (1995). An excellent survey of assessment centre practice is given by Spychalski et al. (1997). A typical assessment centre can be thought of as lasting for two days and comprising of nine stages.

Stage One: Determine the Dimensions

Probably the most crucial stage is to determine the dimensions that the assessment centre will measure. Sometimes, an organization already has a competency framework but, more often, it has a framework that needs modification. Some assessment centres are based on very long lists of dimensions; lists containing as many as 27 competencies have been reported. Very long lists are probably counterproductive; they simply swamp the assessors' ability to make discriminations. Russell (1985) suggests that most lists of dimensions can be consolidated into just four dimensions that capture broad aspects of problem-solving and interpersonal skill. Gaugler and

Thornton (1989) suggest that accuracy of ratings decreases as the number of dimensions increases. The number of dimensions should usually lie between three and seven. A fairly typical list of dimensions is as follows:

- leadership
- emotional stability
- written communication
- motivation
- relationships with others
- planning and problem-solving
- oral communication.

In some assessment centres, the dimensions are weighted. For example, it may be decided that leadership is three times more important than written communication. It is not clear whether weighting dimensions improves the accuracy of the overall ratings of assessment centres. Clearly, very complicated weighting schemes involving decimal points will be confusing and prone to error.

Stage Two: the Exercise-dimension Matrix

Once the dimensions have been established, the exercise-dimension matrix is prepared. The matrix is an essential tool that ensures that every dimension is measured several times and that each exercise measures several things. The construction of the matrix is simple: a grid is produced, with the types of exercises arrayed across the top and the dimensions listed down the side. It is then a matter of considering each cell and judging whether the exercise is an appropriate measure of the dimension. For example, a written intelligence test could be a good measure of problem-solving ability but a poor measure of leadership. The matrix is marked accordingly. A minor sophistication would be to put two ticks in cells where the exercise will be a good measure and one tick in a cell where the exercise would be an acceptable measure. This stage is difficult. It is inherently subjective and requires considerable experience. An example of a simplified matrix is given in figure 20.1. In this example, the matrix clearly demonstrates that there are too many exercises measuring 'relationships' and that the role-play exercise is being used to measure too few dimensions. A revised matrix is therefore drawn up, which tries to equate the number of times each dimension is measured. It is also necessary to equate the number of times each exercise contributes to the total score. It is rarely possible to obtain a matrix that is exactly balanced but, as the next matrix shows, it is usually possible to achieve a close approximation in which every dimension is measured three times, and most exercises measure three dimensions. A further example of a matrix is given by Goffin et al. (1996).

Often, the exercises are linked in order to test how well candidates can perform in longer-term and complex situations. For example, there might be a report writing exercise in which a candidate has to choose and justify which of several sites should be purchased for a retail outlet. This would be followed by a presentation in which the candidate is asked to imagine that he or she is talking to a board of directors about his or her proposals. However, it is unwise to link too many exercises together. If the candidate misunderstands or performs poorly on the first exercise, performance on the second is also likely to be poor. Consequently, it is usually best to use a combination of linked and independent exercises. In practice, the minimum number of exercises is four, so in that case two exercises can be linked and two exercises can be independent.

	Group Exercises	Presentations	In Tray	Report	Interviews	Role Play	Personality Tests	Cognitive Tests
Leadership	✓✓			✓	✓		✓✓	
Relationships	✓✓		✓	✓✓	✓	✓✓	✓✓	
Stability	✓	✓✓			✓		✓✓	
Planning and Problem-solving			✓✓	✓✓				✓✓
Written Communication			✓	✓✓				✓✓
Oral Communication	✓	✓✓			✓✓			
Motivation	✓✓	✓✓			✓✓			

Figure 20.1

Stage Three: Writing Exercises

Guidance on writing exercises was given in section 18.1.4. Generally, the level of difficulty should be moderately above average, and instructions to candidates should be short, so that the exercise does not become a test of speed reading.

Stage Four: Phasing Exercises

It is a task of considerable complexity to sequence exercises into a workable timetable. Resources such as assessors' time, candidates' time and the availability of rooms need to be coordinated. Usually, there is a master timetable and also individual timetables for assessors and candidates. The logistics of an assessment centre can be very complex and it may be worthwhile using a specialist computer package. If logistical constraints permit, it is best to start with an easier exercise that has a high level of realism. This avoids disheartening candidates at an early stage and helps to build rapport. It is unwise to start an assessment centre with an exercise that will be linked to a later one, in order to avoid contaminating later exercises with unfamiliarity or initial nerves. Indeed, some assessment centres start with a short exercise that is not evaluated at all. The final exercise should also be chosen with care. It too should be 'easy' and relevant, so that candidates leave the centre with a 'warm glow'.

Stage Five: Choosing and Training Assessors

An assessing team usually consists of half the number of candidates, plus a chairperson and a psychologist. Ideally, there would also be an administrator. Typically, assessors are two levels above the candidates. The senior managers should be required to act as assessors for at least two assessment centres. This reduces the total training effort and it also helps to ensure consistency between centres. Assessors who wish to attend just one centre can be a half-hearted, irritating inconvenience. The chair is usually a senior person from the human resource function.

Training for inexperienced assessors should involve at least two days for every day of assessment exercises. It should cover the organization, the job, assessment techniques, the relationship between dimensions and performance, skills of observation, and data integration processes and skills. Training should also include attendance at a mock centre, to ensure that the proper centre runs smoothly. Once a cadre of experienced assessors has been built up, it is possible to train subsequent cohorts of assessors with only one or two days of formal training plus time 'sitting by Nellie'; that is, on-the-job training.

Stage Six: the Assessment Centre Itself

Candidates should receive advance written information about the centre. Guidance on the content of this information is given by the Task Force on Assessment Centre Guidelines (2000).

Most assessment centres are hectic and tiring. Unanticipated events occur and contingency plans should be in position lest assessors or candidates fail to turn up. Two particular difficulties are to prevent candidates from conferring and to ensure that assessors arrive at *independent* ratings based solely on behaviour *observed* during the exercises themselves. The most frequently used exercises (Spychalski et al., 1997) are as follows:

- in-trays   81%
- leaderless group discussions, without role assignment   59%
- leaderless group discussions, with role assignment   44%
- interviews   57%
- simulations   54%
- problem analysis   49%
- presentations   46%
- fact-finding   38%
- skills and ability tests   31%
- self-evaluation   31%
- peer evaluation   22%

Usually, different candidates are doing different exercises at any one moment in time. For example, one candidate may be completing ability tests, another may be giving a presentation and the remainder may be completing in-baskets. In general, for each exercise, a candidate is observed by two assessors and each assessor is asked to observe two nominated candidates. It is desirable to have a scheme whereby, over the duration of the centre, assessors observe each candidate for an equivalent number of exercises. Usually, the scheme for matching assessors to candidates and exercises is so complex that it needs to be devised in advance and it is helpful if a computer is available, so that last-minute changes can be accommodated.

Stage Seven: the 'Wash-up'

Plenty of time should be allowed for integration of the marks. It takes about an hour to process the results for one candidate. The process starts with a laborious, exercise-by-exercise, trait-by-trait comparison of the ratings given by the two assessors. If there is a difference between the two ratings, it should be discussed until a consensus within one rating point is reached. It is wrong to simply average discrepant ratings.

Once the ratings have been agreed, they need to be combined into an overall rating (the OAR). The combination of the ratings can be achieved in two ways. First, the assessors can take a *holistic view* and, in the light of all the information before them, come to an opinion on the OAR for a candidate. Second, the component rating can be *mechanically summed* to provide the OAR. Research suggests that the mechanical, arithmetical approach produces OARs with greater validity (Feltham, 1989). Spychalski et al. (1997) report that 84% of assessment centres use the consensus method of obtaining the OAR. The OAR then needs to be translated into decision categories, which are usually as follows:

- Ready for promotion now.
- Ready for promotion except for a few minor points.
- Promotion potential, but significant development is needed. Usually, this involves attendance at another centre in, say, one year hence.
- Discourage from holding ambitions for promotion. (Never darken our doors again!)

The final task at this stage is to itemize development points that should be fed back to the candidate.

Stage Eight: Feedback

Over 90% of centres give feedback to candidates. This should take place promptly. Taking practical considerations into account, this means that feedback should take place within two weeks. Training on giving feedback should be a routine component in assessor training. Very often (70%), the feedback is oral and takes an average of 65 minutes. Spychalski et al.'s (1997) figures suggest that:

- 31% of candidates receive only oral feedback
- 39% of candidates receive both oral *and* written feedback
- 22% of candidates receive only written feedback
- 8% of candidates receive no feedback.

Stage Nine: Evaluation

Evaluation of an assessment centre is vital. Otherwise, an ineffective method might be used to make decisions that make dramatic differences to the course of people's lives, and that may have a vital effect on the organization's profitability. An evaluation also proves invaluable if there is a legal challenge. Despite its importance, evaluation often falls by the wayside and about 40% of assessment centres in the United States are unevaluated. To avoid this possibility, a specific person should be made responsible for evaluation. This person will probably be an internal or an external consultant. At the very least, evaluation should include evaluations of:

- the composition of candidates arriving at the centre
- the composition of candidates who pass and the candidates who fail
- candidate reactions

- administrative arrangements
- data on costs and, if possible, benefits
- distributions of ratings – for majority and minority groups
- reliability of ratings (inter-rater reliability data should be available from assessor pairings and some internal consistency indices of reliability should be possible)
- the content relevance ('validity') of the centre.

About 36% of organizations attempt some kind of predictive validity study of their assessment centres.

20.5 THEORETICAL ISSUES

There are three major theoretical issues concerning assessment centres: the validity gap, policy capturing and dimensions versus exercises.

20.5.1 THE VALIDITY GAP

The validity of assessment centres contains a puzzle. The validity of some of the individual selection methods, such as ability tests, work samples and situational interviews, is quite good – in the region of, say, .53. Yet, meta-analyses such as Gaugler's suggest that the validity of assessment centres is about .37. The obvious question arises, 'Why does this validity gap arise?' There are three possible reasons.

First, the validity gap arises because good predictors such as work samples, situational interviews and ability tests are mixed with poor predictors such as traditional interviews, and the resulting *mélange* has a validity of under .4. If this explanation is correct, the remedy is simple: the design of an assessment centre should exclude predictors, such as traditional interviews that have low validity.

Second, the way in which scores from the individual exercises are combined during the 'wash-up' session may introduce error. It may be that the OARs that emerge are partly dependent on factors such as who is the more dominant of two assessors. If this is correct, 'wash-up' sessions should be abandoned OARs should be calculated arithmetically. Feltham (1989) found that mechanical combination of ratings produced an OAR that was at least equally, if not more, valid than judgmental combination.

A *third* possible explanation of the validity gap is that meta-analyses underestimate the true validity of assessment centres. It could be that assessment centres included in meta-analyses such as that of Gaugler et al. (1987) were too 'catholic' and combined results from a motley collection of assessment centres, which varied enormously in length and composition. It may be that, when only the results from well-organized assessment centres such as AT&T and CSSB are used, the gap disappears.

20.5.2 POLICY CAPTURING

Klimoski and Strickland (1977) argue that assessment centres may not be particularly valid at identifying true ability. They work not by measuring true job performance, but by detecting and magnifying the organizational biases and prejudices in promotion decisions. This is known as policy capturing. According to policy capturing, assessment centres could predict promotion because *both* assessment centre decisions and promotion decisions favour individuals who are good at, for example, projecting a superficial image and who are good at appearing to work effectively in the short term while under observation. In other words, assessment centres may work because they are able to predict 'who is going to get the best ratings from the organisational "big shots"'. To an extent, this criticism is unfair. Most selection methods are validated against superior ratings and most methods are subject to policy capturing. Some people take a totally sanguine view of policy capturing. They say that it is the selector's job to select people that the organization wishes, rather than engage in intellectual imperialism and impose their own theoretical standards and ideas. If the organization chooses to specify the wrong type of person, that is the organization's problem, and the market or other mechanisms will extract the penalty!

20.5.3 DIMENSIONS VERSUS EXERCISES

Researchers such as Sackett and Dreher (1982) and Robertson et al. (1987) have noticed an important feature in the correlations between ratings obtained in assessment centres. It is possible to obtain these correlations in two ways:

- First, it is possible to correlate dimensions (that is, across rows – see figure 20.2). For example, in an assessment centre based on the revised grid reproduced in section 20.4, it would be possible to correlate the ratings of leadership from the group exercise with the ratings for leadership from the role play, and the process could be repeated for the other combinations where the *same DIMENSION is involved.*
- Second, if so instructed, a computer can calculate the correlations for exercises (that is, down columns – see figure 20.3). For example, it would be possible to correlate the leadership rating obtained from the group exercise with the relationship rating also obtained from the group exercise. The process could be repeated for the other combinations where the *same EXERCISE is involved.*

When the two sets of correlations are compared, the correlations for the exercises are significantly higher than the correlations for the dimensions. Empirical evidence from Russell and Domm (1995), using a slightly different definition of 'exercise', found that 'task ratings' produced higher validities than ratings on dimensions. Such findings have a number of important implications. First, they suggest that conclusions about individuals are likely to be more

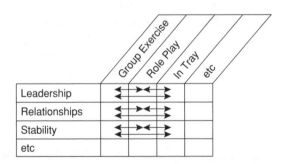

Figure 20.2 Dimension correlations.

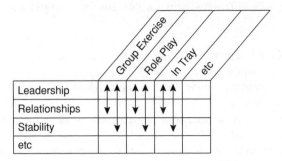

Figure 20.3 Exercise correlations.

valid if related to tasks and situations rather than to dimensions (Feltham, 1989). Second, there are implications for assessment centre design. The findings indicate that it is not necessary to decide on dimensions when designing an assessment centre. It is merely necessary to create a group of exercises that mimic (sample) the activities of the job. Furthermore, with no sacrifice in accuracy, assessors could abandon ratings for the dimensions and make just one rating per exercise.

There may be two reasons why these conclusions may be wrong:

- First, some of the *calculations of the correlations may be inappropriate*. The dimensions of an assessment centre are, well . . . dimensions, in the same way that height, weight and IQ are dimensions, and it is perfectly proper to use them for correlations. The exercises, however, are entities that are described by the dimensions in the same way in which people are entities that are described by height, weight and IQ. It is no more appropriate to correlate exercises than it is to produce correlations between Tom, Dick and Harry. The appropriate statistic for this kind of data is some kind of distance measure. Consequently, conclusions drawn by comparing a set of appropriate correlations with a set of inappropriate correlations may be misleading.
- Second, there may be a *systematic accumulation of error variance* in one direction. A person's observed score on an exercise will depend upon his or her ability (true score) plus a range of coincidental errors, such as the way in which an exercise is administered, the arbitrary details of the scenario (which may give some candidates, but not others, an edge) and the candidate's mood during the exercise. All of these error factors will be relatively constant during any given exercise, and some correlation within exercises would be expected even if there is no correlation whatsoever between the true scores. The situation with dimensions is rather different. There is less reason to believe that error accumulates systematically across dimensions. The scores for dimensions are obtained at different times of the day, perhaps on different days, in different task contexts. Hence there is a greater chance that error will cancel out. There may well be higher correlations for exercises than for dimensions, but the difference is small and can be accounted for by the way in which error accumulates.

20.6 DEVELOPMENT CENTRES

Development centres arose because candidates found that assessment centres highlighted their development needs. A new genre of centre thus evolved. According to Kerr and Davenport

(1989), some of the main differences between a development centres and an assessment centres are as follows:

- Attendance should be preceded by questionnaires completed by the participant, their peers and their subordinates.
- A development centre is longer, because more dimensions need to be measured in order to give detailed feedback.
- A development centre is timetabled more loosely, to allow for reflection and consolidation of lessons learned.
- Frequent, short, positive and constructive feedback sessions are included in the timetable. The amount of feedback given at any one time is limited, to avoid overwhelming the participant.
- In a development centre, similar exercises are programmed after a feedback session, so that participants have a second chance to practice lessons learned.
- A climate is created in which it is acceptable to experiment and make mistakes.
- Assessors do not remain 'detached and clinical'. They act as participating mentors, adopting the roles of co-learners and facilitators.
- In a development centre, exercises should be moderately difficult rather than hard.
- There is a natural progression from building core skills to observed exercises, and then feedback on development centre performance.
- A development centre ends not with a judgement from assessors, but with counselling and an action plan produced by the participant.

Development centres usually require greater resources than assessment centres. For example, they usually involve a higher ratio of 'assessors' to 'candidates', and a higher level of organizational knowledge of development and coaching. Furthermore, they may need 'post-centre' material, such as brochures on personal development and lists of resources that are available to aid personal development.

PART IV

USING TESTS

CHAPTER 21

TEST ADMINISTRATION

THE AIMS AND IMPORTANCE OF GOOD ADMINISTRATION

Proper test administration is vital. There are at least three reasons. First, it increases reliability by eliminating random events and increasing standardization. Where random events cannot be eliminated, they will be noted by an alert administrator, so that they can be taken into account at a later stage. Second, correct administration increases validity by inducing applicants and clients to be as honest as possible. Third, good administration projects a good image of the organization. The main aims of test administration are to:

- reassure the candidates and reduce their anxiety
- inform the candidates of procedures and methods
- collect test information from the candidates
- project a good image of the organization.

Good administration starts with good advanced preparation.

21.1 PREPARATION

21.1.1 WELL IN ADVANCE

As soon as you decide to use tests, you should read the manuals and attempt the tests yourself. Ideally, you should also try to administer the test on 'guinea pigs'. It is a good idea to inform others that you will be using tests in future. It is also worth checking the physical infrastructure, in case rooms need to be modified, furniture purchased or advance permission obtained.

21.1.2 THREE WEEKS BEFORE TESTING

Estimate the number of people you will test and check:

- *Stocks and condition of test materials.* Have either two spare sets or, if the likely number of candidates is greater than ten, a 20% capacity of spare sets.
- *Pencils, erasers and name tags.* Check the *availability of test logs* and *notices* for doors.

- *Stopwatches* and clocks.
- *Room and equipment.* Check that the room is sufficiently large to allow candidates to be seated at a distance that will prevent cheating. Avoid seating candidates at opposite sides of 'boardroom-style' tables.
- *Timetable.* Allow plenty of time for breaks and explanations. If possible, start and end with unthreatening tests. A possible plan for a session involving the AH4 test, the 16PF test and the Rothwell–Miller Interest Test for able candidates might be:

     9.45 Candidates arrive at reception

     10.00 General welcome and introduction

     10.10 Break

     10.15 Rothwell–Miller Interest Test

     10.30 AH4

     11.00 Coffee

     11.20 16PF

     12.15 Thank you and farewell

- Organize *invigilators*. Assume that at least one candidate will be disabled. Consequently, the number of invigilators will be as follows:

Candidates	Invigilators
1–4	1
5–11	2
12–25	3
25–49	4
50–74	5
75–99	6

  If, later, it becomes clear that there are no disabled applicants, the number of invigilators can be scaled down.

- *Prepare invitation letters.* Adopt an open, friendly style. The letter *must* contain:
  - the date, time, duration and venue of testing
  - the contact name
  - the reasons for using tests (in a maximum of three sentences)
  - whether refreshments will be available
  - the role of the test results in the context of the whole selection procedure
  - reassurance that candidates will not be embarrassed or asked degrading questions
  - a request to confirm attendance.
- It is useful to provide other information in order to reduce the amount of official blurb that needs to be given on the day of the tests. The danger is that too much extra information will make the letter daunting and official. Some organizations solve this problem by enclosing an extra sheet of 'Information for Candidates', that contains:
  - a policy statement that people are not assessed under duress, and that they are free to leave at any point, should they wish
  - assurances and details about confidentiality
  - the purposes for which the scores will be used
  - assurances that there will be practice questions
  - assurances that there will be a chance to ask questions

    – a request that people notify the organization if they are disabled or have any special
      requirements
    – a suggestion that mobile phones, pagers and chiming watches are not brought to the
      testing session
    – the form in which the results are retained
    – the time for which results are retained and how they are stored
    – any additional uses to which the results may be put
    – arrangements for feedback of results
    – the policy on payment of expenses
    – a contact name and telephone number that people can call before or after the testing
      session, if they have any concerns.

It is not necessary to labour these points. One or two sentence for each is usually sufficient.
Jargon must be avoided. If 'test takers' guides' are available, they should be included with
the letter of invitation. The letter of invitation should be despatched 10–14 days before
the testing session. Often, it is best to make tentative arrangements by telephone and send
a letter in confirmation.

- Prepare a general welcoming spiel to candidates (see below).
- Prepare a closing spiel to candidates (see below).

21.1.3 TWO DAYS BEFORE TESTING

- Prepare a *list of candidates* and *name badges*.
- Notify *reception* and *security*.
- Prepare a *summary table* or *spreadsheet* for candidates' scores.
- Assemble and check *materials and any equipment*.
- Visit the *room* and check the seating arrangements.
- Adjust the number of, and brief, *invigilators*.
- Check that 'credits' are available for computer tests. If there are insufficient credits,
  contact the publishers to obtain a 'release code' that will allow enough credits.

21.1.4 ON THE DAY OF TESTING

First thing in the morning:

- Remind *reception* and *security* of the testing session.
- Check the room.

Twenty minutes before the testing session:

- Sign out the test materials from the secure store.
- Check the test booklets and other materials for marks.
- Set out the tables or desks.
- Confirm arrangements with invigilators.
- Put signs on doors and in corridors.
- Divert calls and unplug telephones.
- Have stopwatches ready and 'zeroed'.

- Enter the tests used in the test log.
- Enter the names of the candidates in the test log – this reminds testers to use the test log and it familiarizes them with the candidates' names. Any special provisions made for disabled candidates should also be noted in the test log.

 ## 21.2 TEST ADMINISTRATION

21.2.1 THE INTRODUCTORY SESSION

The main invigilator should welcome candidates and give the introductory spiel, which should cover:

- Your name and job title and those of the other invigilators.
- A welcome and thanks for attendance.
- A check that people are being tested with their full consent.
- A check of audibility, and a check that candidates who need spectacles are wearing them.
- Safety arrangements and the timetable, including any refreshment breaks.
- Arrangements for smokers. Usually, smoking is not allowed during the testing session but is allowed during breaks. Indicate areas where smoking is permitted.
- An instruction to candidates to switch off mobile phones and watch alarms.
- A brief description of the tests.
- The role that the tests will play in the selection decision.
- A reiteration that all of the tests will have some practice questions.
- An explanation as to why instructions will be read from a card, even though this seems very formal and unfriendly.
- A check that everyone has the correct equipment, booklets and so on.
- An invitation to candidates to ask general questions.
- The announcement of a five-minute break before the first test.

21.2.2 COMPUTER-ADMINISTERED TESTS

If the tests are administered by computer (see chapter 17), there should be an additional section which:

- reassures candidates who are unfamiliar with computers
- explains pieces of hardware, such as a 'mouse'
- gives candidates a chance to practice with the hardware before the test starts.

There are legal advantages in leaving the candidate to enter his or her own details, such as age, gender, ethnic group and previous qualifications.

21.2.3 GENERAL TEST ORIENTATION

When the group reassembles, the main invigilator should try to reduce tension by avoiding, if possible, the word 'test' and using ploys such as:

- Is everyone comfortable?
- Would any of you like to take off your jackets?
- Do any of you have any further questions?
- Have you switched off your mobile phones and watch alarms?

If the test is marked by computerized sensing devices, remind candidates that they must use the pencils provided. They should be reminded that if they make a mistake, they must cancel the wrong answer using the eraser.

21.2.4 PRACTICE ITEMS

The exact instructions for the test are then *read verbatim*. Usually, the test starts with a few *practice questions*:

- Do not hurry candidates over practice questions.
- Be vigilant to note those who finish the practice questions early, and then turn over to the other pages of the test. Unambiguously remind them that they should not turn over until told to do so.
- If candidates cannot solve the example questions, tactfully ask them to have another look, reading the question more carefully. If this does not lead to the answer, ask 'How are you going about answering the question?' If this does not work, go through the practice question, explaining each stage rather than divulging the correct answer directly.
- Before the test commences, it is usual to ask 'Does anyone have any questions? We cannot answer questions once the test has started.'
- Unless the manual contains express instructions to the contrary, ensure that candidates are aware of any time limits.
- Check that candidates are answering in the required way. Correct candidates who:
  - write the word rather than the number of the answer
  - tick a box rather than using a cross
  - do not fully blacken the appropriate space on a 'mark sense' answer sheet.
- If candidates ask to leave because they decide that the test is too hard:
  - remind them that they have as long as they need to do the practice questions
  - point out that the tests are only a part of the procedure and that they may do a lot better on the other parts.
  However, if all this fails, assist them to leave without further fuss. Reassure the remaining candidates that occasionally some people prefer not to do tests and that they have a right to leave.

21.2.5 MAIN TEST ADMINISTRATION

Ensure that candidates are aware of the time limits that are stated in the test manual. Start the stopwatch. After a few seconds, invigilators should tour the room to observe that that candidates are answering in the correct mode. Beware of candidates who:

- answer across the rows rather than working down the columns, and vice versa
- give two answers to a question without erasing one properly

- answer questions out of sequence
- turn over two pages of the question book
- turn over to start the test before the signal is given.

Candidates who make mistakes should be given discreet guidance. Tours of the testing room should be conducted every few minutes. Make a note of any event in the test log. It is usually tactful to wait a minute between observing an event and making a note in the test log. Be alert to signals and comments that indicate that candidates have taken the same tests previously.

 ## 21.3 ENDING THE TEST SESSION

Stop the test precisely when the allowed time has elapsed. Be firm with candidates who continue working. It is generally best to ask candidates to remain in their seats until all of the papers have been collected.

As test papers are collected, make sure each answer sheet has a legible name. Before you give the signal for people to leave the room, count and reconcile the number of test booklets against the inventory. Ensure that no one leaves the room with either answer sheets or test booklets.

Thank candidates for attending the session. Remind them of the person to contact if they have any concerns. Ask if there are any further questions. You should prepare responses to the most usual questions and comments, which are as follows:

- What is the next step?
- How will I hear the results?
- Do we get feedback on today's tests?
- I didn't finish the test. Am I stupid?
- I feel really bad about some of my answers on the personality test.
- Some of those questions upset me a lot because . . .
- Some of those questions seemed really dubious.
- There is one question where two alternatives could be right.

Make a note in the test log of any questions or comments that might influence the interpretation of the results. Check the question booklets and any other reusable materials, and destroy them if they have been marked. Record such actions in the test log. Make a note of the number of booklets and so on returned to the secure store.

 ## 21.4 MARKING

21.4.1 MARKING SYSTEMS

There are three main types of marking methods:

- *Systematic methods*, which rely on the sequence of responses. These often entail rewriting the answers on to a specially prepared grid. An example of a systematic scoring method is the Rothwell–Miller Interest Test, where each block of answers needs to be copied, in a slightly different order, on to a grid. Be very careful to ensure that replies are copied exactly and that there are no transcription errors.

- *Marking keys*, where the correct answers are printed on a separate sheet, which is held against the answer sheet completed by a candidate. It is vital that marking keys are correctly aligned. Marking keys where one mark is given for each tick visible in a window are notoriously difficult to align. They also make it very difficult to detect candidates who give more than one answer to each question. Different marking keys may be needed for parallel versions of the same test. It is vital to use the correct marking key for the version that is being used (yes – it does happen!). Often, the windows on these keys have different values. For example, a cross that is visible in one window may carry a single mark, while a cross that is visible in another may carry two marks. It is vital to allot marks appropriately.
- *'Self-scoring' forms* have a pressure-sensitive system that transfers the crosses made by the candidate on to a second sheet, which is sealed beneath the answer sheet used by the candidate. When the seal is broken, a grid containing the candidate's answers is revealed. With simple tests (for example, Raven's Progressive Matrices) marking usually consists of crediting answers that fall within defined areas. When a test is more complicated and yields several scores, it is necessary to count answers that fall within complicated patterns given by different bands of colour or shading. This system commands a higher price and its use is increasing. The main problems are that candidates do not use sufficient pressure, or use a soft pencil so that marks are not transferred on to the second sheet. Proper invigilation should ensure that this does not occur. The bands or patterns of colour that must be followed when marking individual scales can be very complex, and it is very easy to overlook some areas that should be included.

Some answer sheets can be *scored by machines*. In principle, machine scoring is quicker, cheaper and more accurate. However, setting up the answer template is often tedious, time-consuming and error prone. A mistake at this stage might mean that thousands of tests are wrongly scored. Furthermore, answer sheets that are creased or crumpled may be rejected.

21.4.2 MARKING TECHNIQUE

All scoring systems require a systematic approach. Bad scoring can add as much as 5% to the error variance. Follow the scoring instructions in the manual precisely. Always use a pen with a contrasting colour. Before marking questions, an answer sheet should be visually inspected for general problems, especially where a candidate gives *two answers* to a question. Follow the advice in the manual. Usually, on ability tests credit is only given for the last answer. Sometimes, candidates *omit to give any answer* to questions. Follow the advice in the manual. Usually, on personality tests, if only one or two questions are unanswered, it is permissible to insert the candidate's modal answer for that scale. Other problems are as follows:

- An abrupt *change in the pattern of answering* – for example, answers suddenly change from being all correct to being all wrong. This may be caused by the *candidate losing synchronization* between the numbering of questions and answers. Reposition the scoring key to restore the pattern of answers.
- The total of correct answers, wrong answers and omitted answers *does not equal the total number of questions on the test*.

- *Subscales are totalled incorrectly.* If possible, arrange an independent check of all arithmetic.
- Answer sheets should be inspected for clues of faking, such as a high frequency (over 33%) of responses in the middle, 'uncertain' or 'natural' category.

21.4.3 COMPUTING COMPOSITE SCORES

Sometimes, scores from subscales need to be combined to provide global scores. For example, the score on Part I of the AH4 (verbal and numerical reasoning) can be combined with that of Part II (abstract reasoning) to give a global score for mental ability. This is a simple process of ensuring that the addition of the two part scores is correct.

However, on other tests and measures the situation is more complex because the different components are given different weighting. For example, an assessment centre may involve four dimensions (interpersonal skills, technical knowledge, mental ability and emotional stability), which a job analysis suggests are needed in the ratios of 3:2:1:1. First, the scores on the dimensions should be converted to a common scale; say, a sten scale. Then they must be accurately combined using the appropriate weights. Thus a candidate who scores 7 on interpersonal skills, 3 on technical skills, 5 on mental ability and 5 on stability would achieve a total Over All Rating (OAR) of 37. Often, it is best to divide the total by the sum of the weights to give, in this, case a score of 5.3. Whilst this score is reasonably comparable to the original stens, it is not actually a sten score (whilst the average will be 5.5, almost certainly the standard deviation will be less than the 2 used in the sten scale). Great care should be taken to use the weight appropriate to each sub-score. The above example shows the limit of the calculations that should be attempted without the use of a computer.

Scores on personality scales are frequently combined to produce other scores. For example, several scores on the OPQ can be combined to produce a score for extroversion. Similarly, several scores on the 16PF can be combined to produce a score on, for example, suitability for the team role of 'resource investigator'. These calculations have complex weighting systems using decimal points. They should be done with the aid of a spreadsheet that has been tested on at least six cases whose combined scores are previously known.

In selection, scores need to be transferred to a summary table or spreadsheet. Care must be taken to avoid transcription errors – especially confusion of 1 with 7, of 2 with 5, and of 0 with 9 or 6. Take special care if two candidates share the same name, such as Patel, Singh, Smith or Zhang. If tests are used for research, similar care should be taken when entering scores on a database.

21.5 SECURITY

Secure storage must be used for all test materials. This means a locked cabinet, to which only bona fide users have access. It is probably best to have two types of secure storage:

- Secure storage for *test materials*, to which only registered test users have access.
- Secure storage for *results*, to which only appropriate people involved in the selection decision have access.

Do not include test results in files that may be inadvertently passed to others. If results are held on a computer disk, ensure that the provisions of data protection legislation are observed. Most data protection legislation includes the provision that if you store identifiable personal information about people in electronic form, you should register with the data protection authorities. They will ask you to specify the kind of data that you hold and the purposes for which it is used. This information must be consistent with that given to people when they were invited for testing. It is particularly important that the data is accurate. An individual has a right of access to personal information. If it is incorrect, he or she can insist that it is put right. Other aspects of data protection are described in chapter 27.

The data on individuals must only be used for registered purposes except, perhaps, at the bona fide direction of appropriate legal authorities. It should never be shared with other organizations and it is often improper to share it with other parts of the same organization. If data is subsequently discovered to have research value, people should normally be contacted for their permission – unless, of course, they agreed to this use at the time of testing. Furthermore, names and other 'open' identifiers should not be included on a computer database. Each individual should be given an identification code. The key that links personal identifiers and the identification code entered on the database should not be stored in the same computer system. It must be securely stored elsewhere.

Other security measures include generating a climate in which it is clear that test materials should not be photocopied. Further points concerning security are as follows:

- As well as test booklets, security of materials extends to scoring keys, administration instructions and answer sheets.
- Dispose confidentially of unwanted, tatty or out-of-date test materials.
- If you leave an organization, destroy tests, take them with you or formally hand them over to someone in the organization who has appropriate qualifications.
- Requests by unqualified people to borrow materials must not be granted. Refusals of such requests should be made in a firm but sensitive way. Usually, these requests are made by people who are either keen or anxious about tests. It is normally worthwhile spending ten minutes with the person and determining the reason for the request. Often, the person's needs can be met in some other way. For example, a short discussion or explanation of tests can remove anxieties. It is necessary to think out, in advance, spiels to refuse requests for inappropriate access. Requests by students, colleagues or friends can be met with ploys such as:

> Of course, I would like to help you. But tests are confidential and I promised to use them only for agreed purposes. If I broke that promise, I could have my certificates withdrawn and you could receive bad publicity. Another candidate might get to know and complain that you had an advantage. It might also mean you end up in a job where you would be unhappy. If you like, I can tell you a little bit about the tests so that you will not be taken by surprise . . .

This would be followed by a short explanation that tests help many people to reveal their strengths; there will no 'trick', embarrassing or degrading questions; candidates should work at a brisk pace; they should not expect to get all of the questions right – and so on.

The situation of consultants who are requested to send tests to a potential client is more difficult, but it must meet with a resolute response, such as:

It is good that you want to check that tests are appropriate to your organization. I know that some people might send you tests but we follow a strict code of ethical conduct, which means that we must respect our agreement with test publishers not to let the tests out of our personal control. If I broke that agreement I could have my certificates withdrawn and your firm might receive bad publicity. You can be confident that I will be ethical and respect agreements that are made with your organization.

However, I can send you copies of practice leaflets that are usually sent to candidates. These give a very good idea of what the tests are about and they will give a very good basis upon which to decide whether they would be appropriate to your company. Even better, I could arrange a short meeting to show you the tests and discuss them with you.

- Never send confidential tests through the post for candidates to self-administer.
- Never allow candidates to take tests away, to finish them in their own time.

21.6 TESTING PEOPLE WITH DISABILITIES

21.6.1 BASIC PRINCIPLES

When first inviting candidates to a test session, ask them to notify you of any special requirements. Under the disability discrimination legislation, an employer of more than 20 people must make reasonable changes to their methods in order to accommodate disabilities. The selection process should be adjusted so that it will give the best possible prediction of how a person would perform in a job when it has been modified appropriately. Often, employees with disabilities can produce work of equal worth by tackling a job in a different way. For example, a blind person is able to read Braille quite adequately by substituting the sense of touch for the sense of vision. The job analysis, the person specification and the tests should take such possible substitutions into account. Often, the objective tests are fairer to candidates with disabilities than measures such as interviews, where erroneous attitudes may influence decisions.

The aim is to place a person with an irrelevant disability on an equal footing with an able-bodied candidate. There is no requirement, out of sympathy, to redress a person's general misfortune and disadvantage: able people may have equal misfortunes and disadvantages caused, say, by redundancy. It is very difficult to decide the exact level of adjustments that are appropriate and fair. Advice may be obtained from appropriate charities. Test publishers can also be a source of help. Government organizations such as the Employment Service are able to offer advice and they may loan equipment or provide grants to purchase equipment.

Physical disabilities are usually visible and the adjustments that are needed may be obvious. Other disabilities, especially neurological disorders, may not be obvious and candidates may be reluctant to disclose them. It is best to make clear that such disabilities will not necessarily be counted against a candidate and that the information will be treated discreetly. The terminology used when dealing with candidates who have a disability is important. Words such as 'epileptic' or 'clinically anxious' should be avoided. In general, it is better to use terms that emphasize that they are people who have a particular condition. Do not, for example, refer to a person as 'an epileptic candidate' but, rather, as 'a candidate who has epilepsy'. Some points of etiquette are as follows:

- Talk directly and make eye contact. Do not treat the candidate as a 'non-person' by talking via the carer. Do not avoid the customary physical contact, such as shaking hands.

- Do not hesitate to *offer* help and assistance, but wait for the candidate to signal his or her acceptance before actually *giving* help.
- Do not be too self-conscious when talking to a candidate with a disability. For example, do not cringe if you use phrases such as 'I see what you mean' or 'look at it this way' to a blind person.

The following subsection gives some guidance on testing people with the specific conditions of dyslexia and with hearing, movement and vision disabilities.

21.6.2 GUIDANCE FOR TESTING CANDIDATES WITH SPECIFIC DISABILITIES

Dyslexia

- Ask when dyslexia was diagnosed and how troublesome the problem is. Ask what modifications would to be appropriate. Some clients or candidates (especially students) have official statements detailing the degree of their disability. It may be appropriate to ask them to bring this statement to the test session.
- The main difficulties arise in processing written material. Often, extra time is needed. Usually, people with dyslexia are allowed 33% more time, but this should be checked with the test publisher or appropriate organization.

Hearing Disabilities

- *Ask*, in advance, *how the candidate prefers to communicate*. Do not make assumptions. Some deaf people can lip read, some prefer sign language and others prefer written communications.
- Initially at least, *communicate directly with the candidate*. Speak slowly and clearly while looking the candidate in the face.
- Provide comprehensive *written instructions*. Do not rely on lip-reading instructions. If written instructions are not suitable, have a signing interpreter.
- *Do not shout*.
- To attract attention, *wave your hand or touch the person* on the shoulder.
- *Use normal non-verbal* cues to put the candidate at ease.
- Check that *non-test measures* are appropriate. Presentation exercises are usually unsuitable and more time may need to be allocated for interviews.

Movement Disabilities

- Ask, in advance, how the disability might influence the test performance and what facilities the candidate thinks would be appropriate.
- Give consideration to the testing *venue*. Avoid unnecessary and long walks. The venue should be easily accessible, so that the candidate is not tired or embarrassed by having to ask for special assistance. Most workplaces *should* already be adapted (with, for example, ramps and appropriate toilets) to cope with basic mobility problems.

- Check whether the *method of responding* requires modification. It may be appropriate to provide large-size answer sheets for a candidate who has difficulty in writing. Sometimes, it might be more appropriate to use an adapted keyboard. Check whether the movement disorder slows the response time. Try to quantify the handicap by comparing the candidate's response time on similar but neutral questions and then adjust the time allowed accordingly.
- If a candidate is a *wheelchair user*, sit down to talk to him or her. Do not lean on the wheelchair. Have a writing surface at a height that is appropriate for a wheelchair user.
- If a candidate uses *crutches*, avoid keeping him or her standing for substantial periods. Have a chair ready.
- Avoid non-test measures that require *incidental fine movements*, such as shuffling papers in an in-tray.

Visual Disabilities

- Ask how the disability might affect performance and what adaptations would be appropriate.
- People with visual impairment may have difficulty *navigating their way* around new environments. Alert reception that a candidate with a visual disability may arrive. When moving about a building, it might be polite to say 'Would it help if you took my arm for guidance?' Help a blind person locate furniture either by verbal comments or, perhaps, by placing his or her hand on the back of a chair where he or she can sit.
- Give *verbal cues as substitutes for visual cues*. For example, when in a group of people, use names as a substitute for eye contact. Similarly, substitute the comment 'Shall we shake hands?' for the cue of holding out your hand.
- Some visual impairments can be minimized by *good lighting* and by the avoidance of glare.
- Some visual impairments can be overcome by using *tests with large type*, and many test publishers will loan tests in special formats. If all else fails, some method of magnification can be considered.
- Some tests are available in *Braille*, but do not assume that all blind people can read Braille. Some computers can synthesize speech from a word-processor file. Alternatively, a reader can be made available.
- A candidate with a visual disability may be able to dictate *responses* – either to a cassette recorder or to another person. The use of Braille or other techniques may mean that the time limit for a test needs to be increased. Computerized voice recognition means that answers may be dictated to a computer.
- Other selection methods may need to be adjusted. Some large organizations have Braille application forms. Other participants in a group discussion need to be briefed that they must always identify the person to whom they are speaking. Interviews require very little adaptation. Although it is theoretically possible to adapt an in-tray exercise to Braille, under most circumstances the Braille version will be unrealistic.

Unfortunately, many other forms of disability exist. People recovering from a serious illness may find a long selection process exhausting. Specific advice needs to be obtained from the appropriate organization or from the test publisher. In general, the pace of the session should be slowed and more time allowed between activities. It is often important to allow extra time for reassurance with explanations and with practice items, since pressure often increases the effects of a disability.

The obvious strategy of 'putting yourself in their shoes' might not be a good one, since different people react very differently and you may make unwarranted assumptions. Above all else, treat people with disabilities as adults.

21.6.3 ADAPTING TESTS FOR PEOPLE WITH DISABILITIES

Make rational decisions about the adaptations that are needed to enable candidates to compete 'on a level playing field'. Check with appropriate people and organizations who may have made scientific assessments of the adaptations needed. If they can offer no advice, it may be necessary to make bespoke adaptations. These should not be made in a nonchalant manner. The following advice may help to decide on the appropriate level of adjustment:

1   Refer to the job description and the person specification, to identify the exact nature of the characteristic being measured.
2   Inspect the test carefully and note:
    • the mental processes involved
    • the input method (that is, the way in which a question is put to the candidate)
    • the output mode (that is, the way in which the candidate indicates his or her response).
3   If either the input mode or the output mode is coincidental to the mental process, changes can be considered. For example, a traditional reasoning test may require candidates to identify assumptions in arguments. The arguments may be presented in a printed booklet and the answers may be given by writing on an answer sheet. In this case, the input and output modes are irrelevant to the mental process being tested. Consequently, it would be permissible for questions to be read aloud to candidates with a visual disability and it would be permissible for candidates who have difficulty writing with a pen to dictate their answers. However, where the characteristic being measured is related to the mode of input or output, no alterations should be made. For example, if the job description for a clerk for a traffic survey indicates that a high degree of clerical speed and accuracy is needed, no additional time should be allowed for candidates with dyslexia, since coping at speed is an intrinsic requirement of the post.
4   Try to establish the impact of any changes that have been made. For example, if a candidate with motor difficulties is to be allowed to dictate his or her answers, a trial could be held among, say, 12 people who do not suffer from the disability. Six people would complete the test twice – first writing their answers and then dictating them. The other six people would also complete the test twice but the order would be reversed. They would first dictate their answers and then write them. This ruse would counterbalance any order effects and learning. Appropriate adjustments to the final score could then be established. For example, if the dictated scores were three marks higher than the written scores (probably because it is slightly quicker to dictate an answer than write it), three marks would be subtracted from the score obtained by a disabled person who dictated his or her responses. Of course, in an ideal situation a sample much larger than 12 would be used. However, in most organizations a trial with 12 people is about as much as would be practically feasible – and few barristers would be prepared to argue before a jury that 12 is an insufficient number!

Carefully document any adaptations and the reasons why they are being made. If, despite all efforts, the adaptations still leave a person with a disability at a disadvantage, make appropriate adjustments at the interpretation stage, perhaps by adopting a larger margin of error, or perhaps by adding an allowance to a score. However, the latter approach involves some risk, since over-compensation may arise. This may be unfair to other candidates, and it may land a person with a disability in a job that is quite unsuitable and which may cause him or her stress or unhappiness.

 21.7 TROUBLESHOOTING

Some problems and suggested responses are as follows:

Problem: A candidate asks if wrong answers are marked negatively.
Response: Follow the instructions in the manual. If the manual gives no guidance, adopt the following principles. For a personality test, say that there are no right or wrong answers and that the issue of negative marking is not relevant. If the test is an ability test, tell the candidate whether or not negative marking is used. If all else fails, say 'I am sorry, I cannot tell you about the marking scheme. If I gave this information to some candidates, it would not be fair on the others. It will be best if you try to give as many correct answers as possible.'

Problem: During the practice questions, it emerges that a candidate grew up in Peru and has difficulty understanding English.
Response: Make a note in the test log. Talk to the candidate and ask how much they feel disadvantaged. Show as much empathy and reassurance as you can. Assess the candidate's fluency in English. Make an immediate note of the conversation and draw the note to the attention of person making the interpretation. Check to see why the problem was not detected at an earlier stage. If it is a sensible course of action (for example, language skills are not an important requirement of the job), administer, or offer to administer, a test such as Raven's Progressive Matrices, which has very little verbal content.

Problem: You are using a written vocabulary test to check candidates' knowledge of words. A partially sighted candidate cannot read the test.
Response: Make a note in the test log. Ask if the candidate needs spectacles. If spectacles are no help, extract the candidate from the group. Administer the test orally and allow the candidate to dictate answers. Administer the test as an untimed test, but make a note of the point reached when normal time limit is up.

Problem: The job requires visual acuity in order to ensure the safety of others. One of the candidates turns out to be visually impaired and cannot do the task.
Response: Make note in the test log. Ask if candidate needs spectacles. If spectacles are no help, extract the candidate from the group and tactfully explain that the job is only open to those with good vision. Establish why the problem was not detected earlier.

Problem: Two days before the test, a promising candidate phones to say that he or she has a physical disability that might affect performance on the test, but which may not affect performance on the job.

Response: Ask about the candidate's disability and seek suggestions about alternative arrangements or equipment. Phone an appropriate charity, pressure group or test publisher for advice. To protect the rights of the majority (yes, majorities have rights too!), ask a disinterested colleague whether the changes would give an unfair advantage. If there is no unfair advantage, implement the changes and obtain evidence that the person does in fact have the disability.

Problem: There is a false fire alarm shortly after a timed test is started.

Response: Quickly note the time. Evacuate in an orderly way. Try to sequester the group and discourage them from talking about the test. If possible, use an equivalent test when you are permitted to return. If an equivalent test is not available, repeat the instructions, restart the test and allow candidates to work for the *balance* of the time. Make full notes in the test log.

Problem: A candidate becomes acutely ill, clutching at his or her chest and gasping for air, about halfway through a test.

Response: Ask the candidate what you should do. Ask other candidates if they have any medical qualifications. Summon medical help. Abandon the session if possible. If this is unreasonable for other candidates, arrange a substantial pause while they, and you, recover composure. If possible, use alternative tests in the resumed session. Make notes in the test log. Send a get-well card to the *malade*.

Problem: An electrician working in the adjoining room causes the lights to go out for two minutes.

Response: Why on earth did you allow an electrician to go anywhere near the test room? Provided that there is some light, halt the test temporarily. Reassure candidates and ask them not to discuss the test. Resume the test when lighting is restored. Allow candidates to continue for the balance of the time. Make a note in the test log.

Problem: A candidate loudly exclaims that he or she does not understand a question and asks for help.

Response: Immediately signal silence. Slowly walk to the candidate and quietly explain that there can be no questions once the test has started. Make a note in the test log.

Problem: Two candidates finish before the end of the test and start to converse.

Response: Immediately signal silence. Slowly walk to the candidates. Explain that others are still working. Ask them to remain quietly in their seats until the end of the test. Do not remove tests and materials from their desks until the normal collection at the end of the session. Make a note in the test log.

CHAPTER 22

NORMS AND PROFILES

When a test or other assessment measure is marked, raw scores are produced. On their own, raw scores are of limited value because they give little information about what a person can do. The fact that Pauline obtained a raw score of 10 on an arithmetic test gives very little information. The test may have been easy or it may have been hard. It may have had 100 questions or it may have had only ten. To be useful, Pauline's raw score must be transformed into some other scale that gives information about how other people scored or how someone with that score will perform a job. Norms are used to transform raw scores into a more useful scale. Normed scores are often most useful when they are given in diagrammatic form, as profiles. Several types of norms exist and it is important to know whether to use norms, which type of norm is appropriate and how normed scores should be profiled.

◤ 22.1 WHETHER TO USE NORMS

Most textbooks on testing place great emphasis on proper norms. In *selection*, this emphasis is misplaced. *So long as selection is 'top down' AND the test is valid and fair, it will always pay to choose the person with the best score.* The use of raw scores or normed scores makes no difference. It is like writing names on a sheet of elastic. However the elastic is stretched or condensed, the names are always in the same order and the top name is always at the top. Norming merely rescales the information by expanding or contracting the elastic sheets into a more useful size: but norms never alter the order of candidates – the top candidate will remain top whatever norms are used. The same conclusion remains when you are using 'top-down' selection to choose several candidates. For example, if you are using *a fair and valid* test to choose the best ten from 100 applicants, simply choose the ten with the highest raw scores. One can use out-of-date norms, foreign norms or no norms, as long as the test is valid and fair.

Researchers should also use norms sparingly. Under almost all circumstances, raw scores should be keyed into computer programs. Statistical analyses should also be conducted on raw scores. Articles and research reports should mainly deal with raw scores. Normed scores can be given after raw scores have been reported – provided that full details of the norms used are given.

However, in many situations norms should be used because they provide additional information. There are some situations in which norms must be used:

- If the test has *differential validity* and one group is disadvantaged. Disadvantage can be counteracted by using separate norms for the two groups. (Note that the fact that one group scores higher or lower than another group is *not* evidence of unfairness or disadvantage). The use of separate norms should be preceded by an analysis similar to those described in chapter 12. If separate norms are used simply on the basis of average scores, the selection system could end up being biased against a group that is genuinely more able.
- Tests are used for *vocational guidance* rather than selection.
- *Different, but equivalent, tests* are used. For example, a company may generally use the AH4 test for selecting apprentices, but it uses the Thurstone Test of Mental Alertness if candidates say that they have recently taken the AH4 in another application.
- *Scores from different tests* need to be compared. For example, an organization might wish to know whether a manager has better verbal than numerical abilities.

 ## 22.2 TYPES OF NORMS

There are three ways of transforming scores: criterion, normative and ipsative. These transformations can give rise to misnomers – criterion-referenced *tests* and norm-referenced *tests*. This distinction is often inaccurate. It is not the *tests* that are criterion- or norm-referenced; it is the way in which their scores are *transformed* into norms. In many cases, the raw scores on the same test can be criterion-, norm- or *both* criterion- and norm-referenced.

22.2.1 CRITERION REFERENCING

A typical statement using criterion referencing might be 'a person with a score of 47 or more will be able to operate the machine to efficient worker standard', or 'a doctor with a score of 82 will be able to make correct diagnoses of cancer in 90 out of 100 patients who actually have cancer'.

In these cases, the test is used to make statements about standards that lie outside the test. Criterion scores are used essentially to differentiate between people who have or have not acquired the skills and knowledge for a designated activity (Anastasi, 1988, 138). The archetypal criterion-referenced test is the driving test, where a pass means that a person has reached the legal standard of competence. Many educational tests are also criterion referenced (for example, a government committee decides what a 14-year-old should achieve in, say, mathematics – students who achieve the standards are considered to be satisfactory and those who do not are considered to be unsatisfactory). Most school and university qualifications are, essentially, criterion-related scores where, in principle, there is an absolute standard upon which employers can rely and where, in principle, every candidate could pass.

The adequacy of criterion referencing depends on the quality of the external standards. Ideally, external standards are set after an empirical study. For example, management could decide which widget makers are good workers and which are poor. A test could be administered and an analysis conducted to decide the score that best differentiates good widgeteers from poor ones. The same test could then be given to applicants and those who score over the differentiating line would be offered a job. The process seems objective but, in essence, it depends upon a subjective decision of who are competent and who are incompetent workers. Most criteria are set by a panel of well-meaning 'experts', who discuss and then decide on the appropriate mark.

Criterion-referenced scores have the *advantage* that they relate directly to actual behaviour and competence. They therefore seem more reasonable to lay people and are more easily defended against a legal challenge.

Criterion-related scores have two main disadvantages:

- *Setting the criteria* is a problem. It is difficult to define the criteria in an empirical way that reflects actual behaviour. Hence criteria may be set in a way that is fundamentally normative and which defeats the purpose of criterion scores. For example, a government committee may decree that what 60% of 14-year-olds achieve is an appropriate criteria and set that level as criteria by which teenagers are judged on, say, a mathematics test.
- *Standards may drift* because of environmental changes, even though performance remains the same. For example, it could be said that over the past three decades, the driving test has become harder, even though the manoeuvres required of candidates have remained identical. Increased road congestion has probably meant that manoeuvres such as parking require more skill. Similarly, the performance for an educational qualification may be the same as the performance many years ago. However, it may be argued, today's students who pass have lower ability because they have had the advantages of teachers who are more focused on the examination system, modular examinations, better visual aids and more photocopied notes. Because criteria are influenced by such environmental circumstances, criteria need to be recalibrated each time there is a change in either the environment or the job.

22.2.2 NORM REFERENCING

Most psychological tests scores are norm referenced. A score is norm referenced when it is translated into a statement of where a person stands in relation to other people who have taken the test. A typical norm-referenced statement might be 'James scored higher than 90% of people on verbal ability', or 'Lucy is in the tenth percentile for intelligence'. All scores based on the normal curve are normative scores. The following are all normative statements:

- Israf's Z score is −3
- Nadin's T score is 35
- Penny's stannine is 5.5
- Luiz's IQ is 143
- Oliver's sten score is 5.5.

With normative scores, some people will always be better than others. The *advantage* of normative scores is that they are less affected by the environment. If I am in the top 10% and the environment gets more difficult, my score will be lower but I will still be in the top 10%. If the environment gets easier, my score will rise but I will still only be in the top 10%. The *disadvantage* with normative scores is that there is no direct link between the score and performance on some external task. I may be in the top 10%, but what does that mean I can actually do?

Normative scores are so important that many different systems have been devised, and except for three very simple systems they are based on the normal curve.

Above- and Below-average Categories

The crudest system of norms merely places people in two categories: above or below average. The only advantage of this system is that it requires very little data – the mean – and so it can be used with small samples and where the scale has poor psychometric properties. This advantage is heavily outweighed by the disadvantages. It does not give much information about the individual and its use encourages the perpetuation of poor measures. This system is so bad that it should only be used in emergency situations, where all else fails.

Fivefold Systems

A fivefold system is noticeably better than the twofold system. It is widely used in many selection situations. There are several versions of this system, but the most frequently used version places people in categories A–E:

A = top 10% of candidates
B = next 20% of candidates
C = middle 40% of candidates
D = next 20% of candidates
E = bottom 10% of candidates.

The advantage of this system is that maximum discrimination is given at the extremes of the spectrum and over-interpretation of scores from poor measures is prevented. The system is easy to communicate to those with little knowledge of psychometrics. Furthermore, it reflects the normal distribution. However, can be very unfair to candidates near a borderline. It is also crude and wastes information when the data has been derived from high-quality measures. The waste of information can be reduced by using pluses and minuses within each category (A+, A, A–, for example) to give, in effect, a reasonably sophisticated 15-point scale.

Some organizations use a different and less satisfactory variation, where:

A = top 20%
B = next 20%
C = middle 20%
D = next 20%
E = bottom 20%.

It is essential to know which system an organization is using, and the two fivefold systems should never be mixed.

Percentiles (and Deciles)

Percentiles are used very frequently. They refer to a person's place in a representative sample of 100 people who have been arranged in the order of their scores. For example, someone with a percentile score of 50 would be the middle person in the queue of 100 people, whilst someone with a percentile score of 98 would be third from the top. It should be noted *percentiles are*

Figure 22.1 An illustration of the 50th percentile.

not concerned with the proportion of questions that a candidate answers correctly – they refer to the position in a queue of 100 people (see figure 22.1).

Percentiles have two big *advantages*. First, they are easily explained and understood. Second, they give finely graded scores that differentiate between people. Percentiles do not demand large samples and can be constructed from the scores of about 200 people. Furthermore, if statistical tables are available, percentiles can be translated into scoring systems based on the normal curve. The big *disadvantage* of percentiles is that they may distort true differences between individuals. In general, they minimize the large differences between people at the ends of the distribution and they magnify small differences between people in the middle of the distribution. For example, on one arithmetic test with 180 questions, the average person at the 50th percentile will correctly answer 90 questions while someone at the 53rd percentile will correctly answer 92 questions – a difference of two answers. However, at the top of the distribution, a candidate at the 90th percentile will correctly answer 140 questions while a candidate at the 93rd percentile will answer about 151 questions – a difference of 11 answers, even though the two candidates are separated by only three percentile points.

It must be remembered that percentiles cannot be added, subtracted or subjected to any other arithmetical operation. Enthusiasts might like to note that this limitation arises because percentiles are ordinal measures.

Sometimes, there is insufficient data to allow the construction of percentiles. In these situations, **deciles** may be used. Deciles are very similar to percentiles, but they relate a person's score to their position in a representative sample of ten people. Deciles are not as 'sensitive' as percentiles, but they are sufficiently refined for most decisions and are less likely to be over-interpreted. Additionally, adequate deciles can be constructed on the basis of a sample of, say, 50 subjects.

Z Scores

Most other scoring systems are based on the normal distribution. The simplest of these systems are **Z scores**. They are encountered frequently elsewhere in this book, but it is most

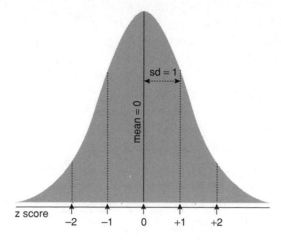

Figure 22.2 Z scores and the normal curve.

appropriate to describe them in detail here. Z scores indicate how many standard deviations a person is away from mean (average). A positive Z score indicates that someone is above average. A negative Z score indicates that someone is below average. For example, a Z score of − 1.5 on extroversion means that the person is 1.5 standard deviations less extroverted than average. A Z score of +2 on intelligence means that a person is two standard deviations more intelligent than the average. The Z score system is the basis of many other systems. It could be considered as a universal scale. A thorough understanding of Z scores is essential before proceeding to other scales.

Z scores have immense theoretical importance, but they are rarely used because they have a number of practical disadvantages:

- They involve + signs and − signs that have a notorious ability to be missed wherever scores are copied. This may have bizarre consequences.
- They appear to be fairly insensitive. Most scores are within the range of −2 to +2. The problem is easily overcome by the use of decimals. However, the use of decimals may seem pedantic and they are easily omitted when scores are interpreted.

The disadvantages of Z scores have led to the development of several other systems that are based on the normal curve and derived from Z scores. The main systems are:

- quotients
- T scores
- stens
- stannines.

It should be noted that all scores based on Z scores can be summed or subtracted – because they are 'interval' measures.

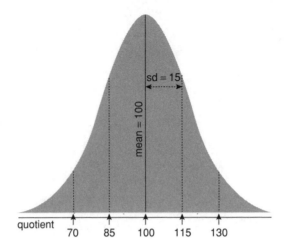

Figure 22.3 Quotients and the normal curve.

Quotients

Quotients were one of the first scoring systems based on the normal curve and they arose from early tests of intelligence. Today, most quotients are based on a mean of 100 and a standard deviation of 15, and fall in the range of 63–137 (−2.5z to +2.5z).

However, some tests, such as MENSA tests and US Employment Service (USES) tests, adopt a slightly different system. They use a standard deviation of 20. Quotients on the latter scale tend to be used in newspaper articles and advertisements, because they tend to give more extreme, and therefore more newsworthy, figures. Unfortunately, this causes confusion: clients with a very desirable IQ of 130 can be disappointed because they compare their IQs with those of, say, 140 that they have seen in the press. To avoid such confusion, IQs should always be reported on a scale that has a mean of 100 and a standard deviation of 15. Figure 22.3 demonstrates the relationship between quotients and the normal curve.

The quotients work well for intelligence tests that are based on, perhaps, 100 questions and where the standard error is about three quotient points. However, in the case of personality and other tests, where each score is based on, say, ten questions and where the standard error is about seven quotient points, the system invites over-interpretation of small differences. Consequently, other systems based on Z scores have been developed.

T Scores

Thurstone, a psychometric guru of the 1930s and 1940s, recognized the dangers of quotients. He suggested a smaller scale where the mean is 50 and the standard deviation is 10. He modestly called this system T scores. T scores normally lie within the range 25–75 (−2.5z to +2.5z), which is very similar to the range found in percentage marks awarded to exams or essays by teachers and academics. The relationship between T scores and the normal curve is shown in figure 22.4.

Unfortunately, T scores also invite over-interpretation when they are used with scales based on, say, 30 questions and where the standard error is about 5.

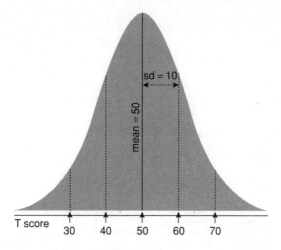

Figure 22.4 The relationship between T scores and the normal curve.

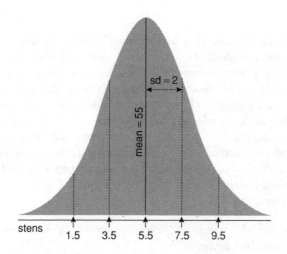

Figure 22.5 The relationship between sten scores and the normal curve.

Stens

Stens are the most frequently used system for personality tests. They have a mean of 5.5 and a standard deviation of 2. Sten scores usually fall within a range of .5–10.5. This is very similar to the range of school marks where assignments are marked out of ten. Stens are easily understood. Furthermore, they are not prone to over-interpretation when used with scales that have, say, ten questions and a standard error of .5. Figure 22.5 shows the relationship between sten scores and the normal curve.

The sten system has two very minor disadvantages. Most people expect scores of this magnitude to have a mean of 5, whereas the sten system has a mean of 5.5. In addition, sten scores often generate half-marks, such as 4.5 or 10.5.

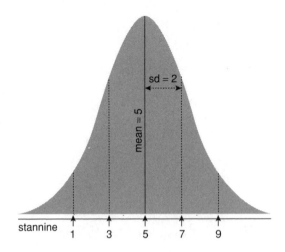

Figure 22.6 The relationship between stannines and the normal curve.

Stannines

Stannines are very similar to stens. They have the same standard deviation, 2, but their mean is set at 5. The mean is therefore identical to the 'average' score used by teachers marking essays and tests. Most stannines scores lie in the range 0–10. Stannine scores are used by a substantial minority of personality tests. Figure 22.6 shows the relationship between stannines and the normal curve.

This multiplicity of scoring systems is extremely confusing to the lay person. Only one system should be used within a single organization. In general, the system that is already used most predominantly should be adopted. If all else fails, the sten system should be adopted as a 'failsafe' choice. However, a selection specialist or counsellor must be able to translate between systems in the same way that a physicist can translate between temperatures expressed in degrees Celsius, Fahrenheit, Raemur and Kelvin. The key is to recognize that Z scores are the central system and there are two actions:

1 Translate from the 'old' system to Z scores by subtracting the old mean and then dividing by the old standard deviation.
2 Reverse the process by multiplying by the new standard deviation and finally adding the new mean. The following tables show the precise steps:

Step one: translate from 'old' to Z

Old score	Action one: subtract the mean of the old system	Action two: divide by the standard deviation of the old system
Z scores	No action needed	
Percentiles	Divide by 100 and look up Z score of proportion in normal curve table	
Quotients	Subtract 100	Divide remainder by 15
T scores	Subtract 50	Divide remainder by 10
Stens	Subtract 5.5	Divide remainder by 2
Stannines	Subtract 5	Divide remainder by 2

Step two: translate from Z score to 'new'

New score	Action one: multiply by the standard deviation of the new system	Action two: add the mean of the new system
Z scores	No action needed	
Percentiles	Look up proportion for Z score in normal curve table and multiply by 100	
Quotients	Multiply by 15	Add 100
T-scores	Multiply by 10	Add 50
Stens	Multiply by 2	Add 5.5
Stannines	Multiply by 2	Add 5

With apologies to statistics buffs, an analogy may help those who are not statistically oriented. An imaginary continent consists of six countries. Country **Z** is the regional superpower. It is central and dominates all others. All routes pass through **Z** and it is compulsory to change currency at its borders. The exchange rates in and out of country **Z** are shown in the snazzy figure 22.7, which allows you to plan any journey.

Enthusiasts might wish to note that many other systems exist. Weschler subscales, for example, use a system with a mean of 10 and a standard deviation of 3. Another system uses a mean of 20 and a standard deviation of 4. The latter is based on the observation that most other systems 'abandon' people who are more than 2.5 standard deviations from the mean. But on some measures some populations are outside this range. Basketball players, for example, are commonly four standard deviations higher than average. It can be argued that psychologists should be interested in their intellectual equivalents, and a scale with a mean of 20 and a standard deviation of 4 should therefore be adopted (David Duncan, personal communication 2001).

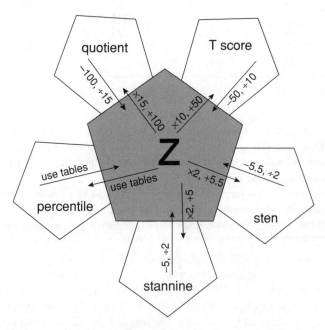

Figure 22.7 A diagram showing translations to and from Z scores.

22.2.3 SELF-REFERENCED SCORES (IPSATIVE SCORES)

Self-referenced scores say nothing about what the person can do (criterion-referenced) or about their standing in relation to other people (norm-referenced). Instead, they give information about the relationship between aspects inside one person. Self-referenced scores are mostly used (along with normative scores) in guidance and development. Statements based on self-referenced scores might be 'You are more assertive than you are generous', or 'Your interest in outdoor activities is higher than your interest in musical activities'. Note that the latter statement would apply to a really fanatical hiker who is a keen musician. The statement would equally apply to someone who dislikes walking and detests music. Self-referenced scores say nothing about the level of the traits or how they compare to the levels in other people – they only say that one is bigger than the other *in that person*. These scores are also called **ipsative scores**. Some tests can only yield ipsative scores. Ipsative tests are described in more detail in section 15.4.

 22.3 NORM TABLES

Most manuals contain norm tables such as:

Raw score	Percentile	Grade	Raw score	Percentile	Grade
75	3	E–	108	63	C+
80	6	E	111	70	B–
85	10	E+	114	76	B
89	18	D–	117	84	B+
93	24	D	122	90	A–
95	30	D+	126	93	A
98	37	C–	131	97	A+
103	50	C			

$n = 200$, mean $= 103$, sd $= 15$.

Using the table, it would be easy to determine that a person with a score of 98 would be in the 37th percentile and, in this system, that person would be placed in category C–. Similarly, a person with a score of 122 would be in the top 10% of the population (90th percentile) and, in this system, would be placed in category A–.

Some test publishers are less lazy and give tables that allow raw scores to be converted into any of the five main scoring systems. An example is given in table 22.1.

Norm tables can be produced in two main ways – generating them from percentile method or generating them from an equation:

- Norms *generated from percentiles* are produced by giving the test to, say, 600 people and arranging the scores in order. The raw score for, say, the tenth percentile would be obtained by looking at the score of the 60th (10% of 600) person. The raw score for the 20th percentile would be obtained by looking at the score of the 120th person (20% of 600) and so on. The normal curve table would then be used to obtain the Z score for, say, the

Table 22.1 An example of a typical norm table

Raw	Percentile	Grade	Quotient	T score	Sten	Stannine	Z score
75	3	E−	72	31	1.7	1.2	−1.88
80	6	E	77	34	2.4	1.9	−1.55
84	10	E+	81	37	2.9	2.4	−1.28
90	18	D−	87	40	3.7	3.2	−.92
93	24	D	90	43	4.1	3.6	−.70
95	30	D+	92	45	4.5	4.0	−.52
98	37	C−	95	47	4.8	4.3	−.33
103	50	C	100	50	5.5	5.0	0
108	63	C+	105	53	6.2	5.7	.33
111	70	B−	108	55	6.5	6.0	.52
115	76	B	112	57	6.9	6.4	.70
117	84	B+	114	59	7.3	6.8	.92
122	90	A−	119	62	8.1	7.6	1.28
125	93	A	123	66	8.6	8.1	1.55
131	97	A+	128	69	9.3	8.8	1.88

10th percentile and this would be used to produce the appropriate quotient, T score, sten or stannine. The *advantage* of this system is that it does not rely on the assumptions that the distribution of scores is normal and yet the scaled scores are always normally distributed. The *disadvantage* is that, in effect, each number in the table depends upon the score of just one person and will fluctuate, sometimes wildly, from sample to sample. This is a crucial disadvantage if the sample size is small, below about 300.

- Norms *generated using equations* are produced by administering the test to, say, 600 people and then calculating the mean and standard deviation. Z scores are then produced, using the equation

$$z = (score - mean)/\text{sd}$$

Finally, quotients, T scores, stens and stannines can be calculated from the using the steps indicated on pages 306–7. Norms generated from equations have the *advantage* that each value in the norm table is, in part, based on every score in the sample and therefore it will be much more stable than a value based on one or two people's scores. The *disadvantage* is that the norms will only be truly accurate if scores are normally distributed. If this is not so, the distribution of the scaled scores will be skewed and not normal. This may limit the range of analytical statistics that they can support.

22.3.1 QUALITY OF NORMS

Tests vary in the quality of their norms. Some give many excellent norms, each based on large, carefully specified samples, while others give a single norm table based on a small, ill-defined convenience sample. Bartram and Lindley (1994) suggest the following criteria for evaluating the sample sizes on which norm tables are based:

more than 2,000   excellent
1,000–1,999   good
500–999   reasonable
200–499   adequate
under 200   inadequate

Often, it is necessary to decide which tests to use on the basis of their norms. Furthermore, where several norms are provided for a test, it is necessary to decide which norms to use.

22.4 CHOOSING NORMS

The main decisions are whether to use subgroup (ethnic, age, disability) norms, employee norms or narrow-band norms.

22.4.1 SUBGROUP NORMS

Best practice is to obtain data on the differential validity of the measure (that is, whether there are different regression equations for different groups). If there is no differential validity, population norms are better because they will be based on larger samples. However, if differential validity exists, group norms will be better *provided that* the norms for the smallest group are based on a decently sized sample – of at least 200.

Unfortunately, life is complex. Some selection methods may be moderately fair. For example, a subgroup that has purple skin may score one standard deviation below a subgroup that has blue skin. However, when performance on a job is measured, the average performance of the purples is half a standard deviation below that for the blues. This means that the test magnifies a true difference. If separate norms are used for the purple group, the blues will be disadvantaged. If population norms are used, the purples will be disadvantaged. The appropriate norms will depend on the priorities of the situation. If public safety and survival are important factors, population norms should probably be used even though they involve some disadvantage to a minority group. This course of action should not be taken lightly. It should be checked against the opinion of a disinterested third party. If this course of action is substantiated, means of redressing the disadvantage by other actions should be explored. If there are no issues of public safety or survival, it is probably better to use subgroup norms and actively consider appropriate means of redress for the majority group.

22.4.2 EMPLOYEE, APPLICANT AND POPULATION NORMS

Sometimes there are norms for existing employees, norms for applicants and norms for the general population as a whole.

In selection decisions it is best, all other things being equal, to use **employee norms**, because this will allow the most accurate prediction of whether an applicant will turn out to be a 'good employee' or a 'bad' employee. Employee norms give data about the group most relevant to the decision. The best employee norms are based on *scores that are collected at the time of hiring*. Unfortunately, norms of employees at the time of hiring take time to accumulate and sample sizes can be small. If it takes many years to accumulate a sufficient sample, the job may change during the interval and some of the data may be out of date. Nevertheless, norms on existing employees at the time of hiring are usually the best option, at least in theory. Sometimes, *employee norms are obtained 'concurrently'* and all those working in a job are tested at a given time. The data will therefore be derived from some people with substantial experience and from some newly engaged employees. These norms should be avoided in selection situations, because they will incorporate the effects of training and experience and will probably underestimate the suitability of new applicants.

Many organizations use **applicant norms**. They are much quicker to obtain, because there are usually far more applicants than people actually employed. Consequently, applicant norms are less likely to be out of date or based on a small sample. The sample will be fairly relevant to a selection decision, but it will not be quite as relevant as employee norms. Applicant norms may be the most relevant norms in vocational guidance where clients are considering their chances of gaining access to a specific organization or occupation.

Norms for the general population may be useful in selection where adequate employee or applicant norms are unavailable. In guidance, it is usually best to use population norms – supplemented by information about specific groups. Information based on specific norms may be misleading. A scientist informed that he or she is in the bottom 1% of Nobel prize winners may feel very inadequate until he or she is informed that Nobel prize winners are a very, very able group and that compared to the general population they are in the top 1%!

22.4.3 NARROW-BAND AND WIDE-BAND NORMS

Decisions about subgroup norms or applicant norms both involve the underlying issue of band-width. General population norms are wide-band norms, while subgroup norms are narrow-band norms. All other things being equal, 'narrow-band' norms are preferable to 'broadband' population norms. Typical narrow-band norms would include 'graduate norms', 'norms for general apprentices' or 'norms for managerial positions'. Narrow-band norms are usually collected in carefully defined situations that are more relevant to the particular situation at hand. For example, the NA4 test has norms for graduate applicants. Consequently, it would be more realistic to use these norms when selecting amongst final-year university students. Narrow-band norms usually distribute relevant candidates over a wider scale. For example, if general population quotient norms of a test of numerical ability are used for graduate mathematicians, the most scores will be crammed into quotients in the range 120–130. When narrower graduate norms are used, their quotients range from 90 to 120. When very narrow norms for mathematics graduates are used, their quotients cover the full range of 60–140. Clearly, a selector will find it easier to identify the most able people when they are spread out along 80 points of a scale than when everyone is crammed into a ten-point range.

However, narrow-band norms have disadvantages. *First*, they make small differences in ability or personality seem large. In guidance, in particular, the use of narrow norms can have negative effects on self-perception. Managers who are told that they are in the bottom 2% of managers might think that they are useless and give up work when, in fact, they would still be quite capable. In vocational guidance, it is often the wide-range perspective that is most useful. In addition, the use of local norms makes the combination of test scores (for example, combining verbal and numerical problem-solving into an index of 'global' reasoning) impossible unless local norms are available for all specific tests that are used.

Other things are rarely equal. Narrow-band norms may have technical disadvantages because they are 'home grown'. The sample size may be quite small and thus contain a large element of random error. The sample for local norms may be deficient in some way and reflect an 'unusual' population. Local norms will also tend to perpetuate the 'status quo' within an organization. Furthermore, some organizations may not have sufficient resources or technical expertise. The norms they produce may be more prone to error.

▲ 22.5 OTHER PRACTICAL AND THEORETICAL ISSUES CONCERNING THE CHOICE OF NORMS

In the previous discussion, we have used the phrase 'other things being equal'. However, norms may differ in their recency, their sample size and the reliability and validity of the test on which they are based.

22.5.1 RECENCY OF NORMS

It is impossible to update norms continually – this would make tests very expensive. Few organizations would be able to afford the tests; less effective people would be hired, prices to the consumer would tend to increase and people might get less satisfaction from their jobs. If the norms are new, there is never a problem. If the norms are old, much will depend upon the rate at which the underlying psychological characteristic changes. There are only minor problems when norms are old and the rate of change is slow. But if the norms are old and the rate of change is fast, old norms may give misleading results.

There is some evidence that average scores on ability tests are rising. The effect of using out-of-date norms with ability tests is therefore likely to disadvantage more able candidates, whose scores are more likely to be circumscribed by ceiling effects – the difference between them and less able groups apparently shrinks.

22.5.2 THE SIZE AND RELEVANCE OF THE SAMPLE

There are usually insufficient people in an organization to produce good norms for a specific job. An organization might only employ, say, 80 accountants and norms based on a sample of 80 people would be inadequate. The problem of size of normative groups is a particularly acute when constructing ethnic norms. In the United Kingdom, ethnic minorities make up about 7% of the population. If accountants constitute 5% of an engineering company's workforce, then the company would need about 57,000 employees in order to amass a sample of 200 ethnic accountants. Very few companies are this large. Furthermore, there is no reason to believe that all ethnic groups are exactly equal, so separate ethnic norms for, say, Afro-Caribbeans and Asians might seem desirable. To obtain ethnic norms at this level would probably require a company with about 114,000 employees. But, is it reasonable to believe that, say, all Asians are the same? Should we not be looking for separate norms for Asians from India and Asians from China, and hoping that we can find a compliant organization with a total employee count in the region of 228,000 people?

22.5.3 NORMS VERSUS RELIABILITY AND VALIDITY

There is no necessary link between validity, reliability and the quality of the norms for a test. If a test's norms are out of date, what should be done? – Change to a test with poor validity, but with up-to-date norms? In most cases, validity should be supreme and it would be best to use the test with the highest validity.

 ## 22.6 DRAWING PROFILES

Profiles help people to understand scores because they present them in a pictorial form. However, tables of numbers have greater scientific use and should always be given, perhaps as an appendix, in a scientific report. Nevertheless, profiles are a potent aid to communication with clients and their employers. Two ways of drawing profiles are incorrect and two ways are correct.

22.6.1 TWO INCORRECT WAYS OF DRAWING PROFILES

Often, profiles join points on a graph to form a line chart, as shown in figure 22.8.

This method is incorrect. It implies a continuity between the scales (for example, January, February, March, April, . . .) – as though the 'Big Five' personality factors constituted an accepted series such as the months of the year. Line graphs are only appropriate when graphing a time sequence.

Another incorrect way is to use bars extending from the bottom of a scale, as shown in figure 22.9.

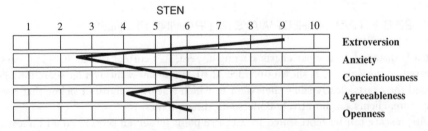

Figure 22.8 Incorrect use of line graphs.

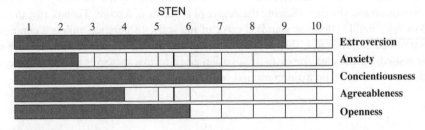

Figure 22.9 Incorrect use of bars from zero.

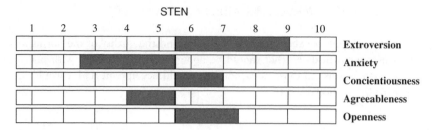

Figure 22.10 The correct use of bars 'hanging' from zero.

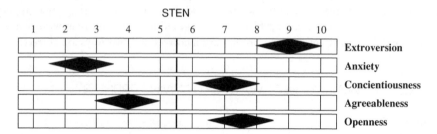

Figure 22.11 The correct use of a marker showing the mean and the margin of error.

This method is wrong because it implies that the scales are fixed ratio measures where the zero point is known. Fixed ratio scales are rare in psychology. For example, we do not know where the zero point is for extroversion.

22.6.2 TWO CORRECT WAYS OF DRAWING PROFILES

Whilst it is incorrect to use bar charts starting at zero, it *is* correct to use 'hanging' bars that are centred on the average, as shown in figure 22.10. We *do* know the average score for a population and the charts clearly show the extent to which a score is above or below that average. Furthermore, clients can intuitively understand these profiles.

Finally, a score can be represented by a centre point (observed score) and an indication of the margin of error (standard error), as shown in figure 22.11.

This is achieved by using either a lozenge-shaped marker or an asterisk to mark the actual score and brackets to mark the margins of error. This method has the advantage of conveying most information and clearly indicating the degree of accuracy of a score. Technically, the width of the lozenge should reflect the standard error of the scale. In practice, unless a computer is used to produce the diagrams, this is unrealistic and the average standard error for the scales on a test is used. Sometimes, the extra information given by this system is a disadvantage, since it distracts a client from the main point of a test score.

CHAPTER 23

INTERPRETING SCORES

Scores that are scaled and profiled give information about how much of a trait a person possesses. However, they do not automatically indicate what a given score means. The process of attributing meaning to a score is called **interpretation**. Interpretation is, in essence, subjectively based upon the knowledge skills and experience of the selector or counsellor. However, this subjectivity must be guided by the technical qualities of a scale and wider information about the trait being gauged. In this chapter, how the technical qualities of a scale constrain interpretations is first outlined. Guidance is then given on how knowledge of a measure's meaning can be accumulated. Finally, detailed guidance is given on the interpretations that can be made from measures of the 'Big Five' personality factors.

 ## 23.1 TECHNICAL FACTORS INFLUENCING INTERPRETATION

The technical factors that influence interpretation are our old friends sensitivity, reliability and validity, which were discussed at length in chapters 9–11. This chapter will only deal with those aspects of these topics that are relevant to interpretation.

23.1.1 SENSITIVITY

It will be recalled from chapter 9 that the sensitivity of a measure is determined by the spread of the *raw scores*. Spread is the degree to which people's scores are bunched together. If the scores are bunched tightly together and everyone gets a similar mark, the interpretation of a score will be severely constrained. Insensitive measures that have raw score standard deviations less than .6 can only support a few descriptive categories, such as low, average and high. A sensitive measure with a raw score standard deviation greater than 1.4 can support many more (seven plus) grades of meaning.

23.1.2 RELIABILITY

Reliability is a crucial factor in interpreting scores. It determines the margin or error surrounding a score. If reliability is high, then small differences between scores are important. If reliability

Table 23.1 The conversion of reliability coefficients to standard errors of measurement in five scoring systems

Reliability	Z scores sd = 1	Stens sd = 2	Stannines sd = 2	T scores sd = 10	Quotients sd = 15
.9	.316	.632	.632	3.162	4.734
.8	.447	.894	.894	4.472	6.708
.7	.547	1.095	1.095	5.477	8.215
.6	.632	1.264	1.264	6.324	9.986
.5	.707	1.414	1.414	7.071	10.607
.4	.774	1.549	1.549	7.764	11.691
.3	.837	1.673	1.673	8.367	12.550
.2	.894	1.789	1.789	8.944	13.416
.1	.949	1.897	1.897	9.486	17.230

is low, even large differences can be due to chance and should not be interpreted. The method of calculating an se_m is given in chapter 10 – section 10.5, which deals with confidence intervals, is especially relevant. Table 23.1 reduces the computational score of calculating the margin of error (se_m) from reliability correlations for the common scoring systems.

The true score will be within one standard error of the obtained score in approximately two out of three cases. In other words, if a score is plotted on a profile and an arrowed bar is extended 1 se_m above and below that score, we can be 66% certain that the true score is within the scores picked out by the arrowed bar.

For example, if an IQ test had a reliability of .90, the se_m would be 4.7. So, if a client were to score 120 on a test, we could be 67% certain that the true score would lie between 115.3 and 124.7 – it is twice as likely as not that the true score would be in the range of 115.3–124.7, as shown in figure 23.1.

The decision to accept an alpha of .33 (that is, that the chance of making a wrong conclusion is 33%) is customary but arbitrary. In some situations, other alpha levels are more appropriate. To find the appropriate margin of error, simply multiply the se_m by the Z score for the level of risk that you will accept. The Z scores for the main alphas are given in the table 23.2.

So, if the client in the previous example who obtained an IQ score of 120 was a little more conservative, and only willing to accept a 25% chance of being wrong rather than a 33% chance of being wrong, the margin of error on either side of the true score would be 5.4 (4.7 × 1.15).

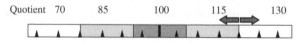

Quotient 70   85   100   115   130

If a test has a reliability of .9 and a quotient of 120 is
obtained, the standard error of measurement will be 4.7
The chances are 2:1 that if the person takes the test a
second time, their score will be in the range 115.3 –124.7

Figure 23.1 The margin of error for a hypothetical quotient.

Table 23.2 Z scores and verbal labels associated with various alphas

Alpha, the level of risk (the probability of being wrong)	Z score	Verbal label
.5	.76	As likely as not
.33	.96	Twice as likely as not
.25	1.15	Thrice as likely as not
.1	1.64	Nine times as likely as not
.05	1.95	Nineteen times as likely as not

In other words, it would be thrice as likely as not that the true score would lie in the range of 114.6–124.4.

Reliability and the se_m have important implications for the way in which profile sheets are designed. It is slightly conservative to say that most personality scales have se_ms of about 1 sten. So, in round terms, with an alpha of .33, it is uncertain whether someone is different from the average unless their score is below 4.5 or higher than 6.5. In other words, 'average' covers a range of two stens, from 4.5 to 6.5. Two stens is therefore a natural way of dividing the sten scale into five equal segments, as shown in figure 23.2.

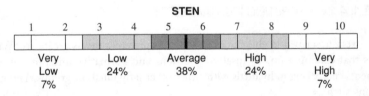

Figure 23.2 Division of the sten scale into five segments.

A score of 6 on the Warmth scale of the 16PF would be interpreted as 'in the middle of the range for interpersonal warmth'. A score of 7 would be interpreted as 'warm', while a score of 9 would be interpreted as 'very warm' and so on.

Some publishers use a slightly different system, as shown in figure 23.3.

This system is not as good. The middle category is too large. It contains 68% of the scores and, consequently, does not differentiate sufficiently between people. Conversely, the extreme categories are too small (2% each) and are rarely used. The unequal widths of the segments (1,

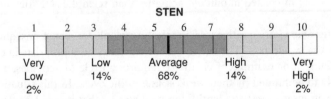

Figure 23.3 An alternative division of the sten scale into five segments.

2 and 4) may mystify clients. Furthermore, there is no obvious relationship between the widths of segments and the scale's margin of error.

23.1.3 VALIDITY

Validity determines the certainty with which inferences can be drawn. To calculate the certainty, square the validity correlation and multiply by 100. The result is the percentage overlap between variances of the test score and the criterion that gives the test score meaning. Validity determines the words used to indicate confidence. One scheme is given in table 23.3.

Table 23.3 Verbal labels and shared variance for selected validity correlations

Validity	Shared variance (%)	Verbal label
.5+	49	Indicates
.4	36	Suggests
.3	25	Is possible

23.1.4 INTERPRETING IPSATIVE TESTS

Ipsative tests were described in chapter 15. Their interpretation needs great care. With ipsative tests or tests that contain a mix of ipsative questions and normative questions, it is wrong to make statements comparing individuals with either other individuals or groups. You *cannot* make interpretations such as:

- Saghu is in the top 10% of the population for outdoor interests.
- Ioannis is more 'sensing' than Karl.
- Derek has no interest in science (even though his raw score is zero)!

Some ipsative tests have tables that invite the conversion of ipsative scores to normative scores. Such conversions 'can be very misleading' (Bartram and Lindley, 1994) and should rarely be used.

If ipsative tests are used, the only permissible interpretations are those that are self-contained within the individual. For example, it would be permissible to say:

- John is more sensing than judging.
- Sangita is more interested in outdoor activities than scientific activities.

It is rarely defensible to use ipsative tests in selecting people for jobs. Consequently, it is better to avoid their use in selection. The use of ipsative tests may be appropriate in personal development and training. For example, if creativity requires a cycle of activities, a person's total creativity is likely to be limited by their weakest link in the cycle. In this situation, it *would* be justifiable to use an ipsative test to identify the weakness so that it could be developed to the point at which it is no longer a limitation.

23.2 THE MEANINGS OF THE SCALES

The previous section said nothing about the meanings of scores. There are so many tests and scales that it is impossible to cover even the main ones. Users need to develop their own interpretation system. This section gives guidance on how interpretation systems should be developed.

23.2.1 SOURCES OF INFORMATION

A major task is to locate sources of information about the meanings of scales – in general, the more sources that are available, the better. The accessibility of resources to aid interpretation should be a major factor in choosing a test. If the only resource is a perfunctory manual published by the test's author, it might be wise to consider another test. If there is information on a test in three relatively independent sources, the test is certainly worthy of consideration.

The *first* indications of a scale's meaning are probably easiest to obtain from a *profile sheet or feedback leaflets* given to subjects. These documents define the scale's meaning to the recipient. A user of a test must be thoroughly familiar with these descriptions, so that they can anticipate and resolve questions or misunderstandings by clients and candidates. Excellent examples of profile and feedback sheets are given by the Quintax Personality Questionnaire (Robertson and Wilkie, 1998). For example, the profile sheet gives a brief description of an introvert as:

> . . . reflective, likes to think before acting. Prefers few interests pursued deeply. Needs time for quiet concentration. Enjoys privacy. Appears quiet and reserved to others.

The Quintax test also has feedback sheets. There is a sheet for every combination of the 'Big Five' personality factors. The sheets are very comprehensive and, as an illustration, extracts from the sheet for an introverted, independent, controlled, tough-minded and emotional person (ILSG-V) are given below. The feedback sheet is arranged into sections:

- *Pen portrait* – dependable, results-oriented, natural organizers . . . preferring to plan and schedule . . . loyal to both people and organizations . . . painstaking with detail.
- *Definition of an introvert in this context* – probably more at home in the inner world of ideas than in the outer world of people and things.
- *Strengths* – an organized and planful approach to work, reliable and dependable, patient and careful with facts and details.
- *Weaknesses* – may not see the wood for the trees . . . may appear inconsiderate to the feelings of others, ignoring everyday interpersonal graces . . . may seem a little unenthusiastic or disapproving to others.
- *Development objectives* – make sure you are considering the feelings of others and express your own feelings in words from time to time . . . make sure you communicate your commitment and enthusiasm.
- *Learning style* – need time for quiet concentration and study, like to get deeply into subjects and prefer the tutor to take the initiative.
- *Time management* – enjoys managing time . . . may be too rigid over plans and schedules.

Quintax feedback sheets are particularly good because they allow for the interplay of personality traits. For example, in a person who is *not* conscientious (for example, ILAG-V), introversion is likely to manifest itself as being:

> less planful . . . more concerned with developing high levels of skill . . . democratic and status free with the danger of failing to work long enough on anyone project for its to bear fruit etc.

Unfortunately, few tests provide such excellent feedback information, which can be used as a first step to interpreting the meanings of scores.

The *second* most convenient source of information about the meanings of a scale will be the *test manual*. It usually gives a straightforward explanation followed by a detailed description of the meanings. The detailed description should refer to validity studies and research reports. The test manual should also refer to scales in other tests that have similar meanings. An example of a good manual description is the OPQ, which has seven scales measuring facets of introversion. The scale with the highest loading on this factor is 'Outgoing' and a low score is associated with introversion. The manual gives the following explanation:

LOW SCORERS
Description: Quiet and reserved in groups, dislikes being centre of attention.
Typical item: I am rather a xxxxx person.
Key behaviour: Quiet and reserved, they prefer to blend into the background on social occasions rather than become the centre of attention. They may feel uncomfortable when there is a lot of noise and high-energy social activity going on around them. Generally, they prefer quieter, less hectic social events.

The *third* source of information about the meanings of a scale is *courses* provided by test publishers and other organizations. Many test publishers have two levels of course. Full courses, which last for about six days, are for people who are new to personality testing. They will cover a wide range of concepts, including the meanings of scales of the publisher's test. About 60% of such courses is devoted to the meanings of scales. Many test publishers also offer 'conversion' courses. These assume prior knowledge of personality testing and do not consider issues such as personality theory or distortion. They are usually shorter and last for 2–3 days, and about 90% of the time will be devoted to the meanings of the scales. In addition, courses usually provide case studies, research reports and equations that are not otherwise available.

The *fourth* source of information about the meanings of scales is *reports* written by others and computer-generated reports. Some clients may have completed previous tests and they may be willing to make them available. The copies can then be inspected and the interpretations made either by other practitioners or by a computer can be extracted. The value of this information depends upon the expertise of the person or the system that generated the report.

Fifth, information about the meanings of a scale is found in *books and journal articles*. Postgraduate theses can also be included in this category. Test publishers will often maintain a list of books, journal articles and theses that mention their test. However, a user should also conduct independent searches. The 16PF 5 is unsurpassed as a test with a deep and extensive infrastructure of books, articles and theses that help understand the meanings of its scales. As examples, some books that can aid interpretation of 16PF scales are:

- Belbin, R. M. 1981: *Management Teams*. Oxford: Heinemann.
- Cattell, H. B. 1989: *The 16PF: Personality in Depth*. Champaign, Ill.: Institute for Personality and Ability Testing.
- Krug, S. E. 1981: *Interpreting 16PF Profiles*. Champaign, Ill.: Institute for Personality and Ability Testing.
- Lord, W. 1998: *16PF 5 Overcoming Obstacles to Interpretation*. Windsor: Assessment and Selection in Employment.
- Lord, W. 1998: *16PF 5 Personality in Practice*. Windsor: Assessment and Selection in Employment.
- Tyler, B. 1996: *16PF Interpretation Guide: Edition 4 and Edition 5*. London: Miller & Tyler.

Some articles that could aid the interpretation of, say, the OPQ are:

- Dulewicz, V. 1995: A validation of Belbin's team roles from 16PF and OPQ using bosses' rating of competence. *Journal of Occupational and Organisational Psychology*, 68, 81–91.
- Matthews, G., Stanton, N., Graham, N. C. and Brimelow, C. 1990: A factor analysis of the scales of the Occupational Personality Questionnaire. *Individual Differences*, 11(6), 591–6.
- Saville, P., Sik, G., Nyfield, G., Hackston, J. and MacIver, R. 1996: A demonstration of the validity of the Occupational Personality Questionnaire (OPQ) in the measurement of job competencies across time and in separate organisations. *Applied Psychology: An International Review*, 45, 243–62.

An example of a thesis that may aid the interpretation of the scales in the 16PF, the OPQ and the Eysenck Personality Questionnaire is:

- Enzer, I. 1994: *The Five Factor Model of Personality and the Measurement of Occupational Interests in a Managerial Group*. Unpublished PhD thesis, UMIST, Manchester.

Personal experience should not be overlooked as a source of information on the meanings of scales. It is often decried by psychometricians and researchers who seek vast eternal relationships that explain human behaviour and might earn a Nobel prize. Their paradigms usually concern effects that apply to large numbers of people. But unless they have samples of thousands of subjects they are unlikely to detect subtle relationships which apply to, say, 5% of people. An experienced practitioner, on the other hand, might be able to identify a pattern on the basis of a dozen cases. Practitioner experience is essential to interpreting the personality profile obtained in unusual circumstances. For example, no psychometric study is available to guide the interpretation of the test results for a client suffering from porphyria – a disease that reduces the production of haemoglobin for the blood, and also makes the skin sensitive to light. The classic example of a porphyria sufferer is King George III (while Bram Stoker may have partly based his fictional character Count Dracula on reports of this disease, and on long-established myths of vampires who came out at night and sought other people's blood). Research using the general population would reveal nothing. A specific study with a reasonable sample would be impossible. Yet, a practitioner who has experienced several cases will be able to interpret a porphyric profile.

Conclusions based on practitioner experience may be less accurate than scientific conclusions, but they are cheap, quick and they can be obtained in situations that defy scientific paradigms. Whilst experiential judgement and case law are useful, care must be exercised. Experience should not be confused with superficial, off the cuff, intuitive judgements. Experiential judgements need to be logical and based upon observable, testable evidence. Long, convoluted chains of reasoning should be avoided. Attribution bias (Ross, 1977), whereby causes are attributed to people rather than their situations, should be resisted.

 ## 23.3 THE INTERPRETATION GUIDE

Information about the meanings of scales quickly becomes so extensive that it is impossible to remember accurately. It is essential, especially during the first 100 interpretations of a scale, to record the information in an 'interpretation guide'. The aim of the interpretation guide is to organize the information so that it can be accessed systematically and easily. The guide can take the form of a computer database or paper dossier. A computerized guide is probably better when written reports are needed. However, a paper dossier is usually better during feedback sessions, where it can be placed on the table among other documents and consulted unobtrusively.

Table 23.4 relates the scales of personality tests commonly used in personality tests to the 'Big Five' personality factors:

- NEO/FFI (Costa and McCrae, 1995)
- 16PF 5 (Conn and Rieke, 1994)
- OPQ (Saville Holdsworth, 1999)
- Quintax Personality Questionnaire (Robertson and Wilkie, 1998)
- Hogan Personality Inventory (Hogan and Hogan, 1992a)
- Myers–Briggs Type Indicator (Myers and McCaulley, 1985)
- Eysenck Personality Inventory (Eysenck and Eysenck, 1991).

The information on each scale will be several pages long and is best divided into three major sections, covering the 'high' pole, the 'low' pole and middle scores. Each of the major sections should cover:

- alternative names
- general information and correlates
- advantages
- disadvantages
- implications for career
- implications for interviews
- implications for long-term development.

The following appendix tables give basic interpretation guides for each of the 'Big Five' factors. It should be clear that the personality dimensions are very broad factors and often they are not unidimensional. For example, not all extroverts are the same (Lord, personal

Table 23.4 The 'Big Five' personality factors and scales of selected personality tests

Factor	NEO/FFI	16PF 5	OPQ	Other tests (EPQ, Quintax, Hogan, MBTI)
Extroversion–Introversion	Warmth Gregariousness Assertiveness Activity Excitement-seeking Positive emotions	Warm Outgoing Lively Forthright Team-oriented	Outgoing Emotionally controlled –ve Modest –ve Outspoken Affiliative Persuasive Controlling	EPQ: Extroversion Quintax: Extroversion Hogan: Sociability MBTI: Extroversion – Introversion
Instability–Stability	Anxiety Angry hostility Depression Self-consciousness Impulsiveness Vulnerability	Emotional Worrying Tense Sceptical	Tough- minded –ve Relaxed –ve Worrying Socially confident –ve Optimistic –ve Social desirability –ve	EPQ: Neuroticism Quintax: Emotional involvement Hogan: Adjustment –ve MBTI: no scale
Controlled–Uncontrolled	Competence Order Dutifulness Achievement-striving Self-discipline Deliberation	Conscientious Self-controlled Practical Cautious	Detail conscious Conscientious Vigorous Forward thinking Evaluative Data rational Achieving	EPQ: no scale (possibly lie scale) Quintax: Organization Hogan: Prudence MBTI: Judging–perceiving
Openness to Experience	Fantasy Aesthetics Feelings Actions Ideas Values	Cultured Experimenting	Conventional –ve Variety-seeking Conceptual Innovative Rule-following –ve Behavioural Adaptable	EPQ: no scale Quintax: Intellectual focus Hogan: Intellectance MBTI: Sensing–intuition
Agreeable–Tough-minded	Trust Straightforwardness Altruism Compliance Modesty Tender-mindedness	Assertive Venturesome Sceptical	Caring Democratic Competitive –ve Trusting Independent- minded –ve Decisive –ve	EPQ: Psychoticism??? Quintax: Criticality Hogan: Agreeability MBTI: Thinking–feeling???

If '–ve' is printed after a scale name, the opposite end of the pole correlates with one of the 'Big Five' factors.

The Hogan Personality Inventory also has scales called 'Ambition' and 'Scholarship'.

'???' signifies that the classification is far from exact.

communication, 2001). In some cases, extroversion is manifest by a high level of energy. In other cases, it is manifest by a high level of sociability, and in yet other cases it is manifest by both high energy and high sociability. The reader should therefore check that the positives and negatives are true in each individual case. If tests giving subscales of the 'Big Five' are used, it will be useful to disassemble the information according to subscales.

It is inconceivable that all phrases are mechanically used in a report or feedback session. Judgement will be needed to decide which phrases should be used. The guide, which was developed from the tests' manuals and personal experience, is by no means exhaustive and users should add their own phrases. Indeed, the present author would welcome copies of any additions!

APPENDIX 23.1 INTERPRETATION GUIDES

High Extroversion

Other names for high scores: Exvia, Outgoing. There is unusually high consensus on this name and the term is used universally with minor differences in spelling. Sometimes, extroversion is split into mainly two components: high energy and sociability. There is less consensus about the names for the components. High energy is also called enthusiasm, surgency, forcefulness and liveliness. Sociability is also called interpersonal warmth, social boldness or group orientation and, perhaps, dominance.

General information: Extroversion is one of the two largest personality factors and rivals stability in size. It was one of the first personality dimensions to be isolated. There is evidence that extroversion is at least partly related to neural functioning. It is contended that the nervous system of extroverts has stronger inhibitory mechanisms. It is as though the nervous system is 'turned down' so that extroverts either find 'loud' environments or they take action to liven up a subdued environment. There is evidence that extroverts take longer to condition. Frontal lobotomy increases certain aspects of extroversion – as does the consumption of alcohol. However, the neurological explanation of extroversion must not be exaggerated. There is also considerable evidence of environmental and cultural influences.

Extroversion seems to increase from morning to evening. It is highest among young adults (16–24), there is then a notable decline in early maturity (25–44) and a further slight decline in full maturity (44–64), but the sociability component may increase with age as people become less shy. Extroversion is moderately heritable – .4 to .5.

There is a high correlation between extroversion and social desirability. In Western cultures, extrovert characteristics are generally seen to be desirable. Leaders tend to have higher extroversion scores than followers.

Potential strengths for individuals with high extroversion:

- able to establish relationships with other people quickly and effectively . . . forms strong attachments to people
- maintains wide circle of friends
- attentive to people . . . able to remember names . . . generous in relationships
- able to adapt and make flexible compromises with people's foibles . . . tends to recall emotions rather than facts

- able to motivate and inspire other people
- will not put on 'airs and graces' . . . will be considered as open, direct, forthright, honest genuine and usually likeable
- easy to communicate with
- tends to dislike school classroom and accepted 'academic goodness'
- tends to be popular; that is, receives sociometric votes
- good at teamwork . . . brings in others who are reluctant to contribute . . . helps others with problems
- joiner . . . gregarious . . . spends a lot of time in the company of others . . . makes group favourable remarks
- takes high profile in interactions, delightful, entertaining, talkative, good speaker, fun loving
- likely to organize clubs and teams
- more responsive to group therapy than individual therapy
- action-oriented, decisive, upbeat, energetic
- positive, optimistic
- comfortable in negotiations, derives pleasure from changing people's views
- likes to be in charge, likely to fill leadership roles (with high independence)
- likes variety

Potential weaknesses for individuals with high extroversion:

- unable to take cold, clinical decisions about people
- may be over-emotional, sentimental and easily influenced (with low stability or low independence)
- may lack self-reliance and initiative (with high agreeableness)
- may depend too much on group approval (with high agreeableness)
- dislikes being alone and may have feelings of loneliness
- may be thick-skinned, brash and pushy
- may come across as domineering and overbearing
- may be seen as too loud and exuberant
- may under-react to environmental danger
- may seek out danger because he or she finds it exhilarating
- may not listen to other people
- better able to receive than give attention
- may exhaust the patience of others
- tactless and lacking in subtlety
- thoughtless about other people's feelings
- openness and directness may discomfort others
- may be too gushing, 'over the top' and talk too much
- may be something of an exhibitionist or self-centred
- may come across as being full of him- or herself, and self-important
- need for being with others inhibits some activities such as reading and study
- interests may change quickly with latest fads or fashions
- may be impetuous or impulsive
- may take on more than can be handled or finished
- does not do well in long-term undertakings
- rarely masters things thoroughly; poor finishers with a long trail of uncompleted projects
- may rush into unsuitable social arrangements

Career implications of high extroversion:

- occupations dealing with people which demand the ability to face the 'wear and tear' of dealing with people (with stability)
- occupations requiring boldness, willingness to take risks and strong nerves (with stability)
- should be wary of jobs concerned with health and safety
- social worker
- psychiatric technician
- employment counsellor
- manager
- business executive
- travelling salesperson
- airline cabin crew member
- firefighter
- explorer
- cook and kitchen help
- football player
- swimmer

Comments on interviews for individuals with high extroversion:

- be careful to avoid dominating the interview; do not talk too much
- do not try to make a friend of the interviewer
- listen carefully to questions
- choose words carefully in order to avoid offending the interviewer
- play interviews in a 'safe and steady' way; avoid any 'stunts'
- be prepared to give examples of projects that have been properly completed
- carefully consider the pros and cons of any job offer

Developmental implications for individuals with high extroversion:

- be more prepared to take 'clinical' decisions about people
- carefully consider the pros and cons before taking action
- avoid taking on too much
- beware of talking too bluntly or frankly to people
- be less prepared to go along with the wishes of others (with agreeableness)
- listen carefully for the meaning behind what others say (with high stability)

Low Extroversion (Introversion)

Other names for low scores: Invia, Non-extroversion, Reserved, Unsociable. Introversion is the opposite pole to extroversion, so the notes on extroversion should be consulted. Some authors suggest that introversion does not exist – it is more accurately described as the absence of extroversion.

General information: Take care when feeding back results. Clients may interpret the word 'introvert' negatively. Note that introversion should not be confused with depression.

Possible advantages for individuals with low extroversion (introversion):

- does not let own emotions colour judgement; not greatly influenced by feelings
- less influenced by social reinforcements such as praise
- objective, analytical (if shrewd and intelligent)
- sets high standards, provides exact information
- has a hard-headed intellectual approach
- more likely to take lead in analytical, goal-oriented discussion and provide constructive solutions
- usually likes things or words
- likes to focus on task in hand
- an independent thinker
- prepared to think deeply and deliberately
- enjoys working alone
- self-reliant and able to handle a professional team (if intelligent)
- may be creative (if imaginative and experimenting)
- reliable, careful and serious
- good at controlling 'downside' risks
- appreciated by supervisors who value a serious, responsible approach
- has few daily fluctuations in mood
- good listener, perceptive (if shrewd and intelligent)
- well-behaved and considerate of others
- effective social skills (if some warmth, people orientation and shrewdness)
- will hold back from criticizing others, will avoid direct criticism of others
- does not need to be the centre of attention
- shrewd and has a good feel for business
- able to spot opportunities, opportunistic (if imaginative and open)
- 'sharp' at diagnosis and identifying 'angles' (if intelligent and open)
- alert to manners, social obligations and social reactions of others (with middle scores on stability)
- able to conceal his or her feelings and emotions
- prefers to give people space to make up their own minds; rarely pressures others
- may over-achieve academically

Possible disadvantages for individuals with low extroversion (introversion):

- too cold or reserved
- places high value on privacy and freedom of choice
- difficult to get to know
- may be seen as snobbish and elitist
- may tend to reject help
- may be shy and live in a shell
- may have difficulty in making social contacts
- does not take people's foibles into account (with tough-mindedness)
- tends to be a 'wet blanket' on social occasions
- is often dissatisfied with group processes
- may reject compromise; able to hold fast to unpopular positions

- colourless
- may be shy and tormented by unreasonable sense of inferiority
- may be inhibited in expressing themselves
- unable to motivate or influence others
- unlikely to be leaders
- inhibited with people and relationships
- cannot adapt to team work
- follows own ideas regardless of the views of others
- over-critical
- negative and over-analytical
- too smart for own good
- difficult to read; colleagues do not know where they stand
- unwilling to take risks, pessimistic
- too dour and cautious
- low tolerance for fear and arousal
- is often more comfortable leaving others to make a decision
- may have a tendency to be under-promoted
- achievements may not be recognized; may be undervalued

Career implications of low extroversion:

- accountant
- artist
- clergy
- electrician
- engineer
- time study engineer
- machine operator
- employment counsellor
- university administrator
- university professor
- biologist
- geologist
- physicist
- farmer

Comments on interviews for individuals with low extroversion:

- be prepared to make an impression, 'larger than life', early in the interview
- give positive non-verbal cues, such as nods and smiles
- do not be pedantically logical
- give positive, upbeat replies
- only be critical or sceptical when it is clearly required
- do not under-estimate your own experience and achievements in order to be 'safe'
- be prepared to talk about achievements obtained in group contexts
- do not look for hidden meanings or motives in interviewer's questions

Developmental implications of low extroversion:

- learn not to over-estimate the importance of logic or under-estimate the importance of emotion
- be more prepared to make compromises for the sake of team spirit
- devise 'positive' ways of giving criticisms or negative information
- make sure that the positive aspects of situations are taken into account
- do not keep things close to your chest; make sure you talk problems over with someone
- be more prepared to show emotional reactions

Note that most introverts are aware that their interpersonal relationships may be strained. Bluntly advising them to improve their friendships with others may make them more self-conscious and be counterproductive.

High Stability

Other names for high scores: Calm, Adjusted, Low Anxiety, Hardy, Secure, Relaxed, Even-tempered, Buddha-like.

General information: The stability–emotionality dimension is one of the largest personality traits. It is rivalled in size only by Extroversion. Heritability is about .4–.5. Stability may have links with low volatility of the sympathetic nervous system or high activity of the parasympathetic system. Men tend to have higher scores on stability than women, but there are no major trends with age or ethnic origin.

Possible advantages for individuals with high stability:

- able to cope with difficult emotional situations
- not affected by emotional situations
- able to cope with stressful situations and pressure
- rarely becomes upset or emotional – consistent
- able to maintain control over emotions
- has stamina and resilience to rise above difficult situations
- able to keep spirits up when going gets tough
- remains cool and does not make a drama out of a crisis
- unruffleable
- brings difficult situations under control
- remains calm when the unexpected happens
- stoic; has realistic expectations
- does not procrastinate
- trusts people and is able to get their trust in return
- able to take on board the feedback from others
- satisfied with life
- able to achieve those things that seem important
- mature, dynamic integration of emotions
- difficult to upset, not easily offended, can ignore insults
- unconcerned with what others think of them

- does not over-react to criticism; unruffled by jibes and insults
- remains cool when things get personal
- helps to maintain group morale, helps team spirit
- finds it easy to relax
- does not project 'inner tensions'
- easy-going, friendly, relaxed
- calm before important occasions
- expects things to turn out well
- sees the positive side of life
- strong ego which may diminish in later life
    - make good spouses and parents (with extroversion and conscientiousness) but may be resented by others
    - may have had difficult childhood (and has therefore learned effective coping techniques?)

Possible disadvantages for individuals with high stability:

- may be too stable and pooh-pooh catastrophic situations
- complacent; difficult to motivate and supervise
- lacking in sensitivity (with extroversion and high self-image)
- may be a reaction to 'burn out' or case hardening
- too nice – car dealer's delight
- easily deceived – prey for confidence tricksters
- others may view them as unambitious
- too relaxed, lacking 'go' (with low conscientiousness)
- robot-like (with groundedness and introversion)
- may have a 'mystical', but positive, coexistence with others
- may be impertinent (if unrealistically confident)
- may under-achieve
- feels little 'emotional pain'
- poor spouses (with introversion, unless they are shrewd!)
- torpid, lacks vigour and drive, languorous
- lives in the present; not too concerned with the future
- rarely accepts blame or shows remorse (with low conscientiousness)
- does not feel responsible or committed – lacks contrition (with low conscientiousness)

Career implications of high stability:
Generally suitable for careers that involve high emotional demands, pressure and stress. Often suitable for posts abroad (away from head office support) or start-up situations. Occupations which, subject to other considerations, might be appropriate are:

- firefighter
- judge

- kitchen worker
- life insurance agent
- education (university) administrator
- airline pilot
- biologist
- physicist
- research scientist
- police officer (if suspicious)
- anaesthetist
- abattoir worker
- finance manager
- special education teacher
- dental worker
- electrician
- psychologist
- flight attendant
- psychiatric worker
- sewage worker
- nurse
- social worker
- athlete
- garage mechanic
- school counsellor

Comments on interviews for people with high stability:

- emphasize competence in stressful, pressured situations
- emphasize resilience to setbacks
- emphasize ability to de-escalate crises
- emphasize ability to get best out of people by trusting them (but only in jobs with benign environments)
- beware of being too 'laid back'; sit in an alert position; respond with energy to questions
- show empathy to questions where people suffer minor frustrations
- show readiness to react to initial signs of things going wrong
- avoid trusting interviewer with information

Developmental implications of high stability:

- make concessions to the way in which some tender souls might perceive you
- learn to empathize with 'tender souls' who are swamped with emotion
- be prepared to act on early warning signs that things are going wrong
- if you are ambitious, be prepared to voice your ambitions
- be wary of people who are trying to sell you a product, service or idea (not with people who have IQs greater than 125)
- beware of impressions of complacency – especially to bosses who are anxious themselves (about 20% of bosses)
- make periodic (monthly?) displays of worry and emotion if boss is not equally stable

Low Stability (Neuroticism)

Other names for low scores: Emotionality, Emotional Involvement, Neuroticism, Anxiety, Non-adjustment, Tender, Sensitive.

General information: Low scores on stability can sometimes be caused by a person encountering a difficult time, such as redundancy or bereavement. This possibility should be checked at, say, an interview. A very low score that has no obvious external cause may require referral to an appropriate professional.

Many tests have several scales that measure this factor and most of these scales are highly intercorrelated.

The 16PF 5 has four relevant scales: Tension (Q4+), Apprehension (O+), Emotionally Changeable (C−) and Vigilance (L+).

Low stability is measured by five scales on the OPQ: Tough-minded (−), Relaxed (−), Worrying, Socially confident (−) and Optimistic (−).

The NEO has six relevant scales: anxiety (N1), angry hostility (N2), depression (N3), self-consciousness (N4), impulsiveness (N5) and vulnerability (N6).

Other tests, such as the Eysenck Personality Questionnaire and the Quintax Personality Questionnaire, have a single scale that measures emotionality (neuroticism and volatility, respectively). Inexplicably, the Myers–Briggs personality questionnaire does not measure this major aspect of personality.

Possible advantages for individuals with low stability:

* gives personal commitment (with control)
* needs to put situations right (with control)
* not easily satisfied, high involvement
* can handle difficult characters (with control)
* has drive and nervous energy to meet deadlines (with control)
* hard to fool (with low extroversion)
* can relate to 'artistic' creativity
* is sensitive to the emotions of others
* strong loyalty and commitment to the organization (with control)
* is often unselfish, humane and virtuous
* is concerned about the way they are perceived by others
* tension provides energy to get things done (with control)
* guilt and worry may motivate performance in benign or tolerant situations that would induce complacency in others

Possible disadvantages for individuals with low stability:
Emotionality is often, but not necessarily, indicative of maladjustment and emotional distress. It is characterized by a preponderance of negative feelings:

* easily annoyed or upset by others
* frequently loses control over feelings
* poorer tolerance of frustration
* may have disturbed interpersonal relationships
* may have recurrent jealous and suspicious feelings

- may be defensive
- guilt-prone; a general sense of inadequacy and loneliness
- worrying; may blame self to much
- may often feel jittery, nervous or on edge
- may over-react to a difficulty
- may be an 'injustice collector' with a chip on his or her shoulder
- may have low self-esteem
- may become excessively worried or agitated before events
- slow to calm down after an incident
- easily affected by adverse criticism

Career implications of low stability:

Avoid jobs that generate an onslaught of emotions, feelings and pressure. Avoid jobs where a momentary loss of control over feelings could have catastrophic or irretrievable effects.

Suitable jobs may, in consideration with other personality factors, include:

- artist
- employment counsellor
- farmer
- priest
- supermarket personnel
- editorial worker
- engineer
- janitor
- university professor
- writer

In general, people with high emotionality do rather worse in their careers than might be predicted on the basis of other factors such as intelligence.

Comments for interviews of individuals with low stability:

- arrive at interview in good time; use waiting time to read or think about something enjoyable; do deep breathing exercises
- control nervous actions and mannerisms – if necessary, sit with hands lightly clasped and legs lightly crossed at ankles
- emphasize ability to respond to emotions of others
- emphasize personal commitment
- emphasize keenness to meet deadlines
- avoid taking offence over small actions or slips by interviewer
- avoid wasting mental effort criticizing or dwelling on own answers given to previous questions
- avoid becoming impatient with interviewer

Developmental implications of low stability:

- avoid taking on other people's problems (accepting other people's monkies)
- do not allow others to pressure you into taking on more than that with which you feel comfortable
- do not blame yourself when things outside your control go wrong

- beware of being impatient with other people when a deadline is approaching
- beware of seeing too many meanings in things – many things happen by chance or carelessness, rather than by conspiracy
- try to attribute positive meanings to events (cognitive therapy); mentally rehearse past successes
- recognize the onset of stress
- develop ways of reducing stress such as exercise, positive imagination, slow breathing and so on
- reserve a part of the available time for leisure and enjoyment

If scores are very low and there is no obvious environmental factor, consider tactfully broaching the possibility of referral to appropriate professional such as a clinical psychologist or counsellor.

High Conscientiousness

Other names for high conscientiousness scores: Super-ego strength, Self-discipline, Control, Willpower, Organization, Structure, Prudence.

General information: Conscientiousness may be defined as the degree to which a person is able to inhibit impulses and direct behaviour along socially desirable lines. It may be linked to moral development, in its widest sense, and people with high conscientiousness are often said to be at the top levels of Kohlberg's (1976) stages of moral development. Many writers have linked conscientiousness to the development of the super-ego. High scores on conscientiousness are often associated with well-being. It correlates with good marital relationships and good parenting. Paradoxically, however, highly conscientious people can have traumatic relationships with rebellious teenage children. Conscientiousness has clear links with leadership. Conscientious people often have achievements beyond those that would be expected from their ability. The trait has a weak positive correlation with success in most jobs. Conscientious people have fewer car accidents.

High scores on scales of conscientiousness have moderate correlations with high scores on lie scales. This could mean either that people obtain high scores by telling lies or that lie scales unfairly stigmatize people who try to uphold high moral standards.

High scores on conscientiousness often modify the interpretation of other scores by emphasizing the positive aspects.

Potential advantages for individuals with high conscientiousness:

- enjoys completing tasks
- tends to push him- or herself to the limit
- able to control short-term impulses; tries to do his or her best
- generally involved with moral concerns of right and wrong
- persevering
- has a sense of duty
- strong super–ego, strong character
- good self-discipline
- aware of what is conventionally good or bad
- checks work thoroughly
- likes work involving measuring and monitoring

- focuses on errors and assumptions
- good social adaptation
- considerate of other people
- scrupulous, punctual and fastidious; even compulsive
- likes to see tasks through to the end
- evaluates information critically
- likes working with statistics and mathematical problems
- sets clear goals and targets for future
- enjoys planning
- has a high regard for etiquette and social reputation
- readily follows organizational procedures
- is prepared to do the job that is expected, even if it is boring
- has high standards for maintaining self-respect
- sticks to deadlines and schedules
- has strategic perspective
- keeps paperwork and records in order
- likes to work in a tidy way
- is an a good organizer and is well ordered
- is purposeful, strong-willed and determined
- takes things at a steady pace
  - is concerned for the common good rather than personal gain
  - is reliable, practical and has common sense

Potential disadvantages for individuals with high conscientiousness:

- perfectionist
- has annoying, fastidious behaviour
- may get preoccupied with details; may be overly pedantic
- finds it difficult to work simultaneously on several tasks
- may be overly conforming
- is intolerant of long periods of high activity
- may be inflexible
- is rigid and authoritarian
- finds it difficult to cope with overload
- resists anything outside his or her immediate experience
- is status-seeking
- may be demoralized by failure
- may be a workaholic
- dislikes working in spontaneous or unpredictable situations
- is rule-bound, rigid, lacks initiative

Career implications of high conscientiousness:
Conscientious people seem suited to jobs requiring attention to detail and adherence to procedures. They also seem suited to jobs where they need to monitor situations and ensure that tasks are completed. Suitable jobs might include:

- airline pilot
- police officer

- bomb disposal technician
- accountant
- pharmacist
- microchip manufacturer
- airline cabin crew member
- firefighter
- electrician
- university administrator
- data-processor
- judge

Comments on interviews for individuals with high conscientiousness:

- prepare thoroughly for interview and create a good impression; little advice will be needed
- avoid dressing too formally for interviews in organizations where flexibility is valued (for example, media jobs)
- be prepared to adopt a flexible approach
- be prepared to speculate freely on 'fanciful ideas' (with tough-mindedness)

Developmental implications of high conscientiousness:

- beware of other people exploiting conscientiousness and taking you for granted
- do not presume that 'correct' behaviour will be valued or rewarded
- be prepared to vary your approach a little from day to day and from situation to situation
- beware of changes in the organization's 'morals' and values
- avoid 'ethical imperialism' and imposing a set of 'morals' on other people

Low Conscientiousness (Pragmatism)

Other names for low scores: Fickle, Uncontrolled, Undisciplined, Disorganization, Adaptable, Flexible.

General information: A low score indicates a person who is unable to control impulses and direct behaviour in a socially desirable way. Low scores are linked to a number of psychological and behavioural problems, but they do not necessarily imply problems. A low score on conscientiousness is very difficult to interpret, because it may arise in several different ways (Cattell, 1989, 123):

- amorality; that is, having few moral values, similar to infants in Kohlberg's second stage of moral development
- moral immaturity, which is associated with neuroticism and primitive moral orientations
- non-conventional morality shown by people who keep rules and values of another reference group
- post-conventional morality, which follows rules that transcend the moral rules of the time
- 'faking bad' by people who pretend to reject current moral standards whilst actually adhering to them

Low scores on conscientiousness are not rare in young people and they are frequently found in 'chronic' seekers of vocational guidance.

A low score on conscientiousness often alters the interpretation of other scores – it usually emphasizes the negative aspects of other scores.

Potential advantages for individuals with low conscientiousness:

- flexible and adaptable
- not hide-bound by convention and protocol
- able to work flexibly, without plans or guidelines
- quick to respond to a crisis
- efficiently expedient and pragmatic
- flexible about deadlines and timescales
- enjoys long periods of high activity
- has imagination and flair
- thrives on activity; enjoys having lots of tasks to do
- looks for achievable rather than ambitious targets

Potential disadvantages for people with low conscientiousness:

- has links with delinquency and sociopathic behaviour (but check other information and scores)
- may have a disorganized approach
- may leave loose ends and unfinished work
- lacks finishing power
- fickle
- leaves other people to check quality of information
- may ignore detail
- uncritically accepts information
- may be careless
- takes quality of work for granted
- may be prone to putting things off
- a tendency to become overloaded with commitments (with extroversion)
- may ignore boring tasks
- lackadaisical in working towards goals
- lacks a sense of direction
- association with mental health problems
- unrealistic as interests change rapidly (with extroversion)
- skimps on planning (with extroversion)
- little control and organization in the long term (with extroversion)
- prefers to leave their time unscheduled and deal with matters as they arise
- may be caught out or surprised by unforeseen events
- tends to be reactive rather than proactive
- impractical and unrealistic
- may be unconventional, impulsive and perhaps irresponsible
- too idealistic for industry (with agreeableness)
- lacks concern for expectations
- too expedient; disregards rules

Career implications of low conscientiousness:
A low score on conscientiousness may be helpful in jobs requiring flexibility, adaptation and imagination, such as:

- salesperson
- musician
- artist
- editor
- marketing executive
- consultant
- researcher
- advertising executive

It may also be useful in jobs involving work in an impersonal, unpredictable market, such as dealers and brokers.

Comments on interviews for individuals with low conscientiousness:

- prepare for an interview carefully and thoroughly; check travel arrangements in detail, in advance
- organize, in advance, facts about your experience and the relevant points that you wish to make
- do not wear clothes that are outlandish or likely to give offence
- do not dwell on too many instances in which you have prevailed by breaking rules and conventions
- try to be consistent with replies
- be clear about long-term goals
- ensure that ideas take practical realities of the situation into account

Developmental implications of low conscientiousness:

- carefully think through the type of person you wish to be and your long-term goals
- pay more attention to the minutiae of completing jobs
- be more concerned about the expectations of others
- avoid, at least unwitting, infraction of minor rules
- try to be consistent from the viewpoint of others
- always explain to others why you make any tactical change
- make sure that your ideas take practical realities into account

High Agreeableness

Other names for high scores: Threat-sensitive, Lacks independence, Unassertive, Pliant, Shy, Socially timid, Submissive, Attention-avoidance.

General information: Agreeableness is fundamentally concerned with the willingness to subjugate personal views in favour of the views of more dominant people or groups. It has many positive features and can be an effective way of achieving goals. It is an important aspect of obtaining promotion if it is coupled with ambition (the road to the top is paved with mimicry!). Agreeable people are unlikely to be either criminal or creative. Agreeableness is characterized by an avoidance of threats, attention and limelight. Agreeableness is high in established leaders, but does not correlate with obtaining leadership. Agreeable people tend to have had a happy childhood, but they become troubled if separated from familiar surroundings.

Agreeableness is negatively correlated with social status; toffs tend to be disagreeable, but servants are agreeable! Agreeableness has an appreciable heredity component.

Potential advantages for individuals with high agreeableness:

- eager to co-operate and avoid conflict (with extroversion)
- willing to do things in ways agreed with others (with extroversion)
- does not alter behaviour according to position in pecking order, generally deferential
- forgives and forgets
- does not feel the need to do better than others and concedes gracefully
- dislikes competition; believes that participation is more important than winning
- humble and self-effacing, but not necessarily lacking in self-esteem or confidence
- seeks to maximize harmony
- has an active concern for the welfare of others
- generous and considerate
- moved by the needs of others, emphasizing the human side of policies
- achieves goals through cohesion
- open to other people's ideas and suggestions
- believes that others are honest and well-intentioned
- gets on well with most people (with extroversion)
- liked by people with high dominance
- accepts majority decisions; prepared to follow consensus
- prepared to make allowances for the personal problems of others
- likes to look for the best in people
- considerate (with control)
- pleasant, affable, relaxed and engaging
- believes what others say; trusts people (with stability)
- frank and sincere (with extroversion)
- makes decisions that take feelings into account
- tends to be experimental and well informed (with openness)
- dislikes facts and figures; prefers opinions and feelings (with anxiety)
- likes routine exchanges, with no risk of saying something 'something stupid'

Potential disadvantages for individuals with high agreeableness:

- gutless, 'scaredy cats'
- obsequious, self-effacing and gratifying
- no personality of their own
- tries to avoid or deaden all stimulation from outside; likes to be cocooned (with low extroversion)
- likes certainty for its own sake – not because unpredictability can involve threats
- low tolerance for fear and arousal, and needs to protect self from threats
- tends to be cautious when making decisions (with low extroversion)
- likes to take time to reach conclusions
- closes off opportunities for personal gain, friendship and adventure
- ill at ease (with anxiety)
- fear of being singled out for attention, especially if it is negative (with anxiety)
- like to live in a shell as a protection and a prison
- feel harsh and strong colours of everyday life as shrill, ugly and painful (with anxiety)
- tend not to take risks and may miss out on opportunities
- may be taken in or manipulated by unscrupulous people (with extroversion)
- has tendency to give in too easily
- avoids conflict by acquiescing to wishes, whims and wants of others
- may avoid confrontation even when necessary (check toughness)
- spouses of people with low dominance resent having to take all the responsibility

- other peoples' pleasure and successes cause animosity
- strong desire to be liked (with extroversion)
- may not be treated with respect, since self-evaluation may be unimportant
- silence, designed to avoid attention, may be interpreted as criticism or rejection (with low extroversion)
- frustrating for those with no desire to assume dominant roles
- too sensitive to hurt other people's feelings (with low independence)
- benefit from spouses who are more adventurous but may become too dependent
- relationships between two agreeable people may flounder for lack of direction
- reluctant to exchange views honestly is problematic even if intentions good

Career implications of high agreeableness:
Occupations in large organizations, especially 'democratic' organizations that are not closely coupled to the market, seem suitable – for example, civil service, local authorities and professional bodies. In addition, the following occupations might be suitable:

- farmer
- janitor
- cook
- waiter

Comments on interviews for people with high agreeableness:

- remember that interviewers will probably have a better opinion of your social skills than you do
- do not underestimate your experience – if asked about experience, start your answer with 'my experiences of . . . is . . .' and then give a succinct description of the nearest examples – others will probably evaluate them more highly than you do
- do not use the words 'merely', 'only' and 'just' when describing your experience
- do not filter out experience that you consider irrelevant – simply describe accurately the nearest experience you have

Developmental implications of high agreeableness:

- develop ways of banging your own drum
- remember that there are no talent scouts in life – if you do not state your claims, no one else will
- remember that 'Nice guys come last!'
- do not rely on your organization to remember your successes – management development departments no longer exist
- do not rely on superiors to argue your case – managers change too frequently to remember your success
- do not rely on superiors to argue your case – they are likely to claim your successes as their own
- keep a 'hero' file that contains any announcements of your successes or letters of congratulations

Low Agreeableness (Assertiveness)

Other names for low score: Dominance, Assertiveness, Dogmatism.

General information: Men have traditionally been more assertive than women, although there may have been a change in recent decades. Assertiveness seems to rise in early adulthood and then declines. Leaders tend to be rather more assertive than their followers. Problems and illness tend to reduce assertiveness. People of high social status tend to be more dominant. Assertiveness does not seem to be related to physical stature, but there is a suggestion that it is related to testosterone levels.

Assertiveness seems to have a negative correlation with school achievement (which may favour docile pupils) but is positively related to college achievement.

Potential advantages for individuals with low agreeableness:

- gets things done (with tough-mindedness)
- is prepared to take responsibility and push things through
- protects boundaries of self, possessions and priorities from invasion
- has no reluctance to express anger when necessary
- does not mind forcing ideas on others
- believes that attack is the best form of defence
- is a fighter who 'never says die'
- enjoys competitive activities and dislikes losing
- plays to win and is determined to beat others
- feels free to participate, raises group problems and criticizes group defects
- tends to distrust other people's intentions and is wary and suspicious
- is unlikely to be surprised when people are unreliable and dishonest
- is unlikely to be easily fooled
- will remain communicative and fluent even when things are fraught (with extroversion)
- is unlikely to be phased by difficult social situations (with extroversion)
- keeps a professional distance from personal problems at work
- is impatient with inefficiency of making decisions by consensus and committee
- will only accept the majority view if he or she is confident that it is correct
- is selective with sympathy and support (with low extroversion)
- is less likely to make allowances for personal problems or difficulties (with low extroversion)
- remains detached from the personal problems of others (with low extroversion)
- is not afraid to be unpopular in pursuit of the truth (with stability)
- seeks to achieve group goals through efficiency and accurate analysis
- is logical
- is hard-headed and unmoved by appeals to pity (with tough-mindedness)
- realists who make rational decisions based on cold logic (with low extroversion and with tough-mindedness)
- makes decisions on logical and reasoned analysis of facts
  - is unlikely to respond to authority
  - does not like being told what to do
  - is prepared to make decisions without consultation (with low extroversion)
  - prefers to follow own approach (with low extroversion)
  - prefers to make decisions alone
  - shows some reserve in giving support to ideas or plans of others (with low extroversion)

Potential disadvantages for individuals with low agreeableness:

- sarcastic, bluffing, upbraiding, quarrelsome
- aggressive, prefers to compete rather than co-operate
- may be perceived as ruthless, poor team player and bad loser (with low extroversion)
- enjoys dominating and controlling others as well as criticizing them
- abrasive approach might cause conflict
- contumacious, aggressive
- may be disruptive of a group and may 'heckle'
- sceptical, critical, dominant and possibly cold and hostile
- regards more straightforward people as naïve
- hard-headed, sceptical, proud, competitive
- willing to manipulate others through flattery, craftiness or deception
- insensitive to social disapproval (with low extroversion)
- prepared to ride roughshod over others
- prepared to disregard majority decisions (with low extroversion)
- confident in taking decisions; may be regarded by others as autocratic (with low extroversion)
- spends little time determining a consensus (with low extroversion)
- prominent, attention-getting
- may believe that he or she is a superior person
- may be considered conceited or arrogant by others (with high stability and high intelligence)
- is self-centred and reluctant to get involved in the problems of others
- is boastful, conceited, aggressive, pugnacious, forceful, egotistical
- lack of modesty may amount to narcissism
- often does not accept group decisions (with low extroversion)

Career implications of low agreeableness:
Low agreeableness may be helpful in occupations that require boldness and courage, and in occupations that require delivering negative feedback to others. Low agreeableness might also be useful in situations in which great objectivity is needed. Some suitable occupations might be:

- athlete/sportsperson
- administrator
- quality control personnel
- judge
- pharmacist
- psychotherapist
- salesperson
- military trainer
- computer programmer
- law enforcement officer
- scientist
- biologist
- physicist
- psychiatrist
- anaesthetist

Comments on interviews for individuals with low agreeableness:

- avoid 'taking over' the interview; do not talk to much
- avoid 'stunts' designed to make an unusual impact on the interviewer
- listen carefully to the interviewer's questions
- do not pick quarrels with interviewers

Developmental implications of low agreeableness:

- take people's feelings into account when getting things done; make sure you keep important people 'on board'
- beware of putting yourself up front and in a vulnerable position

High Openness to Experience

Other names for high scores: Premisia (projected emotional sensitivity), Tender-minded, Sensitive, Feeling.

General information: People who are open to experience tend to evaluate experience in terms of feelings and emotions. They are less attentive to stimuli in the external world, and more attentive to subjective factors that are frequently thought to be processed by the right hemisphere of the brain. Openness to experience is close to Jung's 'feeling' type of person.

Openness to experience is higher in women than in men. It is thought to be largely environmental and cultural in its origin, and may be associated with a sheltered upbringing. Openness to experience has some association with mental breakdown, both psychotic and neurotic, but it must be emphasized that other indicators must be present.

The interpretation of openness to experience is moderated by other personality factors, especially extroversion. For example, where openness is accompanied by warmth, people are likely to be sympathetic, generous and kind; but where it is accompanied by exuberance and energy, it may result in tendencies towards dramatization.

Often, the optimum levels of openness to experience are the middle ranges.

Potential advantages for individuals with high openness to experience:

- enjoys analysing people
- tries to understand motives and behaviour
- may spot problems that are overlooked by others (with control)
- may see him- or herself as a pioneers or mould-breaker
- favours changes and new approaches to work methods (with extroversion)
- is able to adapt to new audiences and circumstances
- is easily convinced of value of new ideas
- focuses on change and improvement
- enjoys brainstorming and originating ideas
- will be seen as imaginative, inventive and artistic
- is intellectually curious and enjoys mental challenge
- is perceptive and sensitive in the best sense of the word (can pick up vibes)
- is interested in theories and abstract ideas
- is patient with abstract theory
- likes to consider wider implications of information before its practical implications

Potential disadvantages for individuals with high openness to experience:

- radical and unorthodox
- regards 'preserving standards' as old-fashioned
- chases after fads and crazes
- has little respect for established values and traditions
- treatment of people may appear inconsistent and unfair
- others may find his or her changeability and flexibility baffling
- others have difficulty coping with constant changes to routine
- may reject tried-and-tested methods in favour of untested new ideas
- may generate so many new ideas and changes that others are overwhelmed (with low control)
- is easily bored by recurrent activities (with low control)
- has his or her head in the clouds
- tendency towards impracticability
- may be anti-authoritarian and rock the boat too much
- is prepared to break or bend rules (with low control)
- dislikes bureaucracy
- may agonize over difficult decisions
- is fussy and nit-picking
- is over-sensitive (with low stability)
- may be clinging and frequently seek help and sympathy (with low stability)
- has a fastidious dislike of 'crude' people and rough occupations
- is inclined to experiment with new solutions

Career implications of high openness to experience:
Careers suitable for people with high openness usually involve challenging the existing situation and pushing at the boundaries of knowledge:

- research worker
- university professor
- executive
- employment counsellor
- artist
- musician

Comments on interviews for individuals with high openness to experience:

- focus your replies on realistic possibilities
- avoid dwelling on the very long term and the wider implications
- do not attempt to communicate too many new or interesting ideas

Developmental implications of high openness to experience:

- make sure your ideas take practical realities into account
- be aware of the way in which others react to your flexibility and changes
- do not try to think too far into the future or take every detail into account

Low Openness to Experience (Down to Earth)

Other names for low scores: Down to Earth, Grounded, Tough-minded, Tough-poise, Low intellectual focus.

General information: Tough-minded people are usually more interested in the situation before their eyes than how things might be in the future or in their imaginations. There is a suggestion that when tough-minded people encounter a situation, the alpha rhythms in their cortices are larger than those of tender-minded people. Tough-minded people generally respond best when they are told about established facts and are presented with practical solutions. There are, at best, only trivial relationships with low scores and age or intelligence.

Potential advantages for individuals with low openness to experience:

- prefers well-established work methods
- is conventional in behaviour and conservative in outlook
- is ready to operate the system as required (with high control)
- solves problems in a pragmatic, practical way
- is down to earth
- is realistic and to the point
- is good at dealing with facts and details
- does not question or analyse reasons
- is tough enough to survive in industry (with low agreeableness)
- is staunch and reliable (with control)
- is more likely to build on the ideas of others and generate them themselves
- behaves consistently across situations (with low extroversion or high conscientiousness)

Potential disadvantages for individuals with low openness to experience:

- has difficulty operating without clear guidelines
- may get uncomfortable when situations or the 'goalposts' change frequently
- is traditional and set in ways
- may need convincing of the value of new techniques
- is over-resistant to change
- prefers familiar experiences to novel experiences
- likes tradition and general nostalgia
- prefers routine and predictable, relatively unchanging work environment
- may adapt badly to life's transitions (with low intelligence)
- is reluctant to leave the present for the future
- prefers to deal with practical issues rather than theoretical concepts
- is less interested in intellectual abstractions and hypothetical debate
- may seem narrow, conventional, lacking curiosity or imagination (with low intelligence)
- is less keen on novelty or variety as a part of their jobs (with low extroversion)
- may have difficulty seeing a situation from a 'new' perspectives
- may be seen as uninteresting (with low extroversion)

Career implications of low openness to experience:
Tough-mindedness is probably appropriate in occupations that have clear goals and a stable, if daunting environment. Suitable occupations might be:

- cook
- mechanic

- nurse
- police officer
- air traffic controller
- train driver
- athlete/sportsperson
- military cadet
- farmer
- nuclear power plant operator
- call centre operator
- semi-skilled worker

Comments on interviews for individuals with low openness to experience:

- be prepared to entertain the longer-term and more fanciful aspects of ideas
- be prepared to give answers that are several sentences long

Developmental implications of low openness to experience:

- be prepared to recognize the advantages of change
- be prepared to consider the longer-term or wider implications of new proposals

CHAPTER 24

FACE-TO-FACE FEEDBACK

Even the most accurate and relevant test scores are of little use unless they are communicated to other people and action taken. This feedback usually takes one of four forms:

- a face-to-face feedback session
- a telephone feedback session
- written reports to organizations
- written reports to individuals.

This chapter covers the first type – the archetypal mode of feedback. It focuses on face-to-face feedback with a client who is seeking vocational guidance. Similar feedback occurs when an applicant is given the reasons why he or she has, or has not, received a job offer. Feedback to applicants is a mixture of the techniques outlined in this chapter and those outlined in chapter 26, on telephone feedback. Face-to-face feedback is perhaps best organized into five sections:

1. Preparation
2. The opening sequence
3. Discussing test scores
4. Ending the session
5. Client aftercare

 24.1 PREPARATION

The crucial feature of a good feedback session is the interactive discussion of the scores. Any other activities, even if they are essential, will detract from this core activity. Good preparation aims to complete as many as possible of the other activities in advance of the meeting, so that as much time as possible can be devoted to discussing the actual scores. Good preparation involves preparing the client and the counsellor.

24.1.1 PREPARATION OF THE CLIENT

A great deal of time can be liberated for interactive discussion of the actual scores by giving the candidate a briefing letter in advance. In many cases, it can be distributed at the end of a testing session. The briefing should be about one page long: its main function is to inform the candidate and induce a positive attitude to the feedback session. The briefing may include the following:

- The *date*, *time*, *location* and *duration* of the feedback session.
- The *names* and *roles* of those likely to be present – usually the counsellor and the client. With the consent of the client, it may be appropriate for another advisor, or perhaps a parent, to be present. Many redundant executives appreciate the presence of their wives at a feedback session. Provided that the client has no objections, feedback generally benefits from the presence of a third person.
- The general *aims* of the feedback session.
- The *basis of feedback* – usually, the feedback is confidential to those present in the feedback room. Occasionally, the counsellor or advisor may be required to give an account of the feedback session to others, such as the sponsoring organization. There is only one hard and fast rule: *the basis of the feedback must be known and willingly agreed BEFORE feedback occurs.*

It will also save time if a brief outline of the *scoring system* is communicated in advance of the feedback session. The briefing note should end with a genuine reassurance that most people find the feedback sessions informal, enjoyable and useful.

24.1.2 PREPARATION BY THE COUNSELLOR

The counsellor should prepare the physical infrastructure, the organizational climate and the framework, and inspect the scores in advance of the feedback meeting.

- The *physical infrastructure* involves making sure that a private, congenial room is available. The optimum situation is one in which everyone is seated around a circular table, in a well-lit, well-ventilated room of moderate size.
- An *organizational climate* needs to be established in which feedback is seen as a prime activity that takes precedence over production crises, personnel crises, the unexpected arrival of a VIP and other eventualities. It should also be understood that feedback sessions must not be interrupted except in emergencies. It is often useful to fix a 'do not disturb' notice on the door of the feedback venue.
- The *conceptual infrastructure* requires the counsellor to have a clear mental framework for the session. The framework can be abandoned or modified at will, but anyone who is giving feedback must have a fall-back structure. The framework will contain a list of, say, seven major headings. Each heading should be approached in the same systematic way, so that the client can readily perceive the pattern. In one system:
  1 The client is asked to estimate his or her score on, say, extroversion.
  2 The actual score on the broad trait, such as extroversion, is given.
  3 The component scores that comprise the general score are revealed.
  4 The client is asked to comment on the results.
  5 If there is agreement, the likely advantages of the characteristic are outlined.
  6 The likely disadvantages of the characteristic are outlined.
  7 The longest stage is a discussion of the implications of the points made in the previous six stages.

It must be remembered that this framework is intended to provide a fall-back structure. It is particularly useful on the first few occasions when a counsellor gives feedback. As experience expands, other approaches can be developed. The main advantages of this approach are that it makes no prior assumptions and it ensures that all aspects of a profile are covered. This method should be abandoned as soon as it seems that an alternative approach is better suited to a client's needs.

A second approach is to focus on the client's problems. The approach works best when the counsellor and the client work together to identify the main issues. Often, these issues are not obvious and may be misunderstood. Accurate problem identification probably requires a process similar to the seven-stage approach outlined in the previous paragraphs. Once the issues have been identified, only those aspects of the profile that are relevant to these issues are considered. Often, there are more issues than can be covered in a single session. In these circumstances, the issues need to be prioritized and the client needs to play an integral part in the prioritization process.

A third approach is to let clients take total control of the feedback process. They might first be asked how they would prefer to receive feedback – in graphical or verbal form; in general terms or in detail; focusing on data or focusing on reactions. It is possible to show clients a blank profile and ask which scores might be most important to them. This approach is very democratic and it encourages clients to take 'ownership' of the process. However, it only works well for those few clients who have a high level of test sophistication. If this approach is used with the majority of clients, it leads to an almost 'random walk' though the data in a way that is unlikely to be productive.

Scores should be examined in advance and the person who provides feedback should attempt to identify likely points of difficulty, contradictions and links with the client's history. In the counselling context, this information is particularly important in identifying the issues that should be addressed during the feedback session.

◣ 24.2 THE OPENING SEQUENCE

The opening sequence should achieve five main objectives:

- To avoid misidentification and providing feedback to the wrong person – which does happen! This can be achieved by greeting clients by their full names. Also, as they are shown to their seats, you should give your name too.
- To quickly verify that they have received a briefing letter and that they have no outstanding questions.
- To ask whether they remember the tests, and 'how they found them'. This is a vital question, since it gives the counsellor an opportunity to detect and deal with any difficulties, negative attitudes or misconceptions that the clients may have concerning tests. It also gives an opportunity to check whether there were any untoward events that were not entered on the test log.
- To reiterate briefly the purpose of the feedback session.
- To briefly remind clients that tests do not cover all the important factors in a decision.

These objectives should be achieved in an open and friendly way, so that good rapport is established. The transition to the next stage is achieved by as statement such as the following: 'As you remember, there were three kind of tests, problem-solving, personality and temperament. We may as well start with temperament.' It is usually best to vary the order in which you present results, so that you are able to start (and possibly finish) with some of the client's 'best' results.

 ## 24.3 DISCUSSING TEST SCORES

24.3.1 ASKING CLIENTS TO ESTIMATE THEIR SCORES

In most circumstances, it is best to ask clients to estimate their own scores before revealing their actual scores. The enquiry can consist of a simple comment such as 'How do you think you did on the problem-solving test? Suppose there was a sample of 100 people who were representative of the [British] population and they were lined up so that number one answered hardly any questions while number 100 could answer almost every problem – where would you put yourself in that queue of 100 people?' This approach has a number of advantages:

- the norm group and percentile scoring system are quickly established
- clients are forced to reveal their own estimates, and this helps the counsellor to decide upon an appropriate way to disclose subsequent scores
- any discrepancy between the clients' self-perception and the actual scores is opened for discussion
- it is made quite clear, at an early stage, that clients are not expected to be passive listeners.

24.3.2 USING PROFILES

The profile should normally be laid on the table so that it is the correct way round for the client:

- If a profile contains several scores, it is usually better to mask scores yet to be discussed with a blank piece of paper. This provides control of the pace of feedback, and ensures that clients are not distracted from the current issue by looking at other scores.
- When the first score is presented, the scoring system (for example, the sten scale) can be quickly explained by a comment such as 'The scale we use is from one to ten. The average is five and a half. Most people are in the middle and there are fewer and fewer people as you go towards each end.' Unless the client is known to be familiar with statistics, he or she should not be distracted with details about normal curves, means, standard deviations and so on. Even with statistically sophisticated clients, such details should be covered only briefly.
- When presenting the results of the first scale of a personality test, it is essential that the client is informed that 'With personality, one end of the graph is not necessarily better than the other end. It depends upon the jobs people do. For example, a high score on extroversion would probably be a bad thing for a person who wishes to be an undertaker.' (Use another example if the client actually has a low extroversion score!)

24.3.3 GIVING INFORMATION ON THE ACCURACY OF THE TEST

Acceptance by the client can be quickly checked by a question such as 'Looking back on this group of scores, do you think that they are accurate or is something awry?' This is a good time to let the client know that 'While tests are more accurate than many other methods, they are not perfect and the results are not gospel – there is always some error in the scores. On the sten scale, the error of this test is about one, so it is important not to read too much into small differences.'

24.3.4 DISCUSSING THE ADVANTAGES AND DISADVANTAGES OF SCORES

If the client accepts the scores, the counsellor can then discuss their implications. If the client disagrees with a score, it is important to explore why this has occurred. Disagreements arise most frequently from semantic misunderstandings – the feedback may have included jargon or a phrase that has a different connotation to the lay person. Restatement with different words frequently resolves such problems. Disagreements also arise because clients use a different framework for their self-assessments. They are likely to compare themselves with people whom they admire or a highly selected group. For example, mangers who have average scores on extroversion frequently consider themselves to be introverted. They compare themselves to managers in general, who tend to be moderately extroverted. Frequently, people base self-evaluations on the comments of spouses – who may have their own perspectives and agendas. For example, a very introverted wife is likely to perceive a mildly introverted spouse as an extrovert.

Usually, scores are best covered in blocks of three or four related scales. For example, in the case of the 16PF it makes sense to discuss scores on all extroversion factors (A, E, L- and Q2-) as a group. Discussing the implications of scores at the end of a long profile may overwhelm or confuse a client, and much will be missed. On the other hand, discussing scores one by one becomes tedious and repetitive. It is better to discuss scores as a group. It is usually best to start on a positive note by drawing the advantages of a group of scores from the client with questions such as 'What would you say would be the likely advantages at work for people with scores like yours?' Then, ask a similar question about the disadvantages.

24.3.5 THINGS TO AVOID

When delivering feedback:

- Do not shirk feedback on 'difficult scores'. Deal with such scores in a matter-of-fact, non-judgmental way.
- Do not give, long-winded, convoluted or technical explanations of the meaning of scales.
- Do not use jargon.
- Do not talk too quickly.
- Do not talk all the time. Allow pauses during which the client can raise any concerns that he or she may have.

◣ 24.4 ENDING THE SESSION

About ten minutes before the end of the session, begin to give closing signals, such as 'Before we start the last section, is there anything you would like clarifying?' or 'Perhaps we should use the last ten minutes looking at the practical implications of the test results.' The implications can usually be grouped into three types: career direction, interview tactics and personal development:

- Implications for *career direction* will involve both contextual and specific comments. The *contextual comments* are often derived from the results from a personality test and will contain guidance on the type of work, such as specialist work (introvert), general management (extrovert) or work involving stressful situations (stability). Contextual comments might also suggest industrial sectors, such as an industry close coupled to the market (tough-minded), a traditional industry (low-openness to experience) or local and central government (agreeableness). In addition, contextual comments often deal with team roles, leadership roles and the appropriate level of contact with other people. *Specific comments* are often derived from the results of ability tests and interest tests. Personality tests may also provide useful information. Often, guidance on the appropriate level of job can be provided by tests of cognitive ability. Interest tests are often accompanied by tables that link interests to certain jobs. For example, outdoor interests may imply that work as a farmer, horticulturalist, adventure camp supervisor or biologist might be appropriate. The average profiles for people in certain occupations are often available for major personality tests. For example, the 16PF profiles for over 80 occupational groups are known. In these cases, additional suggestions can arise from matching a client's profile against the occupational profiles. However, it is important to remember that some individuals may differ from the average because they are *more* suitable than most people for work in a specific occupation! In some situations, especially with young clients whose interests might change, it may be appropriate to discourage targeting specific occupations or vocational courses in favour of keeping options open until their interests have stabilized and they have acquired experience of more areas of work.
- The implications for *interview tactics* may include suggestions on job search. For example, unassertive and 'grounded' clients can be encouraged to take a bolder and more expansive view of job possibilities. Typical guidance on interview tactics might include being careful not to 'take over the interview' (extreme extroverts), being careful to be positive and energetic (introverts) or avoiding being too self-critical when less than perfect answers are given to interview questions (high anxiety).
- The implications for *personal development* cover a wide range of suggestions, such as 'do not blame yourself when things outside your control go wrong' (high anxiety), 'pay attention to the minutiae of completing jobs' (low conscientiousness) or 'make sure that your ideas take account of practical realities' (high openness to experience).

Often, it is helpful to encourage the client to think about that action that he or she should take on the basis of the test results. This can be achieved by comments such as 'Looking back on what we have discussed, what for you are the most important things to do? . . . What would be the first steps in achieving this?' It is important that the priorities and actions are generated by the client, and that the client shows a commitment towards taking action.

The closing stages of a feedback session frequently concern practical issues, such as 'To what extent can I change these scores?' or 'What is the "shelf life" of my scores?' This may be an appropriate stage at which to remind clients of the aspects of ability, personality or other characteristics that are not covered by the test results.

About three minutes before the end of the session, explain what happens next. Some possible next stages are as follows:

- Nothing. ('Good luck. We wish you the best for the future!')
- 'A report will follow within a week.'
- 'Your counsellor [development adviser] will arrange a meeting to devise an action plan.'
- 'Your manager will arrange a meeting to discuss the results.'
- 'A debt collecting agency will call round to collect my fee!'

Finally, ask whether there are any remaining issues. Use comments such as 'As you were coming here, you must have wondered whether we would cover certain topics. Have we covered everything you expected? Are there any final questions that you would like to ask?'

 ## 24.5 CLIENT AFTERCARE

Issues of client aftercare are often ignored until an incident occurs. However, an aftercare policy should be thought out in advance. Much will depend upon, in order, the legal contract with the client, the seriousness of the situation that emerges and the fee that is paid.

In all situations, the legal contract with the client must be fulfilled. A clear written statement of the services provided is an important way of avoiding unrealistic expectations. It is generally better to err on the side of caution. If one hour's feedback is intended, it may be best to inform clients that the feedback will take 45 minutes. If an hour's feedback is then provided, it is clear that contractual liabilities have been met. A wise contract with a client often includes a statement that further work or advice can be provided at a specified hourly rate.

Budgets and costings should include a reasonable level of client aftercare – perhaps 8% of total costs. Sometimes, the aftercare merely involves answering a telephone question or forwarding a leaflet. Sometimes it involves giving additional advice about a specific job vacancy and sometimes it might involve confirming a score to a prospective employer.

Most people feel a nice, warm, human glow when they help another person philanthropically. However, there are dangers and it is important to be practical and even-handed. Hostages to fortune should be avoided. Clients should be discouraged from forming unrealistic expectations about the aftercare that they can expect. Rash statements – such as 'If we can help you in any way whatsoever, have no hesitation in contacting us' – should be avoided. Sooner or later, a client will take the statement literally and impose such a heavy burden upon you that the quality of service you give to other clients might be endangered. If this happens, excuses will be made and a demanding client will interpret them as hypocrisy. It is much better to avoid these situations by making sure that they do not arise. If clients require further services or work that are noticeably beyond what could reasonably be expected from their contracts, they should be informed, preferably in writing, of the hourly rate that they can expect to be charged.

Occasionally, clients with severe, perhaps clinical, problems will be encountered. Action should be guided by two ethical principles. First, selection specialists should only operate within the limits of their competence. They should not try to 'cure' the problem unless they have appropriate qualifications or experience. Such clients should be referred to someone who is qualified to help. However, selectors and counsellors must retain responsibility for that client until he or she has been formally accepted by a colleague who has appropriate training. In most of these cases, it would be inappropriate to charge such clients for the effort involved in maintaining these responsibilities.

CHAPTER 25

WRITTEN REPORTS

There is little point conducting a flawless testing session unless the results are communicated effectively. One medium is the written report. A report is an end product. It is not a chore. Effective reports usually result in a satisfied client, and they can also be a justifiable source of satisfaction to their author.

What matters in any report is the information left in the mind of the recipient. A report may earn plaudits from colleagues because every detail and caution recommended by a pedantic professional body has been diligently included. However, if these details and cautions are so boring that they distract or confuse the recipient, the outcome will be a bad report. A good report should include clear implications for future action and leave the recipient keen to take appropriate action.

Although reports are vitally important, they are time-consuming and costly to produce. Initially, reports can be written at a rate of about four pages per day. After 30 or so reports and have been written, the most frequently used phrases and paragraphs can be made into word-processor macros, and a good report can then be produced in, say, two hours.

It is important to judge the standard of reports in relation to the needs of the recipient and to the fee paid. A car can be useful without reaching the standard of a Rolls-Royce. Similarly, a test report can be useful even if it is shorter than *Pride and Prejudice*. If Rolls-Royce reports are consistently produced for clients who only need – and have only budgeted for – a Lada, other clients who cross-subsidize the report or the personal life of the writer are cheated. However, there should be a clear level below which one should not sink. Avoid situations in which reports consisting of 'just the names and the scores so that costs can be kept down' are produced. People who ask for these types of reports are really saying that they do not value test results sufficiently to pay a realistic price. Minimalist reports of this kind may also be dangerous. Because there is little context to aid interpretation, misunderstandings are more likely.

 25.1 TYPES OF REPORT

There are three main types: reports for individuals, reports for organizations and scientific reports.

25.1.1 REPORTS FOR INDIVIDUALS

Reports for individuals are usually written in guidance and development situations. Important requirements are as follows.

Sensitivity and Tact

The client who receives the report will be much more sensitive to the nuances of words than the writer. If the client is offended, he or she is likely to reject the report and testing will have been a waste of time. Always try to work within the client's 'latitude of acceptance'. *First*, work out the level of negative information that would be appropriate to the client's 'problem' and state of mind. *Second*, prioritize unfavourable information and discard the less important points that might exceed the client's level of acceptance. *Third*, phrase negative information with care. Start with two positive pieces of information on which there will be ready agreement. Then introduce and discuss a negative score. Follow the negative score with two positive ones and so on. Try to end with two positive pieces. Finally, work out words and phrases that will convey negative information in a constructive way.

Clients will be exquisitely sensitive to the nuances of the words used to describe them. Beware of using words that have neutral connotations to the writer, but which have unintended negative connotations to a *client*. Typical examples are 'introverted', 'emotional', 'gay', 'humble', 'sensitive', 'expedient', 'average' and 'thick-skinned'. Without misleading the client, try to be positive and uphold the ethical principle of self-regard. Do not tell people that they are unintelligent: suggest that they would be happiest dealing with familiar problems where they could use their past experience to greatest effect, or where the level of uncertainty and change are not high. Do not tell people that they are unstable and emotional: suggest that they are aware of their personal feelings and those of people around them.

Have no hesitation in using phrases that might appear to be Barnum statements in order to make a point acceptable. For example, you might wish to remark to a client with a very low conscientiousness score that 'there are circumstances in which you tend to ignore protocol'. Technically, this is a Barnum statement, since it applies to the vast majority of the population. The fact that it applies to most people means that the statement is less controversial and less likely to be rejected. Nevertheless, the statement is very useful, since it focuses the client's attention on a matter that might be causing problems. Given a more subtle and wider perspective, the statement is not being used as a Barnum statement, because whilst it could appear in the reports for most people, in fact it is only included in reports about those who have very low conscientiousness scores.

For some clients, tact is a waste of time. They are so thick-skinned that they feel little impact except when hit with a metaphorical baseball bat. These clients are usually extremely stable, assertive and venturesome. Whilst sensitivity will not be at such a high premium with these clients, it should still be employed. Their reports will be shown to other people, such as parents and spouses. If comments seem reasonable, they will get the support of others.

Background Information

The report is likely to be the first report on psychological tests that the client has ever seen. Prior information should not be assumed. An explanation of the scoring systems, the accuracy and the norms used must be included. The actual test results should be preceded by essential information. Other background information should be placed in an appendix.

Absence of Jargon

Jargon can be daunting and can inhibit understanding. Often there is no way for the recipient of an individual report to find out what the jargon means. Keep jargon in reports to individuals to a minimum. Think very carefully before using phrases such as 'Factor M', 'standard deviation' and so on.

The Length of the Report

People like to read about themselves and are highly motivated to read pages upon pages. Clients who have paid for guidance sometimes equate report length with value for money. Consequently, brevity is not at a premium in guidance reports. However, the costs of providing written reports to clients can be very high and it is best to evolve a format that is adequate and can be produced efficiently using a word-processor.

25.1.2 REPORTS FOR ORGANIZATIONS

Reports for organizations, usually in a selection context, need to be more focused. If the organization has an existing report format, it should be followed. The need for tact is less acute in organizational reports, but it is still required. A report may subsequently fall into the hands of the candidate, or it may concern a relative of one of the selectors.

Tables with a consistent format should be used to communicate information quickly and to allow comparisons between candidates. Candidates should be listed in order of suitability and a summary (two or three sentences) of their performance given. Then, a detailed report should be given for each candidate. These individual reports should be ordered so that the report for the most promising candidate is placed first. Great care should be taken before concluding that a candidate is unacceptable or unsuitable. Such conclusions should only be made on the grounds of strong, specific evidence, which will stand up in court. The following categories can usually be defended and will allow the best candidate(s) to be identified:

- *Excellent*. Very high scores across attributes identified in the personnel specification. Usually, this means that a better candidate is unlikely to be found.
- *Good*. Mostly high or very high scores, but one or two less suitable scores – a good, but not perfect, appointment.
- *Acceptable*. A mixture of high and low scores or a set of mediocre scores – employ only if there is pressure to make an appointment.
- *Concerns* (note the euphemism). In this situation, there are two or more very low scores or inappropriate scores. In most circumstances, it would be better to seek other candidates.

25.1.3 SCIENTIFIC REPORTS

Scientific reports are the easiest kind to write. There are well-defined expectations about their contents. Readers are likely to have considerable background knowledge and a high level of jargon can be used. Scientific reports also need less tact. Nevertheless, precautions still need to be taken to avoid the possibility of identification or divulging commercial or embarrassing information. The overriding concern for scientific reports is replicability. Enough information should be given so that other researchers can repeat the study. The writing style needs to conform to a journal's house style: it is wise to consult recent issues of the journal. The style needs to be terse and economical, and the report should be written in the third person. Length is not usually a problem, since most journals will accept articles containing 20 printed pages (30 typescript pages) of relevant material.

 ## 25.2 GENERAL ASPECTS

25.2.1 ACCURACY

A score should never be altered and an untrue score should never be given, even if it might seem that there are good, sympathetic, reasons for doing so. Whatever is written must be true. An impeccable level of integrity must be maintained.

25.2.2 CLARITY

A report must be readily understandable to the reader, whose level of knowledge should be established. The reader should be led gradually from what he or she already knows towards what he or she should know. Clarity is achieved by using short words, short sentences and short paragraphs. Avoid flowery or needlessly complicated language. Use plain English. For example, use the word 'need' rather than the word 'required', or 'help' rather than 'assist'. More complicated vocabulary can be used very occasionally in order to introduce variety and to avoid repetition of the same words.

25.2.3 FOCUS

Reports are not essays, where an author can wander, without restraint, from subject to subject. Reports are written for a purpose and they should fulfil that purpose. A report written for vocational guidance, for example, should actually give explicit guidance on the client's career paths, search tactics and personal development. It is always a good idea to state explicitly, in one or two sentences, the *purpose* of a report. This deters possible misuse and can absolve the author from responsibility for blatant misuse. It is not unknown, for example, for psychiatric patients to obtain test results under the guise of seeking vocational guidance and then use the results to manipulate their counsellor(s). A clear statement that a report is only intended for use in choosing a career path will do much to limit such manipulation.

25.2.4 STRUCTURE

A report is easier to understand if it is clearly structured. The structure should be simple (no more than seven main sections) and logical. It should not start with one thought, introduce a second thought and then return to the original thought. Items should be dealt with in a clear, maybe chronological, sequence. The structure of a report can be conveyed by a consistent system of *headings and numbering*. Numbering systems that use Roman numbers or Greek letters are best avoided: Latin is a dead language and such systems are less informative than a system of arabic numbers (for example, '1.1.1', '1.1.2', '1.1.3' and so on).

White space can do much to make the structure of a report apparent. Headings can be emphasized by one or two leading lines of extra white space. Subsections should be indented. Crowded pages are tiring to read. A 4 cm left-hand margin and 2.5 cm top, bottom and right-hand margins are recommended. This makes a report look more attractive and easier to read. It also makes it look longer and may help command a higher fee! Connoisseurs use different *typefaces*. Sans-serif typefaces such as Arial are used for headings, while serif typefaces such as Times Roman are used for text. Real connoisseurs will use *italics* and **boldface** sparingly. It is a good convention to use italics to emphasize key phrases, whilst special or technical terms are highlighted using bold face.

25.2.5 IDENTIFICATION

Identification is a vital start to a report and should unambiguously state:

- the name of the person completing the test (and that person's age and sex)
- the name of the person writing the report
- the date of the test
- if appropriate, the name of the commissioning organization.

Early sections of the report should also clarify the report's confidentiality and include any disclaimers. In the case of reports intended for individuals, it is *probably* better not to give the names of tests but to refer to them in general (for example, a test of numerical ability) In scientific and selection reports, the names of the tests must be given.

25.2.6 THE RATIONALE FOR USING SPECIFIC TESTS

The rationale for using a specific battery of tests should feature somewhere in the report, but the depth of the description will vary. For reports *to individuals*, a brief rationale is all that is necessary. For example:

A general problem-solving test was included because research has shown that it is relevant to most jobs.

Your personality might be an important determinant in the way that you work and the style of the job that would suit you.

A narrow-spectrum interest test was used because you expressed a wish to know which management function you might find most satisfying.

Individuals are usually more interested in knowing their actual scores and the implications. Many individuals will find the rationale for using specific tests intuitive. Despite exhortations from professional bodies, the rationale for using tests should not get in the way of what a client really wants to know – their scores and the implications. Adopt a user-oriented approach and put technical information in an appendix.

For reports *to organizations*, the rationale for the use of specific tests should be fuller and it should certainly refer to the person specification. Again, the choice of tests is not the key information that managers need, so it should not be given undue prominence. Appropriate tests should be chosen, and one or two sentences in the early part of a report should direct a reader to an appendix where the rationale is set out in more detail – perhaps as a table, where four lines are devoted to the choice of each test.

For *scientific reports*, especially theses, the rationale for using specific tests should be set out in excruciating detail, so that each step in the reasoning can be questioned and checked by an external examiner or referee. The rationale for each test can easily exceed a page as each of the following facets are considered:

- the theoretical underpinnings of the test
- the conceptual relevance to the main thesis
- the construction of the test
- validity
- reliability
- practicality
- the norms (if appropriate)
- previous research use and findings.

In scientific reports, the premium on avoiding jargon is not high. A cynic might say that there is less need for brevity and clarity since, in academic circles, long-winded confusion might be mistaken for brilliance.

25.2.7 AVAILABILITY

The distribution of a report is determined entirely by the agreement reached with the person *before* he or she starts to answer the tests. There must be utmost faith in adhering to this agreement. Any deviation from the agreement must be resisted. Even in exceptional circumstances, deviation is only permissible if written agreement is obtained, without pressure.

Confidential means that the report will be kept secure and will be available only to those people who have a genuine reason for seeing the results. In *vocational guidance reports*, 'Confidential' generally means that the report and scores are only available to:

- the client
- the person administering the test, and their direct secretarial or data-processing staff
- any third party agreed by the client (for example, a parent or another counsellor).

In *selection reports*, 'Confidential' generally means that the report and scores are only available to:

- the person in charge of the selection, and their direct secretarial and data-processing support staff

- the line manager to whom the person appointed will report
- the senior manager (grandparent) of the line manager
- senior managers with responsibility for the selection function
- consultants who have a role in that specific appointment.

Proper security must be arranged so that unauthorized people do not have access to the reports. In selection reports, it is sometimes helpful to have the roles of people entitled to read the report printed on the front cover.

Anonymous means that others will not be able to identify who completed the test. Care should be taken, because individuals can often be identified if only a small group of people is tested. If fewer than 100 people are tested, details of age, sex, place of testing and so on can be used to narrow the field down to a small group. A little devious detective work might then identify an individual person. Although a report may be published in an anonymous form, subjects will almost always be able to identify themselves – so the use of information in any anonymous case study should be with the person's consent and should obey the ethical principle of positive self-regard. Freud was an appalling role model. Not only did he lie about his results, but he felt that his status meant that he could write publicly about his clients in a way that would destroy their already fragile self-regard!

25.2.8 APPEARANCE

Clients may use false cues such as appearance to judge the worth of a report. A cogent and otherwise excellent report can be dismissed because it looks tatty and unprofessional. Professionalism can be communicated by a clear layout and the use of heavier (100 g/m^2) A4 paper. Avoid sending reports printed on unusual-sized paper. There is an optimum level of appearance – anything very smooth can be regarded as flashy and the report can be discounted. An appropriate strategy is to look at other reports in the organization and improve, just noticeably, upon that standard.

25.3 TECHNICAL ASPECTS OF REPORTS

25.3.1 NORM GROUPS

A statement of the norm groups is not strictly necessary when you are involved in 'top-down' selection or research. It is vital in vocational guidance reports, since people like to know with whom they have been compared.

25.3.2 SCORING SYSTEMS

In vocational guidance reports, a brief explanation of the scoring system *must* appear early in the report, since the client needs this information before he or she reads the results. In selection reports, especially for organizations that have been using tests for some time, some prior knowledge can be assumed. It may be appropriate to include a sentence early in the report, referring readers to a full explanation given in an appendix.

25.3.3 ACCURACY OF SCORES

Most reports should contain guidance on the accuracy (standard error) of the test results. This is a technical subject and there is a strong danger that the reader is confused. In *vocational guidance reports*, it is probably best to give a general statement that tests are not perfectly accurate. Then make a simple statement such as 'The margin of error of this test is about [se$_m$] and if you took the test again you can be 67% sure that the new score will be in this range.' The 67% confidence limit is appropriate for most circumstances but other confidence limits can be calculated if required (see chapter 10). Remember that the subject of confidence limits is a technicality that can baffle and alienate clients. In vocational reports, avoid technical terms such as 'alpha level', 'se$_m$', 'standard error', 'statistical significance' or even 'confidence limits'. Keep things simple. Do not trudge through every scale, giving its standard error to five decimal places. In most situations, a general indication such as 'On the 16PF test the margin of error of the scores is about one sten' will suffice. Standard error freaks could put the se$_m$s for each scale in an appendix.

In *selection reports* where there is 'top-down' selection based on one score, it is probably a mistake to mention margins of error at all. Some managers will waste hours agonizing over whether 'given the margin of error of the test, candidate A is any better than candidate B'. Some managers will use the existence of a margin of error to devalue the results of tests and introduce more subjective and less valid information. In fact, with 'top-down' selection based on one valid and fair test, it pays to choose the candidate with the highest score – irrespective of the test's standard error! A less mathematical approach is to use results as successive hurdles (filters), starting with the method with the smallest standard error. Cognitive tests usually have a smaller standard error than personality tests, which, in turn, are usually better than interviews. If there is a field of ten candidates, cognitive tests would therefore be used to eliminate, say, six of the candidates. The less accurate personality test results can then be used to choose, say, the best two from the four survivors. The final choice of the person to appoint can then be made on the basis of the interview results. This approach has two major advantages: it puts the least accurate measure where it can do the least damage, yet it gives an important person who conducts the interview the kudos of making a final decision.

Selection reports should be structured in a way that implies the standard error of the measures. For each candidate, start with a full discussion of the scores on the most accurate test; then proceed with increasingly brief discussions for progressively less accurate measures. Arrange any compilation of results for a field of candidates in a way that reflects the accuracy of the measures. In a table comparing candidates, use the first (far left) column to give the results for the most accurate measure. Use the last data column (far right) to give results for the least accurate measure. List candidates in the order of their scores on the most accurate measure. For example, the following table shows the sten scores of candidates who took an intelligence test (se$_m$ = .5), a personality test (se$_m$ = 1.0) and an interview (se$_m$ = 1.5):

Candidate	Intelligence test	Personality test	Interview
Sam	9	9	8
Joe	9	8	9
Frunella	8	9	6
Algenon	8	7	6
Kim	7	8	7
Kevin	5	4	7
Chris	5	6	9
Tracy	4	7	1
Amar	4	1	6
Blodwin	4	3	3

Presenting data in this way is much better than listing candidates alphabetically or listing the measures in order of administration. It is intuitively obvious that the best candidates are Sam and Joe, and that Sam has only a very slight edge because of a higher score on a more accurate measure. The table makes it less likely that Chris, who was interviewed by the managing director (coincidentally also named Chris), will be appointed. In fact, this table demonstrates that Sam and Joe are such close contenders that the organization may well decide to obtain further information from a presentation exercise before appointing Joe.

25.3.4 DESCRIPTION OF SCALE NAMES

Describing scale names in an accurate and meaningful way to lay people is an important aspect of a good report. Jargon and long-winded explanations should be avoided. A simple description of one or two sentences should be enough. Examples include the following:

- the ability to solve difficult problems involving the kind of numbers used by senior managers (a high-level test of numerical ability)
- the ability to solve many kinds of problems that a typical group of people might encounter (a middle-level intelligence test)
- interest in a wide range of jobs that people with A-levels might consider doing (an advanced occupational interest inventory).

When personality tests are used, it is particularly important to be tactful and sensitive in the use of trait names. It is the meaning used by lay people that matters, since some of the terms considered to be neutral by psychologists have negative connotations in everyday language. Terms such as 'introverted', 'less than average intelligence', 'emotional', 'unstable', 'uncontrolled', 'submissive' and 'sensitive' should be used carefully, if at all.

The website associated with this book gives a number of specimen reports that illustrate some of the points made in the course of this chapter.

CHAPTER 26

TELEPHONE FEEDBACK

More feedback on psychological tests is probably given over the telephone than via any other medium. Usually, there are more unsuccessful candidates than successful ones and their feedback is almost always via the telephone. Even when tests are taken 'in company' and for development purposes, commitments and travel plans sometimes mean that feedback of results has to take place by telephone. Purists might throw up their hands in horror at the thought of telephone feedback, in the same way as bank managers once threw up their hands in horror at the concept of telephone banking. Nowadays, however, people are used to using the telephone and this method of feedback is as natural as face-to-face feedback. Consequently, it is important to develop skills at providing this type of feedback.

▶ 26.1 WHETHER TO GIVE FEEDBACK BY TELEPHONE

The first issue is whether telephone feedback is appropriate. It must be remembered that the telephone does not provide non-verbal cues. Consequently, it is more difficult to judge the reactions of candidates. If feedback is likely to involve information that could evoke strong negative emotions or if it would cause harm, the person delivering feedback will be in a poorer position to detect adverse reactions. If it seems that there is a need to impart any depressing or anxiety-provoking news, it may be necessary use a face-to-face meeting. The situation will need delicate handling, because recipients may be aware that telephone feedback has been given to others and they will draw negative conclusions. The use of telephone feedback with unsuccessful internal candidates is particularly problematic, and face-to-face meetings are generally better, since they give better opportunities to develop positive attitudes. With senior and internal appointments, it is usually better to use face-to-face interviews to give feedback to rejected candidates. Finally, it may seem obvious but . . . telephone feedback is not an ideal medium for candidates with hearing difficulties!

Ironically, perhaps, the telephone may be a better medium for giving feedback on very confidential material. The absence of non-verbal cues and the physical distance involved may mean that the recipients feel more comfortable and less embarrassed about intimate and confidential results.

26.2 SECURITY AND CONFIDENTIALITY

A major concern with telephone feedback is security. There is the danger that an impostor could obtain confidential information. The danger is mitigated if the person giving the feedback has conducted the testing session him- or herself and knows when letters were despatched to candidates. Each letter can be given a code number and it can be established in a tactful way before divulging confidential information. Information should never be given to an incoming caller. A return call should be made after the telephone number has been authenticated. Further checks might include verifying details such as date of birth, postcode, middle name or the reference number given on the top of a letter. It is also wise to briefly check that the person is free to talk confidentially and that he or she is not speaking on a shared line.

Confidentiality extends to all candidates. Some people try to use feedback sessions to obtain information about other candidates. They slip in questions such as 'Can you tell me who got the job?', which is be tantamount to asking 'Who else failed?' Unsuccessful candidates might also ask 'What score (experience, references and so on) did the successful candidate have?' *Information about other candidates should never be divulged, however harmless it may seem.*

26.3 TAKING CHARGE OF TIME

Purists may imply that there is an obligation to devote the whole of one's life to giving feedback to rejected candidates. In an ideal world, this might be true. Unfortunately, the world is not ideal. There are only 24 hours in a day and there are many pressing tasks. The time spent giving telephone feedback to unsuccessful candidates means that there is less time to spend on other activities, such as generating additional income, counselling others, implementing equal opportunities, ensuring the accuracy of other appointments, or maybe even being a good spouse and parent!

A key point is to make an explicit decision about how much time it would be proper, in the circumstances, to devote to feedback for unsuccessful candidates. In general, it will be appropriate to devote 10–15 minutes per person. Where there has been a shortlist of six candidates, this means that about 90 minutes should be allocated for giving feedback. Some people will always want more. Ironically, the more time spent, the higher the expectations will be. Initial helpfulness might signal that you are a sympathetic person, with plenty of time on your hands. Having a policy on the amount of feedback means a fairer and more rational approach to all applicants. It is usually best to notify applicants of their rejection by a brief, courteous and positive letter. Telephone feedback is then used as a sensitive and flexible means of providing extra information for those who think it might be useful. Once there is a clear policy, expectations can be tactfully established at the start of the call. For example, at the start of the call it is possible to comment 'I am clear of commitments for the next 15 minutes. That should give us time to cover most things.' Winding-up phrases, such as 'Are there any specific points you would like to talk about during the last few minutes?' can be slipped into the dialogue after about ten minutes.

26.4 SETTING OBJECTIVES

Once the time limits have been decided, the objectives for the call can be set. In general, there are two objectives: giving a good impression of the organization and helping the unsuccessful applicant.

Rejected candidates want to know why they did not get the job and how they can improve their chances on future applications. They do not want to know all about stens and factor analysis of personality questionnaires. Often, rejected applicants are not interested in detailed feedback on test results. Before discussing any substantive issues, it is wise to emphasize that tests are not perfect and that anything you say or suggest must be interpreted in that context – a different test given at a different time in a different setting *might* not produce the same results – but in fact tests usually do give fairly consistent information. Jargon should be kept to the absolute minimum in order to concentrate on the main objectives. Realistically, all that can be done in most telephone feedback sessions is to give an indication of a person's suitability for the type of job, an indication of two strong points and an indication of one or two weaker points.

Above all else, an unsuccessful candidates need to know whether they should continue to make applications for that type of job. Indications of suitability can take one of three forms, and it is worthwhile building up a spiel for each:

- *Very suitable candidates*, who were pipped to the post by a slightly better ones. The tone of their feedback should be positive and encouraging, but without giving hostages to fortune, such as 'If we have another post like this, you are sure to get it!' If there is some minor problem with the candidates' application or test-taking styles (for example, careful checking that slowed them down) it can be mentioned in a constructive way.
- *Fairly suitable candidates*, who were credible applicants but who had one or two points which put them at a disadvantage. Here, the tone should be mixed. One appropriate format is to start with a positive point, and deal with *one* or *two* negative points, give some idea of how they might be addressed and the timescale needed to address them. The conversation is ended with another positive point.
- *Candidates who are clearly applying for the wrong job*. In theory, there should be few of these cases, because they should have been eliminated at the first sift. Concealing unsuitability is a disservice. Unsuitable candidates will continue to waste their time on inappropriate applications that will bring them continuing disappointment. They should be tactfully told that they were the least favoured candidates, and two or three reasons to support this assessment should be given. The self-regard of the rejected candidates can be improved by saying that the assessment only applies to this specific job and that for other jobs they have many useful qualities. If possible, two examples of 'good' qualities that would be useful in other jobs can be given. Unless a particularly appropriate alternative job springs to mind, it is probably better not to suggest specific jobs, in case the suggestion fails to materialize and a complaint is then made against the advice that they received. The conversations can be ended with good wishes for future applications.

◢ 26.5 ARGUMENTS

It is natural for unsuccessful candidates whose hopes are dashed to feel upset. They should receive the helpful and sympathetic consideration that you would wish to receive if you were in their shoes. Unsuccessful candidates will often try to reopen a decision by adding information or contesting some aspect of the procedure. Listen to their point with care and then summarize what they have said. This helps to clarify the situation and confirm that their point of view has been understood.

If an unsuccessful candidate is able to point out a significant error on your part that would have made a difference to the decisions, you should consider what action should be taken to make amends. If an offer has not been made, the decision should be reviewed openly in the light of the new information. If an offer *has* already been made to another candidate and it has been accepted, there are strict limits about what can be done. You should certainly be prepared to spend more time with individuals who fall into this category, giving what help you can with other job applications. You could use your network of contacts on their behalf. You could also ensure that they are put at the front of the queue for similar vacancies in your organization. You should certainly take administrative action to ensure that the error does not occur in the future. If an unsuccessful candidate reveals, for the first time, information that would have made a material difference, he or she should be counselled to reveal the information at an earlier stage in subsequent applications. It might be even possible to suggest ways in which 'delicate' information can be revealed without embarrassment. There is no need to feel guilty in these situations. The onus on revealing advantageous information rests with candidates themselves.

Occasionally, an unsuccessful candidate will become obsessed with minor issues or ask never-ending questions about details of the procedure. It should be possible to admit that while none of the individual aspects of the selection procedures is perfect, a number of different methods were used in case any single method turned out to be faulty. It should also be possible to say that all candidates were treated in the same way, so that any problems had an equal impact on the performance of everyone – including the person who was offered the job. Always be prepared to admit that people's performance on interviews, tests and other selection techniques varies from day to day. Nevertheless, you are entitled to point out that, in practice, you have to go by people's actual performance on a specific day. To make special allowances for some people could be unfair and subjective. It might also be necessary to point out that it would be unfair if one candidate were able to take a test the second time. It is also possible that rejected candidates have taken the same test before, and perhaps obtained a higher scores and have even been offered posts. Such a situation can often be reconciled by explaining to the rejected candidates that different norms are sometimes used with the same test, and that the scores that they obtained previously are not necessarily comparable with the present scores.

Some candidates will try to cast doubt on a decision by quoting other results or information. Typical attempts might be 'In my last job I did test X and I scored 100%' or 'I have an MBA, so how could I have got such a low score?' This needs careful handling. The MBA or other test may have been completed many years ago, possibly at an institution that did not have particularly high standards, and it may have involved considerable course work, which was completed with a group of other students, under favourable circumstances. It may be possible to deal with the problem by saying that without more information about the course and the assessment you are not in a position to explain the apparent discrepancies. Then simply assert the correctness of your selection procedures, and emphasize that you have to make your decision on the basis of everyone's performance on a given day.

If people become very argumentative, they should be discouraged from using their energies in an attempt to reverse a decision or prove that the methods were wrong. It is probably most beneficial to focus them on the future, with comments such as 'Yes, I can understand how you feel. I have felt like that myself. I have learned that the chance of re-opening the decision like this is very slim and involves a lot of trouble. Even if the decision is re-opened, there is no certainty that the new decision will be in your favour. Quite honestly, the best thing to do is to put it all behind you and focus your energies on new opportunities and applications.' At this juncture, it will be possible to remind the person of your next engagement and suggest that the time remaining is devoted to more constructive topics.

In any event, you should thank all candidates for their interest and give them your good wishes for their future careers.

CHAPTER 27

ETHICS AND DATA PROTECTION

Tests and some other methods of selection are very powerful tools. They should be used in a socially responsible way. All stages of selection, counselling and research must be ethical and observe data protection legislation. Consequently, it is appropriate to end this book with a chapter that deals with these topics.

◤ 27.1 THE NATURE AND HISTORY OF ETHICS

Ethics are abstract ideas about '*Goodness*', '*social responsibility*', '*moral principles*' or '*rules of conduct*'. Ethics may arise in two ways: an act of God or an inherent property of things. Philosophers have discussed ethics since, at least, the time of the ancient Greeks. The five main philosophical approaches have been scepticism, enlightened self-interest, utilitarianism, rights and justice.

27.1.1 SCEPTICISM

Sceptics and sophisticated **Sophists** feel that ethics are largely subjective. That which is considered ethical by one person may be regarded as unethical by another. Usually, but not always, ethics follow self-interest. Whilst a lowly paid worker might consider an income tax rate of 50% ethical, a higher-paid worker might consider 'confiscation' of half of a hard-earned income an unethical act. Furthermore, ethical standards can change dramatically within a generation or two. Each successive generation is convinced that its ethics are better than those of previous generations.

Sceptics and Sophists consider that ethics are often little more than the synthesis of the values of a professional body's ethics committee at one moment in time. Indeed, a cynic might define ethics as a mechanism by which an influential group of people seek to impose their values on others. This is sometimes called '**ethical imperialism**'. **Cynics** believe that actions are either unsuccessful or successful. Successful action puts a person in a position in which he or she can impose his or her values on others. Accordingly, ethics follow the law of 'might is right' and the winner writes the ethical codes. If you have the power, you determine what is, and is not, ethical.

27.1.2 ENLIGHTENED SELF-INTEREST

Other philosophers claim that there is a set of universal principles that should guide human behaviour. An ethical principle that appears in the codes of many professions is *do no harm*. You should not leave the world a worse place than you found it. Improving the world a little is a bonus. Confucius identified this principle of reciprocity. Except in the curious case of masochists, you should not do to others things that you would not like others to do to you. This rule of thumb is often a good guide. When devising a selection system or test, it is worth pausing to ask the question, 'Would I think it reasonable if this were administered to me?' Enlightened self-interest implies a long-term view.

Enlightened self-interest is associated with the philosopher Thomas Hobbes and his notion of the social contract. It is based on the idea that many beneficial communal activities would be impossible if everyone followed their own short-term goals. For example, long-term self-interest means that we should not steal books from libraries. If everyone did so, libraries would cease to exist and we would all be deprived of their benefits. In the context of selection, for example, tests should not be photocopied. If everyone did so, publishers would cease to develop tests.

27.1.3 UTILITARIANISM

Utilitarianism arises from a Lutheran belief that whatever increases the sum total of happiness of God's creatures is right and whatever decreases the sum total of happiness is wrong.

Utilitarianism philosophers include Jeremy Bentham and John Stuart Mill. In essence, the utilitarian approach argues that ethics are based on the greatest good for the largest number of people (that is, the maximization of happiness). The utilitarian approach is fundamentally concerned with consequences of behaviour. The utilitarian approach may imply that the 'means justifies the ends'. If six million people need to be exterminated in order to safeguard the health of 60 million people then, according to an extreme utilitarian, so be it – the six million people need to be sacrificed. Some people may consider such ethics as 'the tyranny of the majority'. Bentham (see Veenhoven, 2003) made a radical claim for his time: when calculating the net effects of good or bad, each person (male or female, black or white and so on) should be counted equally. Bentham's ideas are fundamental to democracy and underlie many of our current ideas. The majority's interests are always paramount because this produces the greatest good for the largest number. The majority can therefore bestow or extract whatever it wishes from the minority. Mill demurred in an aristocratic way. He introduced the notion of the quality. He suggested that it was better to be a Socrates dissatisfied than a fool satisfied.

Many actions in selection and guidance are justified on utilitarian grounds. For example, the rejection of less able candidates is justified because it avoids the heartbreak that follows an inappropriate appointment, where people subsequently find themselves out of their depth. Acceptance of the best candidate is justified in terms of less strain on colleagues, greater organizational efficiency and the benefit to society.

27.1.4 RIGHTS

Philosophers such as John Locke developed the idea of **rights**, which were incorporated in the English *Magna Carta* of 1215, which mainly benefited barons. Locke extended rights to all people and the concept of **human rights** has become a bulwark against the tyranny of the majority. According to Locke, an individual is born with certain rights. He or she does not surrender all of these to the community. French Revolutionaries gave the idea of rights a bad name when they used the rights of liberty, equality and fraternity to justify guillotining thousands of, mainly innocent, people. Thomas Jefferson, a major contributor to the American *Declaration of Independence*, listed the main human rights as 'life, liberty and the pursuit of happiness'. Scores of other rights have since been discovered or invented since Jefferson's time. In some circumstances, the idea of human rights can lead to 'the tyranny of the minority', where a minority can extract disproportionate benefits from others on the basis of their perceptions of their rights – without accepting comparable responsibilities. The two most important codes of human rights are probably the United Nations Universal Declaration of Human Rights (www.un.org/overview/rights.html) and the European Convention of Human Rights (www.hri.org/docs/ECHR50.html).

Ethical claims based on the concepts of rights are frequently encountered in selection and guidance. Candidates may claim rights to be given accurate information and to be treated with respect and consideration. Employers may also claim the right to be told the truth.

27.1.5 JUSTICE

Ethics are bound up with perceptions of **justice**. Some people regard justice as a human right, but it is often treated separately in the literature. Gilliland (1993) identified two main aspects of justice: procedural and distributive. **Procedural justice** concerns the consistency with which rules are implemented. **Distributive justice** concerns the correctness of the final decision in terms of a balance between what a person puts into a situation and the rewards that person receives.

Justice lies at the heart of most selection systems. In a *distributively just system*, the candidate with the highest ability will be selected, since the ablest candidate will contribute most – 'it is only fair that he or she should be appointed'. (However, this 'Anglo–Saxon' notion is not accepted in some other cultures, where family and other obligations take precedence). The more a selection system is related to the job, the higher are the applicants' perceptions of distributive justice (Gilliland, 1994). Ideas of distributive justice also form the basis for much of the thinking on fairness and bias (Tenopyr, 1996).

In a procedurally just system, all candidates will be treated in an equivalent way and asked only for information that is clearly relevant to the performance of the job (Smither et al., 1996). Issues concerning procedural justice are particularly relevant when invasive techniques such as drugs testing (Konovsky and Cropanzano, 1993) and physical tests form a part of a selection system (Hogan and Quigley, 1996).

Procedural justice and distributive justice are conceptually different but, in fact, they are highly correlated (Sheppard and Lerwicki, 1987; Brockner and Wisenfeld, 1996; Leck et al., 1996).

▲ 27.2 PROFESSIONAL ETHICAL CODES

Virtually every national psychology society and institute has an ethical code prominently displayed on its website (see the website that accompanies this book). Ethical issues are described in Elmes et al. (1985) and Smith and Robertson (1993). Francis (1999), on which this chapter draws heavily, considers ethics in the wider context of psychology. Most ethical codes, such as that of the American Psychological Association, are very comprehensive, extend to tens of pages and cover the dilemmas faced across the whole range of psychology. Some of the most useful ethical codes are those developed by the Psychological Society of Ireland and the Singapore Psychological Society.

Some psychological societies have produced specific, supplementary guidance relevant to selection. Two examples of such specific guidance are as follows:

- Rights and Responsibilities of Test Takers; American Psychological Association: www.apa.org/science/ttrr:html
- Code of Practice for Occupational Testing; British Psychological Society: www.bps.org.uk/about/psychometrics13.cfm

Practitioners should be familiar with the details of ethical codes of countries in which they work. However, most ethical codes have six cardinal principles and four other areas:

1 The principle of fair advertising.
2 The principle of competence.
3 The principle of self-regard.
4 The principle of informed consent.
5 Freedom to withdraw.
6 The principle of confidentiality.
7 Respect for social codes and multicultural sensitivities.
8 Relationships with others.
9 Fees and financial arrangements.
10 Rights of selectors.

27.2.1 THE PRINCIPLE OF FAIR ADVERTISING AND ACCEPTING WORK

There is nothing wrong with advertising and promoting good selection and guidance services. If advertising and promotion do not take place, many people and organizations will continue with methods and procedures that are less than optimal. However, the promotion of services needs to be fair and accurate:

- Qualifications, training and affiliations should be represented accurately. Advertisements should avoid comparisons with other professionals since the competing claims might become increasingly acrimonious and lead to confusion.
- Information should not be withheld in order to promote misunderstanding. Selectors, and in particular counsellors, should not solicit 'testimonials' from existing clients, since there is the danger that they might exert undue influence or encounter conflicts of interest. Statements made to the media should be based on appropriate research, literature and best practice. Statements made to the media should be consistent with ethical codes.
- The principle of fair advertising extends to the statements of others – especially others who are paid to promote a service. If others make deceptive or false statements on their behalf, a selector or counsellor must make reasonable efforts to correct such statements.
- Employees of the press, radio, television or other media should not be paid in return for publicity. Paid advertisements must be identified as such.

- Selectors and counsellors should not solicit private consultations from clients who receive, or are entitled to receive, services free through an agency or institution. Employees or consultants should not solicit or undertake work that could be in competition with their employer's organization.

Special considerations apply to researchers. Sometimes subjects ask a researcher to give guidance and advice. Francis (1999) recommends that such enquiries should be referred to another professional. When this is not possible, the situation should be discussed with a senior colleague who has no vested interest. The work should only be undertaken if the senior colleague concurs whole-heartedly.

Teachers, and organizations owned by them, should not have any direct financial relationships with students whom they teach or are likely to examine.

27.2.2 THE PRINCIPLE OF COMPETENCE

The principle of competence means that selectors should operate to high technical and professional standards. Selection and guidance decisions often make dramatic and irreversible interventions in people's lives. Usually, these decisions are necessary and cannot be shirked. However, those who give advice should be competent and qualified. Counsellors should not get involved in situations or use methods where they could not cope should things go wrong. They should always be able to cope with the worst case. A key to observing this principle is to recognize one's own limits and to operate within them.

In a changing world, the principle also imposes the need to extend competence. It is relatively easy to extend *personal competence* by training and development. The main difficulties are to obtain experience in a way that does not harm others, and to avoid the danger of believing that you have reached a level of competence when you have not.

The principle of competence is recognized by *data protection legislation*. This legislation is described in greater detail in later sections of this chapter (pages 373–6). Here, it is sufficient to note that most data protection guidelines require organizations to 'ensure that tests are based on the interpretation of scientific evidence' and 'are only used and interpreted by those who have received appropriate training'. Further, this legislation means that employers must be consistent in the way in which information about applicants is used.

27.2.3 THE PRINCIPLE OF SELF-REGARD AND WELFARE

Human dignity should be upheld. Except in very exceptional circumstances, people should not be harmed – and this includes psychological harm. At the end of selection or testing, people should think as highly of their selves as they did at the start. They should also think as highly of their fellow human beings, especially those with whom they have a close relationship. Consequently, selection systems that include detailed life histories should be handled with care, lest they unwittingly implant false memories involving others. In selection, the principle of self-regard is very difficult to uphold. It is almost inevitable that some rejected candidates will be hurt by a decision. This does not absolve a selector from trying to minimize the damage by, for example, giving reasonable feedback that puts a decision in context.

To protect the principle of self-regard, *avoid selection methods that involve humiliation, embarrassment and harm* to people. In this context, degradation or embarrassment must be seen through the eyes of the candidates, not through the eyes of the selectors, who may have become blasé after years of work in the field. If degrading methods are utterly *and absolutely* necessary, for some reason:

- An *impartial second opinion* from a senior colleague or an 'ethics committee' should be obtained.
- *Candidates should be screened* to exclude those particularly vulnerable to long-term effects.
- *Candidates should be debriefed.* The selection methods should be explained so that misunderstandings are avoided and questions answered. During the debriefing, the investigator should look out for individuals who may be experiencing untoward effects.
- *People should know where to get advice* if they feel adverse effects. In minimum-risk selections, it may be sufficient to remind candidates of contact details given in earlier correspondence. In intensive and high-risk selection methods used for, say, Arctic explorers or astronauts, a face-to-face follow-up meeting should be arranged.

If a selector discovers that there are adverse effects, he or she must maintain responsibility and take the best action until responsibility is formally transferred and accepted by someone who is likely to have greater competence.

27.2.4 THE PRINCIPLE OF INFORMED CONSENT

People have the right to know what they are letting themselves in for before they make any significant commitment. They should have reasonable information on:

- the processes used
- the uses to which the information will be put
- who will 'own' the information
- who is the selector or tester, and what his or her auspices are.

The main issue is as follows: *Can candidates, or the person asking for guidance, understand the implications of the information they are given?* This is particularly important when experiments deal with children or people with mental disabilities, in which case it may be necessary to obtain the consent of custodians. Fortunately, this is rarely a problem in selection situations, but it may arise where, say, parents are obtaining vocational guidance for their children.

Data Protection – General Issues

The principle of informed consent is so important that it has had a major impact on legislation concerning data protection (see also pages 377–9). Most administrations, such as those of the European Union (EU Directive 95/46/EC; UK Data Protection Act, 1998) and Australia, have legislation or regulations to ensure that personal information is used properly. The legislation differs slightly from country to country, and it also changes over time. In this book, it is impossible to provide a comprehensive and totally authoritative account. However, it is vital that practitioners are familiar with the data protection legislation operating where they work. A list of some sources containing further information on data protection legislation in different countries is given on the website that accompanies this book. The following outline is given for general guidance.

The Scope of Data Protection

Selection, research and probably guidance using tests (or other methods such as interviews) are virtually certain to come within the ambit of data protection legislation. In many countries, there may be specific documents or codes that specify how the regulations specifically apply to recruitment and selection.

Regulations usually cover all data, irrespective of whether it is stored on a computer or personal organizer or in a traditional filing system. Selection data is only likely to be exempt if it is stored in such a haphazard way that it would be difficult for someone to extract information about a specific individual. The legislation usually covers all methods of selection, including interview notes. The regulations usually cover references – once they have left the organization that is providing the reference. The only material that can be withheld from the subject is information that reveals the identity of other individuals, such as the author of the reference.

Personal data covered by legislation is likely to include:

- salary and bank account details
- e-mails involving named workers
- supervisors' notebooks in which individuals are identified
- application forms and other personnel records.

Some kinds of data may be designated as 'sensitive personnel data', which are subject to more stringent conditions before it can be stored and used. This may include:

- ethnic origin
- political, religious or other beliefs and opinions
- trade union membership
- physical or mental health or disabilities (for example, sickness records)
- sexual orientation
- convictions, offences or legal proceedings.

Information is usually not covered by legislation if it is 'anonymized' (that is, individuals cannot be identified – either directly or indirectly), or if it is held in summary form (for example, profiles of the age structure of the workforce). Legislation often allows employers to keep 'sensitive information' in order to allow monitoring of, say, equal opportunities, or if it is necessary to defend the organization against a legal case.

The Basic Principles of Data Protection

In general, data protection legislation draws a distinction between data subjects (the people about whom information is held – potential employees, present employees, past employees, agency workers, casual workers and contract workers are covered) and data controllers (the people who store and process the information). The legislation is usually based on eight principles, which say that personal information must:

- be processed fairly and lawfully
- be used for limited, stated purposes and not for purposes outside these limits
- be adequate, relevant and not excessive
- be accurate
- be secure
- not be kept for longer than is necessary
- not infringe data subjects' rights
- not be transferred to countries that do not have adequate protection for personal data.

Legislation usually gives *data subjects* the right to have a copy of the information held about them – within, say, 40 days of payment of a reasonable fee. Data subjects can insist that inaccurate data is corrected and they may seek compensation for damage or distress caused by a breach of the legislation. In some circumstances, they can prevent employers from keeping certain information or from using information in certain ways. Organizations can often withhold information if it relates to criminal investigations, management planning such as promotions or transfers, and negotiations.

In general, *data controllers* must register the data that they collect and the uses to which they are put. Selectors, researchers and vocational counsellors must register if they store data in any systematic way. Information about data controllers is usually placed on public records that can be inspected. Data controllers must ensure that individual line managers and others who use the data understand their own responsibility for data protection and, if necessary, amend their working practices to comply with the legislation. Workers should be made aware of the extent to which they can be criminally liable if they knowingly or recklessly disclose or misuse information. In most countries there is a government official, perhaps a commissioner, who has two main activities. First, he or she will promote good practice by providing information and codes. Second, he or she may enforce the law regarding data protection.

Specific Aspects Relevant to the Principle of Informed Consent

Data protection legislation usually contains many provisions that are relevant to the informed consent of candidates, clients and research subjects. These provisions can be divided into two groups: consent and information.

Consent to hold information about employees is generally *not* needed. Indeed, some authorities consider it misleading to seek consent when people have no real choice. Explicit consent is more likely to be needed if 'sensitive information' is involved. In many cases, even sensitive data can be used without consent if it is needed to comply with legislation, such as equal opportunity laws or statues concerning sick pay.

An application implies consent because individuals in an open job market have a choice whether or not to apply for a specific job. There is no need to explain what will happen to information provided that it is no more than they are likely to expect. However, if it is used for unexpected purposes such as marketing, the applicant's consent must be obtained. Consent can only be assumed for a specific application. Details must not be passed to other employers with similar vacancies, or kept for later vacancies within the same organization, unless the explicit consent of the candidate has been obtained. Signed consent is also required for documents or other information that needs to be obtained from other people and organizations, such as former employers or qualification bodies.

Applicants need considerable *information* in order to check that their rights have not been infringed. The main information that must be given includes:

- The name of the prospective employer (if this is not apparent from the advertisement and so on). The use of a post office box number for the return of applications should not be used to mask the identity of the organization. If recruitment agencies are used, the agency must be identified as such. In general, it is better for agencies to let candidates know the identity of the organization for whom they are working or pass on 'anonymized' details only. Prospective employers must either identify themselves in the particulars of the post or appraise candidates that they have received information about them. In counselling and research, the name of the organization or person providing the service or conducting the research must be clear.
- If applications are to be checked or verified, applicants should be informed of the verification process and methods.

Further important provisions of data protection legislation are given on pages 377–9.

27.2.5 FREEDOM TO WITHDRAW

People are free to withdraw from selection, research or guidance. Only those who are willing should be involved. However, the definition of the term 'willing' may prove to be problematic. Is an unemployed candidate with heavy domestic responsibilities free to refuse a request to complete an in-depth interview? Are employees in a redundancy situation willingly completing a test?

27.2.6 THE PRINCIPLE OF CONFIDENTIALITY

Unless it has been explicitly agreed *in advance*, all information collected in selection is confidential to the data subject, data controllers and decision-makers. Confidential information may encompass people, organizations or materials:

- *Confidentiality to people* means that a candidate's results should never be disclosed to others, such as colleagues, friends, competitors, subordinates or bosses. An ethical researcher would never make a comment such as 'X is a fool. He did badly in the guidance test I use.' Information such as biographical details or attitude scores should also remain confidential. Reasonable precautions should be made to keep information secure and results should be disposed of properly after a set period of time. Data protection laws must be observed.
- *Confidentiality to organizations* is particularly important to external consultants. During an assignment a consultant may learn inside details about the methods, people, procedures and finances of an organization. He or she must be careful not to divulge this information to other people or competitors, even if such disclosure would make the consultant 'seem big' or important in the eyes of a prospective client.

- *Confidentiality of materials* means that when tests are supplied on a confidential basis – so that people with the right contacts cannot look up the answers and obtain an unfair advantage – confidentiality must be respected. Test materials should not be shown to people who do not need to know about them. It is improper, and probably an infringement of copyright, to publish test questions in a newspaper or magazine. There are some situations in which the principle of confidentiality should be breached. This could arise when a guidance client seems likely to be a danger to him- or herself, or to others. It also arises when a selector discovers that a candidate is involved in illegal activities. Even in these cases, a second opinion should be sought from an impartial, senior colleague. Information should only be disclosed to authorities when there is clear legal authorization. In almost all circumstances, the law must be obeyed – even if you have formed a personal opinion that the law is silly!

Data protection legislation (see also pages 373–6) stresses confidentiality. There are five main aspects: data collection, verification, vetting, transmission and storage and deletion. It is also important to note that people have a right to view information about them and to know the rationale behind selection systems.

Data Collection

Probably the best way to preserve confidentiality is to avoid collecting unnecessary information in the first place. If information is not collected, it cannot be used wrongly. Application forms should not be excessive or ask for irrelevant material. Similarly, questions at interviews should be necessary and relevant. In most circumstances it is not necessary to ask people about their lives outside work. Only a minority of jobs will necessitate asking for even relevant convictions. Only a tiny minority of jobs (for example, those involving the care of children or other vulnerable people) will justify asking about 'spent' convictions.

Verification

Data protection legislation acknowledges that applicants may not always provide accurate information. Employers may be justified in verifying the information via, say, references. However, the verification process must be open. Candidates should be informed about the information that is to be verified and how the process will be conducted. If verification involves external sources, applicants should know which sources may be approached. External sources should be reliable and should only very rarely include close colleagues or family members. Usually, external sources should only be approached during the later stages of the selection process, and then only with the written consent of the applicant. Sometimes, information provided by an applicant can only be checked using documents to which the applicant has sole access. It may be tempting to make an offer of employment conditional upon the applicant obtaining such documents and handing them over. This is termed 'enforced subject access' and is a criminal offence under some data protection legislation.

Whenever a discrepancy arises between the information provided by applicants and the information obtained from other sources, it should not be assumed that the applicant's information is incorrect. Further verification may be appropriate. The applicant must be notified of the discrepancy and asked for an explanation.

Vetting

Vetting is a more intensive, intrusive process that goes beyond the information provided by a candidate. Vetting is only permissible where there are particular and significant risks to the employer, clients or others (for example, some finance jobs or jobs involving security). Because of its intrusive nature, vetting should be used sparingly and probably at a late stage in the recruitment process. Comprehensive vetting should be reserved for 'successful' applicants. In order to avoid disappointing candidates and wasting organizational resources, candidates should be warned about the nature of any vetting at an early stage, so that they can withdraw if they do not wish to participate.

In some rare situations, such as the recruitment of prison officers or police officers, it may be necessary to collect information about the family or close associates of the applicant. Such people should, except in extreme circumstances, be informed of the information that is being collected about them and the purposes for which it will be used. Data collected about third parties should be treated with the same care as the data collected about the applicant.

Transmission

Data about applicants should be transmitted in a secure and confidential way. At the very least, internal communications containing personnel data should be placed in sealed envelopes when they are sent to another person. There must be no chance of them lying around on open display on photocopiers, desks or in post rooms. Data sent via the Internet should be encrypted. This applies to data sent by applicants who are making e-applications and all subsequent stages. Personnel data should never be faxed to shared machines, unless a telephone call immediately prior to transmission has established that the lawful recipient is next to the fax machine and able to ensure the confidentiality of the material.

Storage and Deletion

Information on data subjects should be stored in a secure place – generally a locked draw or cabinet, to which only specified people have access. In general, information should be destroyed soon after it has been used. For example, once a candidate has passed vetting, the vetting information should be destroyed – although whether he or she passed or failed vetting can be noted. Data from recruitment should not be transferred routinely to employment records. Only data relevant to employment should be transferred. For example, there is rarely any reason why an applicant's salary in a previous post should be transferred. Data not needed for employment records should be destroyed after a period of time. The period should be determined by business needs but should rarely exceed six months. Sometimes, data needs to be kept for longer periods in order to monitor selection methods or defend an organization against legal challenges. In these cases, the data should be held in 'anonymized' form or it should be aggregated to prevent the identification of individuals.

Viewing Information and Inspecting Rationales

Data protection legislation usually allows data subjects the right to inspect information held about them. This includes test scores, and also interview notes and references. If an automated system (such as scores derived from touch-tone answers to computerized telephone questions) is the sole means of deciding which applicants proceed to further stages, the rationale of the system must be provided on request. Furthermore, in some circumstances the decision should be reconsidered or retaken on a different basis.

27.2.7 RESPECT FOR SOCIAL CODES

Selectors should show sensible regard for the *social codes* and *moral expectations* of the community and clients. For example, an atheist selecting personnel in a monastery should not engage in blasphemous behaviour or cause gratuitous offence. If you cannot be tolerant and courteous to the people in an organization, it is better not to accept an assignment in that organization.

27.2.8 RELATIONSHIPS WITH OTHERS

Many aspects of relationships with clients are covered elsewhere in this chapter. However, it is worth pointing out that selectors should avoid body contact other than customary greetings such as shaking hands or giving a 'pat on the back'. Any form of activity with candidates or clients that could be construed as sexual or likely to reduce objectivity must be avoided.

Ethics relating to other professionals usually concern boundaries and roles. A general principle is to agree, in advance, an orderly, explicit arrangement concerning roles, rights and obligations. Particularly important for researchers is agreement about publication. Unless explicitly agreed, preferably at the start of the study, it is unethical for professors, or other members of the teaching staff, to write articles or assume first authorship of papers based on the work of students. Harassment of other people, especially junior colleagues, should be avoided.

A professional should avoid interfering with or inhibiting the work of another selector or counsellor. Often, an unsuccessful candidate will give partial information about a selection method and ask for a view. It is particularly heinous to give opinions on subjects outside one's own area of competence, such as when a clinical psychologist comments upon the selection methods used in employment. It is equally heinous for an occupational psychologist to intervene in the treatment given by a clinical psychologist.

While the ideas, theories and data of another investigator can and should be scrutinized and criticized, personal attacks should be avoided.

27.2.9 FEES AND FINANCIAL ARRANGEMENTS

There are two major principles concerning fees:

- The *fee structure and terms of payment should be made clear* to clients during, or immediately after, an initial consultation (Francis, 1999). Sometimes, broaching the matter of fees can be 'delicate' and it is often appropriate to send a short letter confirming acceptance of an assignment, together with a sheet setting out the fee rate, the estimated length of the assignment and the terms of payment. Should it become apparent that costs are likely to exceed the initial estimate, the client should be notified immediately.
  - Fees for missed appointments and cancelled meetings often need clarification. As a general rule, some level of fee is appropriate for second and subsequent cancellations.

- Sometimes, a request for help is made in ambiguous circumstances, perhaps in social situations. It is important that this ambiguity is removed at an early stage. If the work is done for a reduced fee, or on a **'public benefit'** (*pro bono publico*) basis, the recipient should be informed of the extent of the financial benefit (Francis, 1999), using phrases such as 'normally, this work would involve a fee of www but because of xxx and yyy we think it appropriate to charge zzz'. If it is appropriate to charge a full fee, the situation can be communicated with phrases such as 'to give proper professional advice on this matter would involve considerable work and a fee of zzz is likely'.
- Up to a limit, public benefit work should be encouraged. 'Gift work' serves two main purposes. It provides a way of returning to society the benefits that you have received. This is in addition to taxes and levies. Second, 'gift work' helps to produce a good public view of selection and guidance. A clear policy of giving, say, 5% of your time as 'gift work' avoids ambiguities and helps you defend yourself against unreasonable demands. Sinclair and Pettifor (1991) give a useful guide to the work that can be undertaken on a public benefit basis.

• The basis of payment should be the conventional *fee-for-service* and not fee-for-outcome. The success of any psychological intervention cannot be guaranteed because many intervening influences, including the actions of the client, are important. A fee-for-service means that the selector will use his or her best skills and professionalism, during an agreed time, to achieve the objectives agreed with the client. Other ethical aspects of finance include prompt payment of bills and, whenever possible, avoidance of arrangements involving barter. Where barter is absolutely necessary, the items bartered should be translated into monetary terms and recorded.

27.2.10 RIGHTS OF SELECTORS

It should not be forgotten that selectors and counsellors have rights too. Clients and organizations should be prepared to:

• make and keep appointments
• treat selectors with courtesy and dignity
• give frank and honest replies to questions
• avoid making trivial, facetious and mendacious complaints
• strongly avoid commissioning two counsellors for the same assignment – if this is absolutely necessary, both sets of professionals should be informed of each other's remit
• avoid altering terms of reference or specifications of work without renegotiating fees
• pay promptly and at agreed rates for services received.

▲ 27.3 UPHOLDING ETHICAL PRINCIPLES

The most obvious way to uphold ethical principles is to avoid violating them yourself. You should also set an example to junior colleagues and members of the public by being seen to be ethical – *without* behaving like a sanctimonious prig! Much depends upon the seriousness of the ethical breach.

Minor Ethical Breaches

When unethical behaviour is encountered in others, the situation can be difficult to handle. The main objective must be to ensure that the unethical behaviour is discontinued. With minor and occasional infractions it is best to take low-level, informal action. Many, probably most, unethical acts are undertaken due to enthusiasm and ignorance of the ethical implications. Here, a light-hearted and informal comment will be sufficient to remedy the situation.

Significant Ethical Breaches

In more serious cases, the appropriate action would be a substantive conversation. In a helpful tone, the dangers of the unethical act can be explained. It is often easiest to emphasize the dangers to the perpetrator (candidates might complain to professional body, certification might be withdrawn, suppliers may cease to provide tests, the organization may suffer from a bad reputation, and so on). Intervention will be more effective if positive hints about how the ethical principles *can* be observed are given. A copy of the appropriate code of ethical conduct or other helpful material – such as, perhaps, this chapter – can be provided for the perpetrator.

Serious Ethical Breaches

Where unethical behaviour is premeditated, mendacious, frequent or serious, stronger action must be taken. The perpetrator should be told, point-blank, preferably in writing, that they are acting unethically and that they should desist forthwith.

A violent reaction can be expected. The perpetrator is likely to make counter-accusations of unreasonable, nosey, bossy and patronizing behaviour. Do not be deterred by such abuse. If the unethical person is your boss, it is probably wise to confide in a third person who can take up the issue on your behalf. If the unethical behaviour has caused or is likely to cause serious damage, it should be reported to the appropriate professional organization, such as the American Psychological Association, the Australian Psychological Society , the British Psychological Society, the Canadian Psychological Association, the New Zealand Psychological Society and the Singapore Psychological Society, test publishers or the people who have suffered as a result. Except in an emergency, wait two days between observing an unethical act and reporting it to others; the delay will help to ensure that you get your thoughts into perspective. When making complaints, make sure that you stick to specific observations that you can prove. Beware of hearsay evidence. Ensure that your complaint is not libellous or slanderous.

27.3.1 ETHICAL DILEMMAS

Many, possibly the majority, of ethical problems are not a simple question of right or wrong. They arise from a dilemma between two sets of ethical considerations. Such dilemmas can often be resolved by placing ethical responsibilities in an order of precedence:

- It is generally agreed that the *rights of the client* (that is, the person across the desk) have the highest priority. In this context, the client may not be the person who commissions the work or pays the bill. For example, an HR director may commission an outplacement organization to offer careers guidance to managers. The outplacement organization may employ a psychologist to administer and interpret tests. In this case, the outplaced manager is the psychologist's client, not the outplacement organization or the previous employer.

- The interests of *the profession* are generally placed second (see Francis, 1999). This may give rise to problems in some organizations, such as the armed forces, where a selector is ordered by a senior officer to divulge information that the profession says should not be divulged to unqualified people. Some armed forces have resolved such dilemmas by creating a specific corps of, say, psychologists. A senior officer within the specialist corps may, for example, demand information, whereas a senior officer outside the specialist corps may not.

There is much less agreement on the precedence of other rights. Much will depend upon precise circumstances. Perhaps, the rights of the *person commissioning* the work and paying the fee should generally rank third and the rights of the *selector or psychologist* should rank fourth. Other, general or unspecific rights will normally rank fifth or below.

BIBLIOGRAPHY

Adams, S. R. 1987: Influence of interviewer counselling behaviours and interviewee mood on applicant perceptions. Unpublished master's thesis, Colorado State University, Fort Collins.

Adkins, D. C. 1974: *Test Construction*. Columbus, Ohio: Merrill.

Adler, A. 1956: *The Individual Psychology of Alfred Adler*, edited by H. L. Ansbacher and R. R. Ansbacher. New York: Basic Books.

Adorno, T. W., Fenkel-Brunswick, E., Levinson, D. J. and Stanford, R. N. 1950: *The Authoritarian Personality*. New York: Harper.

Ajzen, I. 2001: Nature and operation of attitudes. *Annual Review of Psychology*, 52, 27–58.

—— and Fishbein, M. 2000: Attitudes and the attitude-behaviour relation: reasoned and automatic processes. In W. Strobe and M. Hewstone (eds), *European Review of Social Psychology*. Chichester: Wiley.

Alafito, J. G. and Kalt, N. C. 1977: Effects of eye contact on evaluation of job applicants. *Journal of Employment Counselling*, 14, 46–8.

Allport, G. W. 1937: *Personality: a Psychological Interpretation*. New York: Holt.

—— and Odbert, H. S. 1936: Trait names: a psycholexical study. *Psychological Monographs*, 47, 1, whole issue.

——, Vernon, P. E. and Lindzey, G. 1960: *Study of Values Manual*. Chicago: Riverside.

Allworth, E. and Hesketh, B. 1999: Construct-oriented biodata: capturing change-related and contextually relevant future performance. *International Journal of Selection and Assessment*, 7(2), 97–111.

American Psychological Association 1981: *Ethical Principles of Psychologists*. Washington, DC: APA.

—— 1999: *Standards for Educational and Psychological Testing*. Washington, DC: American Psychological Association.

Anastasi, A. 1988: *Psychological Testing*. New York: Macmillan.

Anderson, M. 1992: *Intelligence and Development: a Cognitive Theory*. Oxford: Blackwell.

Anderson, N. R. 1988: Interviewer impression formation and decision making in the graduate selection interview: a theoretical and empirical analysis. Unpublished PhD thesis, University of Aston, Birmingham.

Andrich, D. 1978: Relationships between the Thurstone and Rasch approaches to item scaling. *Applied Psychological Measurement*, 2, 449–60.

Anstey, E. 1977: A 30 year follow-up of the CSSB procedure with lessons for the future. *Journal of Occupational Psychology*, 50, 149–59.

Arnold, J. A., Cooper, C. L. and Robertson, I. T. 1992: *Work Psychology: Understanding Human Performance in the Workplace*. London: Pitman.

Arvey, R. D. 1979: *Fairness in Selecting Employees*. Reading, Mass.: Addison-Wesley.

—— and Campion, J. E. 1982: The employment interview: a summary and review of recent literature. *Personnel Psychology*, 35, 281–322.

—— and Faley, R. H. 1988: *Fairness in Selecting Employees*. Reading, Mass.: Addison-Wesley.

—— and Murphy, K. R. 1998: Performance evaluation in work settings. *Annual Review of Psychology*, 49, 141–68.

—— , Bouchard, T., Segal, N. and Abraham, L. 1989: Job satisfaction: environmental and genetic components. *Journal of Applied Psychology*, 74, 187–92.

Asher, J. J. and Sciarrino, J. A. 1974: Realistic work sample tests: a review. *Personnel Psychology*, 27, 519–33.

Association of Graduate Recuiters 2000: *Going To Work on the Web: Web-based Graduate Recruitment*. Briefing 11. Warwick: AGR.

Atkinson, J. W. 1964: *An Introduction to Motivation*. Princeton, NJ: Van Nostrand.

Atkinson, R. C. and Wilson, H. A. 1969: *Computer Assisted Instruction: Book of Readings*. New York: Academic Press.

Atkinson, R. L., Atkinson, R. C., Smith, E. E. and Bem, D. J. 1990: *Introduction to Psychology*, 10th edn. San Diego, Calif.: Harcourt Brace Jovanovich.

Bandura, A. 1977: *Social Learning Theory*. Englewood Cliffs, NJ: Prentice-Hall.

Bangert-Drowns, R. L. 1986: Review of developments in meta-analytic method. *Psychological Bulletin*, 99(3), 388–99.

Banks, M. H., Jackson, P. R., Stafford, E. M. and Warr, P. B. 1982: *The Job Component Inventory Mark II*. Sheffield: Manpower Services Commission.

Baron, R. A. 1989: Impression management by applicants during employment interviews: the 'too much of a good thing' effect. In R. W. Elder and G. R. Ferris (eds), *The Employment Interview: Theory, Research and Practice*. Newbury Park, Calif.: Sage.

Barrett, G. V., Phillips, J. S. and Alexander R. A. 1981: Concurrent and predictive validity designs. *Journal of Applied Psychology*, 66, 1–6.

Barrick, M. R. and Mount, M. K. 1991: The Big Five Personality Dimensions and job performance: a meta-analysis. *Personnel Psychology*, 44, 1–26.

Barron, F. 1965: The psychology of creativity. In T. M. Newcomb (ed.), *New Directions in Psychology II*. New York: Holt Rinehart Winston.

Bartlett, C. J. and O'Leary, B. S. 1969: A differential prediction model to moderate the effects of heterogeneous groups in personnel selection and classification. *Personnel Psychology*, 22, 1–17.

Bartram, D. 1989: Computer-based assessment. In P. Herriot (ed.), *Assessment and Selection in Organisations*. Chichester: Wiley.

—— 1994: Computer-based assessment. In C. L. Cooper and I. T. Robertson (eds), *International Review of Industrial and Organizational Psychology*, vol. 9. Chichester: Wiley, 31–69.

—— 1995a: *Review of Personality Assessment Instruments (level B)*. Leicester: British Psychological Society.

—— 1995b: The role of Computer-Based Test Interpretation (CBTI) in occupational assessment. *International Journal of Selection and Assessment*, 3(3), 178–85.

—— (ed.) 1997: *Review of Ability and Aptitude Tests (Level A) for Use in Occupational Settings*. Leicester: British Psychological Society.

—— 2000: Internet recruitment and selection: kissing frogs to find princes. *International Journal of Selection and Assessment*, 8(4), 261–74.

—— and Lindley, P. 1994: *Test Interpretation: Level A Open Learning Programme*. Leicester: British Psychological Society.

Bass, B. M. 1958: Famous sayings test: general manual. *Psychological Reports*, 4, 479–97.

Bechtoldt, H. P. 1959: Construct validity: a critique. *American Psychologist*, 619–29.

Begley, S. and Rodgers, A. 1998: You're OK, I'm terrific: self esteem backfires. *Newsweek*, 13 July, 69.

Belbin, R. M. 1981: *Management Teams*. Oxford: Heinemann.

Ben-Porath, W. S. and Butcher, J. N. 1986: Computers in personality assessment: a brief past, ebullient present and an expanding future. *Computers in Human Behaviour*, 2, 167–82.

Bethell-Fox, C. E. 1989: Psychological testing. In P. Herriot (ed.), *Assessment and Selection in Organisations*. Chichester: Wiley.

Bickley, P. G., Keith, T. Z. and Wolfle, L. M. 1995: The three stratum theory of cognitive abilities: test of the structure of intelligence across lifespan. *Intelligence*, 20, 309–28.

Bliesener, T. 1996: Methodological moderators in validating biographical data in personnel selection. *Journal of Occupational and Organisational Psychology*, 69, 107–20.

Blinkhorn, S. F. 1998: Burt and the early history of factor analysis. In N. J. Mackintosh (ed.), *IQ and Human Intelligence*. Oxford: Oxford University Press.

Bolsher, B. I. and Springbett, B. M. 1961: The reaction of interviewers to favourable and unfavourable information. *Journal of Applied Psychology*, 45, 97–103.

Booth, J. F. 1998: The user interface in computer-based selection and assessment: applied and theoretical problems of an evolving technology. *International Journal of Selection and Assessment*, 6(2), 57–60.

Boring, E. G. 1923: Intelligence as the tests test it. *New Republic*, 35, 35–7.

Borislow, B. 1958: The Edwards Personal Preference Schedule and fakeability. *Journal of Applied Psychology*, 42, 22–7.

Borman, W. C. and Brush, D. H. 1993: More progress towards a taxonomy of managerial performance requirements. *Human Performance*, 6, 1–21.

—— and Motowidlo, S. J. 1993: Expanding the criterion domain to include elements of contextual performance. In N. Schmitt and W. C. Borman (eds), *Personnel Selection in Organisations*. San Francisco: Jossey Bass.

Bouchard, J. R. 1996: Genetics and evolution: implications for personality theories. In J. Newman (ed.), *Measures of the Five Factor Model and Psychological Type: a Major Convergence of Research and Theory*. Gainsville, Fl.: Center for Application of Psychological Type.

Bouchard, T. J. 1998: Genetic and environmental influences on adult intelligence and special mental abilities. *Human Biology*, 70, 257–79.

Boudreau, J. W. 1989: Selection utility analysis: a review and agenda for future research. In M. Smith and I. T. Robertson (eds), *Advances in Selection and Assessment*. Chichester: Wiley.

—— and Rynes, S. L. 1985: The role of recruitment in staffing utility analysis. *Journal of Applied Psychology*, 70, 354–66.

Boyatzis, R. 1982: *The Competent Manager*. New York: Wiley.

Bray, D. W. and Grant, D. L. 1966: The assessment centre in the measurement of potential for business management. *Psychological Monographs*, 80, 625, entire issue.

——, Campbell, R. J. and Grant, D. L. 1974: *Formative Years in Business*. New York: Wiley.

Breakwell, G. M. 1990: *Interviewing: Problems in Practice*. Leicester: British Psychological Society.

Bretz, R. T. and Judge, T. A. 1998: Realistic job previews: a test of the adverse self-selection hypothesis. *Journal of Applied Psychology*, 83(2), 330–7.

Bright, J. E. H. and Hutton, S. 2000: The impact of competences statements on resumes for shortlisting decisions. *International Journal of Selection and Assessment*, 8(2), 41–53.

Bristow, M. 2001: Management competencies. Unpublished MSc thesis, School of Management, UMIST, Manchester.

British Institute of Management and Institute of Personnel Management 1980: *Selecting Managers: how British Industry Recruits*. London: BIM/IPM.

British Psychological Society 1999: *Guidelines for the Development and Use of Computer-based Assessment*. Leicester: British Psychological Society.

Brockner, J. and Wisenfeld, B. M. 1996: An integrative framework for explaining reactions to decisions: interactive effects of outcomes and procedures. *Psychological Bulletin*, 120, 189–208.

Brown, B. K. and Campion, M. A. 1994: Biodata phenomenology: recruiters' perceptions and use of biographical information in resume screening. *Journal of Applied Psychology*, 79, 897–908.

Bruner, J. S. and Tagiuri, R. 1954: The perception of people. In G. Lindzey (ed.), *Handbook of Social Psychology*. Cambridge, Mass.: Addison-Wesley.

Burrows, W. A. and White, L. L. 1996: Predicting sales performance. *Journal of Business and Psychology*, 11, 73–83.

Byrd, M. L. 1979: The effects of vocal activity and race of applicant on the job selection interview decision. Unpublished PhD thesis, University of Missouri.

Campbell, D. P. 1971: *Handbook for the Strong Vocational Interest Blank*. Stanford: Stanford University Press.

Campbell, D. T. and Fiske, D. W. 1959: Convergent and discriminant validation by the multitrait–multimethod matrix. *Psychological Bulletin*, 56, 81–105.

Campbell, J. P. 1994: Alternative models of job performance and the implications for selection and classification. In M. G. Rumsey, C. B. Walker and J. H. Harris (eds), *Personnel Selection and Classification*. Hillsdale, NJ: Lawrence Erlbaum.

—— and Pritchard, R. D. 1976: Motivation theory in industrial and organizational psychology. In M. D. Dunnette (ed.), *Handbook of Industrial and Organisational Psychology*. Chicago: Rand McNally.

——, McHenry, J. J. and Wise, L. L. 1990: Modelling job performance in a population of jobs. *Personnel Psychology*, 43, 313–33.

Carlson, K. D., Scullen, S. E., Schmidt, F. L., Rothstein, H. and Erwin, F. 1999: Generalisable biographical data validity can be achieved without multi-organisational development and keying. *Personnel Psychology*, 52, 731–55.

Carrier, N. A. 1963: Need correlates of 'gullability'. *Journal of Applied and Social Psychology*, 66(1), 84–6.

Carroll, J. B. 1993: *Human Cognitive Abilities: a Survey of Factor Analytic Studies*. Cambridge: Cambridge University Press.

Carroll, S. J. and Nash, A. N. 1972: Effectiveness of forced choice reference check. *Personnel Administration*, 35, 42–6.

Cascio, W. F. 1975: Accuracy of verifiable biographical information blank responses. *Journal of Applied Psychology*, 60, 767–9.

—— and Ramos, R. 1986: Development and application of a new method for assessing job performance in behavioural/economic terms. *Journal of Applied Psychology*, 1, 20–8.

Cattell, R. B. 1950: *Personality: a Systematic, Theoretical and Factual Study*. New York: McGraw-Hill.

—— 1965: *The Scientific Analysis of Personality*. Harmondsworth: Penguin.

—— 1966: *Handbook of Multivariate Experimental Psychology*. Chicago: Rand McNally.

—— 1975: *The Motivation Analysis Test*. Champaign, Ill.: Institute for Personality and Ability Testing.

—— 1986: *Handbook for the 16 Personality Factor Questionnaire*. Champaign, Ill.: Institute for Personality and Ability Testing.

—— 1989: *The 16PF: Personality in Depth*. Champaign, Ill.: Institute for Personality and Ability Testing.

—— and Luborsky, L. B. 1947: Personality factors in response to humour. *Journal of Abnormal and Social Psychology*, 42, 402–21.

—— and Schuerger, J. M. 1978: *Handbook for the Objective-Analytic (O-A) Test Kit*. Champaign, Ill.: Institute for Personality and Ability Testing.

—— and Warburton, F. W. 1967: *Objective Personality and Motivation Tests*. Chicago: University of Illinois Press.

——, Eber, H. W. and Tatsuoka, M. M. 1988: *Handbook for the 16PF*. Champaign, Ill.: Institute for Personality and Aptitude Testing.

Chan, D., Schmitt, N., Jennings, D., Cause, C. S. and Delbridge, K. 1998: Applicant perceptions of test fairness: integrating justice and self-serving bias perspectives. *International Journal of Selection and Assessment*, 6(4), 232–9.

Child, I. L. 1968: Personality in culture. In E. F. Borgatta and W. W. Lambert (eds), *Handbook of Personality and Research*. Chicago: Rand McNally.

Chopin, B. H. 1976: Recent developments in item banking. In P. De Gruitjer and L. J. T. Van Der Kamp (eds), *Advances in Psychological and Educational Measurement*. Chichester: Wiley.

Cleary, T. A. and Hilton, T. L. 1968: An investigation of item bias. *Educational and Psychological Measurement*, 26, 61–75.

Clifton, T. C., Mumford, M. D. and Baughman, W. A. 1999: Background data and autobiographical memory: effects of item types and task characteristics. *International Journal of Selection and Assessment*, 7(2), 57–69.

Closs, S. J. 1978: *The Occupational Interests Guide*. London: Hodder & Stoughton.

Cohen, D. 1993: *How to Cheat in Psychological Tests*. London: Sheldon Press.

Cohen, J. and Cohen, P. 1983: *Applied Regression/Correlation Analysis for the Behavioral Sciences*. Hillsdale, NJ: Lawrence Erlbaum.

Commission for Racial Equality 1993: *Towards Fair Selection – a Survey of Test Practice and Thirteen Case Studies*. London: CRE.

Conn, S. R. and Rieke, M. L. 1994: *16PF Fifth Edition: Technical Manual*. Champaign, Ill.: Institute for Personality and Ability Testing.

Connerley, M. L., Mael, F. A. and Morath, R. A. 1999: 'Don't ask – please tell': selection privacy from two perspectives. *Journal of Occupational and Organisational Psychology*, 72, 405–22.

Conway, J. M. 1999: Distinguishing contextual performance from task performance for managerial jobs. *Journal of Applied Psychology*, 84, 3–13.

—— and Peneno, G. M. 1999: Compare structured interview question types: construct validity and applicant reactions. *Journal of Business and Psychology*, 13, 485–505.

Converse, R. P. and Markus, G. B. 1979: Plus ça change . . . the new CPS Election Study Panel. *American Political Science Review*, 73, 32–49.

Cook, K. W., Vance, C. A. and Spector, P. E. 2000: The relation of candidate personality with selection interview outcomes. *Journal of Applied Social Psychology*, 30(4), 867–85.

Cook, T. and Emler, N. 1999: Bottom-up versus top-down evaluations of candidates' managerial potential: an experimental study. *Journal of Occupational and Organisational Psychology*, 72, 423–39.

Costa, P. T. and McCrae, R. R. 1995: *NEO/FFI Manual Supplement*. Odessa, Fl.: Psychological Assessment Resources.

Crews, F. C. 1998: *Unauthorised Freud: Doubters Confront a Legend*. New York: Viking.

Cronbach, L. J. 1951: Coefficient alpha and the internal structure of tests. *Psychometrica*, 16, 297–334.

—— 1970: *Essentials of Psychological Testing*. New York: Harper & Row.

—— 1984: *Essentials of Psychological Testing*, 4th edn. New York: Harper & Row.

—— and Glesser, G. C. 1965: *Psychological Tests and Personnel Decisions*. Urbana: University of Illinois Press.

—— and Meehl, P. E. 1955: Construct validity in psychological tests. *Psychological Bulletin*, 52(4), 281–302.

Cunningham, J. W., Boese, R. R., Neeb, R. W. and Pass, J. J. 1983: Systematically derived work dimensions: factor analysis of the Occupational Analysis Inventory. *Journal of Applied Psychology*, 68, 232–52.

Daniels, A. W. and Otis, J. L. 1950: A method for analysing employment interviews. *Personnel Psychology*, 3, 425–44.

Dawis, R. V. 1991: Vocational interests, values and preferences. In M. D. Dunnette and L. M. Hough (eds), *Handbook of Industrial and Organisational Psychology*, vol. 2. Palo Alto, Calif.: Consulting Psychologists Press, 833–72.

Deary, I. J. 2000: *Looking Down on Human Intelligence: from Psychometrics to the Brain*. Oxford: Oxford University Press.

——, Whalley, L. J., Lemmon, H., Starr, J. S. and Crawford, J. R. 2000: The stability of individual differences in mental ability from childhood to old-age: follow-up of the 1932 Scottish Mental Survey. *Intelligence*, 28, 49–55.

De Witte, K. 1989: Recruiting and advertising. In P. Herriot (ed.), *Assessment and Selection in Organisations*. Chichester: Wiley.

Dollard, J. and Miller, N. 1950: *Personality and Psychotherapy: an Analysis in Terms of Learning, Thinking and Culture*. New York: McGraw-Hill.

Douthitt, S. S., Eby, L. T. and Simon, S. A. 1999: Diversity of life experiences: the development and validation of graphical measure of receptiveness to dissimilar others. *International Journal of Selection and Assessment*, 7(2), 112–25.

Downs, S. 1973: *Trainability Assessments: Sewing Machinists*. Research Paper SL6, Industrial Training Research Unit, Cambridge.

—— 1989: Job sample and trainability tests. In P. Herriot (ed.), *Handbook of Assessment in Organisations*. Chichester: Wiley.

Drakerley, R. J. 1989: Biographical data. In P. Herriot (ed.), *Handbook of Assessment in Organisations*. Chichester: Wiley.

Dreher, G. F. and Sackett, P. R. 1983: *Perspectives on Staffing and Selection*. Homewood, Ill.: Richard D. Irwin.

Dulewicz, V. 1995: A validation of Belbin's team roles from 16PF and OPQ using bosses' rating of competence. *Journal of Occupational and Organisational Psychology*, 68, 81–91.

Dunnette, M. D. 1963: A note on the criterion. *Journal of Applied Psychology*, 47, 251–4.

——, McCartney, J., Carlson, H. C. and Kirchner, W. K. 1962: A study of faking behaviour on a forced choice self description checklist. *Personnel Psychology*, 15, 13–24.

Earl, J., Bright, J. E. H. R. and Adams, A. 1998: 'In my opinion': What gets graduates' résumés shortlisted? *Australian Journal of Career Development*, 7(1), 15–19.

Easterbrook, J. A. 1959: The effect of emotion on cue utilisation and the organisation of behaviour. *Psychological Review*, 66, 183–201.

Edwards, A. L. 1957: *The Social Desirability Variable in Personality Assessment and Research*. New York: Dryden.

Edwards, J. R. 1982: Language attitudes and their implications among English speakers. In E. B. Ryan and H. Giles (eds), *Attitudes Towards Language Variation*. London: Arnold.

Elkins, T. J. and Phillips, J. S. 2000: Job context, selection decision outcome, and perceived fairness of selection tests: biodata as an illustrative case. *Journal of Applied Psychology*, 85(3), 479–84.

Elmes, D. G., Kantowitz, B. H. and Roediger, H. L. 1985: *Research Methods in Psychology*. St Paul, Minn.: West Publishing.

Equal Opportunities Commission 1988: *Avoiding Test Bias in Selection Testing: Guidance for Employers*. Manchester: EOC.

Encyclopaedia Britannica 2000: *Encyclopaedia Britannica: Multimedia Edition*. Chicago: Encyclopaedia Britannica.

Enzer, I. 1994: *The Five Factor Model of Personality and the Measurement of Occupational Interests in a Managerial Group*. Unpublished PhD thesis, UMIST, Manchester.

ERI 2000: Electronic Recruiting Index: performance and emergence of middle market. See www.interbiznet.com/2000.eri

Erikson, E. H. 1982: *The Life Cycle Completed: a Review*. New York: Norton.

Eyde, L. D. and Kowal, D. M. 1987: Computerised test interpretation services: ethical and professional concerns regarding U.S. producers and users. *Applied Psychology: an International Review*, 36(3/4), 401–7.

Eysenck, H. J. 1967: *The Biological Basis of Personality*. Springfield: Thomas.

—— 1985: *Decline and Fall of the Freudian Empire*. New York: Viking.

—— 1986: The theory of intelligence and the psychophysiology of cognition. In R. J. Sternberg (ed.), *Advances in the Psychology of Human Intelligence*, vol. 3. Hillsdale, NJ: Lawrence Erlbaum.

—— and Eysenck, S. B. G. 1991: *Manual for the Eysenck Personality Scales*. Sevenoaks: Hodder & Stoughton.

Eysenck, M. 1998: *Psychology: an Integrated Approach*. London: Longman.

Eysenck, M. W. and Calvo, M. G. 1992: Anxiety and performance: the processing efficiency theory. *Cognition and Emotion*, 6, 409–34.

Feather, N. T. 1996: Values, deservingness and attitudes towards high achievers: research on tall poppies. In C. Seligman, J. M. Olsen and M. P. Zanna (eds), *The Psychology of Values: the Ontario Symposium on Values*, vol. 8. Hillsdale, NJ: Lawrence Erlbaum.

—— and Newton, J. W. 1982: Values, expectations and the prediction of social action: an expectancy-value analysis. *Motivation and Emotion*, 6(3), 217–43.

Feltham, R. 1989: Validity of a police assessment centre: a 19 year follow-up. *Journal of Occupational Psychology*, 61, 129–52.

Fernandez, E. and Boyle, G. J. 1996: Meta-analytic procedure and interpretation of treatment outcome and test validity for the practitioner psychologist. In M. Smith and V. Sutherland (eds), *Professional Issues in Selection and Assessment*. Chichester: Wiley.

Fine, S. A. and Wiley, W. W. 1971: *An Introduction to Functional Job Analysis: a Scaling of Selected Tasks from the Welfare Field*. Washington, DC: Upjohn Institute for Employment Research.

Fishbein, M. and Middlestadt, S. 1995: Noncognitive effects on attitude formation and change. *Journal of Consulting Psychology*, 4, 181–202.

—— and —— 1997: A striking lack of evidence for non-belief based attitude formation and change – a response to five commentaries. *Journal of Consulting Psychology*, 6, 107–15.

Fletcher, C. A. 1985: *Inventories Interviews and Insight*. Occupational Psychology Conference. Leicester: British Psychological Society.

Fletcher, R. 1991: *Science, Ideology and the Media*. Somerset, NJ: Transaction Publishers.

—— 1993: The Miss Conway story. *The Psychologist*, May, 214–15.

Flynn, J. R. 1984: The mean IQ of Americans: massive gains 1932 to 1978. *Psychological Bulletin*, 101, 171–91.

—— 1987: Race and IQ: Jensen's case refuted. In S. Modgil and C. Modgil (eds), *Arthur Jensen: Consensus and Controversy*. New York: Falmer Press.

Forbes, R. J. and Jackson, P. R. 1980: Non-verbal behaviour and the outcome of selection interviews. *Journal of Occupational Psychology*, 53, 65–72.

Forer, B. R. 1949: The fallacy of personal validation: a classroom demonstration of gullibility. *Journal of Abnormal and Social Psychology*, 44, 118–23.

Fox, J. 1970: *Interests and Occupations: Supplementary Manual*. Cambridge: Careers Research and Advice Centre.

Francis, R. D. 1999: *Ethics for Psychologists: a Handbook*. Leicester: British Psychological Society.

Frearson, W. M. and Eysenck, H. J. 1986: Intelligence, reaction time and a new 'odd man out' paradigm. *Personality and Individual Differences*, 7, 808–17.

Frederickson, N., Saunders, D. R. and Wand, B. 1957: The 'inbasket test'. *Psychological Monographs*, 483, whole issue.

Freeman, D. 1996: *Margaret Mead and the Heretic: the Making and Unmaking of an Anthropological Myth*. Harmondsworth: Penguin.

—— 1998: *The Fateful Hoaxing of Margaret Mead: a Historical Analysis of her Samoan Researches*. Boulder, Co.: Westview Press.

Freud, S. 1949: *An Outline of Psychoanalysis*. New York: Norton.

Fromm, E. 2001: *The Fear of Freedom*. London: Routledge.

Fulker, D. W. 1979: The nature and measure of heredity. In H. J. Eysenck (ed.), *The Structure and Measurement of Intelligence*. New York: Springer-Verlag.

Funder, D. C. 1991: Global traits: a neo-Allportian approach to personality. *Psychological Science*, 2, 31–9.

Furnham, A. 1992: *Personality at Work: the Role of Individual Differences in the Workplace*. London: Routledge.

Gallaher, P. E. 1992: Individual differences in non-verbal behaviour: dimensions of style. *Journal of Personality and Social Psychology*, 63, 133–45.

Ganster, D. C., Hennessy, H. W. and Luthans, F. 1983: Social desirability of response effects: three alternative models. *Academy of Management Journal*, 26, 321–31.

Ganzach, Y., Kluger, A. N. R. and Klayman, N. 2000: Making decisions from an interview: expert measurement and mechanical combination. *Personnel Psychology*, 53, 1–20.

Gardner, H., Kornhaber, M. L. and Wake, W. K. 1995: *Intelligence: Multiple Perspectives*. Fort Worth: Harcourt Brace.

Gati, L. 1991: The structure of vocational interests. *Psychological Bulletin*, 109, 209–24.

Gaugler, B. B. and Thornton, G. C. 1989: Number of assessment centre dimensions as a determinant of assessor accuracy. *Journal of Applied Psychology*, 74, 611–18.

—— and —— 1990: Matching job previews to individual applicants' needs. *Psychological Reports*, 66, 643–52.

——, Rosenthal, D. B., Thornton, G. C. and Bentson, C. 1987: Meta-analysis of assessment centre validity. *Journal of Applied Psychology*, 72, 493–511.

Gauquelin, M., Gauquelin, F. and Eysenck, S. 1979: Personality and the position of planets at birth: an empirical study. *Journal of Social and Clinical Psychology*, 18, 71–5.

Ghiselli, E. E. 1966: *The Validity of Occupational Attitude Tests*. New York: Wiley.

Giddens, A. 1993: *New Rules of Sociological Methods: a Positive Critique of Interpretative Sociologies*. Cambridge: Polity Press.

Gillie, O. 1976: Crucial data was faked by eminent psychologist. *Sunday Times*, 24 October.

Gilliland, S. W. 1993: The perceived fairness of selection systems: an organisational justice perspective. *Academy of Management Review*, 18, 694–734.

—— 1994: Effects of procedural and distributive justice on reactions to a selection system. *Journal of Applied Psychology*, 79(5), 691–701.

Glass, G. V. 1976: Primary, secondary and meta-analytic research. *Educational Researcher*, 5, 3–8.

——, McGaw, B. and Smith, M. L. 1981: *Meta-analysis in Social Research*. Beverly Hills, Calif.: Sage.

Goffin, R. D., Rothstein, M. G. and Johnson, N. G. 1996: Personality testing and the assessment centre: incremental validity for management selection. *Journal of Applied Psychology*, 81(6), 746–56.

Goldstein, I. L. 1971: The application blank: How honest are applicant responses? *Journal of Applied Psychology*, 55, 491–2.

Gordon, L. V. 1992: *Survey of Personal Values (SPV)*. Maidenhead: McGraw-Hill.

—— 1993: *Survey of Interpersonal Values (SIV)*. Maidenhead: McGraw-Hill.

Griffit, W. and Jackson, T. 1970: Influence of information about ability and non-ability on personnel selection decisions. *Psychological Reports*, 27, 959–62.

Guilford, J. P. 1967: *The Nature of Human Intelligence*. New York: McGraw-Hill.

—— and Fruchter, B. 1978: *Fundamental Statistics in Psychology and Education*. New York: McGraw-Hill.

——, Christensen, P. R., Bond, N. A. and Sutton, M. A. 1954: A factor analytic study of human interests. *Psychological Monographs*, 68(4), whole issue.

Guion, R. M. 1965: *Personnel Testing*. New York: McGraw-Hill.

Guion, R. M. and Cranny, C. J. 1982: A method of concurrent and predictive designs: a critical reanalysis. *Journal of Applied Psychology*, 67, 239–44.

Gulliksen, H. 1950: *Theory of Mental Tests*. New York: Wiley.

Gustafsson, J. E. 1984: A unifying model for the structure of mental abilities. *Intelligence*, 8, 179–203.

Hackman, J. R. and Oldham, G. R. 1976: Motivation through the design of work: test of a theory. *Organisational Behaviour and Human Performance*, 16, 250–79.

Haefner, J. E. 1977: Race, age, sex and competence as factors in employer selection of the disadvantaged. *Journal of Applied Psychology*, 62(2), 199–202.

Haier, R. J. 1993: Cerebral glucose metabolism and intelligence. In P. A. Vernon (ed.), *Biological Approaches to the Study of Human Intelligence*. Norwood, NJ: Ablex.

Hall, C. S. 1938: The inheritance of emotionality. *Sigma Xi Quarterly*, 26, 17–27.

Halperin, K., Snyder, C. R., Shenkel, R. J. and Houston, B. K. 1976: Effects of source status and message favourability on acceptance of personality feedback. *Journal of Applied Psychology*, 61, 85–8.

Handyside, J. D. 1989: On ratings and rating scales. In P. Herriot (ed.), *Assessment and Selection in Organisations*. Chichester: Wiley.

Hanson, J. C. and Campbell, D. P. 1985: *Manual for the SVIB*, 4th edn. Stanford: Stanford University Press.

Harn, T. J. and Thornton, G. C. 1986: Impact of recruiter counselling behaviours and job related information on engineering applicants in campus interviews. Unpublished manuscript, Colorado State University, Fort Collins.

Harris, M. M. 1998: The structured interview: What constructs are being measured? In R. Eder and M. Harris (eds), *The Employment Interview: Theory, Research and Practice*. Thousand Oaks, Calif.: Sage.

Harris, W. G. 1987: Computer-based test interpretations: some development and application issues. *Applied Psychology: an International Review*, 36(3/4), 237–47.

Hartshorne, H. and May, M. A. 1928: *Studies in Deceit*. New York: Macmillan.

Harvey-Cook, J. E. and Taffler, R. J. 2000: Biodata in professional entry-level selection: statistical scoring of common format applications. *Journal of Occupational and Organisational Psychology*, 73, 103–18.

Hathaway, S. R. and McKinley, J. C. 1940: The Multiphasic Personality Inventory: construction of the schedule. *Journal of Psychology*, 10, 249–54.

Hearnshaw, L. S. 1979: *Cyril Burt: Psychologist*. London: Hodder & Stoughton.

Herriot, P. (ed.) 1989a: *Assessment and Selection in Organisations*. Chichester: Wiley.

—— 1989b: Selection as a social process. In J. M. Smith and I. T. Robertson (eds), *Advances in Selection and Assessment*. Chichester: Wiley.

—— 1989c: The selection interview. In P. Herriot (ed.), *Assessment and Selection in Organisations*. Chichester: Wiley.

—— 2002: Selection and self: selection as a social process. *European Journal of Work and Organisational Psychology*, 11(4), 385–402.

Hewstone, M. and Giles, H. 1986: Social groups and social stereotypes in inter-group communication: a review. In W. B. Grudykunst (ed.), *Intergroup Communication*. London: Arnold.

Hoare, S., Day, A. and Smith, J. M. 1998: An alternative selection instrument: the development and evaluation of situational inventories. *Selection and Development Review*, 14(6), 3–8.

Hoffman, P. J. 1960: The paramorphic representation of clinical judgement. *Psychological Bulletin*, 57(2), 116–31.

Hofstede, G. 1984: *Culture's Consequences*. Thousand Oaks, Calif.: Sage.

—— 1994: *Values Survey Module, 1994 Manual*. Maastricht: University of Limberg.

Hogan, R. and Hogan, J. 1987: *Motives, Values, Preferences Inventory (MVPI)*. Tunbridge Wells: Psychological Consultancy Limited.

—— and —— 1992a: *Hogan Personality Inventory: Manual*. Tunbridge Wells: Psychological Consultancy Limited.

—— and —— 1992b: *Manual for the Motives, Values, Preferences Inventory* (UK adaptation by G. Hyde and G. Trickey). Tunbridge Wells: Psychological Consultancy Limited.

Hogan, R. and Hogan, J. 1996: *Hogan Personality Inventory*. Tunbridge Wells: Hogan Assessment Systems and Psychological Consultancy.

Hogan, J. and Quigley, A. M. 1996: Physical ability testing for employment. In R. S. Barrett (ed.), *Fair Employment Strategies in Human Resource Management*. Westport, Conn.: Quorum Books.

—— and Rybicki, S. L. 1998: *Performance Improvement Characteristics Job Analysis*. Tulsa, Okla.: Hogan Assessment Systems.

Holland, J. L. 1976: Vocational preferences. In M. D. Dunnette (ed.), *Handbook of Industrial and Organisational Psychology*. Chicago: Rand McNally.

—— 1985: *Self-directed Search: Professional Manual*. Odessa, Fl.: Psychological Assessment Resources.

—— 1996: Exploring careers with a typology. *American Psychologist*, 51, 394–406.

Hollingworth, H. L. 1929: *Vocational Psychology and Character Analysis*. New York: Appleton.

Horn, J. L. and Cattell, R. B. 1966: Refinement and test of the theory of fluid and crystallised general intelligences. *Journal of Educational Psychology*, 57, 253–70.

Hornby, D. and Thomas, R. 1989: Towards a better standard of management. *Personnel Management*, 21(1), 52–5.

Horney, K. 1939: *New Ways in Psychoanalysis*. New York: Norton.

Hough, L. M. and Oswald, F. L. 2000: Personnel selection: looking towards the future – remembering the past. *Annual Review of Psychology*, 51, 631–4.

—— , Eton, N. K., Dunnette, M. D., Kamp, J. D. and McCloy, R. A. 1990: Criteria-related variables of personality constructs and the effects of response distortion on those validities. *Journal of Applied Psychology*, 75, 581–93.

Howard, A. and Choi, M. 2000: How do you assess a manager's decision-making abilities? The use of situational inventories. *International Journal of Selection and Assessment*, 8(2), 85–7.

Howe, M. J. A. 1997: *IQ in Question*. London: Sage.

Huang, T. 2000: Human resource management practices at subsidiaries of multinational corporations and local firms in Taiwan. *International Journal of Selection and Assessment*, 8(1), 22–33.

Huba, G. J. 1987: On probabilistic computer-based test interpretations and other expert systems. *Applied Psychology: an International Review*, 36(3/4), 357–73.

Huff, D. 1961: *Score: the Strategy of Taking Tests*. Harmondsworth: Penguin.

Huffcutt, A. I., Roth, P. L. and McDaniel, M. A. 1996: A meta-analytic investigation of cognitive ability in employment interview evaluations: moderating characteristics and implications for incremental validity. *Journal of Applied Psychology*, 81, 459–73.

Hunt, S. T. 1996: Generic work behaviour: an investigation into the dimensions of entry-level hourly job performance. *Personnel Psychology*, 49, 51–83.

Hunter, J. E. and Hirsch, H. R. 1987: Applications of meta-analysis. In C. L. Cooper and I. T. Robertson (eds), *International Review of Industrial and Organisational Psychology*, 2, 321–57.

—— and Hunter, R. F. 1984: Validity and utility of alternative predictors of job performance. *Psychological Bulletin*, 96, 72–92.

—— and Schmidt, F. L. 1989: Meta-analysis: factors and theories. In J. M. Smith and I. R. Robertson (eds), *Advances in Selection and Assessment*. Chichester: Wiley.

—— , —— and Jackson, G. B. 1982: *Meta-analysis: Cumulating Research Findings across Studies*. Beverly Hills, Calif.: Sage.

—— , —— , Rauchenberger, J. M. R. and Jayne, M. E. A. 2000: Intelligence, motivation and job performance. In C. L. Cooper (ed.), *Industrial and Organisational Psychology: Linking Theory with Practice*. Oxford: Blackwell.

Ivancevich, J. M. 1983: Contrast effects in performance-reward practices. *Academy of Management Journal*, 26, 465–7.

Jackson, D. N. 1977: *Jackson Vocational Interest Survey Manual*. Port Huron, Mich.: Research Psychologists Press.

—— 1985: Computer-based personality testing. *Computers in Human Behaviour*, 1, 255–64.

Jacobs, A. and Barron, R. 1968: Falsification of the Guilford–Zimmerman Temperament Survey: making a poor impression. *Psychological Reports*, 23, 1271–7.

Jarvis, W. B. G. and Petty, R. 1996: The need to evaluate. *Journal of Personality and Social Psychology*, 70, 172–94.

Jenkins, J. G. 1946: Validity for what? *Journal of Consulting Psychology*, 10, 93–8.

Jensen, A. R. 1980: *Bias in Mental Testing*. New York: Free Press.

—— 1982: Reaction time and psychometric 'g'. In H. J. Eysenck (ed.), *A Model for Intelligence*. Berlin: Springer-Verlag.

—— 1998: *The G Factor: the Science of Mental Ability*. Westport, Conn.: Praeger.

—— and Sinah, S. N. 1993: Physical correlates of human intelligence. In P. A. Vernon (ed.), *Biological Approaches to the Study of Human Intelligence*. Norwood, NJ: Ablex.

Johansson, E. 1992: *Computerised Testing 'Cytech': Enlistment of Conscripts*. Report FOA PM 55:155 (in Swedish). Karlstad: National Defence Research Establishment.

Jones, M. R. (ed.) 1955: *Nebraska Symposium on Motivation*. Lincoln: University of Nebraska Press.

Johnson, C. E., Wood, R. and Blinkhorn, S. F. 1988: Spuriouser and spuriouser; the use of ipsative personality tests. *Journal of Occupational Psychology*, 61(2), 153–62.

Joynson, R. B. 1989: *The Burt Affair*. London: Routledge.

Jung, C. G. 1977: *Jung: Collected Works*. Princeton: Princeton University Press.

Kallman, F. J. 1951: Twin studies in relation to adjustive problems of man. *Transactions of the New York Academy of Science*, 13, 270.

Karas, M. and West, J. 1999: Construct-oriented biodata development for a selection to a differentiated performance domain. *International Journal of Selection and Assessment*, 7(2), 86–96.

Keenan, A. 1983: Where application forms mislead. *Personnel Management*, 15(2), 40–3.

—— 1989: Selection interviewing. In C. L. Cooper and I. T. Robertson (eds), *International Review of Industrial and Organisational Psychology*. Chichester: Wiley.

Kelly, G. A. 1955: *The Psychology of Personal Constructs*. New York: Norton.

Kellett, D., McCahon, S. and James, J. 1991: Evaluation of personality questionnaire reports. *European Work and Organisational Psychology*, 1(1), 196–210.

Kenrick, D. T. and Funder, D. C. 1988: Profiting from controversy: lessons from the person situation debate. *American Psychologist*, 43, 23–34.

Kerr, S. and Davenport, H. 1989: AC or DC? The experience of development centres. *Proceedings of BPS Symposium*. Bletchley: British Telecom.

Klienmuntz, B. 1984: The scientific study of clinical judgement in psychology and medicine. *Clinical Psychological Review*, 4, 111–26.

Klimoski, R. J. and Strickland, W. J. 1977: Assessment centres – valid or merely prescient? *Personnel Psychology*, 30, 353–61.

Kline, P. 1986: *A Handbook of Test Construction: Introduction to Psychometric Design*. London: Methuen.

—— 1991: *Intelligence: the Psychometric View*. London: Routledge.

Klinger, D. E., Johnson, J. H. and Williams, T. A. 1976: Strategies in the evaluation of an on-line computer-assisted unit for intake assessment of mental health patients. *Behaviour Research Methods and Instrumentation*, 8, 95–100.

Koestner, R. and McClelland, D. C. 1990: Perspectives on competence motivation. In L. A. Pervin (ed.), *Handbook of Personality: Theory and Research*. New York: Guilford Press.

Kohlberg, L. 1976: Moral stages and moralization: the cognitive–developmental perspective. In T. Lickona (ed.), *Moral Development and Behaviour: Theory, Research and Social Issues*. New York: Holt, Rinehart, & Winston.

Koksal, F. 1992: *Anxiety and Narrowing of Visual Attention*. Unpublished manuscript, Bogazici University, Istanbul, Turkey.

Konovsky, M. A. and Cropanzano, R. 1993: Justice considerations in employee drug testing. In R. Cropanzano (ed.), *Justice in the Workplace: Approaching Fairness in Human Resource Management*. Hillsdale, NJ: Lawrence Erlbaum.

Krahe, B. 1989: Faking personality profiles on a standard personality inventory. *Personality and Individual Differences*, 10, 437–43.

Kroeck, K. G. and Magnusen, K. O. 1997: Employer and job candidate reactions to video conference job interviewing. *International Journal of Selection and Assessment*, 5(2), 137–42.

Krug, S. E. 1981: *Interpreting 16PF Profiles*. Champaign, Ill.: Institute for Personality and Ability Testing.

Kruglanski, A. W., Baldwin, M. W. and Towson, M. J. 1983: The lay epistimic in attribution making. In M. Hewston (ed.), *Attribution Theory: Social and Functional Extensions*. Oxford: Blackwell.

Kuder, G. F. 1954: Expected developments in interest and personality inventories. *Psychometrica*, 2, 151–60.

—— 1960: *Administrators' Manual for the Kuder Preference Record*. Chicago: Science Research Associates.

Lafferty, J. C. 1973: *Life Styles Inventory (LSI)*. Reading: Verax Limited.

Landis, R. S., Fogli, L. and Goldberg, E. 1998: Future-oriented job analysis: a description of the process and its organisational implications. *International Journal of Selection and Assessment*, 6(3), 192–7.

Landy, F. J. 1980: Stamp collecting vs science. *American Psychologist*, November, 1183–92.

—— 1985: *Psychology of Work Behavior*. Homewood, Ill.: Dorsey Press.

—— and Farr, J. L. 1980: Performance rating. *Psychological Bulletin*, 87, 72–107.

—— and Rastegrary, H. 1989: Criteria for selection. In M. Smith and I. T. Robertson (eds), *Advances in Selection and Assessment*. Chichester: Wiley.

Lanyon, R. I. 1987: Personality assessment. *Annual Review of Psychology*, 35, 667–707.

Latham, G. P. and Finnegan, B. J. 1993: Perceived practicality of unstructured, patterned and situational interviews. In H. Schuler, J. L. Farr and M. Smith (eds), *Personnel Selection and Assessment: Individual and Organisational Perspectives*. Hillsdale, NJ: Lawrence Erlbaum.

—— and Sari, L. M. 1984: Do people do what they say? Further studies on the situational interview. *Journal of Applied Psychology*, 69, 567–73.

—— and Wexley, K. N. 1977: Behavioural observation scales for performance appraisal purposes. *Personnel Psychology*, 30, 225–68.

——, Sari, L. M., Pursell, E. D. and Campion, M. A. 1980: The situational interview. *Journal of Applied Psychology*, 65, 422–47.

Lawshe, C. H. 1952: What can industrial psychology do for small business: employee selection? *Personnel Psychology*, 5, 31–4.

——, Bolda, R. A., Brune, R. L. and Auclair, G. 1958: Expectancy charts II; their theoretical development. *Personnel Psychology*, 11, 545–59.

Lay, C. H. and Burton, G. F. 1968: Perception of the personality of the hesitant speaker. *Perceptual and Motor Skills*, 26, 951–6.

Leck, J. D., Saunders, D. M. and Charbonneau, M. 1996: Affirmative action programmes: and organisational justice perspective. *Journal of Organisational Behaviour*, 17(1), 79–89.

Ledvinka, J., Markos, V. H. and Ladd, R. T. 1982: Long-range impact of fair selection standards on minority employment. *Journal of Applied Psychology*, 67(1), 18–36.

Levinson, D. J., Darrow, C. N., Klein, E. B., Levinson, M. L. and McKee, B. 1978: *The Seasons of Man's Life*. New York: Knopf.

Lewin, A. Y. and Zwany, A. 1976: Peer nominations: a model, literature critique and a paradigm for research. *Personnel Psychology*, 29, 423–47.

Lindley, P. (ed.) 2001: *Review of Personality Assessment Instruments (Level B) for Use in Occupational Settings*, 2nd edn. Leicester: British Psychological Society.

Locke, A. E. 1976: The nature and causes of job satisfaction. In M. D. Dunnette (ed.), *Handbook of Industrial and Organisational Psychology*. Chicago: Rand McNally.

Lombroso, C. 1870: *Studi clinici ed esperimentali sulla natura, causa e terapia della pellagra*. Milano: G. Bernardoni.

Lopez, F. M. 1966: *Evaluating Executive Decision Making*. New York: American Management Association.

Lord, F. M. 1980: *Applications of Item Response Theory to Practical Testing Problems*. Hillsdale, NJ: Lawrence Erlbaum.

—— and Novick, M. R. 1968: *Statistical Theories of Mental Test Scores*. New York: Addison-Wesley.

Lord, W. 1998a: *16PF 5 Overcoming Obstacles to Interpretation*. Windsor: Assessment and Selection in Employment.

—— 1998b: *16PF 5 Personality in Practice*. Windsor: Assessment and Selection in Employment.

Mabe, P. A. and West, S. G. 1982: Validity of self-evaluation of ability: a review and meta-analysis. *Journal of Applied Psychology*, 67, 280–96.

Mackenzie-Davey, D. and Harris, M. 1982: *Judging People*. London: McGraw-Hill.

Mackintosh, N. J. 1998: *IQ and Human Intelligence*. Oxford: Oxford University Press.

MacLeod, C. and Donnellan, A. M. 1993: Individual differences in anxiety and the restriction of work-ing memory capacity. *Personality and Individual Differences*, 15, 163–73.

Magnusson, D. and Torestad, B. 1993: A holistic view of personality: a model revisited. *Annual Review of Psychology*, 44, 427–52.

Manning, E. J. 1968: Personal Validation: a replication of Forer's study. *Psychological Reports*, 23(1), 181–2.

Mardberg, B. and Carlstedt, B. 1998: Swedish enlistment battery (SEB): construct validity and latent vari-able estimation of cognitive abilities by the CAT–SEB. *International Journal of Selection and Assessment*, 6(2), 110–14.

Matarazzo, J. D. 1983: Editorial on computerised psychological testing. *Science*, 22 July, 221, 223.

—— 1986: Computerised clinical psychological test interpretations: plus all and no sigma. *American Psychologist*, 41(1), 1424.

Mathews, B. P. and Redman, T. 1998: Managerial recruitment advertisements – just how market oriented are they? *International Journal of Selection and Assessment*, 6(4), 240–8.

Matthews, G., Stanton, N., Graham, N. C. and Brimelow, C. 1990: A factor analysis of the scales of the Occupational Personality Questionnaire. *Individual Differences*, 11(6), 591–6.

Maurer, T., Solamon, J. and Troxtel, D. 1998: Relationship of coaching with performance in situational employment interviews. *Journal of Applied Psychology*, 83, 128–36.

Mayfield, E. C. 1964: The selection interview: a re-evaluation of published research. *Personnel Psychology*, 17, 239–60.

McAdams, D. P. 1990: *The Person: an Introduction to Personality Psychology*. San Diego, Calif.: Harcourt Brace Jovanovich.

McClelland, D. C. 1976: *The Achieving Society*. New York: Irvington Publishers.

——, Atkinson, J. W., Clarke, R. A. and Lowell, E. L. 1953: *The Achievement Motive*. New York: Appleton-Century-Crofts.

McCormick, E. J. 1976: Job and task analysis. In M. D. Dunnette (ed.), *Handbook of Industrial and Organisational Psychology*. Chicago: Rand McNally.

——, Cunningham, J. W. and Thornton, G. C. 1972: The prediction of job requirements by a struc-tured job analysis procedure. *Personnel Psychology*, 26, 431–40.

——, Jeanneret, P. R. and Mecham, R. C. 1972: Case study of job characteristics and job dimensions as based on the position analysis questionnaire. *Journal of Applied Psychology*, 56, 347–68.

McCrae, R. R. and Costa, P. T. 1990: *Personality in Adulthood*. New York: Guilford Press.

McDaniel, M. A., Whetzel, D. L., Schmidt, F. L. and Maurer, S. D. 1994: The validity of the employ-ment interview: a comprehensive review and meta-analysis. *Journal of Applied Psychology*, 79, 599–616.

McDonald, K. 2003: Psychoanalysis in its death throes: the moral and intellectual legacy of a pseudo sci-ence. See www.csulb.edu/~kmacd/CrewsFreud.htm

McGrue, M. 1997: The democracy of the genes. *Nature*, 388, 417–18.

——, Bouchard, T. J., Iaconao, W. G. and Lykken, D. T. 1993: Behavioural genetics of cognitive abil-ity: a life-span perspective. In R. Plomin and G. E. McClearn (eds), *Nature, Nurture and Psychology*. Washington, DC: American Psychological Association.

McIntyre, S., Moberg, D. J. and Posner, B. Z. 1980: Preferential treatment in selection decisions accord-ing to sex and race. *Academy of Management Journal*, 23(4), 738–49.

McKenzie Davey, D. and Harris, M. 1982: *Judging People*. London: McGraw-Hill.

McReynolds, P. 1968: *Advances in Psychological Assessment*. Palo Alto, Calif.: Science and Behavior Books.

Mead, M. 1928: *Coming of Age in Samoa*. Harmondsworth: Penguin.

—— 1935: *Sex and Temperament in Three Cultures*. New York: Morrow.

Medawar, P. B. 1975: Victims of psychiatry. *New York Review of Books*, 23 January, 17.

Meehl, P. E. 1954: *Clinical Versus Statistical Prediction: a Theoretical Analysis and Review of the Evidence*. Minneapolis: University of Minnesota Press.

—— 1956: Wanted – a good cookbook. *American Psychologist*, 11, 262–72.

Messick, S. 1975: The standard problem: meaning of values in measurements and evaluation. *American Psychologist*, 30, 955–66.

—— 1980: Test validity and the ethics of assessment. *American Psychologist*, 35, 1012–27.

Meyer, H. H. 1980: Self appraisal of job performance. *Personnel Psychology*, 33, 291–5.

Miller, M. 1996: The invalidity of objective personality testing: a rejoinder to Mark Parkinson. *Selection and Development Review*, 12(5), 1–2.

Miller, K. M., Rothwell, J. W. and Tyler, B. 1994: *Rothwell–Miller Interest Blank*. London: Miller & Tyler.

Mintzberg, H. H. 1973: *The Nature of Managerial Work*. New York: Harper & Row.

Mischel, W. 1968: *Personality and Assessment*. New York: Wiley.

Moloney, D. P., Bouchard, T. and Segal, N. 1991: A genetic and environmental analysis of the vocational interests of monozygotic and dizygotic twins reared apart. *Journal of Vocational Behaviour*, 39, 76–109.

Monahan, C. J. and Muchinsky, P. M. 1983: Three decades of personnel selection research. *Journal of Occupational Psychology*, 56(3), 215–25.

Mondragon, N. and Thornton, G. C. 1988: *Effects of Affirmative Programs of Perceptions of Organisations among White Male College Students*. Proceedings of the 1988 Annual Conference of the Council on Employee Responsibilities and Rights, Virginia Beach.

Moreland, K. L. 1987: Computer-based test interpretations: advice to the consumer. *Applied Psychology: an International Review*, 36(2/4), 385–99.

Morrisby, M. and Fox, G. D. 1995: *Manual for the Morrisby Profile*, 2nd edn. Hemel Hempstead: Educational and Industrial Test Services Limited.

Moscoso, S. 2000: Selection interview: a review of validity evidence, adverse impact and applicant reactions. *International Journal of Selection and Assessment*, 8(4), 237–47.

Mosel, J. N. and Goheen, H. W. 1959: Validity of employment recommendation questionnaires in personnel selection. *Personnel Psychology*, 11, 481–90.

Moses, J. L. and Byham, W. C. 1977: *Applying the Assessment Centre Method*. New York: Pergamon Press.

Mosher, D. L. 1965: Approval motive and acceptance of 'fake' personality test interpretations which differ in favorability. *Psychological Reports*, 17, 395–402.

Mount, M. K., Witt, L. A. and Barrick, M. R. 2000: Incremental validity of empirically keyed biodata scales over GMA and the five factor personality constructs. *Personnel Psychology*, 53, 299–323.

Munro Frazer, J. 1966: *Employment Interviewing*. London: Macdonald & Evans.

Murphy, K. R. 2000: Impact of assessments of validity generalisation and situational specificity on the science and practice of personnel selection. *International Journal of Selection and Assessment*, 8(4), 194–215.

Murray, H. A. 1938: *Explorations in Personality*. London: Oxford University Press.

Myers, I. B. and McCaulley, M. H. 1985: *Manual: a Guide to the Development and Use of the Myers–Briggs Type Indicator*. Palo Alto, Calif.: Consulting Psychologists Press.

Nader, K., Bechara, A. and van der Kooy, D. 1997: Neurobiological constraints on behavioural models of motivation. *Annual Review of Psychology*, 48, 85–114.

Nevid, J. S. 1983: Comments: hopelessness, social desirability and construct validity. *Journal of Consulting and Clinical Psychology*, 51, 139–40.

Nevo, B. 1985: Face validity revisited. *Journal of Educational Measurement*, 22, 287–93.

—— and Sfez, J. 1985: Examinees' feedback questionnaires. *Assessment and Evaluation in Higher Education*, 10, 236–49.

Newall, S. 2000: Selection and assessment in the knowledge era. *International Journal of Selection and Assessment*, 8(1), 1–6.

Newman, J. M. 1978: Discrimination recruitment: an empirical analysis. *Industrial and Labour Relations Review*, 32, 15–23.

Norman, W. T. 1963: Towards an adequate taxonomy of personality attributes. *Journal of Abnormal and Social Psychology*, 66, 574–83.

Norvick, M. R. and Lewis, C. 1967: Coefficient alpha and the reliability of composite measurements. *Psychometrika*, 32, 1–13.

Nunnally, J. C. 1978: *Psychometric Theory*. New York: McGraw-Hill.

O'Dell, J. W. 1972: P. T. Barnum explores the computer. *Journal of Consulting and Clinical Psychology*, 38(2), 270–3.

Office of Strategic Services 1948: *Assessment of Men: Selection of Personnel for the Office of Strategic Services*. Oxford: Rinehart.

O'Reilly, C. A. 1991: Organisational behaviour: where we've been, where we're going. *Annual Review of Psychology*, 42, 427–58.

Ones, D. S., Viswesvaran, C. and Reiss, A. D. 1996: Role of social desirability in personality testing for personnel selection: a red herring. *Journal of Applied Psychology*, 78, 679–703.

Pace, L. A. and Schoenfeldt, L. F. 1977: Legal concerns in the use of weighted applications. *Personnel Psychology*, 30, 159–66.

Parkinson, M. 1996: Time for T: observations on objective personality testing. *Selection and Development Review*, 12(1), 1–3.

—— and Fox, G. 1997: Objective personality testing: a valuable tool. *Selection and Development Review*, 13(1), 10–12.

Patterson, F. and Silvester, J. 1998: Counter measures. *People Management*, April, 46–8.

Paulhus, D. L. 1984: Two-component models of social desirable responding. *Journal of Personality and Social Psychology*, 46, 598–609.

Pearn, M. and Kandola, R. 1988: *Job Analysis: a Practical Guide for Managers*. Wimbledon: Institute of Personnel and Development.

Peters, T. J. and Waterman, R. H. 1982: *In Search of Excellence*. New York: Harper & Row.

Pinel, J. P. J. 1997: *Biopsychology*. Boston: Allyn & Bacon.

Ployhart, R. E. and Ryan, A. M. 1998: Applicants' reactions to the fairness of selection procedures: the effects of positive rule violation and time of measurement. *Journal of Applied Psychology*, 83(1), 3–16.

Porter, L. W. and Lawler, E. E. 1965: Properties of organisational structure in relation to job attitudes and job behaviour. *Psychological Bulletin*, 64, 23–51.

Porter, M. E. 1985: *Competitive Advantage*. New York: Free Press.

Prediger, D. J. 1982: Dimensional underlying Holland's hexagon: missing link between interests and occupations? *Journal of Vocational Behaviour*, 21, 259–87.

Psychejam 2001: Details of anankastic personality disorder; available at www.Psychejam.com/anankastic_personality_disorder.htm

Purcell, K. and Purcell, J. 1998: In-sourcing, out-sourcing and the growth of contingent labour as evidence of flexible employment strategies. *European Journal of Work and Organisational Psychology*, 7(1), 39–59.

Radcliffe, J. A. 1966: A note on questionnaire faking with the 16PF and the MMPI. *Australian Journal of Applied Psychology*, 18, 154–7.

Ramsay, S., Gallois, C. and Callan, V. J. 1997: Social rules and attribution in the personal selection interview. *Journal of Occupational and Organisational Psychology*, 70, 189–203.

Rand, A. 1964: *The Virtue of Selfishness*. New York: Signet.

Rand, T. M. and Wexley, K. M. 1975: Demonstration of the effect 'similar to me' in simulated employment interviews. *Psychological Reports*, 36, 535–44.

Rasch, G. 1980: *Probabilistic Models for Intelligence and Attainment Testing*. Chicago: University of Chicago Press.

Rasmussen, K. G. 1984: Nonverbal behaviour, verbal behaviour, resume credentials and selection interview outcomes. *Journal of Applied Psychology*, 69(4), 551–6.

Raymark, P. H., Schmit, M. J. and Guion, R. M. 1997: Identifying potentially useful personality constructs for employees selection. *Personnel Psychology*, 50, 723–36.

Rees, C. J. 1999: Investigations into the faking-good of personality questionnaire results in the occupational context. Unpublished PhD thesis, UMIST, Manchester.

Reilly, R. R. and Chao, G. T. 1982: Validity and fairness of some alternative employee selection procedures. *Personnel Psychology*, 35, 1–62.

Richardson, M. W. and Kuder, G. F. 1939: The calculation of test reliability coefficients based upon the
method of rational equivalence. *Journal of Educational Psychology*, 30, 681–7.

Richey, M. H., McClelland, L. and Skimkunas, A. M. 1967: Relative influence of positive and negative
information on impression formation and persistence. *Personality and Social Psychology*, 6, 322–7.

Rimland, B. 1962: Personality test faking: express willingness to fake as affected by anonymity and instructional set. *Educational and Psychological Measurement*, 22, 747–51.

Robertson, I. T. and Smith, J. M. 2001: Personnel selection. *Journal of Occupational and Organisational
Psychology*, 74(4), 441–72.

——, Gratton, L. and Sharpley, D. 1987: The psychometric properties and design of assessment centres: dimensions into exercises won't go. *Journal of Occupational Psychology*, 60, 187–95.

——, Smith, J. M. and Cooper, D. 1992: *Motivation, Strategies, Theory and Practice*. London: Institute
of Personnel Management.

Robertson, S. and Wilkie, D. T. 1998: *Quintax Personality Questionnaire: User Guide*. Manchester: Stuart
Robertson & Associates.

Roger, A. 1953: *The Seven Point Plan*. London: National Institute of Industrial Psychology.

Rokeach, M. 1973: *The Nature of Human Values*. New York: Free Press.

Rolland, J. P. and Mogenet, J. L. 1994: *Manuel d'application. Systeme D5D d'aide á l'évaluation des per-
sonnes*. Paris: Les Editiones du Centre de Psychologie Applique.

Rollinson, D., Broadfield, A. and Edwards, D. J. 1998: *Organisational Behaviour and Analysis: an Integrated Approach*. Harlow: Addison-Wesley.

Rolls, S. R. 1993: The validity and utility of Computer Based Test Interpretations (CBTIs) in staff selection decision situations. Unpublished PhD thesis, Cranfield Institute of Technology.

Rosen, B. and Jerdee, T. H. 1976: The nature of job-related stereotypes. *Journal of Applied Psychology*,
61(2), 180–3.

Rosenfeld, P., Giacalone, R. A. and Riordan, C. A. 1995: *Impression Management in Organisations: Theory,
Management, Practice*. London: Routledge.

Rosenthal, R. 1991: *Meta-analytic Procedures for Social Science Research*. Newbury Park, Calif.: Sage.

Ross, L. 1977: The intuitive psychologist and his shortcomings: distortions in the attribution process. In
L. Bekowitz (ed.), *Advances in Experimental Social Psychology*, vol. 10. New York: Academic Press.

Rothstein, H. R., Schmidt, F. L., Erwin, F. W., Owens, W. A. and Sparks, P. P. 1990: Biographical
data in employment selection: Can validities be made generalisable? *Journal of Applied Psychology*, 75,
175–84.

Rotter, J. B. 1966: Generalised expectancies for internal versus external control of reinforcement. *Psychological Monographs*, 80(1), 609.

Russell, C. J. 1985: Individual decision processes in an assessment centre. *Journal of Applied Psychology*,
70, 373–46.

—— and Domm, D. R. 1995: Two field tests of an explanation of assessment centre validity. *Journal of
Occupational and Organisational Psychology*, 68(1), 25–47.

Rust, J. 1996: *Orpheus User Manual*. London: The Psychological Corporation.

—— and Golombok, S. 1989: *Modern Psychometrics*. London: Routledge.

Rynes, S. L. and Connelly, M. L. 1993: Applicant reactions to alternative selection procedures. *Journal
of Business and Psychology*, 7, 261–77.

Sackett, P. R. 1982: The interviewer as hypothesis tester: the effects of impressions of an applicant on
interview questioning strategy. *Personnel Psychology*, 35, 789–803.

—— and Dreher, F. F. 1982: Constructs and assessment centre dimensions: some troubling empirical
findings. *Journal of Applied Psychology*, 67, 401–10.

Salas, R. G. 1968: Fakeability of responses on the Eysenck Personality Inventory. *Australian Journal of
Psychology*, 20, 55–7.

Salgado, J. F. 1999: Personnel selection methods. *International Review of Industrial and Organisational Psychology*, 14, 1–44.

—— and Moscoso, S. 2002: Comprehensive meta-analysis of the construct validity of employment interview. *European Journal of Work and Organisational Psychology*, 11(3), 299–324.

Sanchez, J. I. 2000: Adapting work analysis to a fast-paced and electronic business world. *International Journal of Selection and Assessment*, 8(4), 207–15.

—— and Fraser, S. L. 1992: On the choice of scales for task analysis. *Journal of Applied Psychology*, 77, 545–53.

Sandberg, J. 2000: Understanding human competence work: an interpretative approach. *Academy of Management Journal*, 43(1), 9–25.

Saville Holdsworth 1988: *The Work Profiling System Manual*. Esher, Surrey: Saville Holdsworth Limited.

—— 1989: *Managerial Interest Inventory*. Thames Ditton: Saville Holdsworth Limited.

—— 1991: *Equal Opportunities Guidelines for Best Practice in the Use of Personnel Selection Tests*. Thames Ditton: Saville Holdsworth Limited.

—— 1992: *Guidelines for Testing People with Disabilities*. Thames Ditton: Saville Holdsworth Limited.

—— 1999: *OPQ 32: Manual and User's Guide*. Thames Ditton: Saville Holdsworth Limited.

Saville, P. and Wilson, E. 1991: The reliability and validity of normative and ipsative approaches in the measurement of personality. *Journal of Occupational Psychology*, 64, 219–38.

——, Sik, G., Nyfield, G., Hackston, J. and MacIver, R. 1996: A demonstration of the validity of the Occupational Personality Questionnaire (OPQ) in the measurement of job competencies across time and in separate organisations. *Applied Psychology: An International Review*, 45, 243–62.

Schmidt, F. L. and Hunter, J. E. 1998: The validity and utility of selection methods in personnel psychology: practical and theoretical implications of 85 years of research findings. *Psychological Bulletin*, 124(2), 216–74.

——, Berner, J. G. and Hunter, J. E. 1973: Racial differences in validity of employment tests: Reality or illusion? *Journal of Applied Psychology*, 58(1), 5–9.

——, Hunter, J. E. and Urry, V. W. 1976: Statistical power in criterion-related validation studies. *Journal of Applied Psychology*, 61(4), 473–85.

Schmidt, L. R. 1988: Objective personality tests – some clinical applications. In K. M. Miller (ed.), *The Analysis of Personality and Research*. London: Independent Assessment and Research Centre.

Schmitt, N. and Chan, D. 1998: *Personnel Selection: a Theoretical Approach*. London: Sage.

——, Schneider, J. R. and Cohen, S. A. 1990: Factors affecting validity of a regionally administered assessment centre. *Personnel Psychology*, 43, 127–35.

——, Gooding, R. Z., Noe, R. A. and Kirsch, M. 1984: Meta-analysis of validity studies published between 1964 and 1982 and the investigation of study characteristics. *Personnel Psychology*, 37, 407–22.

Schuh, A. J. 1978: Contrast effects in the interview. *Bulletin of the Psychognomic Society*, 11, 195–6.

Schuhfried, G. 1997: *The Vienna Test System*. Runcorn: Cytech.

Schuler, H. and Funke, U. 1989: The interview as a multimodal procedure. In E. W. Eder and G. R. Ferris (eds), *The Employment Interview: Theory, Research and Practice*. Newbury Park, Calif.: Sage.

—— and Schmitt, N. 1987: Multimodale Messung in der Personalpsychologie. *Diagnostica*, 33, 259–71.

——, Moser, K., Diemond, A. and Funke, U. 1995: Validät eines Einstellungssinterviews zur Prognose des Ausbildungserfolgs. *Zeitschrift fur Pädergoische Psychologie*, 9, 45–54.

Schutz, W. 1989: *Fundamental Interpersonal Relations Orientation-Behaviour (FIRO-B)*. Palo Alto: Consulting Psychologist Press.

Schwab, D. P. 1971: Issues in response distortion studies of personality inventories: a critique and replicated study. *Personnel Psychology*, 24(4), 637–47.

——, Heneman, H. G. and DeCottiss, T. A. 1975: Behaviourally anchored rating scales: a review of the literature. *Personnel Psychology*, 28, 549–62.

Seisdedos, N. 1993: Personnel selection, questionnaires and motivational distortion: an intelligent attitude of adaptation. In H. Schuler, J. L. Farr and J. M. Smith (eds), *Personnel Selection and Assessment: Individual and Organisational Perspectives*. Hillsdale, NJ: Lawrence Erlbaum Associates.

Sheldon, W. H. 1942: *The Varieties of Temperament: a Psychology of Constitutional Differences*. New York: Harper.

Sheppard, B. H. and Lerwicki, R. J. 1987: Toward general principles of managerial fairness. *Social Justice Research*, 1, 161–76.

Silvester, J., Anderson, N., Haddleton, E., Cunningham-Snell, N. and Gibb, A. 2000: A cross-modal comparison of telephoned and face-to-face selection interviews in graduate recruitment. *International Journal of Selection and Assessment*, 8(1), 16–21.

Sinclair, C. and Pettifor, J. (eds) 1991: *Companion Manual to the Canadian Code of Ethics for Psychologists*. Ottawa: Canadian Psychological Association.

Singer, J. L. and Kolligan, J. 1987: Personality: developments in the study of private experience. *Annual Review of Psychology*, 38, 533–74.

Slater, P. 1974: *The Grid Analysis Package*. London: St Thomas Hospital.

Small, S. A., Zeldin, R. S. and Savin-Williams, R. C. 1983: In search of personality traits: a multimethod analysis of naturally occurring prosocial and dominance behaviour. *Journal of Personality*, 51, 1–16.

Smith, P. L. and Kendall, L. M. 1963: Retranslations of expectations: an approach to the construction of unambiguous anchors for rating scales. *Journal of Applied Psychology*, 47, 149–55.

Smith, J. M. 1982: *The British Telecom Survey Item Bank*, vol. 2. Bradford: MCB Press.

—— 1994: A theory of predictors. *Journal of Occupational and Organisational Psychology*, 67(1), 13–32.

—— and Abrahamsen, M. 1992: Patterns of selection in six countries. *The Psychologist*, May, 205–7.

—— and Robertson, I. T. 1993: *The Theory and Practice of Systematic Personnel Selection*. London: Macmillan.

—— and Ryder, P. 2000: The exploratory studies of repertory grids in selection. In *Proceedings of Occupational Psychology Conference*. Leicester: British Psychological Society.

——, Hartley, J. and Stewart, B. J. M. 1978: A case study of repertory grids used in vocational guidance. *Journal of Occupational Psychology*, 51(1), 97–104.

Smith, P. L. and Kendall, L. M. 1963: Retranslations of expectations: an approach to the construction of unambiguous anchors for rating scales. *Journal of Applied Psychology*, 47, 149–55.

Smither, J. W., Millsap, R. E., Stoffey, R. W., Reilly, R. R. and Pearlman, K. 1996: An experimental test of the influence of selection procedures on fairness perceptions, attitude about the organisation and job pursuit intentions. *Journal of Business and Psychology*, 10, 297–318.

Snyder, C. R. and Shenkel, R. J. 1975: Astrologers, hand-writing analysts, and sometimes psychologists use the P. T. Barnum effect. *Psychology Today*, March, 52–4.

—— and Swan, A. B. 1978: Hypothesis testing processes in social interactions. *Journal of Personality and Social Psychology*, 36, 1202–12.

——, Shenkel, R. J. and Lowery, C. R. 1977: The acceptance of personality interpretations: the Barnum effect and beyond. *Journal of Consulting and Clinical Psychology*, 45(1), 104–14.

Sonnentag, S. 1998: Identifying high-performance: do peer nominations suffer from likeability bias? *European Journal of Work and Organisational Psychology*, 7(4), 501–15.

Sparrow, J., Patrick, J., Spurgeon, P. and Barwell, F. 1982: The use of job component analysis and aptitudes in personnel selection. *Journal of Occupational Psychology*, 53(3), 157–64.

Spearman, C. 1904: 'General intelligence' objectively determined and measured. *American Journal of Psychology*, 15, 201–93.

—— 1923: *The Nature of Intelligence and the Principles of Cognition*. London: Macmillan.

Spector, P. E., Cooper, C. L. and Sparkes, K. 2001: An international study of the psychometric properties of the Hofstede Values Survey Module 1994: a comparison of individual and country/province level results. *Applied Psychology: an International Review*, 50, 269–81.

Speilburger, C. D. 1984: *State–Trait Anxiety Inventory*. Palo Alto, Calif.: Consulting Psychologists Press.

—— 1987: *State–Trait Anger Expression Inventory*. Odessa, Fl.: Psychological Assessment Resources.

Springbett, B. M. 1958: Factors affecting the final decision in employment interviews. *Canadian Journal of Psychology*, 12, 13–22.

Spychalski, A., Quinones, M. A., Gaugler, B. B. and Pohley, K. 1997: A survey of assessment center practices in organizations in the United States. *Personnel Psychology*, 50(1), 71–90.

Stagner, R. 1958: The gullibility of personnel managers. *Personnel Management*, 41, 226–30.

Stark, S. 1959: Research criteria of executive success. *Journal of Business*, 32, 1–14.

Steege, F. W. 1986: *Computer Assisted and Adaptive Testing as Part of a System of Measures of Personnel Psychology*. Paper presented at the symposium 'Computerised Adaptive Testing (CAT) Applications: an International Military Perspective' at the 21st International Congress of Applied Psychology, Jerusalem, July.

Steers, R. M. and Porter, L. W. 1979: *Motivation and Work Behaviour*. New York: McGraw-Hill.

Stephens, D. B., Watt, J. T. and Hobbs, W. S. 1979: Getting through the resume preparation maze: some empirically based guidelines for resume format. *The Vocational Guidance Quarterly*, 27, 25–34.

Stern, W. 1965: The psychological methods for testing intelligence. In R. J. Herrenstien and E. G. Boring (eds), *A Source Book in the History of Psychology*. Cambridge, Mass.: Harvard University Press (first published 1912).

Sternberg, R. J. 1988: *The Triarchic Mind: a New Theory of Human Intelligence*. New York: Viking.

Stevens, C. K. 1998: Antecedents of interview interactions, interviewers' rating and applicants' reactions. *Personnel Psychology*, 51, 55–85.

Stewart, R. 1967: *Managers and their Jobs*. London: Macmillan.

Stokes, G. S. and Searcy, C. A. 1999: Specification of scales in biodata form development: rational versus empirical and global versus specific. *International Journal of Selection and Assessment*, 7(2), 72–96.

Street, R. L. and Bradley, R. M. 1982: Speech rate acceptance ranges as a function of evaluative domain, listener speech rate and communication context. *Communication Monographs*, 49, 290–308.

Strickler, L. J. and Rock, D. 1998: Assessing leadership potential with a biographical measure of personality traits. *International Journal of Selection and Assessment*, 6(3), 164–84.

——, Messick, S. and Jackson, D. N. 1967: Suspicion of deception: implications for conformity research. *Journal of Personality and Social Psychology*, 5, 379–89.

Sue-Chan, C., Latham, M. G., Evans, M. G. and Rotman, J. L. 1997: The construct validity of the situation and patterned behaviour description interviews: cognitive ability, tacit knowledge and self-efficacy as correlates. Unpublished manuscript, Faculty of Management, University of Toronto, Canada.

Sundberg, N. D. 1955: The acceptability of 'fake' versus 'bona fide' personality test interpretations. *Journal of Abnormal and Social Psychology*, 50, 145–7.

Super, D. E. 1970: *Work Values Inventory: Manual*. Chicago: Riverside.

—— 1973: The Work Values Inventory. In D. G. Zytowski (ed.), *Contemporary Approaches to Interest Measurement*. Minneapolis: University of Minneapolis Press.

Tarleton, R. 1998: *The Motivational Styles Questionnaire*. London: Psychological Corporation.

Task Force on Assessment Centre Guidelines 2000: *Guidelines and Ethical Considerations for Assessment Centre Operations*. Pittsburgh: Development Dimensions International.

Tenopyr, M. L. 1996: Gender issues in employment testing. In R. S. Barrett (ed.), *Fair Employment Strategies In Human Resource Management*. Westport, Conn.: Quorum Books.

Terpstra, D. E. and Rozell, E. J. 1993: The relationship of staffing practices to organisational level measures of performance. *Personnel Psychology*, 46, 27–48.

——, Mohammed, A. A. and Kethley, R. B. 1999: An analysis of Federal Court cases involving nine selection devices. *International Journal of Selection and Assessment*, 7(1), 26–33.

Thorndike, R. L. 1971: Concepts of culture fairness. *Journal of Educational Measurement*, 8(2), 63–70.

Thorne, F. C. 1961: Clinical judgement: a study of clinical errors. *Journal of Clinical Psychology*, xxiii, 1342 pp.

Thornton, G. C. 1993: The effect of selection practices on applicants' perceptions of organisational characteristics. In H. Schuler, J. L. Farr and M. Smith (eds), *Personnel Selection and Assessment: Individual and Organisational Perspectives*. Hillsdale, NJ: Lawrence Erlbaum.

—— and Byham, W. C. 1982: *Assessment Centres and Managerial Performance*. New York: Academic Press.

Thorsteinson, T. J. and Ryan, A. M. 1997: The effect of selection ratio on perceptions of the fairness of a selection test battery. *International Journal of Selection and Assessment*, 5(3), 159–68.

Thurstone, L. L. 1938: *Primary Mental Abilities*. Chicago: Chicago University Press.

Tonidandel, S. and Quinones, M. A. 2000: Psychological reactions to adaptive testing. *International Journal of Selection and Assessment*, 8(1), 7–15.

Tracey, T. J. and Rounds, J. B. 1993: Evaluating Holland's and Gati's vocational interest models: a structural meta-analysis. *Psychological Bulletin*, 113, 229–46.

—— and —— 1996: The spherical representation of vocational interests. *Journal of Occupational Behaviour*, 48, 3–41.

Tucker, D. H. and Rowe, P. M. 1979: Relationships between expectancy, causal attributions, and final hiring decisions in the employment interview. *Journal of Applied Psychology*, 64, 27–34.

Tullar, W. L. 1989: The employment interview as a cognitive forming script. In R. W. Eder and G. R. Ferris (eds), *The Employment Interview: Theory, Research, and Practice*. Newbury Park, Calif.: Sage.

—— and Barret, G. V. 1976: The future autobiography as a predictor of sales success. *Journal of Applied Psychology*, 61(3), 371–3.

Tupes, E. C. and Christal, R. E. 1961: *Recurrent Personality Factors Based on Trait Ratings*. USAF ASD Technical Report 61–67. Lackland Air Base, TX: US Air Force.

Tyler, B. 1996: *16PF Workshop Notes: Interpreting 16PF Editions 4 and 5*. London: Miller & Tyler.

Ulrich, L. and Trumbo, D. 1965: The selection interview since 1949. *Psychological Bulletin*, 63, 100–16.

Undheim, J. O. and Gustafsson, J. E. 1987: The hierarchical organisation of cognitive abilities: restoring general intelligence through the use of linear structural relations. *Multivariate Behavioural Research*, 22, 149–71.

US Office of Personnel Management 1987: *The Structured Interview*. Washington, DC: Office of Examination Development, Division of Alternative Examining Procedures.

Vale, C. D., Keller, L. S. and Bentz, V. J. 1986: Development and validation of a computerised interpretation system for personnel tests. *Personnel Psychology*, 39, 525–42.

Veenhoven, R. 2003: Happiness. *The Psychologist*, 16(3), 128–9.

Vernon, P. A. 1950: *The Structure of Human Abilities*. London: Methuen.

—— 1960: *Intelligence and Attainment Tests*. London: University of London Press.

—— and Mori, M. 1992: Intelligence, reaction times and peripheral nerve conduction velocity. *Intelligence*, 16, 273–88.

—— and Parry, J. B. 1949: *Personnel Selection in the British Forces*. London: University of London Press.

Viswesvaran, C. and Ones, D. S. 2000: Perspectives of models of job performance. *International Journal of Selection and Assessment*, 8(4), 216–25.

Vroom, V. H. 1964: *Work and Motivation*. New York: Wiley.

Wagner, R. 1949: The employment interview: a critical review. *Personnel Psychology*, 2, 17–46.

Wallace, S. R. 1974: How high the validity? *Personnel Psychology*, 27, 397–407.

Waller, N., Kojetin, B., Bouchard, T. and Lykken, D. 1990: Genetic and environmental influences on religious interests, attitudes and values: a study of twins reared apart and together. *Psychological Science*, 1, 138–42.

Walley, E. and Smith, J. M. 1998: *Deception in Selection*. Chichester: Wiley.

Warr, P., Miles, A. and Platts, C. 2001: Age and personality in the British population between 16 and 64 years. *Journal of Occupational and Organisational Psychology*, 74, 165–99.

Watkins, L. M. and Johnston, L. 2000: Screening of job applicants: the impact of physical attractiveness and application quality. *International Journal of Selection and Assessment*, 8(2), 77–84.

Watts, A. G., Super, D. E. and Kidd, J. M. (eds) 1981: *Career Development in Britain*. Cambridge: Hobson's Press.

Webster, E. D. 1964: *Decision Making in the Employment Interview*. Montreal: Eagle Press.

Weisner, W. H. and Cronshaw, S. F. 1988: A meta-analytic investigation of the impact of interview format and degree of structure on the validity of the employment interview. *Journal of Occupational Psychology*, 61(4), 275–90.

Wesman, A. G. 1952: Faking personality test scores in a simulated employment situation. *Journal of Applied Psychology*, 36, 112–13.

West, J. and Karas, M. 1999: Biodata: meeting clients' needs for a better way of recruiting entry-level staff. *International Journal of Selection and Assessment*, 7(2), 126–31.

Westoby, J. B. and Smith, J. M. 2000: *The 16PF5 Job Spec*. Windsor: Assessment and Selection in Employment (ASE).

Wexley, K. N. and Nemeroff, H. F. W. 1974: The effects of racial prejudice, race of applicant and biographical similarity on interviewer evaluations of job applicants. *Journal of Social and Behavioural Sciences*, 20, 66–78.

Wexley, K. N., Yukl, G. A., Kovacs, S. Z. and Sanders, R. E. 1972: Importance of contrast effects in employment interviews. *Journal of Applied Psychology*, 56, 45–8.

White, N. M. and Milner, P. M. 1992: The psychobiology of reinforcers. *Annual Review of Psychology*, 43, 443–71.

Whitacker 2000: *Whitacker's Almanack 2000*. London: The Stationery Office.

Whyte, W. H. 1957: *The Organisation Man*. London: Cape.

Wiggins, J. S. 1973: *Personality and Prediction: Principles of Personality Assessment*. Reading, Mass.: Addison-Wesley.

Wilkinson, L. J. 1997: Generalisable biodata? An application to the vocational interests of managers. *Journal of Occupational and Organisational Psychology*, 70, 49–60.

Witkin, H. A. and Goodenough, D. R. 1977: Field dependence and personal behaviour. *Psychological Bulletin*, 84, 661–89.

Woodruffe, C. 1992: What is meant by a competency? In M. Boam and P. Sparrow (eds), *Designing and Achieving Competency: a Competency-based Approach to Developing People in Organisations*. Maidenhead: McGraw-Hill.

—— 2000: *Development and Assessment Centres: Identifying and Assessing Competencies*, 3rd edn. London: Chartered Institute of Personnel and Development.

Worland, J. H. 1985: Review of 'Welsh Figure Preference Test'. *Ninth Mental Measurements Yearbook*, vol. 2. Lincoln, Neb.: BUROS Institute of Mental Measurement, 1728–9.

Wright, B. D. 1968: Sample-free test calibration and person measurement. *Proceedings of the 1967 Invitational Conference on Testing Problems*. Princeton, NJ: Educational Testing Service.

Wright, J. C. and Mischel, W. 1987: A conditional approach to dispositional constructs: the local predictability of social behaviour. *Journal of Personality and Social Psychology*, 53, 14–29.

Wright, P. M. and McMahan, G. C. 1992: Theoretical perspectives for strategic human resource management. *Journal of Management*, 18, 295–320.

Yerkes, R. M. and Dodson, J. D. 1908: The relation of strength of stimulus to rapidity of habit formation. *Journal of Comparative and Neurological Psychology*, 18, 459–82.

Young, A. M. and Kacmar, K. M. 1998: ABCs of the interview: the role of affective, behavioural and cognitive responses by applicants in the employment interview. *International Journal of Selection and Assessment*, 6(4), 211–21.

Zubeck, J. P. and Solberg, P. A. 1954: *Human Development*. New York: McGraw-Hill.

AUTHOR INDEX

OCCUPATION INDEX

SUBJECT INDEX

TESTS AND MEASURES INDEX